EXPLORATIONS IN GOVERNMENT

EXPLORATIONS IN GOVERNMENT

COLLECTED PAPERS: 1951–1968

W. J. M. Mackenzie

Edward Caird Professor of Politics
University of Glasgow

Macmillan

First published 1975 by
THE MACMILLAN PRESS LTD
London and Basingstoke
Associated companies in New York
Dublin Melbourne Johannesburg and Madras

Distributed in the United States
by Halsted Press, a Division of
John Wiley & Sons, Inc., New York

SBN 333 14836 3

Library of Congress Catalog Card No. 74-6722

Typeset in Great Britain by
PREFACE LIMITED
Salisbury, Wiltshire
and printed in Great Britain by
REDWOOD BURN LTD
Trowbridge and Esher

Contents

Contents

Acknowledgements

I owe so many personal debts in respect of these papers that I cannot acknowledge them in full here. But I must in particular thank Professor Tony King of the University of Essex for his generous help in sponsoring and developing this book, Professor Brian Chapman of the University of Manchester for consenting to the inclusion of a joint paper which owes its merit to his original work, and my secretary, Miss Sheila Hamilton, for all she did in assembling and organising the material.

The publishers and I wish to thank the following, who have kindly given permission for the reproduction of papers collected in this volume (the footnotes provide details of original publication): Clarendon Press (papers 7, 8, 11, 17 and 18), the *Guardian* (paper 14), London School of Economics and Political Science (paper 5), Macmillan Publishing Co. Inc. (paper 19), Manchester Literary and Philosophical Society (paper 4), Manchester School (paper 10), the *Modern Law Review* (paper 3), Political Studies Association (paper 1), Routledge and Kegan Paul Ltd (papers 15 and 16), Royal Institute of Public Administration (paper 9), Royal Town Planning Institute (paper 6), Turnstile Press Ltd (paper 2), and UNESCO (paper 13).

The publishers have made every effort to trace the copyright-holders but if they have inadvertently overlooked any, they will be pleased to make the necessary arrangement at the first opportunity.

University of Glasgow March 1974

W.J.M.M.

Introduction

When it was decided to re-publish this selection of articles I was asked to contribute an introduction about the discipline of political study as I understood it. As I feared, this proves difficult, since I see 'the discipline' as a group of people rather than as a set of principles, as a continuing debate rather than an enquiry in the style of natural science, as an enterprise which is an integral part of real politics, which involves the myths of power and danger as well as those of legitimate authority and of rational human collaboration.

To describe my own position therefore involves introducing some of the participants in my own internal debate, and I must try to do this in intellectual rather than personal terms. Some of the people concerned are dead, and so are some of the intellectual 'paradigms' (to use a pleasantly ambiguous word). But others are full of life.

I take this in four stages which can be labelled shortly as Scotland, Balliol, Magdalen, Manchester, provided that these are regarded not primarily in a geographical sense, but as patterns of intellectual activity.

Scotland

Most of what I know of the intellectual tradition into which I was born I know only by hindsight, after I grew, not as I grew; but the story has to be told in sequence. My pedigree does not go beyond my four great-grandfathers, born probably about 1780 and flourishing in the first quarter of the nineteenth century. Probably two of them, Mackenzie and McClymont, had risen some distance on the wave of change: one was a parish schoolmaster in Angus, not far from Dundee, the other is described in Glasgow University records as *artifex*: a skilled craftsman, working at Dalmellington on the fringe of the Ayrshire coal-field. A third, Millar, was a small farmer on the Highland border of Perthshire, who is said to have tried shop-keeping and failed. Then he tried

Canada (like so many Scots at that time[1]) and died before he could establish himself. But one of his sons did well in the rising town of Dundee, and the rest of the family came home. Finally, there was William Turnbull, a well-established tenant farmer, at Spittal on Rule, from whom descended many cousins: most notably perhaps Colin Turnbull, now professor at Hofstra University, friend of gurus, pygmies and Tibetan Lamas.

The Mackenzie and McClymont homes must have been poor but ambitious and disciplined, and one can guess that both had lost their Gaelic at least a generation earlier, since each sent a son to University, one to St. Andrews, the other to Glasgow; they did not (like James Mill, whose origins were like theirs[2]) lose their faith at University, but went on into the Ministry of the Church of Scotland. Perhaps this was easier than it had been for James Mill thirty years earlier, in that there was now room for radicalism within the church, combining the force of evangelical piety with a sense of mission towards the poor in the cities. The image of the period is that of Thomas Chalmers, a Fife man (like Adam Smith), born in 1780 and educated (like my Mackenzie grandfather) at St. Andrews, who combined these rather emotional and rhetorical attributes with a shrewd understanding of the political economy of his time, and was a leader in the events of the 1830s which led to the radical split in the Church of Scotland in 1843.

My grandfathers were both on the radical side in 1843, figures of the second or third rank, who perhaps pastiched a style they did not create. Mackenzie was a more prolific author than McClymont, and his history of Scotland survived for a long time as a school text book. It has nothing at all in common with academic history as now understood, though clearly my grandfather had dipped a good deal into old books, as Walter Scot used to do, and clearly he was steeped in the language of Scott's novels, for good and bad about equally. In modern terms, his book was not history but myth-making, and his narrative prose was brisk enough to sustain the Scottish myth of the chosen people of God, a People of the Book, often chastened like the Children of Israel, but heirs to freedom and to a Promised Land.

> A! Fredome is a noble thing!
> Fredome mays man to haiff liking;
> Fredome all solace to man giffis;
> He levys at es that frely levis![3]

Undoubtedly the *Democratic Intellect*[4] became less brisk (as G.E. Davie maintains) after the middle of the century. Enthusiasm declined into cant, and Scottish church politics (though they helped to sustain Scotland's position in British politics, Scotland being as necessary to the Liberal Party then as it is to the Labour Party now) become unbearably tedious. Davie attributes the decline to the insidious influence of English education, but it is at least as plausible to see internal causes of decay in the rise and stabilisation of the new Scottish middle class.

Both my grandfathers left widows to bring up large families on tiny incomes, and the family habit was to be not mean but very careful — 'menseful' was the word I grew up with. But in each of these generations there were men who became comfortably off; and (so far as I can trace) there was no one who slipped back to the status of weekly wage earner. The McClymont kin were on the whole comfortable working farmers or comfortable professional people: and the only capitalist star of first or second magnitude was my father's oldest brother William Mackenzie, founder (in competition with the first of the Flemings) of the investment trust movement in Dundee, one of the links between prudent Scottish savers and the exploitation of new lands in the USA, in Latin America, in Australia.[5] The legend is that when his father died in the 1860s William promised his mother that he would be earning a thousand a year by the time he was twenty (the figure would now be ten times that). He did, and looked after his four brothers very well, in his bullying way: two in the USA, one in Australia, my father established in law in Edinburgh (a page of his Edinburgh account book when he was about twenty may give the flavour).

It never occurred to me to puzzle out then why the weekly sermon (rarely more than half an hour in my time) spelled such an infinity of boredom that to this day I am overcome by yawning at the mere sight of a man talking in a pulpit.

32ⁿᵈ Week 16ᵗʰ

Aug 16   By Balance   £   1 11 6½
                                 1 10 1½
                             _____
                                     1   5

                             £   1   5

to 22nd August 1882.

16	To	Dinner &c. 1/6 Scotsn 1d	1	7
	"	Wax match 6 Ev News ½		6½
17	"	Dinner &c. 1/7 7. Stamp 1	2	7
	"	Scotsman 1 Ev News ½ Stamps 3½		5
	"	Note Paper 5d		5
18	"	Dinner &c. 1/7 Bake 3½	1	10½
	"	Scotsman 1d Ev News ½		1½
	"	Programme for Theatre		1
19	"	Dinner & Waiter	1	4
	"	Scotsman 1 Ev News ½		1½
	"	Sundries 1. Needles 1		2½
20	"	Church		1
21	"	Dinner 10d Ev N&T. 1		11
	"	Scotsman		1
22	"	Scotsn 1 Ev News ½ Dinner 10d		11½
	"	Rooms &c.	18	9½
		£	1 10	1½

Retrospectively, one can see that among middle-class women piety had declined into pietism; and that many men must have been in my father's position, soaked in Bible words and in Calvinist thought, but at heart sceptical. Yet the Sunday service was still an obligation to family and to society: at one time my father found a minister with whom he could talk freely on the basis of honest doubt, but the situation was intellectually off balance, and the reunion of the Church of Scotland in 1928 reflected an exhaustion of energy rather than a harmony of spirit.

Similarly the impulse of Scottish liberalism had died, and politics had re-polarized on the axis of Conservative versus Labour, rather than Tory versus Liberal, the lairds versus the people. My father's first political experience had perhaps been to hear Gladstone in the Midlothian campaign of 1880,[6] and he deserted the Liberals very sadly in 1923 or 1924. My own first experience was the general strike of May 1926, and at the age of 17 I had no opinion except the common opinion of a middle class school, that this was a good chance to go out and bash someone. The very 'English' Rector at the Academy, 'the Wee Man', told me not to be a fool, in his gentle squeaky way; so I never got near the foot-plate of a train, which I had been promised. But how right he was.

I must say I had no inkling then of the Edinburgh Academy as a place lying in the heartland of the Scottish bourgeoisie. For me it was certainly a good school; if I was bad my parents told me I would have to go off to a boarding-school, as some very posh boys did, and the threat was terrifying. Basically the school was organised on the Scottish system as it still exists: five sessions to Lowers, another session to Highers and then for most people (if they were good enough) a move to a Scottish University between seventeen and eighteen, or to an apprenticeship in accountancy or law, with part-time study. But the special peculiarity of the school was its Seventh Class, then a small stream (not more than four or five a year) working purely on Latin and Greek for Oxford and Cambridge scholarships and entrance. We did very well.

The thing was not as narrow as it sounds. On the one hand, we had already taken a wide range of Highers, and they pushed us fast; I passed Higher Maths (including some calculus) when I was fourteen. On the other hand, the VII was very free and very glorious: and I began to read Latin and Greek with some fluency. I think it was Sir Dennis Brogan who taught me the quotation from Ally Sloper – 'A dirty mind is a perpetual feast.' The VIIth room had in the corner an ancient bookcase with a pretty complete seventeenth-century set of the Delphin classics, edited *ad usum Serenissimi Delphini*, for the use of the Grand Dauphin, the son of Louis XIV whom he predeceased. In our class texts of Juvenal, Catullus, Lucretius and so on the dirty passages were conspicuously marked by omission; easy to make good from the Delphin edition but puzzling to understand – there are some Roman vices (such as eating dormice[7], or buggering a man with a fish, preferably a mullet – a preference which has puzzled many scholars) which would still be regarded as exotic.

I think some people were driven pretty hard, but I was lucky enough to be quick, and to have a year in hand, and to be quite unaware of the desirability of going to a far away place called Oxford of which I had heard nothing. I remember being quite startled when our class master, a rather grim man, telephoned with warmth and excitement to say I had won a Balliol scholarship: the third scholarship only, but a year young, a few days before I was seventeen. 'What was Balliol, please?' I masked my ignorance, because clearly everyone thought that a Balliol scholarship was a good thing.

At least, it served to give me what was in effect a sabbatical year within the school. I had gone through the school about a year younger than the class average. Is this a strain on clever children? If it was a strain, I never knew it. How could I? This was my norm. But it made life broader and easier, to be back with my contemporaries, to be very good at some things, a decent average at others, appallingly bad at some.

Balliol
This was 1927, not a vintage year, in terms of students or of dons. The connecting link with Scotland was A.D. Lindsay, 'Sandy' (it was embarrassing to a Scot to be expected to

address elderly dons, face to face, by Christian name or nick name), who had been Master of the College since 1924, and was known to be a 'socialist' (whatever one took that to mean). Sandy was very kind to me personally, but I did not begin to understand his political and philosophical stance until much later. I learnt politics not so much from him as by puzzling about him. I don't find the puzzle to be resolved even by his daughter's able biography.[8]

The puzzle lay for me, and still lies, in the character of Scottish philosophy and theology since the eighteenth century. Since then, and till this day, philosophy has in Scotland been part of a general curriculum rather than a special study: a European[9] rather than English tradition, except in the 'Greats' school at Oxford. The general character of the subject meant that jobs for philosophers were most plentiful in Scotland and in Oxford: but this generality implied certain penalties. One of these was that philosophy could not be 'a fugitive and cloistered virtue, unexercised and unbreathed, that never sallies out and sees her adversary, but slinks out of the race . . . '[10] Indeed it spoke large words to a large audience, and prevailed more by oratory than by analysis. Scottish philosophy acquired an immense reputation in the eighteenth century, which it long retained; yet it is hard to think of a Scotsman of world class as a philosopher who taught in a Scottish university after the death of Thomas Reid in 1796. That wording is a little tortuous, as I have warm feelings towards John Stuart Mill, and indeed to M'Taggart, and there ought in any case to be a game of hunt-the-exception. Some appointments of course were trivial: but the strength of the tradition lay in men who had power over words and therefore over things: for instance, A.D. Lindsay, Professor of Moral Philosophy in Glasgow, 1922–4, Master of Balliol, 1924–49, first Vice-Chancellor of the University of Keele,[11] from 1949 till his death in 1952. Perhaps the last Glasgow professor in that tradition was Lord Franks of Headington (not a Scot but a son of the manse), who succeeded to Lindsay's chair at Glasgow in 1937, and is now Provost of Worcester College, Oxford, after public service in many posts of the first rank. Perhaps Woodrow Wilson had lived in a similar setting, though he was called political scientist rather than philosopher.

This tradition has left me uneasy, as has the pulpit tradition. I am not sure why: perhaps because scholarship was not at the top of the list of duties which these men imposed on themselves and others. Perhaps it was also that they emphasised other people's duties more than their rights. I am conscious of, indeed compulsive and obsessive about what I ought to do, but 'the worst thing in the world' (Orwell's phrase in *1984*) is to be preached at or lectured at about one's duties. Therefore, 'do as you would be done by'; don't preach or lecture duty to other people. Explain, amuse, analyse, but do not seek to impose.

I know that this is an impossible ideal for anyone in a position of leadership, and especially for a teacher. But, tenuous though it is, it seems to bind me more strongly than any antipathy I feel toward the content of 'Scotch felosofy', as the English began to call it early in the nineteenth century. There was a strain of rather harsh utilitarianism ('steam intellect', 'march of mind') and this could not be called extinct till the death of Alexander Bain in 1903. But from the time of Carlyle and Stirling the dominant influences were German, Kant and above all Hegel: if there was a central line of thought it was to link Hegel's logic to Kant's ethic, and it was perhaps a mere matter of social climate that such a philosophy found it easy to coexist with a rigorous Christian theology in its period of decline.

Lindsay undoubtedly stood somewhere to the left of this line in the 1920s: basically a Kantian, but on the move from Hegel towards Marx, after an engagement with Bergson, before 1914. In the 1920s the flexible line of idealist thinking went on through M'Taggart to Oakeshott, Collingwood and Mure. In my time, the idealists Joachim and J.A. Smith still held the most important chairs in Oxford, but the strength lay with the careful old men, Ross, Joseph and Pritchard. Pritchard perhaps foreshadowed analytic philosophy, but Oxford philosophy, strong in numbers, was not in intellectual power and imagination a serious competitor with the Cambridge of that time; Moore, Whitehead, Russell, Wittgenstein. The Cambridge books were there in Blackwell's, but they were difficult, and there was no one in Oxford to advertise and expound them. So for exploration away from the 'great books' I fiddled around with Croce and

Bergson, which really were of no use to me except as language texts.

In fact, Balliol philosophy was not very strong in the hands of Lindsay, Charles Morris and John Fulton. But John Austin was two years junior to me, and he spent the six years 1933—9 very well in grasping the essential problems of modern philosophy: to this after the war he added his own unique gift of philosophic style. But this and Freddy Ayer lay ahead; in any case it was probably not the sort of thing I could do well.

Yet it is possible to surmise that the linguistic side of modern Oxford philosophy owes a good deal to the intense concern of Greats men with the juggle between three languages, English, Greek and Latin. I prided myself on translation into English, not out of it; an exercise in context, style and nuance, for me less impossibly hard that the construction (300 years after Milton) of Greek and Latin prose and verse (John Austin was a master, and won the University Greek Prose Prize in 1931 or 1932; I had merely bulldozed my way by power of translation and general knowledge into the all-round prize, the Ireland, in 1929).

At various times, I have wished that I could exchange this classical inheritance for ease of movement in moderately advanced mathematics and formal logic. The inheritance is itself a language, in that one tends to think in tags (some of them garbled) and their remembered contexts, and this includes Biblical tags and contexts too, the language of religious argument and poetry for nearly 2000 years. One can compare the fate of the classical Chinese culture: a *lingua franca* of great subtlety and very wide human reference is no longer taught, and this makes it very difficult to feel that we share an intellectual language with Hobbes or Milton, let alone Plato or Lucretius.[1 2] One of the problems to which I return later is that of the thinness of texture of political and social writing which lies on this side of the gap of generations in Britain, a gap corresponding to that between British and American education in an earlier period.

Two other things deserve mention, Marxism and poetry. In spite of the Master's reputation for radicalism, Balliol was not a radical college. Most of my contemporaries came from major public schools; very few from grammar schools. In so far as Balliol had a special character, it was that of hospitality to overseas students. These came mainly from the USA and the white Commonwealth. But from the 1880s, when Indians began to enter the old Indian Civil Service, a small number of Indian probationers came to Balliol. Hence the chant from over the wall at Trinity – 'Balliol, Balliol, bring out your black men' – and the allegation that Balliol could support an all-black rowing VIII. This was good for us, as Jowett had foreseen, but it did not add up to political radicalism: there were various intellectual essay-reading clubs in college, but they were much more likely to debate modernism in poetry than modernism in politics. It was generally understood that the Master had read Marx (had indeed written a little book about him) and that he supported the Labour Party. But none of us had much clue about his missionary devotion to extra-mural work in the tradition of Tawney, or about the practical activities of the small student group who tried actively to help the unemployed, particularly in South Wales; though these movements had much to do with the character of the Labour Party in the coming generation – with 'Gaitskellism' as successor to 'Attleeism'. At best, the main body of opinion in college was ignorant about the state of the world but tolerant and even jokey. There was for instance a comic cricket club called the Balliol Soviet which put up notices in fake Russian and set out each Sunday to liquidate the kulaks in the surrounding villages. Alcoholically, it was very successful.

Yet this was a period of polarisation, both in attitudes to Russia and in the organisation of British politics. My own period as student built up from the General Strike to the National Government *coup* in the autumn of 1931: and by that time it was obvious that one's loyalties were engaged and one must vote Labour (as indeed I have done ever since, though tending sometimes towards abstention). In that period Marxism at the simplest level seemed to be the best clue to events. In the next period, that of the Russian purges, the rise of Hitler, the Spanish Civil War, Marxist theory seemed less adequate and more confused, and yet it was in that period read and discussed more fully, and it attracted a flow of confused and eager converts, a number of whom gave their lives in Spain.

The poets were perhaps answerable. I knew no one (except Gilbert Highet, perhaps) who was an 'Oxford poet' or closely in touch with that set. But in the old Mods and Greats school one lived with poetry and with the problems of understanding and translating poetry. I had more or less absorbed the 'Georgians' at school, but next came Eliot and Joyce and Proust and the background of French poetic theory, and then the young men of the 1920s. Frankly, I never got much joy from Auden and Spender; but from MacNeice always, from some Isherwood and (unfashionably) from Roy Campbell.

So far as I can judge, without scrupulous study of dates, it was not till the early 1930s, that there began the charade of images drawn from revolution and war, 'radical chic' of death for a cause. Some died, for instance John Cornford,

> 'On the last mile to Huesca,
> The last fence for our pride'.[1][3]

Magdalen

Perhaps the first decision I ever had to take was not to stay in Oxford but to follow the appropriate Scottish course towards the stability and quietude of law practice in Edinburgh. I was very happy with that, but my father died in 1933 and I grew restless in the Edinburgh calm. Happy coincidence and connection gathered me back to Oxford as a classics don.

Edinburgh law teaching was conducted as a tedious routine of lectures and lecture notes, and the only professor to betray intellectual interest was Willy Wilson, teaching jurisprudence and international law, who actually lectured without notes, chatted with students, extemporised about current events. But an LL.B. came in handy later when I contrived to shift from classics to politics, with little claim to relevant knowledge except in Greats philosophy and in constitutional law (Maitland and Dicey, may they rest in peace), jurisprudence and the law of nations.

For the present purpose, there were two relevant things about Magdalen: that for the first time I found myself in an intellectually ambitious interdisciplinary circle, and that I had to learn political science while I taught it.

Largely through Harry Weldon's wit and judgment Magdalen was then being manoeuvred into a new period in which it sought intellectual rather than social distinction; what had been the softest and easiest College in Oxford, Gibbon's college, that of Oscar Wilde and of Edward VIII as Prince of Wales, became before anyone had noticed a focus of what were then radical politics and leftist talk. The heart of the matter was to use the College's wealth radically: and this meant for us primarily more scholarships, more graduate work, more research fellowships, with selection at each stage on intellectual promise without regard to College connection, athletic talent or clubbability. We made ourselves rather unpopular at Eton and among old Magdalen rowing men, and our radicalism now looks rather old-fashioned. But we moved the place, and we got good students.

At Balliol Kenneth Bell had kept open house for students, and gave a public example of a don's duty to his college (there were other examples in Balliol, but less extrovert). However, that was no intellect, no politics in Kenneth's entourage; whereas in Magdalen both were freely available in what ought to be marked for ever as 'Harry's room'.

Weldon's political philosophy is on record, written in very plain language for all to read. Yet it is continually taken out of context (as was Weldon himself), as an example of the trivialities of linguistic philosophy. In fact, Weldon was in his profession primarily a Kant scholar, who got involved in political writing in a mood of pessimism and protest about wars fought in the name of ideas. In World War I he went almost straight from school into the German offensive in March 1918 and emerged alive but shocked, with an MC and severe wounds. In World War II (indirectly, through my agency) he found himself in uniform again, as staff officer, advocate and personal friend of 'Bomber' Harris. This was in the time of the British night bombing offensive, Cologne, Hamburg, Dresden; places which Weldon knew well and had loved. He also loved Bert Harris. One needs this background to understand the deep hatred of cant, of wars said to be fought for 'democracy' and 'humanity' when they were fought in fact to gain power or to defend oneself against it. In the last resort, Weldon's belief was not far from Blake's, that 'no man ever did good save in minute particulars'. His devotion and helpfulness to individuals, both students and colleagues, were not effectively disguised by his sneering humour and mocking laugh. (Unlike most people he did not expel breath in laughing, but drew it in.)

There was of course an old guard in college, but fading through efflux of time and the strength of new appointments. There were also two great names, Sherrington and Schrödinger, but I knew neither well. Then there was what might be called a young guard, in particular C.S. Lewis and Bruce Macfarlane, men of immense ability and energy but not radicals. But those who talked and drank beer in Harry's room would certainly include John Young and Peter Medawar in biology, Pat Johnson and James Griffiths in physics, John Morris in law, John Austin (but a little austerely) in philosophy. Alan Taylor came just before the war, when the old circle to all intents and purposes broke up; he contributed something new and entirely his own.

It would be pointless to add biographies and note distinctions. What is relevant is Weldon's encouragement by precept and example never to be afraid of scientists. Give them beer, bully them a bit into explaining what they are doing, and take a debatable line about the perplexities that then emerge. Weldon was a good philosopher of science, but never *ex cathedra*.

By 1936 I was happy in Magdalen, restless in classics, in which no specific lines of enquiry opened up. I dabbled in Greek law, in the Latin of the early empire, in the invasion of ecstatic Eastern religions which culminated in the victory of Christianity. But it was characteristic of Oxford organisation that there was no one with whom it would be natural to work.[14] My mind was in fact turning to law and London when the swing of students towards 'Modern Greats', 'Philosophy, Politics and Economics', led the college to recruit a second philosopher and to add a fellow in politics, after the recent appointment of a fellow in economics. This offered me all I could wish, a combination of scholarship and relevance: and my hat was in the ring. But perhaps it was a corrupt appointment, among friends.

One of the pleasantest duties was to get around in Europe, taking good care not to get damaged. I managed to be in Vienna just after Dollfuss was shot in 1934, in Paris just after the Popular Front strikes of 1936, in Geneva when Samuel Hoare made his appeal for sanctions against Italy over the Ethiopian war (I heard him), in the Austrian mountains just after the Nazis walked in, in Prague when Runciman was there, in Russia just before Ribbentrop arrived at the end of August 1939. I was lucky; but regretted that, though I could read and could get by, I was never really fluent in any European language. This, and the language of mathematics, I had lost in favour of Latin and Greek.

I was a cautious traveller and mountaineer, but at least I kept up with my students in terms of knowledge of the ground.

On the other hand, I was reckless in tutoring out of the insufficiency of my knowledge. In those days there were few politics dons in Oxford and we all had to be generalists: I remember only Brogan (later replaced by Charles Wilson), John Maud, R.B. MacCallum, K.C. Wheare, Wilfred Harrison, with Arthur Salter (professor from 1934, after a career in administration) no more experienced in his job than I was in mine. But I should add perhaps Ensor, whose *England 1870–1914* was soon to rival Halévy in influence, and certainly G.D.H. Cole, the total generalist, whom Oxford classified as economics rather as politics or philosophy. As perspective lengthens so Cole emerges above us moles. But it will need great intellectual range and insight to understand Cole in his generation, and he is not to be recommended as a soft option for thesis writers.

I could in fact cope, at least at an introductory level, with 'the great books', with international institutions, with British institutions and constitutional history. Inescapably, as we had no adequate modern historian till Alan Taylor came, I had to learn and teach British political history from 1760 to 1914, international history from 1870 to 1914. The latter was a bore because so much debate still turned on ritual manoeuvres about the origins of World War I and the war guilt question. But in a sense I was taught British history by Namier, though I never met him till I moved to Manchester; and I absorbed completely, perhaps uncritically, the essence

of his method — 'find out who the guys *were*'. Hence I have
always kept trying, with indifferent success, to persuade good
historians to Namierise the present: this has been left too
much in the hands of sociologists, not well briefed about the
intimate details of recent history, and of political pamphleteers (as in the Left Book Club days) to whom we in
political science owe much.

But the heart of the matter for me has been not the
history and analysis of concepts but the working of political
systems. How did this stand in the 1930s? On the one hand,
there was Marxist analysis which was attractive partly
because its prophecies about crisis, imperialism, violence and
capitalist decline seemed to be coming out right, partly
because an appeal to faith, comradeship, and discipline
seemed appropriate in a time of weakness, isolation and
despair. There was plenty of Marxist and quasi-Marxist
literature to hand, but the level of Marx scholarship was low
and the very complex debates among Lenin's contemporaries
had virtually disappeared from the record for the time being,
so that perhaps I depended too much on the works of
Trotsky in exile. But clearly these were the writings of a man,
not of a bureaucracy.

It is more puzzling to assess the status of Western writing
about political systems, but it is important to make some
attempt because on this depends one's assessment of 'the
new political science' which arose in the 1940s.

On the one hand, the text-books were not good. The
American books — 'Ogg', 'Ogg and Ray', 'Ogg and Zink' and
so on — were prepared in a business-like way for a large
college market: but a student brought up solely on them
would have had good reason to complain about their
conceptual emptiness and triviality. The only British book on
that scale was *The Theory and Practice of Modern Government* (1932) by Herman Finer: a marvellous source for
bibliography, including French, German, and Italian references, but rather muddled and long-winded in its analysis, so
that I tended to recommend to beginners the rather
elementary but level-headed book on *Modern Political
Constitutions* by C.F. Strong (1930). Bryce and Dicey had
been familiar Oxford figures till the 1920s, but their views,

formed in the Oxford milieu of the 1880s, were primarily of historical interest in the 1930s. Indeed, the most valuable thing about Dicey was that his *Law of the Constitution* (originally published in 1885) was first seriously attacked by Ivor Jennings in *The Law and the Constitution*, published in 1933. This gave one a chance to teach by confrontation about the problems of a constitutional system. There were some short text-books and relevant government publications about federations, electoral systems, second chambers; there was the Haldane Committee Report[15]; and that was about all. But perhaps one should add the mountain of blue books about local government, a similar mountain (but intelligently anthologised) about the Empire and Commonwealth. Each mountain constituted a PPE special subject; on one sat John Maud enthroned, on the other Kenneth Wheare, sceptics and scholars both.

Yet on the other hand it was possible to put good students in touch with original works of classical quality, and the list was not really very long. There were of course Ostrogorski, Michels and Mosca: Pareto was hard to use, and apparently no one had heard of Max Weber till Talcott Parsons discovered him, just at this time. Not much of Sorel was available in English, but at least he could be used to give life to the pre-1914 debates on pluralism in theory and practice and on sovereignty, in which well-known Oxford figures — Lindsay, Cole, Laski, Barker (Figgis was in Cambridge) — had taken a prominent part, and this gave us at least a cross-reference to Europe. I did own a copy of Esmein, and had heard of Duguit: but Carré de Malberg was the rather special property of C.H. Wilson, who came in 1940 to succeed Denis Brogan, when the latter went to the Cambridge chair. However, we had all had 'Maitland on Gierke', though probably no one had any inkling why Gneist in the 1860s, Redlich at the end of the century, had bothered to study English local government. There were fine essays in quantitative method, by Siegfried in France and Stuart Rice in the USA. The Chicago School led by Charles Merriam was setting new standards in the study of micro-politics, and Lasswell was just beginning to emerge as a conceptual influence, with *Psychopathology and Politics* in 1930, and

Who Gets What When How in 1936. Indeed Merriam's own book on *Political Power*, published in 1934, is a warmer and richer book than those associated with the Dahl/Wright Mills debate in the late 1950s and early 1960s. Nor must one forget A.L. Lowell's books, published before 1914, on *The Government of England* (1908) and on *Public Opinion and Popular Government* (1913), nor the early work of Walter Lippmann,[16] when he was associated with Graham Wallas at LSE. Wallas's own book on *Human Nature in Politics* (1908) had a similar breadth and warmth.

Our perspective for country studies was in effect limited to Britain, America, France with a few side-glances at Switzerland and at the Dominions of the "old" Commonwealth, and there might be not more than two or three books on each. But these were good ones; Bryce on the American Commonwealth (1893), Brogan on America (1933) and also on France (1940), Bodley (1899) and Middleton (1932) on France, Alec Werth's incomparable volumes of reporting from Paris in the 1930s. One might say that there were just enough good 'idiographic' books to indicate the kind of questions that might be asked and answered about a political system – if only one had time.

I think the American reaction away from the pre-war books must have been largely due to the aridity of their own text-books, which we did not read. Perhaps we were lucky, in that our native market was too small for such productions to be viable.

It is true that a year's work was ample to bring one abreast of what was available in academic print. But there was no sense of poverty, at least if the task in hand was to engage a student in exploration rather than in dogmatic doctrine.

'Research' was scarcely yet a concept; the thing was not to 'do research' but to 'write a book'. But it is true that John Maud did what was virtually a piece of 'contract research' on *City Government: Johannesburg*, published in 1938; and when Arthur Salter came to Oxford from the League of Nations in 1934 he began in his business-like way to organise younger class and graduate students into a seminar about what are now called 'para-statal bodies', since the old term 'public corporations' has turned out rather sourly. I was interested in this, and also in civil liberties, an exciting subject in the 1930s which turned out to be quite dead in people's minds when I came back to lecturing about it in 1945. By that time I had served out the war in secretariat positions in London and in Washington, and had been quite close to the in-fighting that goes on between 'the good and the great' (the Lindemann-Tizard story for instance, the controversies surrounding anti-submarine warfare, aircraft production, the bomber offensive). Indeed, I had found it not particularly difficult to act as secretariat to radar and operational research committees, and to record their generally disregarded decisions. Add to this that I had written the equivalent of a part-time Ph.D. thesis for the Cabinet Office on the history of the Special Operations Executive, a gruesome story of personal and administrative tragedies; and I think I had invented for Oxford lectures a subject called 'constitutional theory' which proved much more attractive than 'civil liberties'. The best way to define it may be to refer to Geoffrey Marshall's book of that name (1971) and also to his book on *Parliamentary Sovereignty in the Commonwealth* (1957), Maurice Vile on *Constitutionalism and the Separation of Powers* (1967), Tony Birch on *Representation* (1971). It might be more in the mood now to call it 'the rhetoric of legitimacy' or 'ideology in its linkage function': the idea would be much the same.

Manchester

When I moved to Manchester in 1948 I had really published nothing, and saw gathering round me the Nirvana of the ineffectual College Tutor. And I was married and needed the money.

But by this time I had been infected by the research bug: I remember saying in my interview (the bouts of madness that seize one in interviews) that I thought that empirical research by four like-minded people would be enough to change radically our ideas about British government. (Was I right, at least in principle?)

In addition, I had realized that I knew Scotland, Whitehall, Oxford, a good deal of Europe, but had by-passed England. Travelling regularly by train and car between Edinburgh and

Oxford I had missed industrial England as effectively as if I had flown over it at 30,000 feet. Electoral studies were beginning to emerge at Nuffield, sponsored by R.B. McCallum, Herbert Hicholas, David Butler: but the literature of 'grass-roots politics' (as in the work of Chicago School) simply did not exist. Nothing was 'known' about constituency politics, or about politics and administration in local government, for any date later than Ostrogorski on parties (known to be misleading), that of the Webbs (also known to be misleading) on local government: Gash on *Politics in the Age of Peel* was not published till 1953, Hanham on *Politics in the Time of Gladstone and Disraeli* not till 1959, Vincent on *Pollbooks* not till 1967. We 'knew' immensely more about grass-roots politics from the age of Elizabeth (that of Neale) to the age of Namier than we did about our contemporaries. Such a situation I found to be in a scholarly sense indecent and undignified.

So I was heading into the same area as 'the behavioural movement', but from a different starting-point. I could reckon myself as a disciple of the 'Chicago School', but not of those who came into political study primarily from psychology and who muddled things for all of us by introducing the term 'political behaviour'. They were not in fact consistent in applying the 'behavioural' principles of Watson, Pavlov, Skinner, Eysenck, nor could they have been.

I also responded strongly to American influence in the field of administrative theory. By this time, I thought I knew a good deal about administrators and politicians in Whitehall. And I knew a bit about 'the public administration movement' in the USA, about City Managers as part of the counter-move against bossism and *The Shame of the Cities* (1904), about American local research groups and their loose coordination through the Public Administration Clearing House in Chicago. But I had no inkling of the tradition of self-help among local government officers in the provincial cities of England, canalised by the late Levi Hill of NALGO into pressure on provincial universities to offer part-time academic courses to the able boys who in the days of deep depression left school at fourteen or fifteen and were lucky to get clerks' jobs in the Town Hall. The local authorities (in general) gave no cash support: NALGO were coaxed by their Secretary into giving a little, on the basis of their policy of negotiating for proper pay for well-qualified staff. But perhaps something got done largely because this local pressure came into alliance with philosophers of Sandy Lindsay's temper (J.L. Stocks, for instance, in Manchester) who believed in civic commitment and in the development of talent. Practically all the big civic universities (and this includes the University of London, in one of its aspects) provided non-graduate Diplomas in Public Administration; Manchester was unique in offering two parallel evening degrees, B.Comm. and B.Admin. In fact, Politics as a subject got into Manchester (the first strong department outside the LSE) as a result of this alliance between philosophy and administration. This is not so queer as it may seem if one does not know 'the provinces'. But it had the queer effect that one had to start a Politics department with the politics left out, and it required a good deal of time and patience to inject it.

Besides, I rather think that the University thought they were appointing a professor of public administration, so that I had certain obligations; indeed, there were part-time students there (though never of the same calibre of those in the starved and ambitious days before 1939) who might have something to teach. It appeared very soon that within a broad course including economics, economic history, administrative law and political philosophy the weak sister was the core subject, public administration. It had neither theory nor observation; and in timid hands it might decline into rote learning of statutes, financial devices and Royal Commission reports. As one explored the American scene from a distance (I have lived in the USA only for six months during the war), two things seemed to stand out; on the one hand case-studies of the process of administration, on the other hand the second generation of administrative theory. There were in particular at that time H.A. Simon, approaching *Administrative Behaviour* (1947) in a way much more sophisticated than was the 'behavioural' approach to political behaviour; and Dwight Waldo, whose approach to *The Administrative State* (1948) was similar in method to my

notions of 'constitutional theory' but had been developed in
a different area and within a different tradition.

I still find that these two scholars provide excellent clues
to the intellectual organisation of administrative experience.
It seems to me that Simon may be wrong in his later work in
approaching administrative organisation as an aspect of
'artificial intelligence';[1][8] and that one needs (along with
these two traditions) a third leg which might be called
'administrative culture'. But Simon and his associates have set
a high standard of clarity and rigour, a warning against the
mushiness of so much administrative writing (especially that
of some commissions of enquiry).

Another challenge in Manchester was that for the first time
I found myself in a social science faculty where two
colleagues, Ely Devons and Max Gluckman, had strong (but
not dogmatic) views about the unity of social science; as
indeed had Dorothy Emmet, who was during her time as
Professor of Philosophy a vigorous contributor to social
science seminars. And she too was (one might say) an affiliate
of the Lindsay connection who had worked at Risca in the
Welsh valleys in the 1920s. And Michael Polanyi, of late
Professor of Chemistry, though he went his own way, was
there to remind us that academic frontiers are prison walls to
be resented and bashed down.

Ely Devons and I had not met during the war, but we had
seen the same sets of phony figures about future aircraft
production from two sides, he in the Ministry of Air
Production, I in the Air Staff secretariat, and we shared the
feeling that false figures might nevertheless have an administrative 'function'. And we both knew the late Air Chief
Marshal Sir Wilfred Freeman, who talked the same language
quite freely (though in a more pungent way) and served both
of us as a model of the kind of 'serious' administration that
changes the situation, as distinct from mere bustle or mere
pedantry (supply names if you wish!). In a sense, Cornford's
Microcosmographia was a conceptual source for all of us.

We both met functionalist theory through Max Gluckman,
and I suppose that I learnt political sociology from a social
anthropologist not from a sociologist (I did not read Parsons
and co. till I had to, though Dorothy Emmet visited

Columbia often, and transmitted to us a good deal from R.K. Merton). Indeed, I still think that functionalism is as good a scheme as any with which to approach a continuing small society and its micro-politics. But in the middle fifties I was discussing political theory in terms of the paradox of 'common purpose' — how can 'purpose', a word that *belongs* (as it were) to the individual, be used 'properly' in relation to many individuals without postulating a super-creature whose purpose the common purpose is? This is of course only one way of restating a continuing theme in the history of political thought: and I can think of no answer except that we have multitudes of examples of very individual things held in common, such as language — what is a 'word'? what is a 'concept'? We cannot live without these 'things held in common', and at the end of the day I don't find that community of 'purpose' is harder than community of 'words'. Both problems are very hard: neither can be resolved by defining it away.

However, be that as it may, it did not take long to find scepticism invading one's attitude towards the explanatory power of 'function': it has a nice air of non-teleology, but after all what *is* function except purpose without a purposer — or perhaps God's purpose? And so back to Square One of the argument.

I mention the debate about function in this superficial way to indicate that in our *milieu* it had very little to do with Parsonian functionalism, and that I did not have to struggle with serious attempts to use the latter in explanation till I was with Stein Rokkan in Bergen in 1966; and Rokkan had worked closely on this with Martin Lipset.[19] The functionalism of social anthropology (of Radcliffe Brown and Malinowski) began to break down in the 1950s, analytically and also because it was difficult to use in the context of rapid change in Africa, familiar to Max Gluckman and his colleagues, and also to myself in relation to various constitutional enquiries in Africa in which I was involved at that time. Possibly this breakdown was confluent to the reaction against 'grand' sociological functionalism in the 1960s. But one had very little concern either with the politics of the American academic patronage which were involved in

American functionalism[20] or with the neo-Marxism which welled up from somewhere underground in the 1960s.

1968 changed the intellectual world irreversibly, but by that time our Manchester group had imperceptibly disintegrated. The book on *Politics and Social Science*[21] (written mainly at Bergen in the early months of 1966) was a rather desperate effort to state the outcome of that experience in an impersonal way.

Perhaps I understand now what I was trying to do better than before I wrote the book. The introductory section was perhaps concerned too much with the 'data revolution' and its technologies and too little with the desperate and demanding nature of the problems of world politics, which I do in the end state fairly clearly (on p.306):

> the problem of the character and stability of the state system, the problem of change in the state system, and the problem of the politics of all mankind, the only political unit which can now claim generality in an adequate intellectual sense.

And the logic of the rest of the book was not scrupulously worked out, largely because it emerged *ambulando*, in the process of writing. I rather think that this is a defensible and reasonable way to do it, that is to say that methodology comes after practice, not before it, and I hope that if I go on writing it will not be about method. But here is a provisional attempt at re-statement.

(1) 'Grand theory', at least in its contemporary forms, looks slightly ridiculous in so far as its claims the status of natural science. It never achieves either exact statement or crucial and decisive experiment, and it fails to clarify the relation between fact and value in its operations (not that I can clarify this in my own operations).

(2) In the last generation there has been an impressive gain in the stock of partial theories available to social sciences. Some of these (besides being ingenious and 'insightful') can be and have been worked out and applied in a very scrupulous way. But they seem to me to be 'heuristic' rather than substantive; tools in a kit, golf-clubs in the bag, to be

used variously by experience, judgement and manipulative skill as the context requires.

(3) It was in my mind that the appeal to methods of science was often made by people who had not done science nor read the history of science, so that they picked the wrong bits of that story for application to the creation of social science. The science of man is 'end on' not to physics and chemistry but to biology, as is obvious from the history of anatomy, physiology and pathology and their schemes of functional analysis.

(4) The pioneers in these fields of biology for a long time disregarded patterns of behaviour; they were better at studying the dead than the living — the hunters knew more about social biology than did the anatomists. The balance has been redressed in the last fifty years, and there is now a science of social biology or ethology so well established that we cannot conceive how we ever got on without it.

(5) But the history of that science shows that patient empiricism is needed to disentangle physiological and social factors, and then to put them together. Fundamental terms and definitions are by no means finally settled, and the argument about 'the physiological correlates of behaviour' is still obscure. Yet no one doubts that progress can and will be made by 'scientific method'. What were once mere 'bird-watchers' now have a recognised place in 'normal science'.

(6) Following this line of approach, I should properly have begun from some secure scientific knowledge about *The Limits of Human Nature*[22]. But I did not know enough about it (nor do I now), and I started at the level of human ethology and small group studies, noting that even there ideology intrudes.[23]

(7) There follow social anthropology, the study of organisations, the study of communities; I had lived at close quarters with these disciplines in Manchester and felt that it would be ridiculous to deny the progress made within my working life-span. But it would be equally ridiculous to deny that 'impurities' are built into them, particularly in regard to the selection of problems and the limited scope for observations. It must be added that their presentation is often

'hortatory' or 'normative' in style. However, that need not worry us into total scepticism, since it is common enough in applied sciences, such as engineering, medicine and agriculture, which depend on human organisations and human choices. But we need to be wary.

(8) Finally, the inclusive system in which the investigator is himself a participant. World politics exist and are very dangerous. We simply do not know how to manage the human ecology of a small planet, and we had better find out, rather quickly. That is surely a practical form of knowledge? Yet it also requires some workable kind of political system, even if it is only a system of mutual adjustment and social discipline. And I cannot conceive a political system without myths, symbols, and ideology which are to some extent shared. Thus I am driven back to grand theory, grand conceptualisation, grand myth, which I left behind rather sceptically at the beginning of the enquiry.

The best I can claim for my explorations is that this has been a matter of bringing to bear a number of distinct traditions on what were for me in the 1930s the central problems of my time. There was a tradition of evangelical and practical theology, and of the reaction twinned with it: 'the Minister's bairns are the deil's bairns' – I was only a grandson, but on both sides. There was the equally archaic tradition, launched (like that of Calvinism) in the sixteenth century and now on the verge of extinction, the tradition of language as rhetoric, as grammar, as a 'humane' accomplishment. At least I knew enough of scientists, of philosophers, of lawyers not to fear them as remote and dangerous entities. But perhaps predominant has been a training in the tradition of history as an understanding of unique events in context and in sequence. Dare I mention the one published article (nine pages only) of the best of tutors, C.G. Stone, on 'March 1st, 50 BC',[24] twenty-four hours at the hinge of events? But history must also be understood as myth and symbol, rhetoric and style. In the last resort, Thucydides is the man for me, Thucydides, historian, analyst and myth-maker.

a separate discipline of 'economics', nor of 'sociology'. There is a unity in the problems of social science, and that unity I gladly recognise as the unity of a discipline, child of the humanities, the natural sciences, the healing arts, but distinct from all three.

What then are my present main interests?

Neo-Marxism; social biology; rhetoric and style, symbol and myth; political identity; political adaptivity.

Much the same as in the 1930s? But I have travelled quite a long way.

. . . to arrive where we started
And know the place for the first time.[2][5]

Notes

1. Cf. J.K. Galbraith, *The Non-Potable Scotch: A Memoir on the Clansmen in Canada* (Penguin, 1967). Like his ancestors mine went to Ontario: but of course this was not the only kind of Scots settlement in the wide lands of the Dominion.

2. Born 1773, son of a village shoemaker in Angus: Alexander Bain, *James Mill, A Biography* (London: Longmans, 1882).

3. From *The Bruce* by John Barbour, c. 1320–95; *The Oxford Book of Scottish Verse* (Oxford: Clarendon, 1966) at p.10.

4. Edinburgh UP, 1961.

5. J.C. Gilbert, *A History of Investment Trusts in Dundee, 1873–1938* (London: King, 1939); W. Turrentine Jackson, *The Enterprising Scot, Investors in the American West after 1873* (Edinburgh UP, 1968).

6. See Book VII, Ch.6 of John Morley, *Life of Gladstone* (London: Macmillan, 1903).

7. Preposterous coincidence: I had just corrected this for the press when the BBC showed a film of edible dormice: not English dormice but German descendants of the big fat Roman dormouse (BBC.2, 7.25 pm, 9 December 1973).

8. Drusilla Scott, *A.D. Lindsay. A Biography* (Oxford: Blackwell, 1971).

9. as in the French *bachot.*

10. Milton, *Areopagitica.*

11. W.B. Gallie, *A New University. A.D. Lindsay and the Keele Experiment* (London: Chatto, 1960).

12. An odd thing is that Marx stood on the other shore of this great divide. He was a fine Greek scholar and his doctoral thesis on Greek materialism is a key to understanding what he meant by 'materialism'. Perhaps no classical author is closer to Marx in spirit than was Lucretius. There is an article about this ('Karl Marx on Greek

Atomism', *Classical Quarterly*, 22 (1928) p.205) by my Balliol classics tutor, Cyril Bailey, whose special subject was Lucretius. But I have found no evidence of a direct link.

13. No.425 in Philip Larkin (ed.), *The Oxford Book of Twentieth Century English Verse* (Oxford: Clarendon, 1973).

14. Eduard Fraenkel perhaps, Corpus Professor of Latin from 1935 to 1953; a man to respect greatly, but not easy to work with. I followed in fascination J.D. Beazley's small classes on the identification of Greek vase painters. But that clearly was not for me, and by good or bad luck I never fell in with archaeologists of the younger school, several of whom died young as fighters in occupied Greece.

15. Cd. 9230 of 1918: and see the headnote to Section I, below.

16. For instance, *A Preface to Politics* (1913).

17. There is a useful brief account at the end of the first edition of L.D. White's *Introduction to the Study of Public Administration* (New York: Macmillan, 1926).

18. *The Sciences of the Artificial* (MIT Press, 1969). But a scientific battle still rages over the heuristic scope of that concept: see *Artificial Intelligence: a paper symposium* (London: Scientific Research Council, Apr 1973).

19. S.M. Lipset and Stein Rokkan, *Party System and Voter Alignments: Cross-National Perspectives* (New York: Free Press, 1967).

20. A.W. Gouldner, *The Coming Crisis of American Sociology* (London: Heinemann, 1971).

21. (London: Penguin, 1967)

22. Ed. J. Benthall (London: Allen and Unwin, 1973).

23. *Politics and Social Science*, Ch. 11 and 12.

24. *Classical Quarterly*, 22 (1928) p. 193.

25. T.S. Eliot, *Little Gidding*.

I
Sighting Shots

Logically, this Section should include the first substantial thing I wrote for publication, an essay on 'The Structure of Central Administration' which appeared in a book on *British Government since 1918* published in 1950.[1] But it is rather long, is available in most libraries and contains a good deal of obsolete information: so it would scarcely justify inclusion here, especially as its main point can be stated very briefly — if administration is important it is politics.

At that time students of central administration in Britain were offered no conceptual approach except that given by the Haldane Report on the Machinery of Government, published in 1918 (Cd. 9230). It was by no means a bad example of the administrative theory of its time, but it had become dogma for lack of scrutiny, and returned to us ceaselessly in garbled form both in students' essays and in Establishment debate, at the level (say) of the correspondence column of *The Times*. Fresh from war time experience of defence organisation, and from the shabby history of wrangles between Ministers and Ministries over subversion in Europe, I took it on myself to point out that 'Haldane' simply had no relation at all to the facts of administration and politics in the past thirty years. Administrative history could only be interpreted in terms of power and policy: it was a fact of life that if administrative change was important it would be resisted, the slate could never be wiped clean. I pointed out that the principal authors were Haldane, Morant and Beatrice Webb, all of them saturated in experience of administrative power, all of them astute in handling wires, axes and sharp knives. The clanking of their operations sounds through the woolly official prose; and that had more substantive importance for the future than the pose of irrefutable Benthamite rationality.

I was of course doing my best to be brash and boyish as a belated newcomer of forty; and my ignorance of administrative theory and administrative history was extreme. But I have no desire to recant the main theme, or even such rash prophecy as this:

> The great changes in administration have come about through causes partly fortuitous, partly political, but on the whole outside the range of administrative planning. The political forces are sometimes positive in their effects on administration: as, for instance, in the long-term trend which is raising the status of the Scottish Office or in the brief accidents which made the creation of a Ministry of Supply in 1939 symbolic of a resolute foreign policy, or the creation of MAP in 1940 symbolic of resistance to the end. More often they are negative . . .

The essay which now stands first in the collection may seem rather special, but I think that it should be on the record lest one strand in the development of political studies in the United Kingdom is quite forgotten.[2] It was presented at the second meeting of the Political Studies Association in March 1951, in the days when the PSA was comparable to the Fourth Party of the 1880s who could all go to Parliament in the same cab. The total membership was said to be about fifty. I remember giving the paper to a plenary meeting of perhaps fifteen or twenty in a rather dark little dining room in Magdalen. In a sense it reported my first efforts to explore provincial England, and also my first quasi-political efforts to back the periphery against the centre, and to force on the exalted centre some notion of realities outside its ken — but how often have I had to say to myself 'Victrix causa deis placuit sed victa Catoni.'[3] It seems pointless to add detailed footnotes: but it is important to realise that these were the early days of the Local Government Examinations Board and its examining committee, in which quite a number of us were involved. It has been a hard and difficult business to carry local government training through the period since World War II, and the problem of staffing is by no means resolved yet. But there seems to me to have been more creative life in this than in the separate and parallel development of civil service training.

At the time I thought rather highly of my piece about Oakeshott's famous lecture, an attempt to answer it by playing one tradition against another tradition rather than in a vein of exasperated misunderstanding. But I had not really done my homework in *Experience and its Modes* or on Oakeshott's intricately defined position in relation to idealism and phenomenology. I still think that he is wrong to regard this as *the* central (or even as *a* central) English or Scottish tradition: but it has a strong place in Western thought, and it is unwise to brush it aside, as I was apt to do.

Notes

1. London: Allen and Unwin.
2. It has quite recently been brought to mind in R.A. Chapman's pamphlet, 'Teaching Public Administration' (published by the Joint University Council for Social and Public Administration, London: RIPA, 1973).
3. Lucan, *The Civil War*, I, 128. To paraphrase: 'Gods back winners, but I like losers better.'

1 Public Administration in the Universities (1951)

My main submission is that the academic study of public administration is at present in rather a queer state in this country, and that it would benefit by more hard thought and controversial discussion. As I am anxious to provoke controversy, I will take less than proper precautions to hedge my conclusions; but I trust that over-statement may be forgiven me in a good cause.

First, it may be as well to explain why it seems justifiable to take up a session of the Association with a discussion of this topic, which probably seems from Oxford and from London a very limited and not very significant one. PPE once had a paper called Public Administration, but the conventions of the constitution soon dealt with *that*. Almost from the outset it was understood that all the questions were dummies except those on the history of English Local Government, and law was brought into line with practice when the regulations were last revised. In London 'Public Administration' has a fair share in the attention of the Honours Student specialising in Government; but only within the larger context of general Political Science. There is no question of building an undergraduate course of study round Public Administration.

It is far otherwise in the 'Provinces'. I have made no attempt to collect statistics, but I think it is safe to say that most of our undergraduate students in 'Political Studies' are drawn from two sources:

(a) First, the Diploma in Public Administration, generally taken part-time by evening students. DPA's vary a good deal, and include a great range of subjects, but in theory all of them are built round Public Administration, and the course in Public Administration (we think in terms of 'courses' in the Provinces) is under various names supposed to be the educational hub of the whole thing.

(b) Second, the Diploma in Social Studies, under its different names. This is built round the doctrine of social case-work, and in spite of its oddities that doctrine probably makes a more active educational nucleus than 'public administration'. But social workers cannot be turned loose in the social service state without some knowledge of the mechanism of the state, and (at least in my experience) they are markedly allergic to discussions in the best vein of political science about the role of the American senate, the French Administrative Courts or the British Cabinet. So they also fall into the territory of Public Administration: they are in most Universities quite numerous, and (to put it concretely) a large part of our job is social workers by day, local government officers in the evening, all studying 'Public Administration' – in Manchester both groups work for the B.A. (Admin.) degree, not for a Diploma; but the teaching problem is substantially the same. Probably the political theorists carry much the same type of load: but 'political institutions', and 'international relations' still play quite a small part in the provincial scheme of things.

It would be interesting if someone would write a history of the DPA more complete than the short account in Mr. Hill's little book on the educational work of NALGO; there is a good deal to be learnt from Prof. Waldo's book on the gospel of Public Administration in the USA, and from Miss Macadam's account of the origins of training for social work in Britain. But a history would probably not cast any important light on the academic problems of Public Administration – at least I do not think that our academic ancestors had any more light than we have. The teaching of 'Public Administration' did not begin as an attempt to share knowledge already held by wise men: there was no flavour of University extension about it. On the contrary, it was brought into existence by the concerted demands of pupils seeking a higher intellectual status for their work; also demanding an examination and a step in salary suitable to their 'ticket', but it would be grossly unfair to think of the DPA movement as essentially a meal ticket movement. (It had analogies in the history of the teaching profession.) At any rate 'the hungry sheep looked up'; they were sheep well organised and well led, and most Universities were persuaded to look round and hire some more or less plausible persons whose job it would be first to invent Public Administration, then to teach it — and finally to examine it. It would be unfair to complete the quotation from 'Lycidas'; but fair enough to say that in the interval between the rise of the DPA (say 1925–35) and the war, no one in the Universities had much idea what it was all about. I should except London, where there was much crying in the wilderness by Dr. Robson and Dr. Herman Finer; but in a sense a majority of British Universities had in these years accepted a Webbian principle about the training of administrators without having any Webbians at hand to carry it out. I suppose that our founding fathers are on the one hand the Webbs, on the other Mr. Hill and NALGO, and to them we owe bread and butter as well as inspiration; but we also owe it to them to clear our heads a little about what we are doing.

This seems to be urgent now, for at least four reasons:

(a) First, the DPA in its old form has outlived its usefulness. The local government service has by its own action closed the higher ranks of the profession to anyone who has not acquired by examination a qualification equivalent to a degree; this policy may or may not be correct — there is a good deal of controversy about it — but if it is upheld it is in effect a challenge to the Universities to continue the teaching of Public Administration at a standard higher than that of the present DPA.

(b) Second, Political Studies have now emerged from the war as a fairly coherent discipline; we have a fair measure of agreement about what we mean by teaching Political Science. I won't attempt to define it, but I think would be a common ground now that Public Administration is a corner of the picture not academically intelligible except in relation to the whole. Apart from the DPA and its kin, what we are trying to do now is to train political scientists (or if you like, to educate ordinary citizens through political science) so that they can apply their training for themselves in the field in which they work later; it never really occurs to us that some people think we should be training administrators.

(c) Third, more doubtfully, I think we can say that there has been a corresponding stabilisation in the field of social studies as a whole. The air is thick with verbiage about the integration of the social sciences, but through the haze we can dimly see that there are other groups of persons engaged in activities which are in part quite sensible — psychologists, econometrists, social anthropologists, and so on: and we can see that there is a relation between what they are trying to do and what we are trying to do. It is no longer safe to write off our colleagues in other departments as cranks and crackpots.

(d) Fourth, and this is perhaps a reason of a different order, there is a considerable uproar going on in the USA about the new science of administration — business administration as well as public administration. It is not very easy to assess what this amounts to, but at any rate it is a much more sophisticated approach to the subject than ours, and we cannot let it pass without establishing our position in relation to it.

I hope there are sufficient reasons for digging this rather tender plant up by the roots to see how it is getting on. I should like to consider it under three heads:

  (i) Teaching hitherto.
  (ii) Research hitherto.
  (iii) What next?

Teaching Hitherto

What have we taught so far in the average 'course' in Public Administration — which may of course have had other titles such as 'Central and Local Government'? Would this be a fair summary?

(a) A smattering of history, from about 1832, with special reference to the civil service, local government, the public services. The standard of work has been '1834 and all that' a few dates and a few cliches: there has certainly been no attempt to teach either historical perspective or the use of historical evidence. It is perhaps scandalous that we have been so reckless in encouraging young administrators to treat official papers as good evidence for facts: apart from that, the weakness is not altogether our fault. The professional historians have written virtually nothing of critical value on

British government since 1800, and it would be a little hard for us to do more than teach the authorised version.

(b) Second, a little law: some elementary constitutional law, some local government law, but (rather surprisingly) hardly anything of the law governing the relations of the official to the citizen. Our law is certainly worse than our history; and to a lawyer it is beneath contempt. It is totally 'unlawyerly', because it evades all unsettled issues, it evades the precise and painstaking use of technical language, and it cares nothing for the interlocking of the legal system to form a whole. We *could*, if we tried, learn more law: the low level is perhaps less excusable than in history.

(c) Third, there is what I can only call 'current affairs': read (or take lecture-notes on) the latest official reports, and discuss them as if writing for *The Economist*. This is a difficult art, because it involves criticism and prophesy by deduction from major premises passed off as universally acceptable but so far as possible concealed. But perhaps it is only difficult for us because we were in our youth taught by logicians; it would be fairer to say that it is the mode of political argument natural to man and that success in it (as formerly said of Greek verse composition) 'not infrequently leads to valuable preferment'.

(d) Fourth — but this is controversial — I think we have most of us fought shy of a science of administration or principles of administration of the type we associate with Mr. Urwick, Mr. Milward and Mr. Brech. We have not perhaps been intellectuals of the highest order, but we have had our pride: at least there was one branch of study at which we could sneer as less respectable than ourselves.

Was all this worth doing? Paradoxically enough, I think it was. It was and is quite possible to examine in this curious subject fairly and with good discrimination. There was nothing wrong with it as a test of hard work, accuracy and mental agility: but of course (more or less in the words of Macaulay) a properly conducted examination in Choctaw or Sanskrit would achieve that. Has what we taught been worth learning, except as a training in how to jump through specially constructed hoops?

For the ordinary plain man I think it has. The best teachers have been thinking in terms of the plain man's view of administration, and any plain man who has 'done' Public Administration has a reasonably good orientation in the jungle of British government: he knows in a general way where to go to find the right official. But what we have not done is to teach anything whatever to the official about what to do or what not to do in his job. Officials who have been through the course probably have gained some notion of 'where they fit it': they may also have gained what NALGO was aiming at in particular – an improved sense of status and of professional unity. But we have certainly not taught them anything, even negatively, about public administration. One reason is that we have not tried – none of us has taken very seriously the much-advertised launching of the new science of administration. Another is that we have been very busy: the curious amalgam known as Public Administration covers a very wide range of miscellaneous information, and it changes rapidly. We have been much too busy keeping our heads above water to think academically about 'scope and method', and there is still an ocean of information to explore. But I would urge that if we are to do a job worthy of a University we must occasionally stop accumulating and analyse; and analyse academically. The first thing we have to teach administrators is academic doubt – the difference between certainty and uncertainty; perhaps the second is academic precision of speech; and these are relatively easy for us to learn ourselves.

Research Hitherto
Between the wars the number of researchers was so small that any discussion is bound to be a little *ad hominem*: it is hard to think of more than half-a-dozen names altogether. But it might be said that the tradition is descriptive and critical.

(a) First, an administrative institution is *described*, in its history, law and contemporary working;

(b) Second, it is *criticised* by reference to principles drawn from outside the study of administration: the object is not to elucidate or verify principles of administration, but to criticise administration by reference to what may be crudely called 'common-sense'. Of course the best researchers formulate these standards with a good deal of care, but their authority for the standards is their belief that 99 per cent of their readers will accept them if they are properly formulated.

This kind of research I very strongly believe to be a good thing. But it has two severe limitations.

(a) Its method is historical — 'description' is in fact contemporary history — but it is history with half the relevant factors left out. We should not dream of accepting as complete any of our own descriptions of twentieth century institutions if they purported to be descriptions of fifteenth century institutions. Sometimes we deceive ourselves, but generally we know well enough that we have left out half the story. It is almost impossible in contemporary history to be complete, or nearly complete; first, there is the vast size and complexity of the scene; second, there is the limitation of access to evidence; third, and perhaps most important, there is the difficulty of saying what we know — some of it may be libellous, certainly a great deal of it is tactless and it will not make smooth our future relations with our witnesses if we publish it.

(b) Second, there is is the fact that this research is 'angled' not to the administrator but to the public. No doubt it does the administrator good to have some light and air let into his office, but our criticism is intended primarily to guide politicians and the public. It is very hard, for instance, to imagine that any Town Clerk or City Treasurer could get any help with *his* problems from any of the books (except legal books) hitherto published on local government. Here too, we have (on a small scale) been doing a good job, but not a job in Public Administration.

One point emerges from this which I might make here and 'carry forward' to the next section. This 'traditional' technique is not dead and need not die: but it would add to its vitality if it were backed by some proper studies of nineteenth century administration. I know that a great deal has been done for medieval administration and something for that of the seventeenth and eighteenth centuries; will no first-rate historian tackle the history of the public offices — or of individual local authorities — in the nineteenth century? The material is all there, one can get at almost every scrap of paper relevant to great administrative issues, and the participants are mercifully dead. Cannot we get the historians to set standards for us −, standards in the assessments of evidence of the modern type, which has so many pitfalls of its own: standards in concreteness, in seeing the problem all round, with all or almost all the factors relevant to it? Everything I have to say later is rather speculative: this field is white for the harvest now.

What Next?

In this section I shall make no distinction between research and teaching, because I am sure that, whatever has happened in the past, they must not be separated in the future. No institution can teach up to University standards unless it is − researching is too formal a word but − continuously sceptical about the issues fundamental to its teaching; and I very much doubt whether a research institute can live intellectually for long without the discipline of teaching.

Perhaps there are four alternative or complementary lines:

(a) Go on as we are. I certainly do not regard this as either harmful or useless: but in itself it represents frustration. To work only in Public Administration as it now is, is to work in a subject without a top storey: there are masses of material, no design, not even a hypothesis. We shall certainly never achieve academic respectability − that is complete only in dead subjects − but I do not see that we can cease to struggle towards it.

(b) Abandon Public Administration as a separate subject: or rather merge it in the general question of political science − 'How is Britain governed?' We know where we are with that question; we know that we can never completely answer it, but we know what is relevant to the answer. If we approach from this end we put public administration in the general context of political science; there is a tradition of analysis which we can teach, and in it the line between politics and administration is of some importance but not cardinal importance. Government is a whole, with various lines of cleavage in it, running criss-cross.

To put this formally, it means that there is no more DPA or B.A. (Admin): instead there is a Diploma or Degree in Political Science, in which the central papers are the three traditional ones — Political Theory, British Government, Comparative Political Institutions. The subject matter of our old Public Administration need not be killed: but now it will come in as ancillary and optional subjects — Local Government, the Central Department, National Services, each of them including, inextricably mixed, both political and administrative issues.

I have no doubt this is the cleanest cut. All I would say against it, is that it seems a little feeble. After all, there *is* such a subject as Administration. The evidence is that any good administrator can quickly reject out of a sample of humanity those who are *not* potentially administrators; and can tell those whom he retains a great deal about what not to do. He may not be able either to pick winners or to make outstanding work out of ordinary work: but the negative wisdom of the administrator is immense, and much of it is certainly not sub-conscious or inarticulate. On the contrary, many administrators are extremely talkative about it, though quite unmethodical. This *is* a branch of human knowledge, and it is rather a discredit to academic persons if they cannot put it into a rather better order. The University administrator does well to note the precepts in Cornford's *Microcosmographia Academica*, and perhaps Sir Henry Taylor was of some value to civil servants in his day. But no one else has even tried.

(c) Third, we might try to make ourselves useful. It is certainly not to the disadvantage of Political Science that some parts of it are beginning to have a cash value; it is to the good academically as well as practically, that politically important persons need the services of men trained in public opinion surveys, propaganda analysis and so on. The Russians would probably describe our subject as training in the art of espionage; and I do not see why we should not accept the definition. The best evidence that we know something important about the structure of politics is that we can produce techniques for quick, accurate and economical political analysis.

In Public Administration the exact equivalent is a little hard to find, but it seems to lie in the general direction of O & M widely construed. By this I mean not the higher criticism of higher organisation, but the analysis of the flow of business in offices whose terms of reference are specific and whose performance is measurable. The virtue of this is that it begins with those things about an office which can be treated as objective and measurable: an area small at first, but capable of expansion by persistent research based on a wide knowledge of techniques in use in social analysis. Hitherto we have despised O & M, and I think they have despised us: and there are at least two reasons for this antipathy. *First*, it must be admitted that very few of us know enough to teach: we do not know the first thing about large offices, and we know less than the first thing about the techniques relevant to economy in offices — cost accounting for instance, or business machines.

Second, we have been inclined to say that the design of forms and all that is not the sort of thing to be done in a University. This, I am sure, is snobbery: the criticism of forms leads one a long way back into the social sciences. The application is humble, but the principles are extremely complex and uncertain. It would be a very fair test of ability to ask a man first to learn, then to teach, the techniques involved in a great form-factory like the Ministry of National Insurance; if it is well done, the process of teaching and examining in a University forces the crude mass of material into an orderly form, and focuses attention on the unsolved problems. There are practical reasons such as the difficulty of arranging demonstrations which make this form of teaching hard for us; but so far as I know the subject has not even been considered, and this is still a gulf fixed between University teaching and the type of knowledge which men use in office management.

(d) Fourth, we might go all scientific. Get a good map of social sciences — carve out a territory for administration (I am afraid the 'Public' would have to go: it is hopelessly 'unscientific') — people our zone with principles begotten according to the best rules of hypothesis and verification.

This strikes me as a noble enterprise, and also as the greatest possible fun. One begins by reading all the other social sciences: one frames a definition of Administration: then one generates hypotheses, and makes a nice plan for verifying them by case study — and if you have nice cases, case study is as much fun as hypotheses. I am very strongly in favour of trying it, even to the extent of making all professorial committees meet in glass observation-chambers: but I don't think it will work — not because I disagree with the method, but because I think there is no space empty on the map. I can only indicate the argument here. Without haggling over words, the most promising type of definition of the field of Administration as a social science is something like 'purposive group action'. The only likely method of achieving hypothesis and verification in the fields is by working at first with small relatively self-contained groups: natural or artificial microcosms. It is most unlikely that by case-study one can *prove* anything about administrative microcosms — even the smallest of them is much too big and complex: it is also most unlikely that statistical techniques will help, because it is singularly difficult to get a satisfactory 'unit of account', except on the level of routine operations — and this approach rather scorns routine operations (what fascinates its exponents is the problem of adaptation). If this is our field then it seems that it must be studied in small groups, and small groups are already the subject of psychology, social psychology, social anthropology. This is quite a big enough crowd, and the issues would emphatically not be clarified by the addition of a specialist in purposive action. Nor is it any use trying to divide administrative groups from others: if we are looking for the principles of purposive action in groups our first hypothesis is that they are likely to be the same for 10 ants or 10 rats or 10 Waggs-Waggas or 10 professors or 10 Assistant Secretaries. Of course, the hypothesis might be displaced, but we cannot begin by assuming away the uniformity of nature.

Therefore I do not think that we ought to become administrative scientists. Nevertheless, two things may be well worth doing:

(i) First, we ought to know much more than we do about the development of the study of groups and of individuals in relation to groups. This is difficult because so much of the literature is verbose and badly written, and we may need guidance from our colleagues. I suspect that the concrete body of knowledge so far produced is small, but not unimportant: and I do not see why we should not incorporate in our teaching those bits of it which are likely to be of service to administrators: it is certainly part of our job to cast our net wide on behalf of our pupils, and to share with them any useful fish which we catch.

(ii) Second, it will be all to the good if some people with experience of administration and with training in political science get bitten by this bug and transform themselves into sociologists. They will certainly bring to sociology knowledge which it lacks and problems which it has missed: they may give it valuable reinforcement, and they will certainly make some of its conclusions very interesting to us. But there is no use kidding ourselves that they will find the missing science of administration: on the contrary, they will become professional sociologists, and return no more.

Conclusion
May I now sum up this rather arbitrary argument?

It seems to me that the worst thing in our teaching is that it does not inculcate a sense of its own limitations. In some ways we are doing quite well; but we lack a point of view from which to judge our performance. We are unlikely to get this unless we can move further ahead of our pupils, and further ahead of the mass of printed matter with which we are flooded by the Stationery Office. This means partly research: partly a good resolution to read more widely and critically even at the expense of neglecting our monthly batch of official publications.

As regards research, and its repercussions on the development of teaching:

(a) Of 'traditional' research I should say much the same as of 'traditional' teaching; much of it is excellent, but it should be more explicit, both in the terminology which it uses and the criteria it employs. (Standardisation would be the ideal, but an explicit statement of definitions and assumptions is the first stage.)

(b) I can think of nothing more likely to raise standards than the production of some first-rate studies in Victorian administration.

(c) It would also set a standard if we began to measure ourselves against the practical needs of the administrators. At present our cash value is low. One cannot imagine the Treasury or a great county borough turning to a University department of government for technical assistance on any problem of administrative organisation, and they are not even very ready to turn to us for advice about training. In fact we are of little use because we don't know enough or know the wrong things; perhaps with due humility over a period of years we might in the end overcome that handicap.

(d) If anyone wants the pure science of man in society, I think he has come to the wrong shop for it here; Public Administration, in so far as it is related to science, is the application to a complex of practical problems of fag-ends of a great many different sciences, some of which are themselves far from pure. Nevertheless, Public Administration poses endless unanswered problems about political man: it is an admirable jumping-off point, and if anyone cares to jump I hope he will have a wonderful time.

2 Political Theory and Political Education*

The subject of this paper is very old and could readily be stated in terms of Plato's *Republic*; the implication of the title, 'Political Theory and Political Education', is that I want to state it in terms of an inaugural lecture which was given by Professor Michael Oakeshott in March 1951, when he took over the famous Chair of Political Science at the London School of Economics, held previously only by Graham Wallas and by Harold Laski, who had died in the spring of 1950. Oakeshott's lecture is called 'Political Education'[1] : it is not important for the present purpose that you should have read it, because its theme is simple and is stated in rather cloudy and beautiful prose, from which it will be a pleasure to quote.

I should add perhaps that I have in mind also four other books, T.S. Eliot's *Notes towards the definition of culture*, George Orwell's *1984*, Harold Nicolson's biography of *Benjamin Constant*, and Professor E.R. Dodd's book on *The Greeks and the Irrational*, all written by very intelligent men in face of the political situation as they saw it at the end of the 1940s, a period which you will remember pretty well. (This is one advantage enjoyed by adult students, which they seldom appreciate: for the ordinary undergraduate 1949 is now unknown country, in the limbo between the end of

*From *Universities Quarterly*, IX, no. 4 (Aug 1955). This paper is based on a lecture given to a small conference of former students of residential colleges for adult education, which was held at Holly Royde in January 1955. Since it was written I have found the same line of argument much more professionally stated in an article by Mr. J.W.N. Watkins: 'Political Tradition and Political Theory', *Philosophical Quarterly*, Oct 1952: but he is less concerned than I am with the problem of teaching, so I have let this stand untouched.

history and the beginning of news). I want to use Oakeshott as a basis for discussion; but I mention these other books because his lecture is (to use a word that he favours) part of a 'conversation' — a 'conversation, not an argument' (p.20) and they help to indicate the conversational mood of that period.

He sets the theme in the first paragraph, after the cutomary tribute to his predecessors: Graham Wallas, who never preached and always had faith that the way to improve human affairs was to apply intelligence to them, by 'the Art of Thought', as he called it in the title of a famous book[2] : and Harold Laski, who always preached, used learning primarily for rhetorical effect, and seemed often to prefer fact to fiction only in so far as fact might serve better to persuade and to amuse. Not that it is put in this way by Oakeshott, but the contrast is written plainly between the lines. Oakeshott ends his exordium, with great fairness and modesty: 'They were both great teachers, devoted, tireless, and with sure confidence in what they had to teach. And it seems perhaps a little ungrateful that they should be followed by a sceptic, one who would do better if only he knew how.

This contrast between three eminent men — Graham Wallas, Laski, Oakeshott — puts in personal form the abstract issue that I want to discuss. I feel it in a personal form myself because various accidents have put me (like Oakeshott) into the position of political educator, a very odd by-product of our educational system. The notion of 'political education' is perplexing enough in itself, and matters have been made worse by recent experience of forms of political education which (most of us agree) are both efficient and detestable. For argument's sake these perplexities can be arranged in a nice dialectical thesis and antithesis — and here I go along with Oakeshott — but I do not feel, as he does, that the pieces then click together with Marxian precision at the end of the story.

I

First, there are two things against which we all react, naïve scientific optimism and political sermons; here it may be neatest to reverse Oakeshott's order, and to take preaching first, social science second, because my generation went through them in that order. This is perhaps not true for you, because the great political preachers were bred in the period before 1914, and there are only scattered survivors left, now that Laski and Lord Lindsay of Birker have both gone. My own reaction against sermons came very early in life, as both my grandfathers were ministers of the Church of Scotland who 'came out in '43' –,the Disruption of the Church of Scotland in 1843, a more important date in Scottish history than '45, for better or for worse. In 1745 Prince Charles destroyed only the peculiar life of the Highlands, which was in any case an anachronism, a mere appendage to the substantial life of Scotland. But the quarrel which split the Church of Scotland marked the end of a middle-class tradition that had made Scotland the wonder of Europe in the eighteenth century: for the image of men like Hume and Adam Smith, Burns and Scott, it substituted the image of the Scots Sabbath and the elders of the Kirk. The Scots 'meenister' replaced the Scots 'feelosofer' as the world's stereotype. Holy Willie was in the saddle, and has never been thrown off. Or perhaps he is dead, and it is only his ghost that troubles us. At any rate, he is a pleasanter character now than he once was: but on the other side of the account he has lost that fire and rigour which made him a power in the nineteenth century.

The minister's bairns are notoriously the de'il's bairns: an upbringing in one or other of the branches of the Church of Scotland has inoculated many boys for life against the temptation to preach. The English tradition is less familiar to me, but I suspect that by the middle of the 1920s (I first went to Oxford in 1927) much the same thing had happened to the upper middle-class in England. The religious revival of the early nineteenth century found one of its forms of expression in the revival of the public schools, for which Arnold of Rugby set the tone: high intellectual standards and plenty of sermons, a tradition which (like the tradition of the Kirk in Scotland) had elements of greatness in it, and which did immense things in English life. In Oxford it met the revival of Platonism and the delayed impact of German philosophy: and became what can be called (in a sort of shorthand) the Balliol tradition. Not that this current was

ever dominant even in Balliol, or that it was confined to
Balliol: but there is a thin strong thread of continuity, from
the election of Jowett to a fellowship in 1838 to the death of
Lord Lindsay of Birker in 1952. This might be called a
tradition of preaching to the best intellectual people in the
best intellectual way. I do not of course mean simply
preaching lay sermons in chapel, though that was part of it[3]:
and I do not mean that this was some sort of devotional cult.
On the contrary, it was an extremely practical form of
politics. The best students were taught to preach the best
sermons, and were fixed up with the best jobs. I speak
cynically, but only because that is how those outside the
circle felt about it. The influence of the circle was very
powerful, and almost wholly for good, in the field of adult
education among many others. Indeed, this has been one of
the big things in English intellectual and political history; far
bigger than the Fabians, a rather random collection of
personalities, who gave themselves credit for much more
collective influence than they possessed.

Do not therefore construe the word 'sermon' in a
derogatory sense. Sermons attempt to persuade by style and
imagery, like the great sermon on hell-fire in Joyce's *Portrait
of the Artist as a Young Man*: they also use argument, and
the case for political theology can be put in three propositions, which are disputable but not absurd:

First, it is dangerous to act in politics without principles;
one must have a policy.

Second, it is intellectually indecent to accept political
principles without severe scrutiny, and without setting them
in relation to the best thought of mankind.

Third, the most fundamental of these principles is that the
next generation should be brought up in the same principles.

To revert to faintly cynical phraseology, here is how
Oakeshott puts the same thing:

'As I understand it, a political ideology purports to be an
abstract principle, or set of related abstract principles, which
has been independently premeditated. It supplies in advance
of the activity of attending to the arrangements of a society a
formulated end to be pursued, and in so doing it provides a
means of distinguishing between desires which ought to be

encouraged and those which ought to be suppressed or redirected.' (pp. 11—12).

Now I am not sure how strong has been the general and popular reaction against this attitude to politics in Great Britain; probably not strong, because the popular reaction in favour of it was not really strong either. General opinion, I think, has quick day-to-day shifts against a very long and slow ground-swell; intellectual opinion has an intermediate rhythm. I do not think that ordinary public opinion would be at all alarmed by two quotations which horrify Professor Oakeshott: ' "Every schoolboy in Russia", wrote Sir Norman Angell, "is familiar with the doctrine of Marx and can recite its catechism. How many British schoolboys have any corresonding knowledge of the principles enunciated by Mill in his incomparable essay on Liberty?" "Few people", says Mr. E.H. Carr, "any longer contest the thesis that the child should be educated *in* the official ideology of his country" ' (pp. 13—14).

Sir Norman Angell and Mr. Carr shock Professor Oakeshott, and I think they would shock almost all university teachers of politics to-day: the current has set in a new direction. It would take us too far afield to explain how this has happened: there has certainly been a combination of many factors which tell the same way. Personal reaction against an older generation; contemporary taste in poetry and art; recurrence to an older and more continuous tradition in English philosophy; the prestige of natural science; the horrifying examples of what ideological indoctrination can do. I doubt whether the question of faith or loss of faith in religion has much to do with it; Christianity is big enough to accommodate both schools of thought, and perhaps Christian existentialism is part of the same reaction from general principles towards individual action.

The case against indoctrination was stated in its extreme form by George Orwell in *1984*. This has been taken up recently as if it were a tract directed against Russia; but Orwell was certainly as hostile to indoctrination by social pressure as to indoctrination by physical torture — indeed social pressure was for him almost a kind of physical force. His own experience of the Ministry of Love was at Eton and in the Burma police; and he knew many dialects of double-think beside the Marxist one.

II

I hope then that the reaction against sermons can be taken as a fact. I think that there is also, though less violently, a reaction against the idea of science in politics. The idea of creating a positive or empirical or realistic science of society goes back a long way – to Machiavelli, perhaps to Thucydides, Aristotle and Polybius; the strength of the tradition has varied proportionately to the prestige of natural science, but it has never died out completely. Late in the nineteenth century that prestige grew so strong that it was the dominating myth of the Western world, and the fashion was that social science must become more like natural science, so that the new society might be built as an engineer builds a bridge. This seized on the imagination of people everywhere and provided language for many different factions.

The case against this movement is now equally familiar. Science, it is said, can solve some of the problems of society: it cannot solve any of the problems of politics, strictly defined. Politics in the narrowest sense is concerned with policy: with ends, and with 'arrangements' for decisions about ends. This is not engineering nor is it science. Empirical study can clarify the choice of policy, and can help to execute policy: but it cannot create policy, and if this is misunderstood, it may obscure the nature of policy. Oakeshott puts the same point in sharper terms: 'From a practical point of view then, we may decry the style which approximates to pure empiricism because we can observe in it an approach to lunacy. But from a theoretical point of view, purely empirical politics are not something difficult to achieve or proper to be avoided, they are merely impossible; the product of a misunderstanding' (pp. 10–11).

This is harsh enough language to make one feel uncomfortable. Certainly my university generation – in the bitter period of the 1930s – thought it honourable to conceal strong political emotions under a mask of zeal for science in

the study of society, and I do not think that there has been
the same general reaction against science as against late
Victorian political piety. Nevertheless, intellectuals trained in
a critical tradition soon found grounds for distaste: on the
one hand, in the nauseating jargon used by German and
American sociologists to conceal banality of thought, on the
other hand in the equally nauseating Russian pretence that
Marxism has (like Moral Rearmament) some private pipe-line
to the Almighty, by virtue of the magic word 'science'.

Perhaps there is better ground for a change of attitude in
the changing climate of science itself. Its power is greater
than ever, but the words which now reach the layman are
'relativity', indeterminacy', 'the expanding universe'. Science
seems to have discarded the concept of 'real' objects standing
by themselves in 'empty' space, and to hitch the whole
universe to the observer and his operations. Doubtless all this
has been half misunderstood. Yet it has been built into a new
mythology of science, colouring the language and thought of
the last thirty years. Paul Valéry sums this up appropriately:

> Notre savoir tend vers le pouvoir et s'écarte d'une
> contemplation coordonnée des choses: il faut des prodiges
> de subtilité mathématique pour lui redonner quelque
> unité. On ne parle plus de principes premiers: les lois ne
> sont plus que des instruments toujours perfectibles. Elles
> ne gouvernent plus le monde, elles sont appareillées à
> l'infirmité de nos esprits: on ne peut plus se reposer sur
> leur simplicité: il y a toujours comme une pointe persis-
> tante, quelque décimale non satisfaite qui nous rappelle à
> l'inquiétude et au sentiment de l'inépuisable.[4]

Undoubtedly, there has been what some sociologists would
call a 'cultural lag' in the growth of this new attitude to
science. Some people still rush to make social science more
like the natural sciences, while others are backing out. This is
a normal and proper state of affairs, but the disorder is such
that the political educator certainly cannot now comfort
himself in his difficulties by the hope that properly organised
research will in the end give all the answers. Natural science
and social science are plainly in the same boat: they sink or
swim together.

III

This then is the thesis — a rather untidy thesis, in duplicate: and the antithesis, which does not follow neatly in sequence, is despondent negation. Sermons and science are both out of fashion. To be specific, it is now difficult to take with a clear conscience either of two very promising lines in teaching politics. It is hard to take the Laski line, to elucidate principles and to put the world right in the light of them. It is equally hard to take the Graham Wallas line, to observe and analyse and cautiously indicate lines of progress — unless one is prepared to rest content with technique, and to discard policy. Conscience is a nuisance in these matters, because great teaching can be done in both these ways, and has not yet been done in any other: at least not in any other which can be described as a frontal attack on the problem of teaching politics. I make this reservation, because I could make a strong case for some indirect approach through the seemingly irrelevant, in the tradition of 'Greats' — Latin prose, for instance, and algebra, and Thomist theology, or some other odd combination. In the right hands and in the right environment these may be the best tactics: but here and now we are conmmitted to the frontal attack, by various factors in the educational system which are quite beyond our control. We must therefore set out ruefully in search of a synthesis, as Oakeshott does.

His own synthesis is simple enough. The activity of a politician is like the activity of a natural scientist or like the activity of a cook.[5]

> The cookery book is not an independently generated beginning from which cooking can spring; it is nothing more than an abstract of somebody's knowledge of how to cook: it is the stepchild, not the parent of the activity. The book, in its turn, may help to set a man on to dressing a dinner, but if it were his sole guide he could never, in fact, begin: the book speaks only to those who know already the kind of thing to expect from it and consequently how to interpret it (p. 15).

Speaking as a rare user of cookery books, I feel that this is rather hard on them; it is amazing what a good book will do for a bad cook, who has faith in it and is careful. But this really does not affect the point: even the bad cook cooks within a tradition, because he — and the eaters who can't cook at all — know what is good cooking and what is bad cooking. What is more, good British cooking is not the same as good Chinese cooking, or good West African cooking or even good French cooking. The analogy and the appropriate tag are very old: 'de gustibus non est disputandum', which might be translated 'it is pointless to compose a logical exercise about cookery.'

The equation between cookery and politics[6] can be set up without difficulty. 'Taste' in politics is British taste or French or Russian taste or American taste, each of them consisting of or embodied in 'a traditional manner of attending to the general arrangements of a society' (p. 15). An ideology is an abridgement of a particular tradition; this may be necessary and even useful if an attempt is to be made to copy or export the tradition, but the abridgement is always secondary and may prove dangerous. One danger is that the ideology may be substituted for the tradition, so that the servant becomes the master. Another danger is that we may get muddled in the process of abridging the tradition, and may try to give the abridgement a completeness which is really impossible, by 'filling it out, not with our suspect political experience, but with experience drawn from other (often irrelevant and misleading) activities, such as war, the conduct of industry, or Trade Union negotiation' (p. 18).

The safeguards which Oakeshott recommends for protection against these dangers can be summed up as nationalism, scepticism and pessimism. 'The knowledge we seek is municipal, not universal' (p. 24). 'Politics can never be anything more than the pursuit of intimations;[7] a conversation, not an argument' (p. 20). 'In political activity we sail a boundless and bottomless sea; there is neither harbour for shelter nor floor for anchorage, neither starting-place nor appointed destination' (p. 22). In all this there is great truth. Some may think that it smacks a little too much of the mood of Ecclesiastes — 'What profit hath a man of all his labour which he taketh under the sun?' 'Much study is a weariness to the flesh': but no harm in that — this is one mood of human truth. But what is the political educator to do with it?

IV

What Professor Oakeshott recommends is what Professor Oakeshott can do supremely well. It is, briefly, to write history like a poet.

The historian is bound by the evidence, because only exact use of evidence will convince; he is also bound by the language of his own time, because there is no other language in which he can speak to living men. A society *is* in a sense its own history: it is held together in part by an image of the past held in common. Homer in recording Greek tradition made the Greeks a people — one could almost define Hellenes as people brought up to know Homer by heart. The role of the epic poet has passed to the historian. All true historians (like poets taught by the Muses) write the truth: some historians also help to make the tradition which they record.

This poetic analogy is not unfair to Professor Oakeshott,[8] who insists continually on 'intimations', on individuality, on complexity, on knowledge of detail, on the analogy between politics and language. Poetry (or the poetic art in prose) is the only way in which these things can be communicated (only a poet could say of himself 'volito *vivus* per ora virum'); it is familiar that poets are politicians, for are they not 'the unacknowledged legislators of the world'? Fair enough: but is this not perhaps a lot to ask from a Professor of Politics?

V

In part, therefore, my criticism of Oakeshott is that he calls himself a sceptic, and is in fact a Utopian.

This is plainly true in one rather humble sense. Political science has got into the educational system, and that is no place for poets.[9] Can you picture George Orwell as Professor Blair? There is a lot of sordid business with syllabuses, and local government promotion examinations, and the pass mark of 40 per cent, and the selection, pay and careers of university teachers and other honest persons. The system in its nature standardises and conscripts: things distasteful and to be resisted. But are they best resisted by ignoring them? or is it best to accept, study and mitigate? This is an open choice, but my own inclination is to face the problem rather than to evade it. To borrow Professor Oakeshott's quotation: 'Spartam nanctus es, hanc exorna.'

The second point, almost equally sordid, is that there are people who want to be taught not traditions but facts. There is a great deal of information about government which is required (for instance) by civil servants and local government officers and social workers and Trade Union officials going about their business; a practical demand, similar to that satisfied in other European countries by courses and text-books in public law. In England so much of the practice of government is outside the law that lawyers hardly aspire nowadays (as did Bryce and Dicey and Anson) to teach realistically about public affairs: and the process of instruction is laborious because so much of the information needed has to be pieced together from original sources, so as to keep pace with perpetual change. There is therefore a continuous and unsatisfied demand for the sort of courses and text-books which people need for practical training and for daily business, and the need can be met only by political scientists.

This practical kind of knowledge is within the tradition to which Oakeshott refers, and it can be taught so as to be a vehicle of tradition. But the method of teaching is governed by considerations more appropriate to the writer of cookery-books than to the epic poet. We must have cookery books: for heaven's sake let us apply our minds in order to make sure that they are good ones.

My third and last point is larger. It can be raised by saying (for the sake of argument) that I disagree wholly with Professor Oakeshott about the political tradition within which we live. His lecture ends: 'And the more thoroughly we understand our own political tradition, the more readily its whole resources are available to us, the less likely we shall be to embrace the illusions which wait for the ignorant and the unwary: the illusion that in politics we can get on without a tradition of behaviour, the illusion that the abridgement of a tradition is itself a sufficient guide, and the illusion that in politics there is anywhere a safe harbour, a destination to be reached or even a detectable strand of progress. The world is the best of all possible worlds, and *everything* in it is a necessary evil' (p. 20).

These 'illusions', it seems to me, are themselves a part, though not the whole, of our political tradition; and are one of its great excellences. Such is their power that Professor Oakeshott's last sentence — a very French sentence, I think — is in itself repugnant to the character of the English tradition.[10] Or so it seems to me.

What then? Do Professor Oakeshott and I have a 'conversation, not an argument'? Surely we can have neither conversation nor argument unless we proceed in a very theological and scientific manner to define some of our terms. We are talking about a society. What society? Cambridge University? England? The whole of Britain, subsuming England, Wales, Scotland and Ireland? The Western World? What activities does our political society include? and by what marks are we to know its bounds? We are talking about a tradition. By what marks are we to know the content of a tradition? How is truth about the tradition to be distinguished from falsehood? 'By their fruits ye shall know them' is a maxim which sifts very slowly indeed, and it is scarcely practicable to wait a hundred years in order to discover who was right. We want to converse about it with Professor Oakeshott now: and unfortunately the Greek for that sort of conversation is 'dialectic'. 'A life without exact argument is no life for man': if we believe that, we have abandoned the poets and we are back with the preachers and the scientists.

The quotation which I have just given is from Plato's *Defence of Socrates*, and it is inscribed on the little memorial to Jowett in Balliol College Chapel. If we accept it, does it mean that we are back in the pulpit and back in the nineteenth century, with Benjamin Jowett and the late Lord Lindsay? I am now almost bold enough to say that it does. We are impelled to compile cookery-books and to argue about them: in politics an argument is in the last resort an argument about what to do, and the conclusion of it is· policy. There are different ways of preaching policy, and the academic way is not that of the practical politician. Confusion between these ways is disastrous, as disastrous in adult education as in the university: but it seems to me to be impossible, utterly impossible, to talk about politics without incurring a share in responsibility for action. You will notice that this impossibility is a moral and personal impossibility, not merely a logical one: in fact I have reached not a synthesis, but my own starting-point, a reluctant traveller round a circle.[11]

VII

I hope that I have not confused a plain enough issue by pinning it to personalities and to the text of a particular essay. It may help discussion if I put the matter briefly again, in a very bald way.

The strongest academic traditions in political education in this country have been, first, to teach principles at the stiffest level of intellectual debate which the pupil can stand: second, to teach empirical method and the use of evidence, with due precautions to ensure that the limits of the method are understood. Professor Oakeshott reacts against both branches of the tradition, and so do most of us, because we are sick at heart to see the harm which they can do.

His reaction is into a poetical or epic approach to the tradition of English history: here it is hard to follow him, partly for lack of his gifts, and partly because he leaves unsatisfied cravings which have a right to exist, though they have no right to be satisfied. They may be summed up prosaically as a desire for something that one can get one's teeth into: there has never been anything to satisfy this except theology on the one hand, empirical science on the other. What Professor Oakeshott offers is not a synthesis but an option, and to me the old devil seems better than the new.

I have no doubt that the search for principles in politics is a romantic illusion. But my taste is for the romantic rather than for the rococo, and there is after all a well-known remedy for romance. As old Stein has it in *Lord Jim*:

> One thing alone can us from being ourselves cure! The way is to the destructive element submit yourself, and with the exertions of your hands and feet in the water make the deep, deep sea keep you up. So if you ask me — how to be? . . . For that too there is only one way . . . In the destructive element immerse . . . To follow the dream, and again to follow the dream — and so — *ewig* — *usque ad finem.*[12]

1. Bowes & Bowes, Cambridge, 1951.

2. See also his Huxley Memorial Lecture on *'Physical and Social Science'* (1930).

3. Summed up by the parody of a sermon by Jowett in W.H. Mallock's *New Republic*, published in 1877.

4. From *Au sujet d'Eurêka*, published in 1924. I am indebted for the quotation to Mr. Frank Sutcliffe's recent book, *La Pensée de Paul Valéry*.

5. The cook is Platonic [cf., for instance, μαγειρική in the *Gorgias* (500 B)], and he is also in Graham Wallas, *The Art of Thought*, p.26.

6. The equation between cookery and natural science is more complex, since the scientific community is international: but (as Professor Michael Polanyi has pointed out) taste, judgement and tradition are essential to it.

7. Graham Wallas was also interested in 'intimations' (*The Art of Thought*, pp.97–108 and 119–32), but as a stage in thought, not its culmination.

8. Elsewhere Prof. Oakeshott refers to 'the poetic character of all human activity' or 'of all human moral activity'; but this seems to raise rather different questions. ('The Tower of Babel', *Cambridge Journal* (1948), Vol. II, pp.77–8).

9. To quote the malicious Mallock again, parodying Herbert Spencer: 'progress is such improvement as can be verified by statistics, just as education is such knowledge as can be tested by examinations.'

10. It is one of F.H. Bradley's aphorisms, from the Preface to *Appearance and Reality*. But Bradley's trick was to balance one aphorism by another.

11. Both Mr. Mabbott and Prof. Oakeshott have used the metaphor of the topless tower; 'the circling of the rising spiral' (Mabbott, *The State and the Citizen*, p.10). I find no comfort in this at all.

12. Perhaps I should add that this quotation was meant to be a reference to Conrad and not to later writers. I have now traced it through I.A. Richards, *Science and Poetry* (1926): Wyndham Lewis, *Men without Art* (1934): Stephen Spender, *The Destructive Element* (1938) and *The Creative Element* (1953) — and it haunts Spender's autobiography (*World within World* 1951). But that is another story.

II
Local Government in its Context

I am not sure that I can claim to be a 'local government man' – but 'I have been faithful to thee, Cynara! in my fashion.'

I have never even stood for election – cowardice perhaps, but what Ward Committee would have had me, except perhaps in some rural backwater? I have been in and about a good many Town Halls and City Chambers, both in Britain and in East Africa, and I am addicted even to the smell of them, so different from the smell of Ministries. But one has to get used to ambivalences. 'Policy is for the committee, its execution is for the officials.' The committee members love to discuss cases and are pretty good at it, collectively, but one is lucky (or is it unlucky?) if even the chairman and vice-chairman understand anything of the jargon and the compromises involved in national policy for (say) housing or education. 'The committee-room is the work-shop of local government' (attributed to Laski) – God help us if our work-shops are like that. And so on. One is inclined to pick up Nietzsche's phrase – *Menschlich, all zu Menschlich* ('human, all too human'); and perhaps this is as it should be.

The first paper really belongs to Professor Brian Chapman, as it is based entirely on his unpublished doctoral thesis about the theory, law and practice of regionalism in Italy from the foundation of the Kingdom in 1860 to the Republican Constitution of 1948, which survives with only minor amendments. My contribution was merely to absorb it into the structure of debate with Dicey about sovereignty and federalism.

The subsequent history the regional system in Italy has been of immense interest: it almost seems possible that Professor Ambrosini's ingeniously formal scheme may have

political life in it, in the setting of Italian politics. But it is
something of a joke that the British had ignorantly and
empirically worked themselves into a rather similar pattern
for Scotland, Wales and Northern Ireland; and that they tried
to export it. So far as I know, the Colonial Office was
unaware of this article and of the Italian concepts. But
several times they were stuck with the problem of finding a
compromise between federal and unitary government, and
they fumbled about intelligently in this constitutional area;
particularly in Ghana in the later 1950s,[1] and in Kenya (the
Swahili for regionalism was *Majimbo*) in the early 1960s. But
it didn't work there: and now we have to rework it for
ourselves, in the 'United Kingdom', as it is ironically called.

I have excluded various conference papers, which were fun
at the time, and also a lecture on 'The Conventions of Local
Government',[2] which was to have been given at LSE in
February 1951 – but I caught mumps from one of our
children (an illness which I do not recommend). The
invitation was an honour, and I took all the trouble I could
to develop and illustrate a position. This was stated in terms
of the theory of the law and conventions of the constitution;
it tried to apply that theory to the working of local
government, and thus to indicate the applicability of the
principle I had applied to the Haldane Report – important
administration is politics. Of course, I had not enough
material to work on, and it is only in recent years (in effect
since the creation of the Social Science Research Council in
1965) that students of politics, as distinct from students of
administration, have had a chance to savour the quality of
local politics, and its immense range of personality and
colour. That period was one of intense and abortive argument
about local government reform, explored in many reports
and pamphlets and summed up in the Trustram Eve report,
the second report of the Local Government Boundary
Commission, 1945–49. This was a very able document, as
well argued as the Haldane Report, and brushed aside as
swiftly by political events. All students of local government
mourned Nye Bevan's contemptuous treatment of the Eve
Report, and I had no wish to separate myself from them. But
I thought that the trend of the debate showed more concern

for the life of local government than understanding of its character.

The lecture grew cumbersome in its argument, and was cluttered with some efforts at quantitative, analysis which were never very good and are now out of date. So I have excluded this article, and its two successors in a minor debate about 'local government in Parliament'.[3]

In the end, we got statutory reform, for London in 1963, for England and Wales in 1972, for Scotland in 1973. The new statutory forms are not much more lovable than the old ones, and in due course there will be new complaints and new wrangles. But meantime there is a bustle of activity in local government; patterns have been torn across and must be re-shaped, and there is room for innovation and flexibility, personal and political.

At the same time, prospects look better than ever before for a realistic study of local authorities as political entities, and perhaps this has been to a small extent due to the 'style' and to the research activities of the Herbert Commission and of Maud I (the Maud Committee on 'people in local government'), of which I was a member. The report of the latter came out in a rather confusing form, as it was a negotiated acceptance by first-rate local government people of a model offered by very good civil servants and very good business men, after debate and compromise. I had not much to contribute because I thought the compromise was unreal: but there were no hard data with which to fight it. True, we had commissioned a study by the Government Social Survey, and this made real advances. *Epur se muove* – at the beginning we excluded questions about party affiliation because 'everyone' said it would be embarrassing; at the end 'everyone' was grumbling that we had missed an essential part of the picture.

The Herbert Royal Commission was a different kind of body, in that by accident it fitted the space allocated in the model proposed in my 1951 paper.[4] It was working within a precisely foreseeable time-span for a government which had power (the power of timing) for legislation, and was led by a formidable combination of Minister, Henry Brooke, and Permanent Secretary, Dame Evelyn Sharp. We were seven in

all, including the Chairman; Sir Edwin Herbert (the late Lord
Tangley) led us into a crisp pattern of work, in that we each
had a topic, we each had a region of London; that is to say,
we each had as it were cross-specialisms, by topic and area.[5]
We had some funny disagreements, as between 'big' and
'small', 'town' and 'country': but the method of work had
unified our perspective and we all saw quite clearly what we
had to do.

I don't mind saying that the drafting of Chapters 3 and 4
of the Report (which deal with Economic and Social Factors,
and with Historical Development and Present Structure) was
largely mine, based of course on masses of work by other
people. Certainly it should be said emphatically that Chapter
5, simply entitled Evidence, was produced by the Chairman
alone, though with the applause of all. It is so lucid, weighty,
and witty that it should somehow be anthologised for
students and fellow sufferers.

I am not sure that there is much to be said now for my
1952 lecture on The Government of Great Cities except that
in Manchester I followed hard on the heels of Ernest Simon
and that we were both ahead of the band-wagon. The paper
led quite directly to the appointment of Leslie Green as
Simon Fellow in 1957 and to his book on *Provincial
Metropolis* published in 1959. The line leads straight from
Ernest Simon's work before 1939 to this paper, to Leslie
Green's book, and to the creation of Greater Manchester by
the Local Government Act of 1972. Sometimes, I must
confess, I have an uneasy feeling that the structure of living
has now changed, and that we have been planning (like
generals) for the previous war. But, nevertheless, things move.

The lecture on Theories of Local Government came
straight out of Sir Edwin's Chapter 5, though written of
course in my idiom not in his.

> Semper ego auditor tantum numquamque reponam
> Vexatus totiens?
> ('We have to listen to a lot of rubbish as part of our job:
> are we never to get a word in ourselves?')
> Difficile est satiram non scribere
> ('In the circumstances, the hard thing would be not to
> write satire.')[6]

Perhaps the only comment needed is that if I had had more time and space I should have liked to amplify the last section, that on the metropolis as a natural phenomenon. I should have made more clearly the contrast, indeed the contradiction, between the two conceptual sources of current debate: J.S. Mill's concept of local government as an arena of political decision; the ecologists' view of local government as a natural growth, part of the interchange between man and environment. I am warmly in favour of both views, but I have had no more success than naive orators and interest groups in getting them to cohere intellectually.

Last in this section is a paper given at the Golden Jubilee conference of the Town Planning Institute, in June 1964. It is relevant to recall the conjuncture of events. The London Government Act, based substantially on the Herbert Report, had become law in 1963. Its first elections were held in 1964 and placed Labour in a very strong position both in the Greater London Council and in the London Boroughs. Accordingly, no more was heard of Labour threats to repeal the Act and re-establish the LCC, Labour's symbol of victory in 1933, of resurgence after the disasters of 1931. In 1963 came the report on traffic in towns, and for the first time the general public heard of Colin Buchanan: a symbolic figure — but symbolic of what? To his report was annexed a report on administration, with the late Lord Crowther in the chair, and Lord Holford and T. Dan Smith among its members. The idea of making this combination was right: as appears in the paper, I was not very happy about its execution.

There followed immediately the victory of the Labour government in October 1964; the episode of the Department of Economic Affairs and its Regional Economic Planning Committee (I was a member of the one in the North West); the rejection of workable schemes of local government reform in England and Scotland, and another horrifying period of 'royal commissioning', which led in due course to local government 'reform' in both countries, on lines that nobody liked — it was probably right to abolish what they abolished, but what replaced it will need five years at least to establish itself. Meantime, decisions and non-decisions continue. One is reminded of Belloc's little poem: 'The

Garden Party', which ends

> . . . they married and gave in marriage,
> They danced at the County Ball,
> And some of them kept a carriage
> And the flood destroyed them all.[7]

Notes

1. Dennis Austin, *Politics in Ghana: 1946–1960* (London: Oxford U.P., 1964) pp. 303, 327, 380.

2. Published as an article in *Public Administration* (Winter 1951) p.345.

3. 'Local Government in Parliament', *Public Administration* (Winter 1954) p.409.

4. ' . . . it is unlikely that any big local government bill will be promoted except by a government which can see its future secure for a year or two ahead, which has no great party programme of legislation, and which is not greatly troubled by crises in foreign affairs.' (p.354).

5. The internal organisation of the old Local Government Board was rather like this.

6. Juvenal, *Satires*, I, lines 1 and 30, crudely translated.

7. *Complete Verse* (London: Duckworth, 1970) p.219.

3 Federalism and Regionalism*

During the fifty years of the Irish Home Rule controversy, from about 1870 to about 1920, the question of regional devolution was one of first-rate political and constitutional importance in this country. Since the creation of the Irish Free State in 1921 the English (though not the Scots and the Welsh) have almost forgotten that regionalism can be a constitutional issue. A great deal has been said in recent years about administrative regionalism, and about regions as a cure for the *malaise* of English local government, and about geographical regionalism as a reasonably scientific way of classifying human habitats: but all this talk has reacted very little on politics and on constitutional theory. Yet the political importance of these issues has grown, and may grow further; and it is perhaps time to take another look at the orthodox constitutional doctrine as it has been handed done to us by Dicey.

This doctrine poses the sharp alternatives of Austinian jurisprudence; legal sovereignty is indivisible, therefore in any country either it resides in the central legislature or it does not reside in the central legislature.[1] If it does not reside in the legislature, the true sovereign is elsewhere and has delegated his powers separately to different authorities. There may be a constitutional division of functions between legislature, executive and judiciary: or between central legislature and local legislature: or there may (as in the USA) be both divisions. In such cases one may be puzzled to say where true sovereignty lies: does it lie with 'We, the people of the United States' or with 'we, the nine old men of the Supreme Court'? But it is clear that it does not lie with the

---

*From *Modern Law Review*, XIV, no. 2 (Apr 1951). Joint author: Brian Chapman.

central legislature, as sovereignty in the UK lies with
Parliament. The magic of the British constitution resides in
the Sovereignty of Parliament and in the Rule of Law, two
interlinked ideas: it is logically impossible to mitigate the
Sovereignty of Parliament except by constituting a new
sovereign. To do so would be Federalism, and Federalism
would be a disaster to English interests as well as a
revolutionary change in the constitution. This is the theme
which Dicey pursued in almost all his later works.[2] The
doctrine, though not its political conclusions, are still there in
Professor Wheare's book on *Federalism*, the first edition of
which appeared in 1946.

There are two possible lines of comment. One is to attack
the Sovereignty of Parliament itself, by casting doubt on
Dicey's explanation of the authority of the constitution. In
his view it owes its authority ultimately to the law of the
land, and the law of the land owes its authority to
Parliament. This doctrine is not altogether satisfactory even
on legal grounds,[3] but these need not be argued here. The
main point is that it just does not match our normal usage of
the word 'constitution'. Whatever we mean by it, we do *not*
mean the unlimited sovereignty of Parliament. The Act of
Union with Scotland, adopted in 1707, forbade the introduction of lay patronage into the Church of Scotland: lay
patrons were introduced by an Act of Parliament of the UK
passed in 1712. This Act was itself legal, and it did not lead
to illegal consequences: but it was a perfectly plain instance
of what we mean by an 'unconstitutional act'. Similarly, it
would be natural to say that the sovereignty of the
Parliament at Westminter is already morally and practically
(though not legally) limited by the rights of regional bodies.
It would plainly be unconstitutional for Parliament to abolish
the Court of Session or the General Assembly of the Church
of Scotland: it has been declared by a recent Act that it
would be improper for the Westminster Parliament to cede
Northern Ireland to the Republic of Ireland without the
consent of the Parliament at Stormont[4] : and it would be just
as unconstitutional to abolish the teaching of Welsh in Welsh
schools and to close the Welsh department of the Ministry of
Education without some expression of Welsh consent. Even
the status of the Channel Islands and of the Isle of Man has

considerable constitutional sanctity. If one looks at the situation as it is, and not at legal theory, there is no doubt that regionalism of a kind is already part of the constitution of the UK. This is not merely a statement about the extent to which it is expedient for Parliament to exercise its powers — Dicey's 'external limit'[5] : it is also a statement of what is generally felt to be right and proper. There are things which Parliament could legally do, but which it does not do because a majority of its members think them wrong. In this the constitution is above Parliament, not subordinate to it.

But one may also attack the doctrine on logical grounds, as well as on grounds of normal usage. Is it really essential to legal principle to draw a rigid line between unitary and federal constitutions, as between black and white? The object of this paper is not to answer that question, but to state a case for consideration by those better qualified to judge. There have in Italy since 1945 been discussions, theoretical and practical, which raise important issues not hitherto considered in this country.

Italy did not from Roman times until 1870 form a political unit: the sentiment of Italian nationality had from the later Middle Ages been a strong factor in the politics of all those who spoke Italian, but their political organisation and history were very diverse, and their economic progress no less so. It is not surprising that several of the publicists of the Risorgimento thought in terms of a federation, or even a confederation, and not of a unitary State. When the time came their doubts were swept aside by an irresistible combination of fact and theory.[6] Theory laid it down that between federalism and unity no compromise was possible; and in 1860, when the union of Piedmont with the Kingdom of Naples and Sicily was new and precarious and when the North and South in America were on the verge of civil war, there could be no doubt which was the right choice. Italy chose unity, not federalism: the Piedmont constitution of 1848 was extended in 1860 to all Italy except Rome and Venezia, and these were added in 1870. That constitution was what might be called a good Orleanist constitution: a marriage of the centralising and popular traditions of the French Revolution to the British invention of constitutional monarchy. The constitution was unitary, and within it

Parliament (or the King in Parliament) was by usage sovereign in a sense which would have been as acceptable to Robespierre as to Dicey. What is more, it carried with it an administrative system on the Napoleonic model: Italy was until the fall of Fascism a 'prefectoral State'.

This was perhaps the best that could be done in the 1860s: but the contrast between centralism in theory and diversity in practice was one of the factors which produced a sense of strain and unreality in Italian democracy before 1914. It expressed itself most glaringly in the contrast between North and South, between an Italy as advanced as any State in Western Europe and one as backward as some countries of the Middle East — or as Ireland was in the 1840s; but there were also lesser 'regional' problems, such as those of Sicily and Sardinia. These were divisions between people who shared a common language. In 1919 Italy acquired in the North-East substantial German and Slovene minorities, whose political importance was even greater than their numbers because they inhabited a strategic border region. Some attempt to grapple with both problems, the old and the new, was made between 1919 and 1921, but they seemed insoluble, and this was one among many factors which made the way easier for the Fascists, who were prepared to deny that the problems existed.[7] Mussolini produced a sham solution for the problem of Left and Right in politics: he merely ignored the existence of regional divergences within Italy.

There were thus long arrears to be settled when the war of 1939 was over and the time came to write a new Italian constitution. It was obvious that the German and Slóvene minorities could do serious damage to Italy's international position if they were not given fair treatment. Another small linguistic minority, that of the Val d'Aosta, had become politically conscious. It is not clear to what nationality the Valdostians belong, for they are not without qualification Italian and they are certainly not French; and they are a border folk in a position of some strategic importance. The economic situation of the South had not improved; and its politics had been complicated by the Allied advance through Sicily, Sardinia and the old Kingdom of Naples, which unwittingly created forms of regional self-government in areas which had never been able to secure self-government under the Kingdom of Italy. By 1946 all Italian parties were committed in different degrees to an attack on centralisation and bureaucracy, and when the Constituent Assembly met in June, 1946, it could not avoid facing the question of regional devolution, political as well as administrative, though it had little precedent in the traditions of the Italian State.

Fortunately there now existed a constitutional formula which offered, or purported to offer, a third alternative which was neither a federal nor a unitary State. This had been put forward by Professor Gaspare Ambrosini, of the University of Rome, in a number of articles published between 1933 and 1935[8] : their subversive tendency seems to have escaped the notice of the Fascist authorities. Professor Ambrosini examined in detail the constitutions of a number of countries which could not readily be classified either as federal or as unitary States, although some of them claimed to be either one or the other. His main instances were Austria (not 'Austria-Hungary') both before and after 1918, the Spanish Republican constitution of 1931, the Weimar constitution, and the Soviet constitutions of 1924 and 1936. To this list he tentatively adds the British constitution in respect of the special status of Northern Ireland and Scotland, and the pre-war constitution of Yugoslavia. On these cases he built the theory of a 'State characterised by regional autonomy', which he distinguished both from the federal and from the unitary State.

The point at issue can be seen most clearly if it is approached through the Continental jurists' distinction between *autarchic* and *autonomous* bodies within the State. Both types of bodies possess corporate personality and a measure of local discretion. The former, *autarchic* bodies, draw their personality and powers from the legislature of the State: English local authorities, for instance, are autarchic bodies, in that their status, including their charters, can always be modified by Act of Parliament, if Parliament so determines. *Autonomous* bodies draw their personality and powers not from the legislature but from the constitution. The constitution has also created the central legislature; it may have given it larger powers, but not a superior status. This would describe the position of the States within an undoubted federation such as the USA or Australia.

So far, this is old: what is new is a distinction drawn within this latter class. Its basis is not in Professor Ambrosini's original articles stated anywhere with clarity and finality: but this absence of a perfectly sharp dividing line is an essential part of the theory. He makes three points, explicitly or by implication. *First*, in federal States the member States are represented *as such* in the highest legislative body of the federation. *Second*, normally the members of a federation have existed as independent States before federation, whereas 'regional' bodies derive their juristic existence solely from the constitution of the State; the constitution of a federation is in some sense a treaty, it has a 'contractual origin.' *Third*, federal States are those in which the autonomous bodies possess at least some 'national' or 'sovereign' powers (of course they cannot possess all such powers, or they would be independent States): regional States are those in which autonomous bodies exist but do not possess any 'national' or 'sovereign' powers. Perhaps one should say 'do not possess such powers *as of right*'; their claim as guaranteed by the constitution, written or un-written, extends only to existence and to non-sovereign powers. Greater powers may be given them, but that will be only at the discretion of the central legislature. This third point is in a sense a generalisation of the first two. It is not in Professor Ambrosini's articles fully explicit, and it is the most difficult of the points to apply legally; nevertheless it is essential to the development of the theory. The essence of the theory is that there is ample constitutional experience to justify the substitution of a scale of unity — in three stages, but there could in principle be more — for the traditional dichotomy between federal and unitary States; and it is only by applying this criterion that one can obtain what might be called a gradation of Statehood.

This is a scanty summary of a doctrine which draws much of its strength from examples, and it is scarcely a sufficient basis for criticism. But two points may be made, telling in different directions.

In the first place, the academic doctrine of the federal principle, though elegant, is somewhat sterile. Professor Wheare is irrefutable when he defines the federal principle as 'the method of dividing powers so that the general and regional governments are each, within a sphere, co-ordinate and independent': but he is not interesting, and indeed for most of his book he is engaged with other and more interesting matters. What Professor Ambrosini has done is to accept this criterion, but to add a second. The federal State is not merely a State marked by the federal principle: it is one in which the federal units possess a real share of sovereign power. Where the sovereign power is not divided there is no true federation. This seems much more promising. We have all in our minds some vague classification of State powers in order of magnitude and could plot some sort of curve reaching upwards from the power to change the shape of postmen's helmets to the powers of peace and war and of public order. When we want to know whether a State is centralised or decentralised we ask in real life not about the federal principle but about the point where the division of central and local powers falls on this scale. It is an empty form to say that a State is a federation if the units (or, on the other hand, the central government) have no power *except* to regulate postmen's helmets.

It should be added that Professor Ambrosini discusses the effects of practice as well as those of formal law, and certainly believes that regionalism, in the sense of a guaranteed existence, can be conceded or withdrawn by constitutional usage as well as by law. His 'regionalism' is a sub-species of Professor Wheare's 'federalism': but this recognition of usage goes futher than his principle of the gradation of powers in blurring the sharpness of the distinction. This, too, is a gain in descriptive realism.

On the other side, although this new line of classification is welcome to the political scientist, it may not be so welcome to the lawyer. It confuses the picture because it introduces a distinction of a new type: Ambrosini's distinction between autarchic and autonomous is a distinction of law within the framework of Austinian jurisprudence, his distinction between federal and regional is a distinction not of law, but of fact: it is an appeal not to a formula but to the judgment of the 'reasonable man'. The distinction between sovereign and non-sovereign powers is hard to pin down in any form of words, because the significance of a power shifts according to the historical context: even the power to design postmen's helmets would be a sovereign power if the shape of helmets became symbolic of great issues. There would be an international incident of some importance if one of the German *länder* chose to dress its postmen in the uniform of the SS. It may be possible with ingenuity to frame definitions which will be helpful, though not exact: but even then 'federal' and 'regional' will not lie in opposition to one another, but in continuity, as segments of an unbroken slope. A court of law which attempted to decide cases on this basis would in marginal cases perform a political, not a legal function.

There are various mitigations of this difficulty. In the first place, it does not look, from the text of the Italian Constitution, as if the matter will be very troublesome in practice. The Italian Supreme Court may have to decide whether or not the central legislature has interfered with the guaranteed *existence* of the regional governments: it may have to decide on the scope of particular powers and duties enumerated in the Constitution: it may in difficult cases call to its aid the general doctrine of regionalism. But it does not seem that there is anything in the Constitution which turns on the legal meaning of the word 'region', as clauses of the American Constitution turn on the meaning of 'commerce' or 'general welfare' or 'due process of law'. In the second place, one branch of law, international law, has already had to face this issue in questions affecting the recognition of States. The decision to recognise or not to recognise is a political decision: but it would be accepted fairly generally that the decision would be contrary to law unless certain conditions were fulfilled. It is a question of *fact* whether these conditions are fulfilled or not: but lawyers have succeeded on the basis of precedents in enumerating in some detail conditions such as independent power to make peace and war and effective authority in foreign affairs, and in indicating the sort of evidence which might show that these conditions have been met. Some progress has been made in this quarter in defining at least the main contours of the gradation. Finally, the regionalists can answer the federalists with a *tu quoque*. Regionalism may involve some legal knots; but they cannot be worse than the knots tied by the Founding Fathers in 1787.

However the balance of argument stands, this is certainly not a doctrine to be lightly put on one side: it was admirably fitted to the political situation of Italy in 1947, and it was deliberately chosen as the basis of the Fifth Title of the Constitution, which deals with regions, provinces and communes. The first draft of this title was produced by a sub-committee of ten members of the Constituent Assembly, whose chairman and rapporteur was Professor Ambrosini himself, and there were no fundamental changes during later discussion.[9]

The title contains twenty articles, some of them likely to pose difficult legal problems, and there is a good deal in it not covered by this summary. Italy is divided into nineteen regions, five of which are 'special regions' whose status is to be defined individually by separate constitutional laws. These five are the regions which raise political problems of special difficulty: Sicily, Sardinia, the Val d'Aosta, Trentino-Alto Adige, where there is a German-speaking minority, and Friuli-Venezia Giulia, which still contains some Slovenes even after the readjustment of the frontiers in favour of Yugoslavia. When the Constitution was adopted in December, 1947, Sicily had already secured a statute of its own, accepted by the Constituent Assembly. Statutes for Sardinia, Val d'Aosta, and the South Tirol were promulgated by laws of the Republic in January, 1948: that for Friuli-Venezia Giulia awaits a formal settlement of the frontier dispute with Yugoslavia. What follows applies strictly only to the fourteen 'standard regions', which correspond pretty closely to the historic divisions of the peninsula; but it will in general be true also of the five special regions. The boundaries of the regions in the first instance follow those of existing provinces (ninety-one in number), which they group together. Provinces or communes which request it can (after a local referendum) be transferred by ordinary law from one region to another: but it requires elaborate procedure followed by a change in the Constitution to amalgamate two existing regions or to create a new region by sub-division. In this sense the *existence* of the regions is guaranteed by the Constitution.

An ordinary law of the Republic will define the system of election for regional councils: these councils will themselves approve (by an absolute majority of their members) a regional statute defining in detail the administrative and legislative procedure of the region, which may include the use of the initiative and the referendum. These statutes are subject to approval by the central legislature, which may refer them back to the regional councils for reconsideration: but if the disagreement cannot be reconciled by compromise the final decision would (it is believed by Italian jurists) rest with the Constitutional Court, not with the central legis-lature.[10]

The regional council elects its own chairman: in addition it elects from among its members the President and Junta of the region, who are the heads of its administration and might be described as its Prime Minister and Cabinet.

So far this is fairly straightforward: there follow three critical matters, legislation, finance and central control.

(a) *Legislation.*

There was a clash of opinion here of some importance. One group wished to divide functions in the traditional federal manner: exclusive powers of the centre, exclusive powers of the regions, concurrent powers.[11] A second group considered that the Constitution would slip from regionalism into federalism if any powers were given exclusively to the regions. This latter view prevailed in form, but after concessions in debate which leave the final position some-what obscure. A single list of topics is given for which the region 'makes legal rules within general principles enacted by the central legislature, provided that these rules do not conflict with the interests of the nation or of other regions'. This seems to mean that for the enumerated subjects the State can in future legislate only in general terms: detailed provisions, which would previously have been made by the equivalent of 'statutory instruments', will in these cases be made by the regional councils – and by them only. But they cannot even in this sphere modify State law: nor can they (it seems) take the initiative until general principles have been centrally enacted.

Outside this sphere the central legislature can delegate rule-making power to the regions it if wishes.

The sphere in which the regions appear to have a monopoly of rule-making power is pretty wide, and not closely defined. The list is as follows:–

Regulation of offices and administrative organs subordinate to the region.

Communal boundaries.

Local police in towns and country.

Fairs and markets.

Public assistance, personal health and hospital services.

Technical education and financial aid to students.

Local museums and libraries.

Town planning.

Tourist trade and the hotel industry.

Tram and bus services of importance within the region.

Roads, water mains and public works of importance within the region.

Lake navigation and harbours.

Mineral springs and hot springs.

Quarries and peat bogs.

Game.

Freshwater fisheries.

Agriculture and forestry.

Handicrafts.

The list can be amended only by a change in the Constitution.

(b) *Finance*

The problem of local finance, which seems acute in England, is ten times worse in Italy, where the gap between the richest and the poorest areas is very wide. The experiment in regionalism has little prospect of success unless the State can redistribute resources between regions on a large scale without destroying regional autonomy in the process. This riddle may be insoluble: the Constitution certainly makes no attempt to solve it. It lays down only that the regions may hold property, that the legislature must allocate to them by ordinary law sufficient revenues for their 'normal' expenses, and that it may in special circumstances make grants for particular purposes. The only comfort which this article gives to the poverty-stricken South and Islands is that it refers to them specifically as possible beneficiaries of this discretionary power.

(c) *Control*

By contrast, the question of control in other spheres is very elaborately handled. By way of preface, it should be said that it is plainly intended that the central government should use the area of the region for the administrative decentralisation of those services which it retains in its own hands. It is provided that a 'Commissioner of the Government' will reside at the capital of each region, will superintend all central government services within its area, and will 'co-ordinate' them with the regional services. It is to be emphasised that this gentleman is not a prefect, that he exercises no 'tutelle administrative', and that he reappears in only one of the articles dealing with control. These may be arranged under three heads:—

(i) *Administrative*

An 'organ of the State' will have power to quash administrative acts of the regions on legal grounds (roughly the equivalent of ultra vires, although Continental administrative courts take a rather wider view of their powers than do the English courts). It may also have regard to the policy of such acts, but if it does so it has power only to refer them back to the regional council, with a statement of its objections.

There was much argument as to the proper form of this 'organ', and it was ultimately left to ordinary law (not constitutional law) to decide. The constitution prescribes only that the 'organ' shall be decentralised: but it adds in the same article (perhaps as a hint) that the lowest tier of the hierarchy of administrative courts is in future to be located in the regional capitals. This had hitherto been in the provincial capitals, which may in future retain only 'sub-sections'.

(ii) *Political*

In certain circumstances the President of the Republic (which means in practice the Prime Minister and Cabinet) may dissolve a regional council: the decree must state reasons, and must have been submitted (for advice, not for approval) to a standing committee of the two Houses of the Legislature, which is to be set up for regional questions. The effect of dissolution is that the regional government is taken over temporarily by a commission of three citizens of the region, who are to hold fresh elections within three months.

There are five sets of circumstances which may call these reserve powers into action: acts by the regional council contrary to the Constitution; serious illegalities; reasons of national security; refusal to remove a regional President and Junta guilty of unconstitutional or illegal acts; failure to reach a decision on the appointment of President and Junta. These are politically very large powers; but they are clearly the minimum which is necessary if the central government is to bear its responsibilities for national defence, internal order and the continuity of administration.

(iii) *Legislation*

It is rather difficult for a foreigner ignorant of Italian procedure to say how far the articles so far summarised give any party a title to sue in the Supreme Court on an issue of constitutional law.[1][2] There is no doubt about the position under the next article. All laws passed by the regional council require the counter-signature of the Commissioner of the Government; he must either append this within thirty days, or refer the law back on the grounds that it is ultra vires or that it is contrary to the interests of the nation or of other regions. The regional council may override this veto by a majority of its membership; if it does so the Government may give way or they may press their objection within fifteen days. If the objection is a legal one they must take it before the Supreme Court; if it is one of substance they must refer it to the legislature. The latter will mean making the matter one of confidence in two Houses in which the Government must maintain a majority, so that it is not to be undertaken lightly; and it is for the Supreme Court to decide whether the issue is one of law or of substance.

These three points together make an elegant and logical structure which fits Professor Ambrosini's theory well. The central government has certain general reserve powers: these are great powers, but not of a different order from those held by the Government of the United States under the war power and the guarantee of a Republican form of government. Within its own sphere of legislation the regional council is protected by the Supreme Court, but this is not an absolute protection; it may be overridden on grounds of national interest, but the procedure laid down is such that this is not likely to happen except on major issues. The Italian Parliament, like all free parliaments, has a crowded time-table; the Government will be reluctant to add to its business, and if it does it may well find hostility on its own side of the house to any hint of centralisation. Within its administrative sphere, as defined by State and regional law, the regional government is autonomous and subject only to check for ultra vires, and to some undefined but mild supervision of the substance of its decisions.

It should be added (finally), to complete the picture, that the Constitution recognises the corporate existence of provinces and communes within the regions, but it gives them no guarantees[13]; the regional governments will (it seems) be responsible for the general supervision of their administration. But all this is far from clear: it was understood in the Assembly's debates that the provincial prefect would be abolished; but he is still there.

What can be said by way of comment? It must be understood that as yet we can comment only on the text. The Constitution was adopted in December, 1947; in March, 1951, the structure of regions is still not complete and in working order.

In the first place, this title is like the rest of the Italian Constitution: a good piece of craftsmanship. The drafting is plain and economical, and the articles fit together to make a structure of great theoretical elegance. In these respects the

Italian Constitution puts most other post-war constitutions to shame.

Second, one is bound to emphasise that the draftsmen's hearts failed them when they came to finance. But no federal draftsmen have done much better; and in other respects the regional framework looks practical as well as elegant. It is plainly right to recognise the special position of the two islands and the three frontier regions. It is only in these cases that regionalism in some form is a political necessity. These five problems *must* be solved if Italy is to survive as a State within its present frontiers: the constitutional theory of regionalism may give the framework of a solution, but it would only do harm to impose a standard pattern upon all five. None of the fourteen 'standard regions' has ever in this century dreamt of secession, and they are relatively safe ground for a theoretical experiment in devolution.

Third, the legal pattern is very close to Professor Ambrosini's ideas. The existence of the regions jointly and severally is guaranteed by the Constitution. Their powers are not guaranteed, and their activities can in the last resort be legally controlled by the central government and the central legislature. But there are elaborate provisions which encourage the central authorities not to intervene except on issues of great national importance; it is to be expected that over a period of time constitutional usage will grow up to protect the regions in the exercise of a considerable range of powers, if they have sufficient vitality to use them.

Fourth, these ideas seem to have general applications of some importance. We are not, in the United Kingdom, likely to sit down now and write a constitution for ourselves on the Italian model: but Italian theory is applicable with only minor adaptations to our present situation. The United Kingdom is already a regional State, in respect of Northern Ireland, Scotland and Wales: once this is recognised it should be easier to face the issue of Home Rule for Scotland and Wales free from the old bogey of separatism. Regionalism is not a step to separatism, but a safeguard against it.

The position of the two 'kingdoms' and the 'principality' may be compared to that of the Italian 'special regions'; the problem of self-government within England has something in common with the problem of the Italian 'standard regions'. 'Home Rule all round' and 'Back to the Heptarchy' are cries which do not awake much popular response at present: but if anyone wishes to experiment with them here is a model ready to hand.

There is likely to be a more direct field of application in the countries now emerging from the colonial stage. Hitherto the textbooks have urged them to choose between unitary and federal government: a very awkward choice for a country like Nigeria. Such a country will stick forever if it attempts with inadequate resources to develop a dominating central government: it will stick no less certainly if it breaks into federal units and gives these units (some of which will certainly be very conservative) an absolute guarantee that in certain fields they can disregard the national interest. The regional solution would give an absolute guarantee (for instance) to the corporate existence of tribes and emirates, as entities within the State, and a rather less rigid guarantee of their territorial limits; but it would subordinate their demands to the necessity of creating a State strong enough to stand on its own feet. There are other cases which come to mind, such as the Gold Coast or Indonesia, where a colonial Power has imposed unity on diversity. The unity is an asset too precious to dissipate, and yet it can scarcely be maintained unconditionally with the resources at the disposal of these States. No formula can solve such problems, but the lack of a formula may make them harder. Perhaps Professor Ambrosini's formula is to be commended particularly to African constitutionalists.

Notes

1. Dicey in his eighties seems to have mellowed on this point, as on some others. In *Thoughts on the Scottish Union* (1920) (p.100) he admits that the Austinian doctrine need not be true as an account of a real situation, and was not true of the relations between the Scottish Parliament and General Assembly from 1690 to 1707: his claim is only that inconvenience will result if it is not followed.

2. *England's Case against Home Rule* (1886); *Letters on Unionist Delusions* (1887); *A Leap in the Dark* (1893, reissued 1911); *A Fool's Paradise* (1913). *Thoughts on the Scottish Union* (1920) is a much more open-minded and stimulating exercise on the same theme.

3. Dicey himself would complete it by saying that Parliament uses its absolute discretion 'constitutionally' when it acts so as to promote the greatest happiness of the greatest number. 'On any wide view of large public questions expediency will be found to be only another name for justice' (*England's Case*, p.13). But Dicey's utilitarianism is not very austere: he is always ready to mitigate the reader's instinctive dislike of this argument by distinguishing between 'the law of the constitution' and 'constitutional morality' (*e.g.*, *England's Case*, p.246).

4. Ireland Act, 1949 (12 & 13 Geo. 6, c. 41).

5. *Introduction to the Law of the Constitution* (8th ed., 1931) p.74.

6. 'The sagacity of Italian statesmanship rejected the plausible scheme of an Italian Federation': Dicey, *England's Case*, p.66.

7. Mussolini, cited in *The Times* of August 15, 1950: 'The southern question does not exist'.

8. These articles were collected and republished in book form in 1944, shortly after the liberation of Rome: G. Ambrosini, *Autonomia Regionale e Federalismo*, Rome, 1944.

9. The text of the Constitution is not yet available in English. What follows is based on the Italian text, edited with notes on the course of the debates by Falzone, Palermo and Cosentino: published by Colombo (Rome), 1948.

10. G. Balladore Pallieri, *Diritto Costituzionale (secondo la nuova Costituzione)* Milan, 1949, pp.248–9.

11. Professor Ambrosini had himself in his original article in 1933 required that in a regional State the regions should possess some exclusive competence. (*Autonomia Regionale e Federalismo*, p.13.)

12. The provisions governing the competence of the Constitutional Court are contained in Constitutional Law No. 1 of Feb. 9, 1948, which certainly concedes to private parties the right to raise constitutional issues, subject to some limitations.

13. They are in the sense of Professor Ambrosini's definitions, 'autarchic' but not 'autonomous': but the Constitution itself is not consistent in the use of these terms.

4 The Government of Great Cities[*]

I must begin by attempting to limit my field somewhat. There is an immense literature about modern cities, and in particular about the form of city which is distinguished from others by several rather clumsy titles — megalopolis or the metropolis or the conurbation. These have slightly different shades of meaning, and I have chosen the phrase 'great city' partly because it is better English, but also because it can cover these various aspects without implying judgments about history or politics.

This literature deals with almost every aspect of life in great cities; there has been detailed comparative study of the geography, the sociology, the physical framework of city life. On this basis there has been created a secondary literature that of city planning; almost every great city in the world has its plan, the product of long research, beautifully produced, and due to be completed in the time of our great grand-children. In fact, these plans are Utopias. Like other Utopias, they may be powerful instruments of change; but what intervenes between Utopia and action is government, and little has been written on the comparative politics of great cities. This is surprising; the matter is of supreme importance to the planners, and it is also one of the central problems of democratic government.

It is easy to illustrate this. In England and Wales 17,000,000 people, two-fifths of the population, live in London and in the five other conurbations recognised by the Registrar-General; Scotland is even more effectively dominated by the great city on the Clyde. In the United

*From *Memoirs & Proceedings of the Manchester Literary and Philosophical Society*, XCIII, no.5 (1951–2). Percival Lecture, 1952.

States 42,000,000 people, about a third of the population, live in cities of over 1,250,000 inhabitants. The proportion in Western Germany is perhaps about the same; and France is the sort of exception which proves rules. The only great French city, in this sense, is Paris, and Paris contains only about one-eighth of the population of France. Nevertheless, for many purposes France is a city-state, and its acropolis is Paris. This domination by great cities has been accepted as one of the marks of the Western way of life; we have been arguing for a long time about the correct form of government for industry, yet there is a case for saying that the political problem of great cities is even more urgent. At least these two together should be central themes in our discussions of practical democracy, and yet the second never seems to have been taken seriously. Much has been written about the government of individual cities, and very little about the common fund of international experience.

This was the train of thought in my mind when I suggested a title for this lecture, and as I went on I saw more clearly than at the outset that I could not possibly live up to it. The problem is too big and the literature is too scattered. Nevertheless, I think I may be able to state a number of issues which are worldwide, and to indicate very superficially how they arise and how they are related to one another. I am going to take four problems; first, the potential dominance of the great city in national politics and the measures taken to limit its power; secondly, the frontier problems of the great city; thirdly, the problem of finding, within the unity of the city which is too vast for the citizen to comprehend, some lesser unit as a basis for individual participation in government; fourthly, co-ordination and direction in the government of cities. The burden of my song is that these four issues are inseparable, and that the essence of our dilemma lies in this inter-connection.

Perhaps I should add that what started this train of thought was the problem of how to teach students about the government of the great city in which we live; a great city which has no name and no boundaries, although it is certainly one of the great cities of the world. It is convenient by way of illustration to take some figures for what the

Registrar-General calls in his bald way 'the South-East Lancashire Conurbation'; but of course his boundaries are arbitrary and there are many other versions with as good a claim to recognition; some are larger and some smaller. Our population in 1951 was a little under 2,250,000, second in the census figures only to the London conurbation, and roughly comparable to the metropolitan areas of Rome or Hamburg or Detroit or Boston or San Francisco; a good deal behind the giants, but obviously a little sister of the giants, and not a big sister in the older family of unified and corporate cities — you remember Jerusalem as it is described in the Psalm, "builded as a city that is compact together".[1] The area of our city was about 380 square miles, rather oblong in shape from North to South, but effectively within a radius of fifteen miles from Manchester Town Hall. On this basis the density of population is relatively low; and this may serve as a warning that not much is to be learnt from figures of population density in metropolitan areas, as they depend on where the administrative boundary is drawn, and that begs all our questions.

It is more interesting to recall that our city includes all or part of nine primary and independent units of local government (that is to say, two counties and seven county boroughs), and no fewer than forty six secondary units, county districts of various kinds. You can reckon for yourselves the formidable army of elected persons who are involved; I make it 1,703 councillors, and one might add 252 aldermen. It is not so easy to calculate the number of public servants engaged in the work of the city; it is not easy even to get a satisfactory figure for the employees of all the local authorities, and it would not mean much if we had it, because of the fortuitous division between national and local and privately-owned services. Certainly, not less than 100,000 workers are needed to provide essential services for 2,500,000 people: I give a round figure to indicate the scale of operations, but please do not ask me how it is calculated. The area, finally, is represented in Parliament by thirty three Members, a body of men who could, if they were united, exercise very great influence in the House of Commons as it is at present constituted.

I am not lecturing about Lancashire, and I will not return to it; one could produce similar illustrations from America or Germany or France, but these figures may bring international problems a little closer home. We are merely a case (a bad but not an extreme case) of a very common disease.

But really I should avoid the word 'disease', which suggests criticism of a kind which would be quite out of place. It is only a miracle of organisation which makes life possible at all for 2,000,000 people in this corner of England; our local administration is admirable, and in a political sense the system fits us comfortably, like an old pair of shoes. Those whose job it is to work the system do so very well, and probably do so without a great sense of strain. Nevertheless, the word 'disease' might stand, as a convenient short-hand for two things; first, that there is a pattern of factors, a relation between conditions of government and other conditions of life, which we can see repeated elsewhere; second, that this pattern contravenes all that the classical books of democracy say about proper forms of urban government. So much the worse for the classics, perhaps; but at least there is a 'disease' here in the sense that theory and practice are out of joint.

Perhaps I might now start from the last point which these local figures indicated, the importance of the conurbation in the politics of the state. There are some American instances in which the process has gone so far as to become farcical. The metropolitan area of Chicago contains two-thirds of the population of the State of Illinois;[2] metropolitan New York contains three-quarters of the population of New York State, and, on top of that, three-quarters of the population of New Jersey.[3] In both these cases there has been a long history of gerrymandering, of attempts by the dwindling majority in the State to perpetuate itself by over-representation of the small towns and of the country-side, and so to keep the city at bay, and also perhaps to earn blackmail for the simple country legislators and their constituents. In addition, there are cases, of which New York is one, in which a single metropolitan area is divided between two States of the Union; Detroit is even divided between two sovereign States, the USA and Canada. This sort of case in some ways is beyond human aid, as nothing can be done except by calling in question the

whole structure of national government. But in practice
common sense is fairly strong, and there is enough informal
co-operation to make life possible.

But Paris is a better test case than Chicago or New York or
London, because in Paris the issue has been faced, and it is
possible to see what a solution involves.[4] Paris, of course, is
still of dominant political importance in France. Its power to
upset governments by force has declined, but it is still
considerable, as was seen in the events of Februrary, 1934
and August, 1944. In addition, Paris contains about one-third
of French manufacturing industry, it pays about half the
taxes collected in France, and it dominates French intellectual life. Successive regimes have been unable or unwilling to
control the physical growth of Paris, which has expanded
across old administrative boundaries. In a similar situation
British governments have ignored the administrative needs of
London; the French have accepted the logic of administration, but at the expense of self-government. Almost the
whole conurbation is included in two interlocked administrative units, the Ville de Paris and the Department of the Seine.
These administrations are in principle distinct, but they are
responsible only to two men, both agents of the central
government. These are the Prefect of the Seine and the
Prefect of the Police — two officials of immense power, but
controlled by the division of power between them and by
their direct dependence on the government of the day
through its Minister of the Interior. The Ville de Paris has its
elected municipal council, the Department has a similar
departmental council; all the little Communes of the Department have their councils and also their elected Mayors. But
there is no Mayor of Paris; and in any case all these councils
are for most purposes advisory and not executive. Wise
Prefects respect public opinion and handle Paris delicately;
much delicacy is needed when (as at present) the Government is of one political colour and the majority at the Hotel
de Ville is of another. But on the whole Paris belongs to
France and not to the Parisians; it has been given its unity,
but not its freedom, and perhaps it could not be given its
freedom without adding another element of instability to a
dangerous situation. So far as I know only one great capital

has secured both unity and a fair measure of self-government, and that was Greater Berlin in the days of the Weimar Republic, under the Charter of 1920. But self-government did not include 'police', a word which had a wide meaning in Germany even in the days of the Republic.

All these instances illustrate my first problem, that of state control over the great city. You will notice that they are also related to the second problem, that of administrative boundaries. Here the issues very often seem to be local. But notice (in the first place) that one gets much the same sort of local issues the whole world over. Here is a paragraph from a book about American cities,[5] written without reference to conditions outside America, which I quote almost in full because I think it will suggest some parallels at home:

> Opposition in a suburb about to be annexed is usually based on anticipated consequences such as the following: (1) the substitution of the incompetent or corrupt government and the low standards of service obtaining in the city, for the competent, clean government and high standards of service which have been maintained in the suburb; (2) an increase in taxes (in territories in which the taxes at the time are lower than in the city); (3) the applying, in the case of a wealthy district, of a portion of the taxes paid by it to poorer portions of the annexing city; (4) the assuming of a portion of the large debt previously incurred by the annexing city; (5) the lack of any intimate knowledge of the conditions of the suburb on the part of the city authorities; (6) the necessity of waiting its turn, as a district or ward of the city, for improvements which as an independent unit it could provide at its own discretion; (7) relative inaccessibility of city authorities or their inattentiveness to the needs of annexed territories; (8) the inapplicability of the city's general police regulations, some of which may be too restrictive and others not restrictive enough; (9) the control of the enlarged city by another political party than that which is in control in the suburb; (10) the merging of the people of the annexed area with a great cosmopolitan population largely of a different race, nationality and religion, of a lower culture, and subject to the control of undesirable politicians; (11) the loss of the name and identity of the suburb; (12) the disappearance in the annexed territory of that live com-

munity spirit and interest in local affairs essential to development and good government; (13) the introducing of an innovation which may not work as well as the existing system which has been tried and has given reasonable satisfaction; (14) where the territory happens to lie in another county, its disruption from the old county and loss of some of the county's resources.

These arguments are all related to local issues, and there is an equally good stock of local arguments to be used the other way. But notice also (in the second place) that the law under which the battle is fought is national law. There are for instance some American states which permit what their writers call 'forcible' annexation; a popular vote is taken in the great city and in the district to be annexed, and if the majority of the whole is for union it is held that democracy has been satisfied. In other states the votes are counted separately, so that the voters in the district in dispute can veto annexation. Thus there is a sense in which the question is always settled nationally, and not locally; the scales cannot be held precisely even, and they are tipped one way or the other, for or against the great cities. Sometimes, as in Lancashire, the influence of the state on such matters is remote and rather intangible; there are very rarely cases in which the state intervenes to help the great cities; much more often it is influential in a negative sense, by what it does not do.

It is for instance astonishing that London in its present form can be governed at all. Its two largest independent units, the LCC and the Middlesex County Council, are ruled by majorities of opposite parties; but at least they live fairly close together in Westminster and Lambeth. The rest of Greater London, about a third in population and about half in area, is governed from remote county towns and county boroughs;[6] and responsibility is also shared with *ad hoc* authorities of many different kinds, such as the Metropolitan Water Board, the Metropolitan Police, the London Transport Executive, and the four strange Hospitals Regions, each of which extends from an apex in central London to a broad base in the country-side far beyond the metropolitan area. No man could devise a tidy form of government for a place like London, and it would be silly to try; but the system need not be as confusing as it is. There have been, at each stage of London's growth, plenty of plain and obvious improvements in government which could have been facilitated by the central power, and many of these improvements have in the . end been made; but they have always lagged behind events. The Metropolitan Board of Works would have been a good device in 1800, but it was set up in 1855; the LCC might have done wonders in the 1850s, but it was not set up until 1888, when its opportunity was almost past. Recently there has been serious controversy about the execution of the Greater London plan; the plan has been agreed, but it is not agreed who should act on it. There was a split in the committee appointed to report; the minority were for a new local government body, which would represent all the authorities concerned and would possess executive powers; the majority were prepared only to give advisory powers — in other words, no powers at all. The late Government compromised by placing the responsibility on the narrow shoulders of a civil servant in the Ministry of Town and Country Planning (as it then was), supported only by a committee of civil servants; it is not very likely that the present Government will act otherwise.

Thus far, I have illustrated the forms of local opposition to the enlargement of administrative areas, and the way in which these local factors operate in the context of national suspicion about the overweening greatness of conurbations, in particular of the capital city. Now, the most effective of all local arguments against amalgamation is that it is certain to reduce the field of representative self-government within the great city. On the figures which I gave earlier, we have here in 'South-East Lancashire' one elected person (and I exclude aldermen) for every 1,500 of the population. New York, when it adopted its present Charter in 1936, was so tired of what Walt Whitman (who was an experienced New Yorker) called 'the never-ending audacity of elected persons' that it reduced the scope of representation to a council of 25 for a population of 7,900,000; that is not quite the whole story, as New York also votes to elect a mayor and a good many other officials, including many judges, but the contrast is valid. In

Paris there is almost as great a contrast between the suburbs and the central area of administration as in New York. The Department of the Seine and its Communes have about 2,300 councillors for a population of 2,000,000; the Ville de Paris has 90 councillors for a population slightly larger, and its Arrondissements and Quarters have no elected councils of their own.

Consolidation is likely to diminish the number of citizens who take a direct part in government. On the other hand, even the most democratic theory must impose some limit on self-determination for the parish pump. It is generally true that existing representatives and officials constitute an interest which may oppose change even when their electors favour it; and the moral case for the great city is often better than that for the small fry.

But that is not the end of the matter. Centralisation may be preferable to anarchy, but no one likes a form of government in which services touching the daily life of millions are directed by people whom they do not even know by name. This is not likely even to be efficient. When Lord Simon and his party of investigators were in Moscow in 1936,[7] the city had a central assembly of 2,100 members and 23 local assemblies with about 6,000 members in all. This meant there was about one representative for every 450 persons; and the representatives were organised in a complicated structure of committees which included numerous officials and co-opted members. The arrangements are doubtless now different in detail; but I quote the case to show how essential the Communist Party thinks it to carry with it a large active element among the passive population of a great city. Even where election is a farce and power is highly centralised, it is still thought necessary to broaden the base of government. It is good tactics to economise officials, and to force officials to act with and through amateurs.

In America and in Germany one fairly often meets decentralisation which results from a bargain at the time of annexation; this is fortuitous and often temporary, but there have also been a number of more deliberate experiments which have had some success. The town planners' answer is apparently to retain strict control at the centre, but to plan for neighbourhoods which will have sufficient sense of unity to develop their own local institutions. As we know in Manchester, a community association can act as a very effective pressure group, and it is right that when there is community of interest it should express itself in political pressure. But pressure politics is not a form of government, indeed it is a formula for power without responsibility, which is the negation of government. Neighbourhood units will not solve the political and administrative problem unless there can also be neighbourhood responsibility; and this is not at all easy to combine with the administrative unity of a great city, which is for many purposes very tightly knit.

Berlin and London have both made striking experiments, neither of them with complete success. Berlin was unified by its charter of 1920 and at the same time was effectively decentralised to twenty Bezirke, each with its own council; but the politics of Berlin in that epoch were confused and dirty, and opinions differed about the success of the experiment.[8] In London, the division between the LCC and the Metropolitan Boroughs, which grew naturally out of the old structure of Vestries, was resented at first by the majority of the Council, as a political trick designed by a Conservative Government to frustrate their policies and limit their influence; and there is no doubt that awkward situations can arise between Councils of different party colours. Yet it seems now, fifty years after their birth, that the Boroughs have made a secure place for themselves. Twenty-eight Mayors and a Lord Mayor, with appropriate trimmings, may be rather too much compensation for the very prosaic appearance of the LCC, but they make a good show, and (what is more important) their councils spread the responsibility of government pretty widely. In the LCC area there is one representative for about 2,250 persons, and London is one of the few cities where the ratio of participation thus defined is higher in the consolidated than in unconsolidated areas.

This is one form of democratic decentralisation; another is the constitution of elected authorities for special purposes. It is not very long since School Boards and Boards of Guardians were wiped out in this country; similar bodies still survive in many places in the USA. For instance there are said to be over 1,000 distinguishable public authorities in the metropolitan area of Chicago, which has a population of about 5,500,000. Many of these authorities are trivial, but even the inner city itself is governed by six or seven loosely connected *ad hoc* bodies. In this country, directly elected *ad hoc* authorities have vanished, and in their place we have got *ad hoc* agencies of the central government, each independently responsible to Westminster and Whitehall. One of our staff attempted to take a census in Manchester last year,[9] and found over forty offices of one sort or another each of which could fairly be described as a regional headquarters, Some of these belonged to Government departments, others to public corporations of various types; their areas of action were not uniform, but in general they extended a good deal beyond the limits of SE Lancashire. A few of their functions are clearly local, others are clearly national; but the nature of most of them is betwixt and between, and the advance of the central government into this debatable ground has helped to blur the boundaries of the great cities and to weaken their unity. Something of the same sort is happening in the USA; in France the confusion is partly mitigated by the existence in each Department of the Prefect and his staff, who are a point of reference for all public services in that area, whether they are central or local. The Prefect has been given a bad name because of his importance in local politics, and in part he deserves it; but where politics are less turbulent than in France – in the Scandinavian countries for instance – local unity is helped and not weakened by the existence of a single centre, even if that centre is an official of the central government; and there has not for years been any suggestion that the Fylkesmann in Norway or the Landshövding in Sweden play an improper part in politics.

I have now, as you see, passed on my fourth and final point. Effective participation implies decentralisation; decentralisation exaggerates the problem of co-ordination, and that problem is already hard enough. It is now only the British who attempt to run city government without a strong focus in a single person. In Germany the Burgomaster and his inner council, the Magistrat, have traditionally been professionals, and it looks as if Germany has resisted our rather foolish attempt to impose the British committee system and is continuing in her old ways. The Maire in France, like the Burgomaster in Germany, is elected by the Council; he is less highly qualified than his German counterpart, nevertheless he embodies in his Commune the authority of the French state, and he often holds office continuously for many years. In the USA practically all great cities now work on the 'strong Mayor' system; a Mayor is directly elected, and is given powers which make him at least as strong against his Council as the President is against the Congress of the United States. Even the Irish have begun to revolt against the British model; in Dublin, Cork and Limerick there are now 'city managers' with effective power.

None of these systems can fairly be called undemocratic; nevertheless they depend for success on the personality of one man, and the English generally prefer to take refuge in a committee. This means in effect that if co-ordination is to be achieved at all it must be achieved either by private influence or by political party. If we must choose, we will choose the latter; but, as London has found, co-ordination by party can be an awkward arrangement where there is decentralisation and the second tier of authorities may differ in party colour from the first. It is easy in general to make a case for the consolidation of government over regions or great cities; but if we are asked 'Who is to co-ordinate the new governments?' we can, with our system as it is, give no answer except 'political parties'. Co-ordination by party is better than nothing; but its disadvantages are so plain that they are a serious obstacle to change. None of the exponents of elected regional authorities have worked out which regions would be Conservative and which would be Labour; but the local politicians will work this out at once, if regional schemes ever look like becoming practical politics, and they will guide their actions accordingly. They are quite right to do so; that is their duty within the system as it exists. But it is a factor which rules out a good many of the paper schemes for reorganisation.

May I now in conclusion briefly summarise this argument? The great city in all countries is now so great that the state looks jealously at it; it is reluctant to give it unity unless it can also strengthen state control. This national jealousy abets local jealousies, and together they generally prevent administrative frontiers from advancing to the natural frontier of the city. The muddle which ensues will usually be ascribed to 'vested interests', and this is partially true; but the situation is not improved by an attempt to consolidate all power in the city at a single centre. Such an attempt generally breaks down at the outset, because it offers nothing to conciliate the two oppositions, national and local; even if it were initially successful it might well fail later, because the basis of its government is too narrow. We are more likely to make progress if we attempt to design a city government of a federal type, and some cities have done so with a measure of success. But federation poses anew the problem of co-ordination; always difficult, and particularly hard for the English, who are wedded to the committee system and to the party system. We are brought back thus to the connection between local politics and national politics, which cannot be broken.

I hope this is a recognisable description of a situation found in slightly different forms in the larger Western countries. In each country and in each great city there is a complex situation which resists purposive direction and permits change only through a sort of competitive system in which the competitors are units of government, great and small. Sometimes the national government is sufficiently dominant to impose a pattern, as has been done in Moscow, in Paris, and in some other European capitals. But if the national government is as weak in such matters as are the governments of Britain and the USA there can be no human control except by local initiative. Such initiative will meet opposition which has a measure of right on its side; unity of government should not, and indeed cannot, be attained except by a process of concession and compromise. Democracy and unity cannot otherwise be combined.

Notes

1. Psalm 122,3. The Book of Common Prayer translates it even more relevantly as 'a city that is at unity with itself'.

2. 5,500,000 out of 7,897,241 (1940 figure).

3. Metropolitan area of New York, 12,900,000. In New York State, 9,600,000 out of 13,479,142, in New Jersey 3,300,000 out of 4,160,165. (The State figures are from the 1940 Census).

4. I am much indebted here to Dr. Brian Chapman of my department, and in particular to an unpublished article by him on the Government of Paris, which will appear in a series of studies in the government of great cities edited by Prof. W.A. Robson of the London School of Economics. Prof. Robson's book is likely to be the first serious attempt at a comparative study.

5. Committee on Metropolitan Government of the National Municipal League, *The Government of Metropolitan Areas* (New York 1930) p.89.

6. The county towns of Surrey, Kent, Herts and Essex at Kingston, Maidstone, Hertford and Chelmsford, and the County Boroughs of East Ham, West Ham and Croydon.

7. Sir E.D. Simon and others, *Moscow in the Making* (Longmans, 1937).

8. There is a valuable recent book on German experience of decentralisation: W. Bauer, *Dezentralisation der Grossstadtverwaltung* (Göttingen, 1951).

9. J.W. Grove, *Regional Government in England, a study of the North West* (Institute of Public Administration, 1951).

5 Theories of Local Government *

I ought at the outset to brush aside one or two misconceptions that might arise from the title of this lecture. There *is* no theory of local government. There is no normative general theory from which we can deduce what local government ought to be; there is no positive general theory from which we can derive testable hypotheses about what it is. In fact, the subject is a very base one, if we measure it by academic standards; it has seldom been treated with elegance and precision, and if you scan the textbooks of political thought you will find no accounts, or very shoddy accounts, of theories about local government. An odd thing, because there has certainly been in Britain in the last 150 years endless discussion about it; not theory perhaps, but certainly talk, certainly ideas.

May I steal from Sir Patrick Abercombie[1] a quotation in French, from Verhaeren, whom Sir Patrick calls the poet of town planning?

> Sur la ville, donc les affres flamboient,
> Règnent, sans qu'on les voit
> Mais évidentes, les ideés.

To translate very roughly: 'A city is afire with human suffering, but ideas rule it; the eye cannot see them, but they are plain enough.' In America, Boston (it is said) is not a place, but a state of mind; similarly with London, or indeed any city. As Geddes put it, a city is more than a place in space, it is a drama in time.

*This paper was one of a series of public lectures given during the Lent and Summer Terms 1961 at the London School of Economics and Political Science and published by the School (*Greater London Papers*, no. 2 (1961)).

So I want to attempt some analysis of talk about local government in England. But to avoid another misconception, may I say that this analysis came after the writing of the Royal Commission Report,[2] not before it or during it. We wrote our reflections and recommendations about London as it is now; it is merely an academic hobby of mine, after the event, to trace origins and preconceptions. Only since I have attempted this have I realised how much remains unexplained. I offer a very superficial analysis and will be satisfied if it stimulates more systematic exploration.

The English Tradition

My starting-point, and also my conclusion, is that in some sense or other local self-government is now part of the English constitution, the English notion of what proper government ought to be. Challenge the English to define their beliefs about local self-government, and they become involved in the maze of ambiguities which I shall try to trace. Nevertheless there *are* such beliefs, surely, as fixed and idiosyncratic, as (for instance) English beliefs about the Crown. To take a few examples at random.

The wording of the Royal Commission's terms of reference is more succinct than that usual in such documents, in so far as they affect local government, but it has the characteristic double-barrelled form: "to recommend what changes . . . [and so on] . . . would better secure effective and convenient local government'. Mark you, not 'better to secure effective and convenient administration through local government or in other ways'. Local government is not secondary but primary; it is axiomatic.

An excellent academic illustration is to be found in an exchange of articles in the journal *Public Administration*[3] in 1953 and 1954 between Professor Langrod, an eminent Polish lawyer who is now a Professor in Paris, Dr. Leo Moulin, a Belgian civil servant, and Mr. Panter-Brick of this School. For the two Europeans (or should I say Continentals?), local government is something which is subordinate to democracy and may even be hostile to it — the more vigorously local it is, the more hostile to national democracy. 'There is no justification', says Professor Langrod, 'for asserting that there exists an inevitable tie of reciprocal dependence between democracy and local government. Democracy does not come into being where local government appears, nor does it cease with the disappearance of the latter.' And Dr. Moulin: 'All these practises [of local politics] are so contrary to the most elementary democratic ethics, so foreign to the least austere public spirit, that the citizen is bound to be – and is – confirmed in his most a-moral political ideas and in particular in the practice and the exploitation of parochialism pure and simple without regard for the claims of the wider community.' Mr. Panter-Brick puts the English position correctly, succinctly, and may I say obscurely? 'Local government not only engenders sympathy [by demanding that one another's point of view and one another's interests be mutually appreciated and taken into account], it also tends to guard against too much enthusiasm, against that disinterested but misguided benevolence which in its enthusiasm fails to count the cost.' *Surtout, pas trop de zèle*, as Talleyrand is supposed to have said.

A third instance of the reality of our collective convictions is the ease and unanimity with which it was agreed to export British local government to former colonial territories, first in India, Burma and Ceylon, then in Africa and elsewhere. If Professor Langrod and Dr. Moulin are right, this was a much more dangerous experiment than to introduce national elections by universal adult suffrage; and the evidence from West Africa certainly makes one see more clearly the point of what these two scholars were saying. But not in England, not even in the administration in the colonies, were any doubts expressed. The policy of local government in the colonies – roughly the policy of Mr. Creech-Jones and Sir Andrew Cohen – went through with as little opposition as a proposal for a royal tour.

The paradox to be explained is this ethical commitment to an extremely vague notion of local self-govenment; I am not sure that I can explain it, but at least I can produce a set of propositions for debate.

Government and Property

My first proposition is that nothing was heard of this ancient doctrine of the constitution until after 1832. Obviously it is hard to prove a negative, and I have done no more than make a rough check in obvious sources, such as Bolingbroke, Montesquieu, De Lolme, Burke, Hallam, John Russell. But I would submit that the key word was then not local self-government, but property and its diffusion.[4] The magistrates in the counties were the men of position and substance, the men with an estate in land, the local guardians of the king's peace in virtue of their property, inherited or acquired. In the chartered cities and boroughs the same concept held; the freemen owned (subject to complex rules of procedure) the property of the borough, as they owned (and could sell) its parliamentary seats and the right of holding its paid offices. The 1835 Report on Municipal Corporations concedes that some corporations gave an indication by the secrecy of their transactions that they felt 'some sense of impropriety' in the way they handled their money.[5] Nevertheless it was *their* money; the concept of the distinction between public and private property was struggling to be born, but was not yet clear.[6] Reform was in a sense made in the interest of private property and a free market economy: but in delimiting spheres it did not reduce the sphere of public office. It increased it at the same time as it increased the sphere of private property. In this sense the age of laissez-faire was an attack on an old notion of property in the name of a new notion of property. It was primarily in the name of property that magnates and corporations fought the Reform Bills from 1830 to 1832. One might quote Burke as saying that 'to love the little platoon we belong to in society is the first principle (the germ as it were) of public affections.'[7] But I fear that by platoon he meant family and political connections, not loyalty to any borough.

I do not find that local self-government had any place in Whiggism, old or new, or that it had much to do with the 'unbought grace of life'[8] or the 'partnership in all science, in all art, in every virtue and in all perfection'[9]

Local Government Versus Democracy
My second proposition is that the radical reformers of the 1830s and 1840s agreed heartily with Prof. Langrod and Dr. Moulin against Mr. Panter-Brick. Local self-government, they thought, is the enemy of democracy; democracy will by its

very nature destroy local self-government. One may as well quote Chadwick himself, in a famous *Edinburgh Review* article of 1836. The head-notes of the pages are 'Fallacy that Local Government is Self-government'; 'Rapacity of the Local Job-ocracies'. 'These bands in truth formed petty oligarchies, which we should call job-ocracies, who maintained their hold over the persons of the pauperised labourers and the purses of the ratepayers by pertinacious blackguardism and every low art. Rapine or violence is the characteristic of a rude age; fraud and jobbery of an age more advanced.' To this brutal description he adds brutal philosophy:

> It is now admitted by all, that the Poor Law Act could have been carried by no other than a Reformed Parliament. To these, if any such there were, who, for any purpose, aided that change with the view of obtaining, instead of a stronger, a weaker government, we should submit for study the observation of Hobbes: 'And whosoever, thinking sovereign power too great, will seek to make it less, must subject himself to a power which can limit it; that is to say — TO A GREATER'.

The same doctrine is stated ten years later, with more grace and more amenity, in an article by John Austin in the *Edinburgh Review*[11]. This is a defence of centralisation — the French system which Chadwick was supposed to have copied — on the basis that no other form of government is possible for a civilised society. This follows logically from the nature of sovereignty; it follows practically from the character of a sophisticated and civilised society; in such a society centralisation will do good; in a stupid, brutal, Russian sort of society it does harm, because it tries to control and is foredoomed to fail. 'We may say that centralised government is synonymous with regular administration. But this regular administration is related to administration not completely extricated from primeval disorder, as a body of law, arranged in a well-made Code, to a body of law immersed in its natural chaos.' In fact liberal democracy should hate muddle and should be as hostile to archaic local authorities as to archaic law. Parish government and Dickensian Court of Chancery go together. The shambling despotism of the Czars would be favourable to both. Bureaucracy in Weber's sense and democracy make another pair.

There could be no better statement of the traditional position of European liberals as still held by Professor Langrod and Dr. Moulin; but that was in 1847 and I can find no later utterance in England which showed the same self-confidence. Indeed there were cracks already in the reforming front, theoretical and tactical. In a sense, the reform of Municipal Corporations in 1835 was disastrous. That bill was introduced from mixed motives; indeed, the Commissioners' Report betrays some consciousness of its own electoral implications. But once passed it transformed the arena of debate. The bill was hard to resist at the time except by arguments politically destructive, to the effect that a man could do what he liked even with public property, so long as he acted within the letter of the law. Even young Mr. Disraeli, most devious of debaters, could find no better argument than to denounce the act as a 'covert attack on the authority of the English gentry' in order to 'play the game of a London party'.[1][2] But once elected, the corporations whether Tory or Whig were new made; they stood not by property, but by the vote. They were local sub-parliaments, and they shared alike in the claim to stand as the elected equals of the Westminster Parliament. It there were still corruption and oligarchy, the answer (it was said) should come through the vote of local men, not by the interference of Bashaws or oligarchs, in Somerset House or Gwydyr House. Henceforth, big boroughs and small, Radical and Tory, Manchester and Leeds, side by side with (shall we say, for instance) Canterbury and York, Chichester and Barnard Castle, were all alike members of one body, backed by an electorate of rate-payers. The Association of Municipal Corporations did not appear till the 1870s, but the way was plain for its emergence as a sort of Estate of the Realm, something analogous to the Convention of Royal Burghs in Scotland, which had contrived to maintain its continuity unbroken since the middle of the 16th Century.

Local Government and Historical Rights.
This brings me to my third proposition. The idea that local

self-government was part of the ancient English constitution
was somehow invented or re-discovered in the years between
1836 and 1847; in 1849 it found its classic utterance in a
work by Joshua Toulmin Smith, of which I ought to give the
whole title-page, a splendid piece of Victorian typography:

GOVERNMENT BY COMMISSIONS
ILLEGAL AND PERNICIOUS

The Nature and Effects of all
COMMISSIONS OF INQUIRY

And other Crown-Appointed Commissions.
The Constitutional Principles of
TAXATION:

and the Rights, Duties, and Importance of
Local Self-Government.

By J. Toulmin Smith, Esq.,
of Lincoln's Inn,
Barrister-at-Law.

'It is not almost credible to foresee, when any maximum OF
FUNDAMENTAL LAW of this realm is altered, what dangerous
inconveniences do follow' — Coke, 4 Inst. 41.
'New things which have fair pretences are most commonly hurtful
to the Commonwealth: for commonly they tend to the grievous
vexation and oppression of the subject, and not to that glorious
end that at the first was pretended.' — Coke, 2 Inst. 549.
LONDON:
S. Sweet, 1, Chancery Lane.
1849.

The book itself is nearly 400 pages long, garrulous, repetitive,
cluttered with unreal learning, and it is only one of a flood of
works by the same man. In spite of this it has real style and
sentiment, and there is much in it which has never been said
better. Will you bear with me while I read one rather long
paragraph?

Local self-government may be actual and immediate, as
when all attended by the gemote, when it became an

actual Folk-mote,* and which even now is the case at
parish meetings and others; or it may be representative, in
which case the representatives are of course immediately
responsible to their brethren of the district by whom they
are appointed. By institutions of local self-government
alone is it possible that the interests of districts can be
properly protected. By their existence alone can the full
discussion and understanding of those interests be ensured.
By their existence alone can be ensured that jealous watch
over the encroachments of those entrusted with the
management of the more general affairs of the nation
which is necessary to prevent gradual usurpation of any
arbitrary power. As the protection of local rights and
interests is thus best secured, and the mode of dealing with
them necessarily best understood and most effectually
carried out, so are the minds of all thus better prepared to
understand and deal with affairs of more wide and general
interest. It is, again, an extraordinary security against
violence and anarchy that, by these local institutions,
opportunity is given for legitimately and peaceably expressing the national will, and thus is prevented the
adoption of measures which shall excite dissatisfaction and
discontent. Freedom of opinion, freedom of discussion,
the preservation of all free institutions, and the progress
and full development of all the resources of any state
unquestionably depend, as will be more fully shown
hereafter, on the maintenance of local self-government by
the general governing body. It is because local self-
government stands in the way of empirical legislation on
hasty crotchets and idle schemes that it is, above all things,
hated by the authors and friends of Commissions and of
Central Boards. It is because local self-government ensures
that every proposition shall be really inquired into,

---

*'It is very interesting to notice the universal habit of holding
folkmotes inplied throughout the Anglo-Saxon laws; and the
sanctity attached to them. Thus we find extremely heavy penalities
denounced against the disturbers of the folkmote. 'If he disturb the
folkmote by drawing his weapon, one hundred and twenty shillings
to the ealderman as penalty;' – Laws of Alfred, §38. And the
possible occasion for them even on the most holy festivals is
admitted. Thus: 'Sunday-marketing we also earnestly forbid: and
every folkmote, unless it be for matters of much need.' – Laws of
Cnut, §15.'

discussed, and thoroughly understood before it is adopted,
that it is, just now, the object of such special dislike to
those who delight in nostrums and new experiments; and
that it has become the mark for their ceaseless attack.

For national and human progress local self-government
forms the surest guarantee, affording as it does so many
nurseries where emulation and individual enterprise are
sure of bringing forth continual results whose benefits can
never be confined to the corner of their birth. Under a
system of centralization no idea can diffuse itself unless
first made palatable to the, necessarily, self-elected few
who guide the great machine, and who are, as necessarily,
however honest, the least able to judge of the wants of the
community.

Local self-government is the rock of our safety as
a   free   state;   the   only   absolute   security   for   the
maintenance of the fundamental laws and institutions of
the land, on whose maintenance wholly depends our
peace, prosperity and progress.

It is easy to laugh at Toulmin Smith's history, and even to
doubt his disinterestedness. As barrister, he practised most
successfully on behalf of some very shady local clients in the
long war against Chadwick which ended with the latter's
defeat in 1854; and he certainly put together a repertory of
arguments by which any abuse can be defended for ever on
the ground that it has existed for a long time. He may be
classed perhaps with other rather shady defenders of Magna
Carta, like John Wilkes and Francis Burdett.

But it would be a mistake to under-rate him. For one
thing, he was only part of a wider historical movement,
which flourished both in this country and in Germany.
Perhaps Victorian and Prussian Gothic were part of it;
certainly it included a devotion to Tacitus's account of the
anarchic self-government of the Germans when they with-
stood the Roman Empire, it included deep and serious
interest in Teutonic languages and origins, and it instigated
scholarship which became more balanced and precise as the
century moved on. This was the idealisation of Teutonic
institutions as against Roman institutions, of German and
British politics as against French politics, of historical
thinking as against what Professor Oakeshott calls 'an

abstract principle, or set of related abstract principles, which has been independently premeditated.'[13] Very few British scholars understood what the Germans were up to; even great German scholars, like Gneist and Redlich (Gneist more than Redlich), retired from long study of English *Communal-verfassung oder Self-government*[14] full of false notions they had brought with them. Gneist's version is about as odd as Wagner's contemporary version of German city government in the Meistersingers. Yet in spite of these absurdities the defence of shabby London vestries against the tedious operations of unimaginative reformers meets here a great movement of European thought. What is more, the imprint remains. Once the absurdities have been skimmed off, Toulmin Smith's idea of responsibility to communities remains to puzzle us still as an essential part of our thinking about democracy, an element not present in (for instance) French or American thinking.[15]

The Utilitarians Change Front

My next proposition is that the intellectual advance guard of the reformers had begun to retreat from the front line even before the counter-attack was launched in force. The new utilitarianism of J.S. Mill's generation admitted the proposition so violently denied by Prof. Langrod and Dr. Moulin, that experience in local government is good for the training of citizens in national politics. Go back to the 1820s and one would find that intellectual society agreed unanimously with our continental colleagues. Here, for instance, is Hazlitt in 1825, discussing the poem from which Britten drew the opera *Peter Grimes*. 'The whole of Mr. Crabbe's *Borough* is done so to the life, that it seems almost like some sea-monster, crawled out of the neighbouring slime, and harbouring a breed of strange vermin, with a strong local scent of tar and bilge-water.' Was Peter Grimes in training for democracy? Scarcely.

There is a sarcastic phrase current among social scientists, at least in Manchester: 'It's all in Aristotle.' One could say as effectively 'It's all in Bentham.' I have done a little scouting in the nine volumes of the *Works*, and can say with some confidence that in general the old gentleman thought much the same as Hazlitt. True, he talks of local sub-parliaments, as part of the 'public opinion tribunal': but these merely co-exist with a formidable hierarchy of prefects and sub-prefects, local headmen and their deputies. The conception is Roman or Napoleonic, not remotely Anglo-Saxon. But tucked away in a footnote there is this, written in 1830[16] as advice to the French in constitution-making. Bentham emphasises the danger of federation, the advantages of subordinate legislature. Among their listed advantages is 'having in each sub-legislature a *nursery* for the supreme legislature; a school of appropriate aptitude, in all its branches for the business of legislature.' Oh, for the shade of Peter Grimes. It is this theme that is taken up, perhaps independently re-invented, by John Austin and John Stuart Mill in 1847, in the article already quoted about centra-lisation and in the first edition of the *Political Economy*[17]. There is of course an even more familiar statement of it in Mill's *Representative Government*, which though it was not published till 1861 (why have we had no centenary?) sums up the debates of these years. One set of abbreviated quotations should be enough.[18]

> The plan of representative sub-Parliaments . . . must hence-forth be considered as one of the fundamental institutions of a free government . . . Two points require an equal degree of our attention: how the local business itself can best be done; and how its transaction can be made most instrumental to the nourishment of public spirit and the development of intelligence . . . that portion of the opera-tion of free institutions which may be called the public education of the citizens.

Notice here three things.

First, when Mill says that local government is 'henceforth' to be regarded as fundamental he is not going over to the camp of Toulmin Smith, and accepting some sort of natural rights doctrine, 'nonsense upon stilts', whether justified by appeal to reason or to the Anglo-Saxons. As utilitarian he is convinced by the events of his lifetime; not so much by the failure of Chadwick to beat down the vestries, as by the revolutions of 1848, the failure of Russia in face of the Crimean expedition, the experience of the East India

Company in the Mutiny, the experience of the United States faced by civil war.[19]

Secondly, the ground of general utility[20] is not abandoned: a local authority exists to provide services, and it must be judged (like a Board of Guardians or Board of Health or (later) a School Board) by its success in providing services up to a standard measured by a national inspectorate. The gains of the Chadwick epoch are not to be sacrificed: local authorities are subordinate, not ultimate or primary as Toulmin Smith and the Germans were apt to maintain.

But (and this is the third point) to admit that local government exists also for 'the public education of the citizens' introduces a new concept of free government. This is still a matter of the utility principle, but the measure of happiness has changed. Free government is a less tidy, deodorized, unselfish business than it was; free government admits the need of some at least of the qualities developed in local government, even in Crabbe's *Borough*, qualities of tradition, continuity, a sense of the practicable, a refusal to be bewildered by generalities. In one sense then Mill postulates a central government more conservative than did the older generation of utilitarians who prized these qualities very little. If challenged, he would (I am sure) have said that he was as radical as they, but that he saw that this was the practical way to get forward most quickly to a utopia which would be both sanitary and free. A fair enough answer, but it shows how times had changed. Not only had the panics of bankruptcy and cholera receded; the rather soft-boiled enthusiasms of Harriet Taylor, Mrs. Mill, had replaced the geometrical passions of the first reformers. The theory of local government is no more than a squiggle in the corner of this canvas, but it belongs to the whole picture. Toulmin Smith accidentally relates English local government to one great issue of European thought: John Stuart Mill more consciously and carefully relates it to another.

The Blended Orthodoxy
This is not the whole story,[21] and I have another chapter to add before I sit down. But for most purposes one can take it that the orthodoxy still stands. English local government is

justified because it is a traditional institution. It is justified
because it is an effective and convenient way to provide
certain services. It is justified because we like to think that
our central government needs the kind of qualities which are
best trained by local self-government. One could illustrate
this orthodoxy again and again; for instance from G.C.
Brodrick's contributions to the first volume of Cobden Club
Essays on local government in 1875 (Brodrick, later Warden
of Merton, was a member of the London School Board);
from lectures delivered in this School in 1897 by Sir
Lawrence Gomme, then Clerk to the London County
Council;[22] from Prof. C.H. Wilson's contribution to the
Nuffield College essays in local government published in
1948. Here is one quotation only, from a Conservative
Political Centre pamphlet of April 1961 which has just
turned up in my mail.[23]

> It may thus be said that we, in Britain, are living in a
> fully-fledged democracy in which nearly every adult man
> and woman can play his or her part in administering the
> affairs of the country. Local government itself is a call to
> civic service of the highest order for the benefit of the
> community at large. The local councillor, moreover, has
> the unrivalled advantage over the Member of Parliament in
> that he can see at first hand how the Statutes work, how
> theory is translated into practice, and what a Parlia-
> mentary decision can mean to the happiness of the
> community. The local council, whether it be in a parish,
> rural or urban district, borough or county, is an expression
> of the British genius for self-government and is rightly
> jealous of any encroachments by the Central Government.

This is quite a sufficient cloud of witnesses, and I don't
think I need be ashamed to say that if after the event one
scrutinised the Report of the Royal Commission one would
find all these propositions among its inarticulate major
premises.

The Concept of the Metropolis
But so far I have said not a word about London. This is not
unfair to the authors I have quoted, who don't on the whole
treat London as a special case. But it may be unfair to my

audience, and it certainly omits two issues of doctrine which seem to me to be of the highest importance.

The first of these was alluded to in a *Times* leader of 22nd May last — Whit Monday — perhaps a provincial rather than a metropolitan festival. The leader attempts to soothe an indignant Scot who had attacked the National Coal Board for use of 'the impertinent word provincial'. Scotland, of course, is not a province, it is a kingdom; true, there is a united kingdom, but the leader-writer errs grievously in referring to Scotland as *a* part of *the* kingdom. But unquestionably there is in England a contrast between the Metropolis and the Provinces. How did it arise? And has it any significance in the theory of local government?

I think two points are fairly plain. First, this is a Londoner's kind of geography, not an upper class or establishment geography. There is a much more snob geography which distinguishes between 'in town' and 'out of town' — are you one of those who go up to town or do you go down to London? A class indicator as decisive as any in Nancy Mitford; and with it goes a geography which Miss Mitford should elaborate — the Home Counties, the Shires and so on. This needs elucidation; I suspect that the provinces are outside its ken entirely, since they include (from this point of view) only Thirsk, Aintree, and some grouse moors.

Secondly, I think it is fairly plain that the word metropolis began to compete with the word London some time towards the end of the eighteenth century, when it became conclusively plain that the City of London was not a capital city in the same sense as Paris or Vienna or Berlin. In the time of Wilkes, even at the time of the Gordon Riots in 1780, the City was still a great power in its traditional opposition to the Court. But the City was already becoming a private club, not a geographical expression. Colquhoun, writing of river police in 1800, had no option but to write that his subject 'may be said to affect a considerable proportion of the men of Property in the whole of the Metropolis',[24] because if he had said 'in the whole of London' his sense would have been obscure, ambiguous, even silly. Our predecessors hammered the point home in their Second Report in 1837 by referring to 'the vast extent of uninterrupted Town which forms the Metropolis of the British Empire ... It may be assumed [they say] that the limits of the City of London embrace less than a ninth of the population of what may be considered in a general sense the Town of London.'[2][5] Perhaps it would have been better if they had stuck to this phrase, 'the Town of London': but the legislature was already committed by the Metropolitan Police Act and other enactments to the anonymous label of 'metropolis', and this stuck until the London School Board came into existence in 1870. I think the Royal Commission was modest in proposing another step forward in 1960.

As a Scotsman and a provincial may I digress to say that the claim of London to be a metropolis is philologically quite unsound? The word is Greek: a metropolis is the mother city of its colonies, Britain as a whole was the mother city of the colonies of settlement, as certain Greek cities mothered Greek colonies which they did not claim to rule. But 'province' is Latin, and describes a territory conquered and subjected to a governor: a view of the situation as distasteful to Manchester as to Edinburgh. The French still speak correctly of *Le Métropole* to mean France in relation to its overseas territories: but English usage has had the upper hand, and the world wide problem of 'metropolitan areas', in which American foundations invest so much, means historically the problem of places which have got into the same geographical and administrative mess as London.

Is London an Exception?
There are however certain problems about London — the metropolis — which might be held to set it apart, outside the framework of local self-government: it is (or was) the capital city of an empire and it is very big. Do the ordinary rules apply? My first proposition is that the debaters never reached agreement about this; there is no orthodoxy, but a scale of views.

At one extreme there is Mr. Disraeli — old Mr. Disraeli — when he wrote *Lothair*, published in 1870: 'It is a wonderful place', said Lothair, 'this London; a nation, not a city; with a

population greater than some kingdoms, and districts as
different as if they were under different governments and
spoke different languages. And what do I know of it? I have
been living here six months, and my life has been passed in a
park, two or three squares, and half a dozen streets'. So
Lothair leaps into a hansom, crying ' 'Tis the gondola of
London,' and is carried off to strange adventures;[2][6] What has
this to do with local government? That is the metropolis; all
that is appropriate for a metropolis is some Metropolis
Management Act. Not surprisingly, John Austin is on the
same side;[2][7] 'the respective territories of local governments
(or rather their respective populations) must not be sufficiently extensive to give them a moral weight rendering
their dependence precarious.' Translated into blunt English:
no central government dare give power to a great capital city,
lest it be challenged by an equal authority. London Rome,
Paris, cannot be municipalities.

A second school sits on the fence, croaking 'either' — 'or'.
To this school belonged our predecessors in 1837.[2][8]

In one particular, and that a most important and practical
one, the opinion of Parliament had been already declared
by the establishment of a Metropolitan Police, under the
orders of Commissioners appointed by, and immediately
dependent upon Your Majesty's Executive Government.
We scarcely anticipate that any argument can be brought
forward to show that this system can be partially right. We
can see no middle course for the establishment of an
efficient Police throughout the Metropolis, between
placing the whole under a Metropolitan Municipality, and
entrusting the whole to Commissioners, or other similar
officers under the immediate control of Your Majesty's
Government.

Other topics suggest similar conclusions, as the pav-
ing, sewage and lighting of the streets, which, as
it seems to us, can never be so economically and efficiently
performed in one town as when superintended by an
undivided authority; and the only real point of consideration is, how far these duties for the whole Metropolis
could be placed in the hands of a Metropolitan Municipality, or how far they should be entrusted to the officers
of Your Majesty's Government.

It will be obvious that this is close to the position of the recent Royal Commission 125 years later: but we were driven off the fence by the intensity of general belief in the doctrine of local self-government, of general disbelief in Ministries and Commissions, a doctrine which our predecessors helped to found.

Then thirdly, there is the school of Toulmin Smith, for whom nothing has reality but the ancestral parish pump. Here is a passage which suggests some of the obstinacy, perhaps noble obstinacy, of this view.[29]

> The Parish must be felt to be a *Unit*; of which each man forms a part. Men must realise the universally-proved truth, that no people, nor any neighbourhood, nor any set of men, nor any man, was ever yet made good, moral, clean or safe by Act of Parliament, or by the appointment of salaried functionaries; but that the only hope and assuredness lie in every man feeling and acting up to the obligations of the relation in which he stands to the neighbourhood where he inhabits. In this year of grace, that needs no gloss.

The Metropolis as a Natural Phenomenon
I now come to my final point: this is a big one, but I must have some respect for limits of time and patience. The doctrines I have described so far were pretty complete by 1870; within the limits of human frailty English local government and Parliament in relation to local government have striven to live by them. In most of England something reasonably effective has been made of the triple doctrines of ancient right, modern services, and active citizenship; in London ambiguity has been sustained so successfully that a Royal Commission in 1960 said much the same (unawares) as its predecessor of 1837. Has nothing happened since John Stuart Mill?

Yes, a great deal has happened, but this middle-aged heresy has not yet become new orthodoxy. The story is one associated with names such as those of Patrick Geddes, Halford Mackinder, C.B. Fawcett, Patrick Abercombie, Lewis Mumford, and one could illustrate its variants at length from

their works. As it has always had close association with this
School, may I limit my references to papers read by Patrick
Geddes to meetings of the Sociological Society held here in
1904, 1905 and 1906: James Bryce was then President of the
Society, Charles Booth was in the chair at two out of the
three meetings. There are two papers on 'Civics: a Concrete
and Applied Sociology', one paper on 'A suggested Plan for a
Civic Museum and its Associated Studies.'[30] I shall not quote
any of Geddes's rhetoric: here is an example of Geddes writing
plain and practical prose. 'To realise the geographic and
historic factors of our city's life is the first step to
comprehension of the present, one indispensable to any
attempt at the scientific forecast of the future, which must
avoid as far as it can the dangers of mere utopianism.' And
here is rhetoric by a commentator, Israel Zangwill, the once
famous novelist:

> I fancy the general idea could be conveyed to the man in
> the street under the covering of 'the human shell'. This
> shell of ours is the city. It is the protective crust we have
> built round ourselves. In a smaller sense our house is our
> shell, but in a larger sense each house is only a lobe of the
> complex and contorted whole . . . The human shell is not
> merely geometrical and architectural, like those of pagan
> or beaverish communities; it holds and expresses all those
> differences by which we are exalted about the bee and the
> beaver. It is coloured with our emotions and ideals, and
> contorted with all the spirals of our history. And all these
> manifestations of humanity may be studied as system-
> atically as those of lower orders of creation, which have till
> recently monopolised the privilege of pin and label.

I think that Zangwill's balance between science and
romance is about right. On the one hand, this is a practical
and empirical doctrine; by observation, and only by observation, can one discern structure. On the other hand this is a
doctrine of intense love and respect for the object studied, as
the highest of natural objects. And 'natural' here has the
accustomed ambiguities; in so far as we can understand
nature we must conform to it — except by conformity to
nature we cannot direct nature. What is natural is right; yet
we may seek by patient understanding to control nature. One

86 *Local Government in its Context*

may gibe and say this is all in Aristotle: but the sociological movement of the late nineteenth century put old notions of natural law in quite a new setting, the setting of a world society and metropolitan cities. From the same stem came Halford Mackinder's generalisations about world geography, Fawcett's essays on the Provinces of England, Patrick Abercrombie's plans for cities, and above all his plans for London. The lesson is that to govern we must strive to understand structure and to follow what we understand; work done against the grain is fruitless.

This is, I think, the common doctrine of social science today, a necessary doctrine, and the philosophers must be left to cope with its ambiguities. May I say only, as a student of government, that it seems to omit, or to slip easily over, the thing most essential in politics, common purpose and will, consciously asserted? So I prefer for peroration to end with a quotation not from a geographer or sociologist but from a historian and administrator, Sir Laurence Gomme, once Clerk to the LCC and one of the greatest spokesmen of local government.

> Whenever the great community which now answers to the name of London cares to exert itself in claiming rights over her own destiny, these rights will be conceded in all essentials. The new ideal will be found here. The old ideal, lost and gone for ever in the finished history of the old city, will give place to the new ideal emanating from the pulsation of the men and women who desire London to be great in happiness for those who claim it for their home. . . . There is a dormant force in London which desires the greatness of London in health and happiness, and this once aroused to the full will mean a great ideal and a great result.[3 1]

Notes

1. *Town and Country Planning*: Oxford University Press, 3rd ed. 1959, at p.82.

2. Royal Commission on Local Government in Greater London — *Report*. Cmnd. 1164. HMSO 1960. (Herbert Report).

3. Vol. 31 (1953), p.25 and p.344; Vol. 32 (1954), p.433.

4. A good example is Burke, *Reflections on the Revolution in France*: World's Classics ed., Vol. IV, p.55.

5. Para. 113.

6. Nor is it always clear even now. This for instance in *The Times* of June 4th, 1961: quoting the chairman of a RDC. 'This proposal would rob us of half of our rateable value. Our attitude is that we will give up nothing at all.'

7. *Reflections*, World's Classics ed., Vol. IV, p.50.

8. Ibid, p.83.

9. Ibid, p.106. There is a (metaphorical) reference just below to 'the municipal corporations of that universal kingdom' and the moral limits on their liberty.

10. Vol. 63, pp.504 and 524.

11. Vol. 85, January—April 1847, p.221.

12. *'The Spirit of Whiggism'* (1836): 1885 ed. of the *Runnymede Letters*, p. 289.

13. *Political Education* (1951): see *Philosophy, Politics and Society* (ed. Laslett), Blackwell, 1956, at p.5.

14. The title of Gneist's contribution to controversy within Prussia, published in 1863. Redlich's book, published in Vienna in 1900, has a different academic background and political colour.

15. A student put this neatly in an exam paper this session — 'Ours is a rather 'lumpy' self-government, and quite often small sections bear greater influence than their size merits.'

16. Bentham to his Fellow Citizens of France: *Works*, ed. of 1843, Vol. 4, Footnote on p.429.

17. Toulmin Smith picked this up promptly: see *Government by Commission* (1849) at p.258 and its reference to a review of the *Political Economy* in the *Edinburgh Review* of October 1845 (at p.334).

18. *Representative Government* 1st ed. 1861, pp.267/8.

19. This perhaps scarcely does justice to the influence of De Tocqueville's interpretation of these events. See the quotation from *Democracy in America* (first published in English in 1835) which opens the first chapter of Dr. V.D. Lipman's *Local Government Areas, 1834–1945*, and Bagehot's acknowledgment in *The English Constitution* (Works: 1915 ed., Vol. 5, p.364) that De Tocqueville 'founded what may be called the 'culte' of corporations'.

20. cf. the first Report of the Royal Commission on Municipal Corporations, 1835, at p.49. 'In their actual condition, where not productive of positive evil, they exist in the great majority of instances for no purpose of general utility.'

21. Bagehot's *English Constitution* (1867) reinforced Mill, in a lighter vein, e.g. pp.306 and 362.

22. *Principles of Local Government*: Constable, 1897.

23. Local Government Series No. 1: *The Work of Local Government*: CPC, April 1961.

24. *A Treatise on the Commerce and Police of the River Thames* (1800). Preface, p.11.

25. Report, p.2.

26. New edition of 1878; p.111/2.
27. *Edinburgh Review*, Vol. 85 (1847).
28. Report, p.4.
29. *The Parish* (1854), p.546.
30. To be found in three volumes published by Macmillan in 1905, 1906 and 1907 as *Sociological Papers*.
31. *The Governance of London* (Unwin) 1907; at p.406.

6 Administrative Aspects of 'Buchanan' and 'Crowther'*

This paper is being written at the end of April 1964 to be delivered in June. One of the most significant facts about Buchanan is that things may happen in these two months to make this paper obsolete before it is delivered.

From my point of view, these are two reports using different methods to handle different problems. I shall have some things to say in a critical and controversial spirit both about Buchanan and about Crowther: but this is itself an indication of where we now stand. There was an age 'B.B' — before Buchanan — and we shall never go back to it. Not the urban environment, but argument about the urban environment has been radically changed, we have learned to talk a new language, Buchanan language, and the result is that we can discuss issues that were never properly discussed before.

Because the situation is changing rapidly, I have tried to anchor this paper to a rather formal analysis of the issues. This I have divided into three sections, 'Buchanan', 'Crowther' and 'the rest', and I have tried under each heading to analyse tacit assumptions as well as the published text. In doing this I have tried to concentrate on political and administrative issues in which I have some competence. These are perhaps not as important in a practical sense as the economic and financial issues discussed in Mr. Woodham's paper.

'Buchanan'

(a) Premises which are emphasised

I think the structure of Professor Buchanan's argument is as

*From *Journal of the RTPI*, L, no. 7 (Jul/Aug 1964).

follows:
  (i) Traffic is a function of activities, involving starting-points and destinations (*paragraph 72*).
 (ii) In towns, these starting-points and destinations are (almost entirely) buildings; therefore town traffic is a function of buildings and their uses (*paragraph 80*).
(iii) Extrapolation of existing trends (fig. 38 on p.27) and study of comparable countries gives us a working notion of the probable increase in road vehicles over the next twenty years.
 (iv) Even if we wished to stop this increase, it would be politically impossible to do so in a democratic society. Economically, nothing can stop it except a major slump; there is no technological alternative in sight.

From these premises it follows that there will be severe damage to environment (see for instance *paragraph 22* and what follows), expense due to delay (fig. 13 on p.15), personal frustration (*paragraph 11*), and accidents (*paragraph 15*).

This is a closely-knit argument, set out in such a way that each step can be tested. There may be technological doubts; but from my own knowledge I can find no point at which to challenge it except that it puts in the forefront the question of damage to environment. This sets a serious problem to economists and others engaged in cost/benefit analysis, because the evidence of our eyes tells us that the public has not hitherto cared a great deal about damage to the environment. I agree with Professor Buchanan that they ought to care more, and that they would care more if they were given better leadership in these matters. But one notes that this raises some nice questions about leadership in a free society.

(b) Other premises
The terms of reference of the enquiry were 'to study the long term development of roads and traffic in urban areas and their influence on the urban environment'. This restricted the argument by postulating that there exists now a workable distinction between urban areas and other areas — in plain English, between town and country — and that this dis-

tinction is to be maintained. In the words of the Report, 'a sensible relationship is to be maintained between developed areas and open country' (*paragraph 10*).

   This seems to me to be much more controversial:

   (i) I have lived much of my life in Central Scotland and in North-West England, and I see there no sign whatever of 'a sensible relationship' between town and country which should be 'maintained'. Perhaps Greater London can be described as 'a great town'; in the Report of the Royal Commission on Local Government in Greater London we took that view (nudged to some extent by our terms of reference) and we sought to draw out the administrative consequences of this. But it is not easy to find any sensible relationship between town and country in the great Victorian industrial areas. To achieve this might be a possible objective for re-development; but one could only get there by bulldozing much existing development out of the way.

   (ii) So far as one can judge from preferences expressed through purchasing power, what the British choose is not town or country but suburb. This is also Victorian; the first generations of rich business men were bound to the industrial areas, and they brought the Italian idea of a villa into a rather crazy relationship to Victorian industry — industry and commerce surrounded by Venetian villas. As villadom sank in the social scale it was compressed into suburbia, and much town-planning thought has not been about planned towns but about planned suburbia. I think it is a weakness that in this report so little is said about suburbia. Surely most existing suburbs can absorb the flood of cars with only minor adaptation, and the car (especially the second car) tremendously improves living conditions in suburbia? In fact, I rather like living in a suburb, and I should like to hear much more about the future of the suburban environment.

   Then there is one paragraph which states very clearly but without emphasis a single point of tremendous importance. This is *paragraph 446*, headed 'Static or Expanding Towns'.

'We have not considered the problems of towns in a state of
continuous expansion . . . A plan for continuous expansion
would have to be based quite differently — probably on some
concept of transport corridors, with lateral development.'
Here again the Report is constrained by its terms of
reference; although in this instance it seems that the
Committee set its own terms of reference, and cannot blame
the Minister of Transport. Without some constraints one
cannot write coherently at all; but if one chooses the wrong
constraints one may get *reductio ad absurdum* — a deduction
of consequences that 'proves' the constraints to be intolerable. Peering into the future, I should guess that in the next
twenty-five years the chances are at best 50—50; and indeed
that we are, after 2000 A.D., more likely to get 'continuous
expansion' than to get 'planned expansion' stopping when
planned towns reach 'a given future size'. The first generation
of New Towns has begun to illustrate the difficulty of
stopping at 'a given size'; one has to ask also whether the
detailed studies encourage one to accept or reject this basic
assumption about the future character of urban development.

(c) Feasibility Studies
Here I should like to make explicit an analogy that may well
have been in Professor Buchanan's mind. It costs about as
much to develop a new type of aircraft as to build a new
town; they are both technological operations of great
complexity, to be carried out in a period of rapid technological change. The Treasury, the scientists and the Defence
Services have all been acutely aware of the need to proceed in
such a way as to minimise the grave risks of wrong and
wasteful decisions, and in 1961 the Zuckerman Report set
out the sequence of steps to be followed. A defence
department will state operational requirements; it says 'give
us the weapons for such and such a task'. Adventurous
scientists will sketch answers which stand up pretty well
logically and technologically under criticism from other
scientists. There is the present situation, A; there is a future
situation, B, which is regarded as scientifically possible. But a
feasibility study is needed before we can decide about
attempting to move from A to B. What will the move from A

to B cost, in terms of cash and resources diverted from other projects? How long will it take to move from A to B? In fact, will B be obsolete by the time we get there? I suggest that the four studies, of Newbury, Norwich, Leeds and Oxford Street might well be looked at as 'feasibility studies' in this sense.

Perhaps the Report rather blurs the lines between an operational requirement, a scientific exercise, and a feasibility study. But in any case these lines are never perfectly clear, and the Report gives most of the data needed for an answer about feasibility. I am not qualified to give that answer; I simply suggest something to illustrate the shape of an answer. There are various factors; the optimum date of completion; a date (later than the optimum) after which completion would be useless; the number of Newbury's, Norwich's, Leed's, and Oxford Streets which have to be dealt with. A very rough assessment would be that we could deal with the Newbury's and the Norwich's quite well in the next twenty years; we could make an impact on the problem of Leeds and its peers, though we could not complete the whole thing; we could not possibly complete the Oxford Street project except as a unique case — but it is only one of at least 50 such blocks in Central London, and their problems cannot be dealt with one by one. That is to say, in Central London we must either limit ourselves to palliatives or look elsewhere for a technical solution.

I may be entirely wrong about these conclusions, but this need not affect the argument. More work needs to be done, but we have here data for a decision, data not quite complete, but fairly easy to work up for logical and coherent use. But what about the decision-making process itself?

(d) The Model of Decision-Making

I have perhaps been writing so far in an amateurish way about planning questions; my object has been to lead the discussion to a central point in the political philosophy of the Report. I could put this briefly by saying that 'Buchanan' takes a lofty view of democratic politics, the South East Study takes a low view, 'Crowther' takes no view at all.

There are two points in the Buchanan report itself:
(i) There is a great choice to be made by 'society' very

soon. 'Society will have to ask itself seriously how far it is
prepared to go with the motor vehicle' (*paragraph 68*).
'The choice facing society . . . ' (*paragraph 459*). Conditions 'in the next ten years or so, will demand an
almost heroic act of self-discipline from the public'
(*paragraph 481*).

(ii) Society will choose rightly if it chooses rationally; and
rationality requires coherence and integration —
'transitivity of preferences', in the jargon; 'a smooth,
continuous and fully integrated policy, without the
discordances that are apparent at present' (*paragraph
471*).

This is a very lofty view of the ideal we should set
ourselves. If we described how in fact we go about our
business we should get a rather different picture. The process
of decision-making in a democracy is very complex indeed. In
it there are at least four elements, each complex:

(i) There are those who have strong collective interests in
development and who organise themselves to push these
interests. There are national, regional and local interests;
there are hard cash interests, and there are also altruistic
and aesthetic interests. Professor Buchanan as an
inspector in charge of enquiries has had a ring-side view
of these pushing and struggling interests.

(ii) There are millions of individual citizens each of whom
takes his own line about choice of vehicles, choice of
house, of holidays, of routes, of jobs. One reason why
the attractions of the car-owning society are so irresistible is that it is a sort of consumers' democracy. It
cannot be bossed about; millions of individual choices
add up to a public choice which is almost unchallenge-
able.

(iii) Then there are many professional bodies (of which the
Town Planning Institute is one) which exist largely to
set standards. They decide who is qualified, they
support the judgement of the qualified man, they seek to
demarcate tolerable and intolerable conditions. They
have immense influence, but they have no power of
decision.

(iv) Finally there are the elected persons who preside, listen, and decide — or fail to decide. Who shall blame them if they choose not to decide? This is often the safest choice.

Certainly the authors of the South East Study take the low view, not the high view of our political process.

> For practical reasons, it is unlikely that a great part of the development . . . could take place until the 'seventies . . . First the schemes must be discussed and provisionally agreed — subject to full examination by local enquiry: outline and then detailed plans must be drawn up: and the statutory processes of designation and land acquisition must be gone through. After all that, it will take time before the building rate touches its maximum. (p.79).

> So far as the basic problem is concerned, there is little choice . . . At this stage it is difficult to make any reliable forecast . . . Nobody who has examined the history of planning in London and the South East since the days before the war can fail to be conscious of the possibility of error and of the possibility of social and economic changes that may overturn basic assumptions. There is no way of avoiding mistakes when planning for a long period ahead (pp.100–1).

Selective quotation can never be completely fair; but I do not think one can be in doubt about the rather earthy flavour of this political philosophy. The authors stress the fallibility of all men, including themselves; the law's delays; the impossibility of radical legislation; the scramble of competing interests. Nothing is quite certain; all decisions are provisional; at best the planner may be able to see trouble coming and to improvise dodges in order to minimise it.

I do not say this to criticise Buchanan as Utopian or the Ministry's planners as defeatists. One cannot possibly throw away either view as false. It is true that in the next five years we are facing a situation in which a choice lies open, and that if we do not choose we abdicate control of part of our future. But it is also true that in any form of human government the odds are against clear choice and rational decision; we can attain these good things only partially, and even then by a great effort.

'Crowther'

This brings me to 'Crowther' and to some aspects of the administrative problem. It seems to me that the central weakness of 'Crowther' is that it says little about policy-making, much about the execution of policy.

Its main argument can be stated quite briefly:

(a) The following are needed but are not enough:

(i)   Urban motorways
(ii) Public transport
(iii) Limitation of the use of cars in towns

(b) In addition, the situation requires the reshaping of towns and cities. But the present administrative machinery cannot do this:

(i)   Planning decisions are diffused between many central and local authorities, and are in any case negative in style.
(ii) Co-ordination is also negative in style;
(iii) The financial pattern is confused;

(c) A new administration must be designed to provide for four things:

(i)   A clear statement of national objectives;
(ii) Over-all planning for each urban region;
(iii) Detailed plans for re-development;
(iv) The execution of works.

The argument then makes no further reference to national objectives, but proceeds to a discussion of regional development agencies.

(a) Organisation at the Centre

Crowther thus skips Westminster and Whitehall, proceeding direct to the regions. Clearly this misses the essence of the difficulty; how can regions execute a policy if there is no policy? Professors rush in, where commissions fear to tread: there seem to me to be two rather different issues here.

First, there is a problem of organisation at the political level. I take the liberty of quoting some sentences from Samuel Brittan, writing about economic planning in *The Observer* of 3 May 1964.

One obvious formula for coherence is to have a small committee of really senior Ministers to decide spending priorities. This was advocated by Lord Plowden in the draft of his famous report on public spending, but was later blue-pencilled. In the USSR the four or five top members of the Government were responsible not only for their own specialities but collectively for the whole field of Government spending.

Could the Chancellor of the Exchequer, and the Foreign and Home Secretaries forget their departments and get down together as a team? Probably only if the Cabinet were to have really effective personalities, who could forget about their departments for a while. It might have worked in 1945–50, with Bevin, Cripps, Dalton, Morrison and Bevan. It would be unlikely to work under this Government, or the next.

Decisions about spending land are at least as important as decisions about spending money; decisions about land once taken are hard to reverse and their effects stretch very far. The work cannot be done by a single department; it concerns at least the departments of Housing and Local Government, Trade, Agriculture and Food, Transport, Power, Defence, perhaps others as well. These organisations are going concerns, and not much is to be gained by switching blocks of work from one department to another, unless other conditions are also met. There can be no fundamental change unless the leading men of the party in power are prepared to give an issue high priority, and then to let it be handled either by one powerful minister or by a group. If this condition is met, then it is relatively easy to extemporise an organisation, as was so often done under Mr. Churchill's leadership in World War II. If it is not met, a coherent policy cannot be made and sustained.

Secondly, there is a problem of what has been called 'administrative style'. The conclusion I should draw from the clash in philosophies between Buchanan and the South East Study is two-fold.

(1) The authors of the latter seem to mistake the purpose of 'models' and 'feasibility' studies. Their line of thought would lead them to condemn these as utopian; in fact they are as necessary in engineering the urban and rural environment as in any other sort of engineering. A problem is set us when we

look vaguely into the future and see something there that we do not much like. How can we act rationally to minimise costs, increase benefits? The individual more or less consciously thinks up, ponders, and accepts or discards alternative courses of action. Society cannot face such choices at all unless it is consciously organised for intellectual action. This does not mean a monolithic planning organisation; on the contrary, it needs a loosely constructed organisation, within which there are independent individuals capable of imagining alternatives, and independent critical organisations capable of analysing and weighing rigorously the consequences of each alternative. To return to my earlier example, it would help decision about the Oxford Street block if we had another model based on other assumpttions — for instance the exclusion from the area of all vehicles except goods vehicles moving to one or two carefully designed unloading areas within it, from which there could be distribution by small trolleys, electrical or manual, limited to separate tracks or pathways, and associated with lifts inside the buildings.

As a nation we need better model-building agencies somewhere, bold, fertile and also rigorous. It is rather characteristic of our age that Utopias are out of fashion. They rarely appear unless disguised as science fiction, and then the authors (George Orwell for instance) sketch models of evil rather than models of good. Model building is only respectable in this field if one calls it cost-benefit analysis. I am not being ironical when I say that we need a much better organisation for the construction of alternative Utopias. We should perhaps look for this, as the economists have done, in the ill-defined area between Government, organised interests, and the universities, where one finds such organisations as the National Economic Development Council and the National Institute of Economic and Social Research.

(2) Perhaps it requires a different temperament to make not a model but a working plan, and then to fight the plan through to execution, through a maze of disappointments, compromises, and extemporisations. Most administrators do, in their lives of belittling experience, acquire something of the world-weariness of the authors of the South East Study,

and the confusion of British planning procedure favours that attitude. But there is such a thing as administrative nerve, and here it seems to be failing. Could our administrators not think perhaps a little more boldly, feel a little more confidence in themselves? If the statutory procedure causes dangerous delay, why not change it? If local authorities block action by mutual jealousy, why not displace them? And so on.

This will lead to the fair comment that planning administrators cannot change their style unless they are backed by politicians and the electorate. But one should add that the politicians have few ideas of their own about how administration works; political backing is needed, but administrative style can be changed only from within the administration. Might I beseech them to try it? They will find that rigorous model-building and confident executive action are both in fashion among the younger generation.

(b) Regional Development Agencies

The 'Crowther' argument runs as follows:—

The existing authorities are to remain, perhaps with the changes recommended by the Local Government Commissions.

New agencies are to be created on the model of the New Town Corporations; i.e. they are to be appointed bodies, with their own executive staff and their own financial resources, subject to limited control from Whitehall. The Agency's job will be:

(i) To co-ordinate and stimulate local planning authorities so as to produce a regional plan.

(ii) To remit detailed planning to the existing planning authorities, but subject to some control through its financial powers.

(iii) To carry out the work itself 'unless it was satisfied that the local authority could do it as well and as quickly'.

Then, finally, the Committee adds two or three paragraphs on 'real costs' and 'money costs'; paragraphs which are optimistic but vague.

Mr. Woodham has much more authority in this field than I have, and I should be very ready to accept his diagnosis. My first reaction was to think that this plan was in some respect too radical, in others not radical enough.

(1) It seems to me that there are three issues so big that they must be handled nationally. One is the modernisation of the construction industry. The second is the invention of financial devices which will enable us to keep a proper proportion between the amount spent annually on vehicles and the amount spent annually on roads and other lines of movement. The third is the preparation of a national framework for regional planning, a matter to which I refer again below. I do not see that the Crowther development agencies could handle these three tasks effectively.

(2) On the other hand, we should not be too ready to repeat the sequence of events after 1945. It was judged then that some tasks (the hospitals service, for instance, and the distribution of electricity and gas) could not be carried out by existing local authorities. The conclusion drawn was not that local government should be reorganised, but that new agencies should be created; hence further confusion twenty years later. There are some signs now of a change of heart in local government, of a recognition that effective reorganisation is the condition of survival. I admit that there are signs pointing the other way, and that some authorities still stand about with heads in the sand, presenting small or large posteriors to the indifferent public. I should agree that this is probably the last battle, and that if local government is not modernised in the next two or three years, the 'Crowther' case for death by a thousand cuts can no longer be resisted. It will then be time to find other agencies to do the nation's business.

Regional Government

This brings up the question of the alternatives to local government. 'Crowther' proposes *ad hoc* agencies; a year ago, in speaking at the annual conference of the Institute of Municipal Treasurers, I emphasised an alternative which seemed more in keeping with the present state of our administration. This was a development of the existing eleven

central government regions (Scotland and Wales each constitutes a region with important special institutions of its
own). At one time there existed in England outside the towns
a framework of direct administration, through the Home
Office, the Lords Lieutenant, and the Justices of the Peace.
But since local government reached its present shape, towards
the end of the nineteenth century, the practice in time of
crisis has been not to displace local government, but to plant
representatives of the central government in each of the great
cities, so as to speed up the dealings between central and
local government. There has been flux and re-flux; the central
government spreads out to reach the regions in a crisis;
withdraws in quiet times. I do not think there is any doubt
that regional government in this administrative sense is now
growing stronger, after withdrawal during an epoch which will
probably be known to historians as the feeble 'fifties.

Last year I argued against what I called constitutional
regionalism, the creation of elected regional authorities
throughout the island. This seemed to me to be not viable
politically except in Scotland and Wales, because there was so
little public demand; and perhaps disastrous administratively
because the pattern of movement and settlement in England
is changing very fast, and the trend is perhaps not towards
intensified regionalism but to dispersed settlement in an
interlocking national pattern. To put this in another way, I
am not anxious to strengthen the North against the South,
but to destroy the distinction between North and South, and
it seems to me that events are moving that way.

This may be written off as the view of England taken by a
Scotsman, who can not shake off the idea that all England
lies to the South, except perhaps for some parts which were
unfairly lost by Scotland in unlucky wars. But I have before
me Fabian, Bow Group and Liberal publications; I also have
newspaper accounts of a recent lecture given by Sir Keith
Joseph; and they all seem to be moving, each at their own
pace, in the same direction. There is a general desire for
administrative decentralisation; there are glances towards
elected regional authorities. But in the end the difficulties
make the authors pause, except for what concerns Wales and
Scotland; and they settle for some form of advisory regional

council to act in concert with the regional offices of Whitehall. Some authors propose that such councils should become elective later on if public opinion demands it, others evade this issue, since it may frighten off the existing local authorities. But all propose administrative improvements, none produces a plan which displaces the existing framework of local government.

Such unanimity could be ground for suspicion, and of course there are quite strong arguments against this pragmatical alliance. Responsibility may be lost in a headless structure of regional offices. Local authorities may find one more excuse for ignoring the problems of obsolete boundaries and powers. Appointed advisory bodies are often no better manned than elected councils. Nevertheless, I think these risks should be taken, so long as we emphasise the needs to be met, and develop some real passion in meeting them.

To put this in sociological jargon, I should prefer to stress function rather than structure. Speaking on this subject to the IMTA Conference a year ago, I suggested that four functions were not properly discharged in the English regions at present. I called these liaison, consultation, intelligence and publicity, and I hope you will excuse me if I recur to this briefly. By *liaison* I mean quick and easy communication between local authorities and an effective agent of the central government as a whole. By *consultation* I mean that there should be, as it were, an open forum in which local authorities and other interests within the region can face one another, battle for their own points of view, and realise that they have a joint interest in a quick and realistic compromise. By *intelligence* I mean not so much brains — there is in fact no academic monopoly of brains — as authentic information, collected, checked, consolidated and made available to all who need it, including the general public. But more than this is needed for *publicity*. In most regions of England the discussion of public issues at regional level has in fact declined steeply, as the technology of mass communications has improved. There has been much talk and little action about the cultivation of local public interest through radio and TV. Meantime, the local morning press has dwindled, evening papers (the *Manchester Evening News* for instance) try hard in difficult circumstances, but there is no effective debate in print about things that deeply concern the ordinary man. London is no exception; its local and regional affairs are very ineffectively treated by the press. This is just as much a matter of technological change as is the advent of the motor car; similarly, its effects cannot be allowed to go by default. One needs to engineer new channels for communication, and there are people with experience and skill in this.

In a sense, all these functions, liaison, consultation, intelligence and publicity, are functions of communication. There are, in addition, functions of execution, and it may be that new techniques of construction prescribe new forms of organisation, such as public corporations or consortia of local authorities. But you will recognise here a theme of much recent discussion about decision-taking in big organisations. A complex organisation, whether in business or in government, exists only through its network of external and internal communications; the making and execution of decisions can be no better than the network. I feel a strong conviction about the need to improve *communications*, in this sense. I feel an equally strong conviction that the *executive organisation*, the construction agency, must swiftly follow the requirements of technology. Granted, that such agencies exist to further and to execute good decisions: yet I find it much harder to say anything in general terms about the right organisation for taking planning *decisions*. Indeed, I am not certain that there is a single right organisation. The regional structure of the country is itself in process of a radical change; no two regions are exactly alike (or even closely similar) in internal structure; local authorities with identical legal powers may be very different in their operation; the complexities of Whitehall are not put there by bureaucratic malice, but reflect complexities of technologies and pressures. Only national leadership backed by national awareness can cut through this net. We know a little about how to engineer these things, but not much.

There, I think, I should stop, and briefly recapitulate.

First, the explicit premises of Buchanan. I skipped rather quickly over the agreed parts of the argument, so I ought to repeat now that they seem to me decisive and revolutionary. One problem alone worries me in my capacity of student of politics; how is public taste to be evaluated in a cost-benefit study?

Secondly, there are two 'inarticulate major premises', to borrow a phrase from American jurisprudence. There is (first) an assumption that there is an environment to preserve. For perhaps two-fifths of us, there is not an environment to preserve, but an environment to destroy and recreate. There is (second) an assumption, explicit but not emphasised, that we can plan towns to reach a given size, then stop. This is not realistic.

Thirdly, there is an analogy between engineering aircraft and engineering towns. The Concorde supersonic airliner will probably cost as much as the reconstruction of Norwich: both problems are partly technological and partly political. The best analysis of procedures in one sort of engineering is to be found in the Zuckerman report, and it would be interesting to follow this analogy even more closely than Buchanan has done.

Fourthly, there is a stimulating contrast between the political theory of the engineer, Buchanan, and the political theory of Ministers and administrative civil servants, embodied in the South East Study. I should not be happy to abandon either view. The Ministry seems to be ignorant of the function of model-building as an instrument of decision. Alternative assumptions need to be followed through rigorously before we can choose rationally. But, equally, the engineers expect too much of ordinary mortals. There is an old tag from Cicero, which might be translated: 'We do not live in Plato's Republic but on this dung-hill called Rome.'

Finally, there is Crowther, and my reactions will be obvious from what has gone before. Frankly, the argument seems to me to be below the level of the occasion. There is a level of national decision-making, which Crowther ignores. There is a level of regional and local administration, and here the committee gives an answer of a rather superficial kind.

At the national level, I think that a change of administrative style is more important than juggling with committees and departments. I can assure top people who are hesitant that in the younger generation of scholars and executives there is a great drive towards a new administrative style, a style which combines caution and rigour in thought with energy in action. This may sound brash, but it was a long-dead Victorian civil servant who enunciated the maxim 'the imperative must have priority.' In other words, when an issue *must* be faced, face it decisively.

At the regional level, I find the question of structure very puzzling: at present the shape of England changes every year, and it is moving into uncharted territory. Hence I stress two things, and readers of recent empirical studies of management will know where they come from. First, that function has priority over structure, and that the primary function is communication. Secondly, that executive organisation comes next, and must be ready to respond instantly to technological change.

But I retire baffled in face of the central problem, that of national awareness and national leadership.

III

Africa

There is a useful legend that somewhere in the heart of the British system there is an annotated index of 'the good and great' — those apt for service on official committees. Clearly I got on to it for the first time when I was 'parachuted' into Tanganyika in 1952, age forty-three: and it begins to look as if I have (very properly) been retired from it in my sixties. How these things are done is a question one does not ask: presumably I gave satisfaction, or I should not have been picked, certainly on the whole I took satisfaction.

I have always been more interested in 'governments' than in 'parties', but governments are by nature discreet and difficult to research. I cannot avoid the awkward conclusion that to study government one must participate in government, and this has grave risks. One is that unpaid service may imply an exchange: one is there as someone's stooge and must not speak out of turn. Another is that one is tactitly pledged to discretion. Also, one may take on unawares the attitudes of the very pleasant people with whom one is working. Finally, there are serious risks of boredom and futility: one may be a token member, learning nothing and contributing nothing.

I think I have been lucky: but I can't conceal from myself that it has made me in a sense an 'establishment figure', a proper object of contempt.

It had never occurred to me to become an amateur of developing countries in general, Africa in particular. I had always wanted to move into 'comparative government', once settled in Manchester, but if things had worked out otherwise, I should have chosen Europe rather than Africa. But in that phase, there was scope for the 'in-and-outer' under the aegis of the Colonial Office, no hope whatever of access and funds and leisure for work in Europe.

My knowledge of Africa is really very limited: and perhaps (like many 'thesis-miners', British and American) I exploited

African resources to make tools for attacking non-African questions. But I was lucky in that I had two marvellously knowledgeable and perceptive assistants, Peter Johnston in Tanganyika, Roman Rostowski in Kenya; and in that my brief allowed me to go out and look, and did not condemn me to sit in an office in the capital and hear evidence. Perhaps my 'Africa' is merely a country of the mind: at least it seems real to me.

This love affair provided the ideas for two books: *Free Elections* (1958) and — with Kenneth Robinson and other contributors — *Five Elections in Africa* (1960). There was also a good deal of report-writing; and there was something of a campaign to defend and improve the training of middle-level black administrators in the period of transition. The Report of the Bridges Committee (I was Vice-Chairman) on Training in Public Administration for Overseas Countries probably reads in a rather smooth and platitudinous way. But from my point of view it was part of a tussle (waged along with various good friends) to hold up the hand of the administrator 'in the bush', the managing clerk in the office, in face of encroaching chaos. Probably I romanticised the framework of Roman administration, of Napoleonic adminis-tration, of the 'examination-wallah' in India. My friends and I knew these Africans and their potentialities, felt that (like clerks in English local government and civil service) they needed self-respect, mutual respect, professional standing, and that to create these might be a latent rather than a manifest function of a good training system. The creation of the Committee was a success, its report was for me a partial failure, in that the Committee deadlocked as between my emphasis* on the job to be done 'in the bush' and an equally romantic emphasis on the need to dramatise Britain's post-imperial concern as a leader towards non-Communist development. We compromised and recommended both approaches, which could be portrayed abstractly in the images of Dudley Seers and the Institute of Overseas Development at Sussex, Arthur Livingstone and the Depart-ment of Overseas Administrative Studies at Manchester.

*Stated briefly in an article in *New Society*, 27 Feb 1954.

Surprisingly, the compromise was honoured, and neither line was starved of funds. But I cannot see clearly what (if anything) we contributed severally and jointly to the main trends of decolonisation. In relation to these, I reproduce here only two formal academic 'set-pieces', which will (I hope) still convey the intellectual atmosphere of the 1950s.

The establishment of independence for India, Pakistan and Burma in 1947 made it certain that in the next period movement could only be in one direction, towards independence. Britain had neither the motivation nor the resources to fight a long series of colonial wars; the problem was not one of empire-building but of how to quit an empire with a certain dignity, self-satisfaction, and even smugness. But very few people had a sufficient range of knowledge to foresee what was inevitable; there was some resolute opposition to overcome, especially where there were European settlers linked politically to elements in Britain, and there was a large vaguely 'imperial' sentiment to be re-educated very cautiously.

The talking-point therefore, and it was held to irrespective of the political party in power, was that independence must be given, but only to viable, stable and democratic governments. I call it a talking-point rather than a policy, because the terms were undefined and undefinable, and it was against the rules to name dates.

Viability tended to mean big units: and in British thinking big units meant federation, because all the books traced federal experience, through the USA and Canada to India, Pakistan — and where next? Certainly the Colonial Office legal advisers knew how to draft federal constitutions, and the financial experts could suggest lines of bargaining over tax resources. But I am glad that I was never mixed up in the process of federation-making: I never concealed my opinion that the Central African Federation created in 1952 was not a federation but a fiddle, and I rather think that the middle ranks of the Colonial Office thought (as I did) that it represented a spearhead of South African advance into East and Central Africa, and that the problem was where and how to halt that advance without fighting a third South African war. Luckily the dominant Afrikaner regime was astutely cautious, and the Zambesi has become the frail barrier between different styles of life.

Apart from federation, the key points were stability and democracy, that is to say, administration and elections, and the hardest problem in a personal sense was to avoid being deeply involved in double talk. Some double talk there had to be; one knew that administration and elections could *never* mean the same thing in Dar-es-Salaam or Kampala as they do in Bournemouth or West Ham. After all, their meaning is not the same with us as it is in Chicago or Pennsylvania, Bordeaux or the Midi, Moscow or Soviet Georgia, or (for that matter) in Belfast and Londonderry. But there were substantial things to be done: in fact, to encourage coherent party organisation and to Africanise the administrations. Looking back, these seem like neo-colonial aspirations; looking forward at the time, from the Congo collapse at the end of 1959, it seemed as if much of East and Central Africa would go the same way, leaving a power gap to be filled by South Africa. Our feeling in the 1960s was one of deep relief: we had squeezed through a closing door before it slammed shut against us, and we had gained a breathing-space of at least relative stability. How did I come to use the word 'we'? A strange set of tacit alliances and personal connections, now wholly dissipated. 'We' are out of the story now, and it has made a new start.

7 Representation in Plural Societies*

All British political parties are committed to the further development of self-government within the Commonwealth and to the establishment in due course of new states which can choose for themselves whether to remain in association with the United Kingdom and the other 'Realms'. There are disputes about the pace and tactics of change; but the facts of the situation give us no choice about the direction of advance. We are therefore now engaged in a period in which decisions about the choice of constitutional devices are of extreme practical importance, and it is of particular importance that local politicians in the Colonies, as well as the Colonial Office and the party politicians at home, should be well 'briefed' on the possible effects of various courses of action. The number of devices available to us is basically quite limited, though each of them can be used in various forms, and the range of combinations is very great. There are only seven matters of first-rate importance to be included in a handbook for British constitution-makers: electoral systems, parliamentary procedure, Cabinet government, a non-political civil service, federations, Dominion status, the British system of local government. There has been first-rate research and there are first-rate textbooks on all except the first of these; the nature of the electoral system is fundamental to the structure of self-government, yet practically nothing has been written on electoral experience in any Commonwealth country except Great Britain and the 'settled' Dominions.

This gap is masked in practice because it is not usual to include anything about elections in the constitution itself;

*From *Political Studies*, II, no. 1 (Feb 1954).

there is virtually nothing about electoral systems in the constitution of the Central African Federation,[1] or in the most recent constitutions of Nigeria,[2] or in the most recent documents about the Federation of the British West Indies. Vagueness has the advantage that it by-passes some very controversial issues and leaves scope for manoeuvre outside the four corners of a constitutional document: but it means that some major problems are never really faced. Is the British experience of electoral systems exportable to countries which differ from Britain in political experience and in degree of internal unity?

The problem of political experience is perhaps not so serious as we once thought. In the nineteenth century (the great age of the printed word) it was an axiom that illiterates could not effectively participate in representative government, and not even radicals disputed this (indeed they drew from it conclusions about the duty of the State towards education). But as we have learnt more about pre-literate societies we have come to have considerable respect for their good sense, at least as regards matters within their ordinary experience. At the same time the work of British government has become steadily more technical and more remote from the experience of the ordinary man. We are therefore less certain than we were that the average British elector is politically more literate than the electorate in India, or Ceylon, or the West Indies. Perhaps he is; but even if he is, the difference is one of degree and not of kind, and the old arguments for bringing all 'within the pale of the Constitution'[3] still hold good.

The question of unity is much harder; Great Britain is now remarkably homogeneous, and perhaps the working of our electoral system depends on that unity. There was one deep fissure, that between English and Irish; and the electoral system made it possible to drive in a wedge there that split the old United Kingdom. We will be forced in the next few years to take decisive action about the development of elections in plural societies, in particular Malaya, East Africa, and Central Africa, and it is by no means certain that the careful studies made of the British system tell us anything valuable about what will happen in these different conditions.

There is no textbook on the operation of electoral systems in plural societies,[4] and there is no basic material from which to write one. There has been considerable experience in India, Pakistan, Ceylon, and the West Indies, to name only large instances: but no one has studied it, as they have studied (for instance) the development of legislatures. After the work on elections done during the last eight years in this country, it would be fairly easy for trained observers to adapt themselves to strange social conditions and to record objectively what happens when the English system goes overseas: but this would be a long job, and it is perhaps Utopian to expect it. The present essay is an attempt to see whether it is possible to find agreed ground about matters of principle. It is necessarily abstract in character, but it will serve its purpose if it narrows the field of dispute and directs attention to issues which can only be resolved by first-hand observation.

If one is to proceed methodically, one must think first of the purpose which an electoral system is designed to serve. In constitution-making the British can think only in terms of responsible Cabinet government, in which 'the government' is created by and directs the policy of an elected assembly. We do not, in a cool hour, deny that other systems, such as Presidential government or 'government by assembly', may be both practical and democratic. But it is no use thinking that English constitutional lawyers could ever write a constitution on these lines; or that (if they did) British experience would give new countries any support in the attempt to work it. Our terms of reference are thus partly settled by events, and within them it is possible to put the object of an electoral system fairly simply from two points of view.

Looking at the matter first from a general or public point of view — a view, as it were, above and outside the system — our purpose is to enable the government of the country to be carried on in a democratic way. These words imply a good deal. They imply that there *is* a country and that it is to be *governed*: that is to say, there is a political unity of some kind which either exists or is to be gradually created, and within it there is to be unity of policy and some measure of central direction. They also imply, by saying that it is to be democratically governed, that it is to be governed *from within* — not as part of a colonial system in which the initiative in the last resort lies outside the country — and that this government is to be *democratic* at least in the minimum sense that it is not primarily dependent for survival on the 'three powers' of modern dictatorship — the army, the secret police, and the propaganda machine.

But purposes cannot be assessed in this Olympian way by political leaders within the system; for them an electoral system must be looked at in terms of its benefits to their group or party or race. They must, to do their duty by their followers, consider whether particular electoral proposals will help or hinder them in a stuggle for power; in so far as they fail in this, they weaken their own position as leaders. These are facts which must be accepted if we are to construct democracies. Democracy is not a system in which there is no struggle for power; it is one in which the struggle for power is carried on under rules which all the contestants recognise more or less explicitly, and which are on the whole obeyed. These rules exclude absolutely the use of military power or police power to gain or maintain political power within the system (though they may be necessary to defend the system as a whole); and they impose rather less precise limits on the political use of economic power either by wealthy men or by trade-union leaders. Democracy is impossible unless some code of this sort is pretty generally accepted; one object in creating an electoral system is to promote and maintain this acceptance; and the acceptance will certainly break down if any large interest finds that it can exercise power better outside the electoral system than inside it. There are limits to the truth of 'private vices publick benefits' in politics as in economics. But private purposes supply much of the energy needed to serve public purposes; no electoral system can be democratically effective unless it *both* creates a government for the country *and* gives power in shaping that government through the electoral system to those who possess power outside the electoral system. To put this more bluntly, an electoral system must be founded on realities, and not on aspirations. An electoral system can do a little to shape the future, but only if it recognises the existence of the present, which includes the past. Too wide a gap between aspirations and reality can produce only electoral humbug and the negation of democracy.

If we pass on from purpose to mechanism, we find that the first problem in colonial electoral systems is to define the 'country'. Local citizenship generally begins to emerge out of rules for the control of immigration into a colony, but the legal rules rarely create a recognisable status of local citizenship until the issue is explicitly raised by the problem of elections. Even then, the problem of citizenship is not always considered as a whole, and the 'active citizenship' of the voter may be called into legal existence before the 'general citizenship' of the country, which is logically prior to it in any ordinary system of law.

The natural starting-point in a British territory is now 'citizenship of the UK and Colonies' as defined first in the British Nationality Act of 1948,[5] and this raises two issues. The first problem is to split off from this single unified citizenship separate electorates suitable for local purposes: what measure of local attachment to a colony is necessary for effective local citizenship? This is normally answered in terms of residence as a legally permitted immigrant, and local circumstances allow a good deal of variation. It would rarely be right to dispense with a residence qualification entirely. Great Britain does without it, but can only do so because the number of immigrant citizens is relatively quite small; and Northern Ireland is for obvious reasons less generous.

The second problem is that of the anomalous status of 'British protected persons'; a large part of the population in West, East, and Central Africa and in Malaya are citizens of British protectorates, but not citizens of the United Kingdom and Colonies, so that they are in a legal sense not members of the State that governs them. In day-to-day business the effects of this inequality of status are negligible, and any British protected person may seek citizenship of the United Kingdom and Colonies by naturalisation, with the assurance that the procedure is little more than a formality.[6] But the matter may be politically important, because under the electoral law of the United Kingdom any citizen of the United Kingdom and Colonies may be registered as an elector if he is resident here and is otherwise qualified, but a British protected person may not. The puzzle could be solved if all British protected persons sought naturalisation and were given it: but this does not occur to simple people, and it may cost them money — not a great deal, but enough to deter the very poor. It could also be solved if the Colonial Office were prepared to carry through the annexation of all Protectorates and Protected States, as it carried through the annexation of Sarawak in 1946. There are some legal difficulties about this, in particular the special position of Trust Territories; there are more formidable psychological difficulties, because 'protected persons' tend to cling to their 'protected' status, in the belief that it gives them some special claim to the protection of the British Parliament and of British public opinion against local oppression. There is therefore no easy way to get back to logic, and the choice is between two illogical solutions: the West African solution, which admits protected persons as well as citizens to full political rights, even though they are technically aliens, and the solution in Northern Rhodesia, now copied in Nyasaland,[7] which excludes protected persons altogether from the electoral register, but puts no special obstacle in the way of naturalisation. Of these solutions the second is rather better in logic; surely the first is better in politics? It is logical to demand that a man should make his choice once and for all between protected status (with some inferiority and some privileges) and citizenship (with full equality of rights and obligations). But the choice is hard to make in so clear cut a form: unity is more likely to come smoothly if protected persons are brought unconditionally 'within the pale of the constitution'. If they accept the rights offered, 'protected status' and its special psychology will wither away together as soon as the rights are effectively exercised.

The issue of citizenship is one of a number of issues which together make up the electoral problem, and the answers we give to these first questions depend partly on our attitude to those that follow. We are almost always met next by the issue of the plural society, arising in the conspicuous form of the inter-mixture of races in a society which is economically unified. Discussion of elections is apt to begin — and to end — with the question of Separate Rolls or Common Roll. This is undoubtedly of grave importance, and nothing here written is intended to suggest the opposite. Nevertheless, it is apt to become an obsession, and it is important to reduce it to due proportion. Plural society is most conspicuous where there is a conspicuous difference of colour; but all 'great societies' are in some degree 'plural'. In pessimistic moods we grumble about the 'split mind' of modern man. But we do not really regret it, nor do we pine for a standardised Utopia of 50,000,000 wholly interchangeable units. The existence of strongly differentiated groups within the State has always created grave difficulties for representative government, but we have in this country adapted ourselves pretty well.

Since 1830 we have moved through various phases into what seems to be a fairly stable compromise. The most effective defenders of the old unreformed English electoral system stood on the ground that an electoral system must follow the structure of society, and that the eighteenth-century system did so on the whole, and could be amended piecemeal in so far as it did not. The most effective exponents of reform denounced this as an attempt to obstruct the moving forces in society, and stood on the equally strong ground of the equality of all citizens under the law — each should count for one and no one for more than one. The solution of 1832 was in practice a compromise not unfavourable to the old régime, but it was carried under the banner of equal suffrage, and from 1832 to 1948 successive changes have all been in the direction of 'one man one vote'. Nevertheless, the energy went out of this movement as soon as experience was gained of elections in large and hetero-geneous constituencies. The attack on 'arithmetical democracy', which had been a conservative cry in the 1830s, began to be an 'advanced' cry in the 1890s; and there was a period in which all sorts of active-minded people, both intellectuals and working-class leaders, played with the idea of the 'plural state' as the correlative of plural society. An electoral system (they thought) can work without humbug only within the natural groupings of society: it cannot solve the problems of national government because the State is now too big and diverse to attract the direct loyalties of its citizens.

Elections were first introduced in India during this phase
of British opinion;[8] the British governments which sponsored
them denied that they were preparing the way for representative government, but it does not seem to have occurred
to anyone at the time to denounce the new system as one
inherently incapable of development. About 1900 the communal view of representation was the 'modern view', and
those who supported it claimed to have a new and true view
of democracy.[9]

Since 1918 these doctrines have been twisted to serve as a
basis for régimes of open brutality, and liberal opinion in the
West has swung back again. We have returned to the doctrine
of the mid-Victorian radicals, that majority rule is the proper
basis of authority, but we make certain reservations in
practice. We do not let logic carry us into the mathematics of
proportional representation or even into the simple arith-
metic of equal electoral districts: and we are quite well aware
that there are powerful associations of many kinds which
exercise great influence outside the mechanism of the
electoral system. These reservations cause theoretical difficulties; nevertheless, there is almost complete agreement that
in the last resort authority rests and should rest with a
Cabinet dependent on a majority in the House of Commons,
and that the House of Commons should derive from an
electorate composed of all adult citizens and led by great
national political parties.

This doctrine is not the only strand in British constitutional thought, but it is the only doctrine at present
available for export; the older 'pluralist' doctrine, which
justifies separate electorates, is now ruled out of court for a
number of strong reasons. These are not so much arguments
for a single roll as arguments *against* separate rolls; but they
are negatively very powerful, because they appeal to facts
within the recollection of all of us.

There is nothing inherently more disgusting about separate
representation of guilds or communities than about the
separate representation of states in the Upper House of a
Federation. Both are breaches of 'one man one vote, one vote
one value': both interpose an organisation between the
elector and his representative. But communal representation

has been associated by some of its own advocates with the doctrine of the *Herrenvolk*, which is repugnant to all decent men and women. 'Communal representation' now carries two implications: that if there are separate electoral rolls one of them is the 'best' and most elevated roll: that if there are separate electoral rolls it will generally be found on close inspection that electoral law has been so 'cooked' as to ensure permanent domination by those in the 'best' roll. This association of ideas has been built up by harsh experience, and it will not quickly be dispelled.

It is also usual now to point to Indian experience as showing the fatal effects of communal representation. The Government of India Act of 1935 was the first to enact communal representation by constitutional statute,[10] and the results were conspicuously absurd. There were (for instance) eleven categories of seats in the 'popular' House of the central legislature: two Provinces had fourteen groups of seats each. This result had been achieved after nightmare negotiations, in which Indians demanding self-government seemed impelled in spite of themselves to demand an electoral system which would make self-government impossible, because it would make a stable majority impossible. It was unjust but natural to suspect that the British had set this train of events in motion with Machiavellian foresight so as to preserve their own position for ever: it was also natural to break the system by organising parties strong enough to override the elaborate system of subdivision. The Congress and the Muslim League proved that safeguards of this kind are valueless in practice if they have no general acceptance; they also served to prove that communal representation may widen a gap not at first unbridgeable. We have before our eyes the bloodshed of partition and the wrecking of the economic unity of the Indian peninsula; perhaps communal representation was not to blame, perhaps it is no more than a scapegoat. But the emotional impact of events is such as to lend great force to the theoretical arguments advanced against it beforehand.

These arguments were put plainly and emphatically in the Donoughmore Report on the Constitution of Ceylon, which was published in 1928, and it is worth quoting again the often-quoted words of the report. 'In surveying the position in Ceylon we have come unhesitatingly to the conclusion that communal representation is, as it were, a canker on the body politic, eating deeper and deeper into the vital energies of the people, breeding self-interest, suspicion, and animosity, poisoning the new growth of political consciousness and effectively preventing the development of a national or corporate spirit.'[11] This is intemperate language, and it goes much beyond the evidence. But the Donoughmore formula worked well in Ceylon, and it has been strengthened by its success there. A recent report of equal authority, that of the Waddington Commission on the Constitution of British Guiana,[12] has no fault to find with the working of common-roll elections there, and the system has worked without disaster in other mixed communities such as Trinidad,[13] Mauritius,[14] and Bermuda.[15] No one imagines that under 'common roll' all things are perfect, but there have been no disasters to discredit the system. The troubles in British Guiana cannot be attributed to 'common roll', as no other system has ever existed there. On the other hand, to mention separate rolls calls to mind the troubles of India, Kenya, and South Africa; the separate Maori roll in New Zealand seems to work well, but it is not very plausible to suggest that it could be imitated in other conditions.[16]

The case against separate rolls therefore holds the field, partly because of a swing in doctrine based on European experience, partly because of the experience of the Commonwealth countries during the same period. The presumption is that a single roll should be used wherever possible; the problem is to know what is possible. The cases which must be faced next (in effect Central and East Africa and Malaya) are more difficult than any yet encountered during the 'common roll' phase of British opinion, and a disastrous failure in any of them would have wide effects. A move has been made, or must be made soon, because in each colony there are now local interests so strong that it is impossible either to govern against them or to suppress them. But within each colony these local interests are utterly disparate in numbers and education, even when they are fairly evenly balanced in social and economic power. What single-roll system can be found in

Kenya, to accommodate 30,000 Europeans, 90,000 Indians, and 5¼ million Africans? Or in Malaya, to accommodate 2½ million Malays, 2 million Chinese, and half a million Indians? In both cases the work of each race is economically essential to the country in so far as the economy is above the level of primitive subsistence farming: the contribution of each section (though it cannot be measured) is roughly of the same order, each is in its own way effectively organised, and each has power to disrupt the economy thoroughly by its own particular form of strike action. In each section the actual number (not the proportion) of men anxious and able to see the country's problems as a whole and to carry some administrative responsibility is about the same. How can one design an electoral system which recognises the brute facts of the situation and yet avoids the full weight of the arguments against separate rolls?

The easiest answer is that in these circumstances it cannot be done. If it cannot be done, either there will be no elections, of there will be elections on separate rolls. In either event the 'imperial' guiding hand must remain, as a colony cannot be handed over either to dictatorship or to anarchy: but imperial guidance is a temporary expedient at best, and the British are as keen to shake off the responsibility as the local inhabitants are to assume it. There is therefore every reason for searching farther, unpromising though the search is.

A common-roll system is unworkable unless there is a minimum of mutual confidence between groups in a society and a certain balance between voting power and other forms of power. On both these counts it would be ludicrous in a situation like that of Kenya to run government on the basis of 'one man one vote, one vote one value'; the situation would explode the political framework at once, and it is not at all certain (apart from imperial support) who would win the ensuing civil war. That is to say, arithmetical equality is likely only to throw the situation back into anarchy and so into pure colonial government, the point from which we started.

It is therefore necessary to make a compromise on the basic principle of equal franchise. In principle, the problem is the same as for the various British authors who puzzled themselves in the mid-nineteenth century over the impending 'tyranny of the majority' and tried to find 'fancy franchises' which would let in the rising elements in society without transferring power to those who could sway the penniless and illiterate. The devices proposed were very ingenious, and it is not easy to think of better ones; votes might be graduated by taxable property, by education, by profession, by personal savings, by public office. There are some difficulties in adapting these schemes to colonial territories, but these could probably be overcome but for a more fundamental difficulty.

The Victorians thought of their problem in one dimension only, that of social class: for all but a few diehards and a few revolutionaries the problem was to let the electorate and the distribution of political power expand in step with the change and growth in the numbers of those holding social and economic power. To put it as crudely as they often put it themselves, the problem was to refresh an old governing class without destroying it. In practice the problem was solved pretty well without recourse to anything more ingenious than mild gerrymandering of constituencies and a gradual extension of the franchise on the basis of property alone. Simple devices are always preferable to complicated ones, and British experience may be more exportable than British theory. But neither simple nor complicated Victorian devices fit well into colonial conditions, where the problem has not one dimension, but two, the dimension of social class and that of what (for lack of a better word) we call race. The common-roll franchise of Southern Rhodesia derives from the slogan 'Equal rights for all civilised men south of the Zambesi'; there seems to be not much wrong with it — except the fears that it has aroused for the future. As can be seen from the pages of *Punch* and Kipling, the Victorian upper middle class did not take kindly to invasion by *nouveaux riches* and 'examination-wallahs'; nevertheless, it made a very wry face and swallowed what was good for it. Can a white governing class be expected to absorb in the same way brown or black politicians, businessmen, civil servants, and school teachers? And can brown or black be expected to put up with the sort of snub which the Victorian 'climber' accepted on his way up into 'society'? We continue to hope so; but on the spot emotions are strong, immediate interests are even stronger, and there is not much faith in gentle transition. White reaction to a Victorian 'quality' franchise is to fear that it will mean sooner or later that white is swamped by other colours, as the 'quality' of the other colours rises. The reaction of 'other colours' is to fear that a white government will in the end sabotage such a franchise, either by denying advancement in the other races, or in the last resort by destroying the 'common' franchise before its effects begin to be felt, as Dr. Malan seeks to do in South Africa. Where these attitudes prevail, the introduction of a common-roll franchise is a gamble to be taken only in the light of a very close knowledge of local conditions; the gamble may be made a little safer by further precautions of two kinds. The first is to earmark seats for members of different races, without separating the electorates; the second is 'honest' gerry-mandering, such as has been used in Ceylon.

The first is bound to be complicated. But it is perfectly possible to require, for instance, that the elected members of an (imaginary) Legislative Council should be (perhaps) 4 Europeans, 3 Indians, and 7 Africans: to divide the country into 4 'European' constituencies, 3 'Indian' constituencies, and 7 'African' constituencies, in which the candidates must belong to the appropiate 'race'; and to put the qualified voters in each constituency on a common roll, European, Asian, and African voting together on the same qualification. The qualification would be chosen with care, so that there is a reasonable balance between the number of voters of each race; and there must be some guarantee (for instance by requiring a large number of nominators of the appropriate race) that racial candidates command real support among their own people, and are not mere 'stooges'.[17] Subject to these complications, the thing can be done; its disadvantages are that it maintains a separation of races in law both for nomination and for candidature, and that it may muddle the voters and leave room for misrepresentation.

There can be no doubt that part of Ceylon's good fortune was that it was able to avoid complexities of this kind by very simple 'gerrymandering'. There is a considerable concentration of Tamil population in the north, but the Tamils constitute only about a quarter of the whole population of the country. The Soulbury Commission of 1945[18] recommended very strongly that the Donoughmore 'common-roll' system be maintained, but added that the Boundary Commission set up to delimit constituencies should take account not only of numbers of voters and area of constituencies, but also of 'community of interest, whether racial, religious or otherwise'. The result is that there is a fairly adequate guarantee of reasonable representation of minorities within the 'common-roll' system.[19] This is psychologically possible where there is a certain degree of natural segregation, so that constituencies have been (as it were) earmarked for different races by the hand of God. After all, certain constituencies in the United Kingdom are more or less effectively earmarked in the same way for members of particular nationalities or churches or trade unions. No one complains of the Welsh monopoly of practically all Welsh constituencies, or the NUM monopoly of coal-mining constituencies. The matter is not so easy where the earmarking is conspicuously man-made, as in 'White Highlands' or native reservations: but there is still some chance that the principle of the common roll may be saved by a little 'honest swindling' over the way in which constituencies are delimited.

There is, of course, a point beyond which it is better to discard a principle than to save it by evasion: but the availability of these two devices means that there is some room to manoeuvre between the alternatives of 'common-roll' and 'separate rolls', which at first sight seem to be ideological and practical opposites. It also means that there are devices which can give one side some assurance against the dangers to themselves of a common roll, and the other side some assurance against the social and moral inferiority of separate racial rolls. Like all constitutional devices, these are only of practical importance if we recognise the factor of time. No situation can be preserved for ever by any safeguards whatever: you cannot sit either on bayonets or on entrenched clauses. But safeguards have some delaying power if they are freely negotiated and constitutionally entrenched. Sometimes delay is dangerous; but there is some ground to hope, looking at the world as a whole rather than at local incidents, that race is declining in importance as a source of division. Everyone's economic interests are against it; with few exceptions organised religion is against it; the political interests of the USA, the USSR, Britain, and France are against it. Strong social forces tell the other way, and are a standing temptation to adventurers. But this is perhaps one of the rare cases in which time is on the side of the angels, and it is not absurd to introduce 'safeguards' in order to buy time.

I have not included proportional representation among these possible safeguards. In theory the neatest of all safeguards is 'common roll' (with qualifications designed to give some sort of numerical balance of races over the country as a whole), accompanied by the single transferable vote in multi-member constituencies. One practical difficulty is that in a thinly populated country multi-member constituencies have to be very extensive; but apart from this the scheme looks perfect. It guarantees a seat to any group in the constituency which can rally a share of the votes equal to

$$\frac{\text{(votes cast)}}{\text{(seats to be filled} + 1)} + 1:$$

and it gives even smaller groups a substantial bargaining power which may affect the general tone of politics in the country. The fatal weakness is that people are frightened of anything that requires even simple mathematical operations. This is obvious to anyone who has had to explain the single transferable vote to groups of students of low second-class or good pass degree standard. The principle is simple and can be made clear to anyone of average intelligence — if he concentrates hard and if it is explained two or three times. But very few can reproduce what they have understood unless they are made to 'do sums' fairly regularly under supervision; and very few of those who reproduce the formula right in examination papers do so in a way which would be clear as an explanation to the ignorant. Quite a simple-minded population *could* be taught to use the single transferable vote, but it would need a continuous and deliberate effort of teaching kept up until the idea had sunk into everyone's mind. It is different if the thing can be put visually and not arithmetically; there are some reports that the system has been worked with complete success in open elections where voters line up physically behind candidates; candidates with the shortest lines are in turn eliminated, and their backers are told to withdraw or to vote for someone else. But this clarity of choice cannot be combined with secret ballot except by the system of 'ballotage', under which there is a second ballot to choose between those who reach the 'final'; this seems impracticable (and perhaps objectionable) on other grounds.

In a sense John Stuart Mill was worried about the problems of the plural society, though he used other terms, and it is not surprising that Mr. Hare's system came to him as a gleam of light in darkness. But experience suggests that the system will only work as intended if the electorate make a serious and sustained effort to understand it, and this is too much to expect either of European farmers and miners, or of Indian storekeepers, or of Chinese business men, or of African schoolteachers and local chiefs. There may be exceptional cases in which the electorate show real interest in the mechanics of elections, and are prepared to put up with repeated explanations about proportional representation; and it may be possible sometimes to use simple devices such as the alternative vote, the second ballot, the limited vote, or the right to cumulate votes, which the electorate can visualise more easily. But in general, proportinal representation is not of much value as a safeguard because it is not well enough understood to give any feeling of confidence to those whom it should protect.

There is another group of problems which arises in colonial elections: the illiterate voter, the open vote, and the necessity for a 'pyramid' of indirect elections. So far very little has been written about this by outside observers,[20] but newspaper reports and official optimism suggest that in favourable conditions these difficulties can be resolved much more easily than was once thought. The able and experienced illiterate (a good village headman in India or Africa, for instance) is not really less capable of following political issues than a literate, at least in a society where important news does not travel only by the printed word; of course, both illiterates and literates include many political innocents who vote with their natural leaders — but this is true all the world over. Nor does secrecy of the ballot for illiterates prove to be very hard to arrange — so long as there is an administration which commands popular confidence, and that is a condition which is necessary everywhere, if any electoral system is to be worked at all. The problem of indirect election is more difficult, because it is related to the much larger problem of the emergence of political parties. African and Eastern native society is generally tribal and is often highly localised, and it is difficult to find unity of issues even in a single constituency unless the voters are given some organisation to stand between the multiplicity of individual votes (often locally grouped[21]) and the single choice of a man to represent them. In Western societies this gap is filled by political parties; probably the constitution-makers of the French Revolution were right to say (in the absence of the concept of political party) that elections by a large electorate to a relatively small assembly must be indirect if they are to have any democratic content at all. But indirect elections are the simplest of all to manipulate from above, and all Western experience suggests that the invention of political parties (though we know its dangers) is a better way to organise an electorate. The implication of this is that it may in a colonial territory be necessary to begin with indirect election, because there is no other way of giving a representative character to the assembly: but that indirect election should be dropped as soon as political parties on a national scale are strong enough to bear responsibility. This is an awkward decision, because nascent parties are seldom very wise or very scrupulous; luckily, strength is more important in this context than wisdom or honesty, and the decision is generally forced by effective pressure at the time when it becomes necessary.

This is in a sense a digression, as it leads into the very large question of how political parties emerge and operate in undeveloped countries, and this goes much beyond the matter in hand. But these matters are relevant to the problem of representation in plural societies in that they suggest a difficulty not otherwise foreseen. The argument so far has given priority to the question of inter-racial co-operation, and has followed the analogy of Victorian England in suggesting that this can only be achieved by extending a share in government across the boundary between races, so that natural leaders in each race carry a share of general responsibility for the country. This in turn implies limited franchise as the condition of mutual confidence; and limited franchise implies that many will not have the vote. For instance, the price of working towards an effective common-roll franchise in Central African or East African territories may be the disfranchisement of the large majority of Africans: 'common roll' cannot be combined in the same constituencies with wide suffrage of the type now fairly well established in the Gold Coast and Nigeria. Common roll may therefore tend to favour the powerful or educated African at the expense of the simple African. This is the strongest objection to common-roll schemes because it is one designed to meet liberals on their own ground, and to show up an inconsistency in their attitude. Liberals may say 'Do we contradict ourselves? Very well then, we contradict ourselves', and stand pat. There is a contradiction in theory: but it may in practice be wisest to attack the great evil, race discrimination, and let class discrimination wait its turn. This is a matter of tactics to be settled by those with an intimate knowledge of local conditions; all that political theory can do is to reiterate the sort of warnings given by economic theory, that we cannot have everything at once, choices must be made, and if they are not made rationally they will be made irrationally.

It may be worth ending with another warning of the same platitudinous kind. Every electoral system is a sort of confidence trick. We have in Britain a reasonably unified society, and we have a very well-established administrative system. But even in these favourable conditions elections only work because we believe they are going to work. Our electoral laws contain elaborate guarantees for honesty and secrecy: but these guarantees are unenforceable against a dishonest administration and a corrupt or subservient judiciary. We believe our civil servants to be impeccable and our judges above suspicion: but if we (or any substantial proportion of us) really doubted and began to run a whispering campaign of doubt, the electoral system could not stand the strain. Here there are only tiny signs of weakness, for instance the reiterated Conservative insistence in the 1950 campaign that the ballot really *is* secret:[22] in Western Europe and in most parts of the USA the system keeps going in spite of suspicions more loudly spoken and substantiated by better evidence; a few steps farther, and elaborate paper systems cease to be electoral systems in our sense at all, because they give no sense of free choice and therefore of consent. In illiterate societies, and still more in plural societies, the strain will be heavier than it has been in the West, and the only assurance of success is in the tradition of confidence in the civil service and in the judiciary. This has been fairly well established in British colonies, but it will in any case be under strain as responsibility is transferred to local men. Competence and honesty in administration are necessary to efficient self-government; public confidence in them is necessary to democratic self-government. The problems of law, administration, and politics do not exist in separate compartments, and cannot be solved separately.

Notes

1. The Federation of Rhodesia and Nyasaland (Constitution) Order in Council, 1953. SI (1953), No.1199.

2. The 'Richards' Constitution (Nigeria (Legislative Council) Order in Council, 1946, No.1370) and the 'Macpherson Constitution (The Nigeria (Constitution) Order in Council, 1951, No.1172).

3. Mr. Gladstone in the House of Commons on 11 May 1864 (*Parliamentary Debates*, 3rd series, vol.175, col.324), following a line very close to that of J.S. Mill in chapter viii of *Representative Government* (published 1861).

4. There is some useful discussion in general terms in Marjorie Nicholson, *Self-Government and the Communal Problem* (Fabian Research Series No.126, April 1948), in chapter iii. 3 of Martin Wight, *The Development of the Legislative Counciil 1606–1945* (1946), and in chapter v of *Problems of Parliamentary Government in Colonies*, ed. S.D. Bailey (special issue of *Parliamentary Affairs*, vol. vi, 1952/3).

5. 11 & 12 Geo. 6, ch. 56. See also J. Mervyn Jones, *British Nationality, Law and Practice* (1947), and Clive Parry, *British Nationality* (1951).

6. The statutory references are: British Nationality Act of 1948, s.10, s.30, and the Second Schedule, ss.3 and 4: The British Protectorates, Protected States and Protected Persons Order in Council 1949 (SI 1949, No.140). The legal oddities of the position are explained very clearly by Mr. Clive Parry, op. cit., pp. 10, 94, 154.

7. Reuter bulletins in the *Manchester Guardian*, 23 Oct. and 1 Dec. 1953; report in the *Observer*, 25 Oct. 1953.

8. The crucial dates are the Indian Councils Act of 1892 (55 & 56 Vict., ch. 14) and the Morley—Minto Reforms of 1909, embodied in the Indian Councils Act of that year (9 Edw. 7, ch. 4) (see e.g. Sir Reginald Coupland, *The Indian Problem*, 1942, pt. i, p.24). Neither of these Acts enacts any electoral system, and there was comparatively little discussion of the possible choice of systems. Communal elections were introduced by Regulations made under the Acts. The Montagu—Chelmsford Report (Cd.9109 of 1918) proceeds on the new footing, that India is ultimately to gain 'responsible government' within the Empire; and it contains the first classic statement of the doctrine that communal electorates are incompatible with effective majority rule (paras.226—32). These views did not prevail; the Act of 1919 (9 & 10 Geo. 5, ch.101) delegated power to legislate about elections, and this was used in accordance with the old policy.

9. It is usual to date the beginning of this movement from Penty's book on *The Restoration of the Guild System*, published in 1906, but the material for his thesis was already to hand. The Webb's *Industrial Democracy* was published in 1897, 'Maitland on Gierke' appeared in 1900: the Taff Vale Case was decided in 1901 ([1901] AC 426), *Free Church of Scotland v. Lord Overtoun* was decided in 1904 ([1904] AC 515).

10. 25 & 26 Geo. 5, ch. 42, First and Fifth Schedules.

11. Cmd. 3131 at p.39. Quoted (eg) in S. Namasivayam, *The Legislatures of Ceylon* (1951), at p.59; cf. Jennings and Tambiah, *The Dominion of Ceylon*, at p.33. Lord Donoughmore was an important member of Mr. E.S. Montagu's mission in 1917—18 (see Supplementary Paper No. 1 to the Montagu—Chelmsford Report), and the connexion of thought is obvious. The Report of the Simon Commission, published in May 1930 (Cmd. 3568—9), shows little sign of this influence.

12. Colonial No.280 of 1951. For earlier history see Sir Cecil Clementi, *A Constitutional History of British Guiana* (1937), in particular Pt. III, ch. ii (f).

13. For Trinidad see Hewan Craig, *The Legislative Council of Trinidad and Tobago* (1952).

14. For Mauritius see Appendix G to Bailey, *Problems of Parliamentary Government in Colonies*, and Cmd. 7228 of 1947.

15. For Bermuda see Cmd. 7093 of 1947. I have not seen the report of the joint committee of the Bermuda Legislative Council and House of Assembly, issued in March 1948.

16. Cyprus has had separate rolls for Christians and Moslems (Greeks and Turks) since elections were introduced in the 1880s; they

seem to have had little to do with the various troubles of the island, and were to be retained in a mitigated form even in the abortive British proposals of 1945 (Colonial No.227 of 1945).

17. Or 'shoneens' as Lord Morley called them in introducing the Indian Councils Bill of 1909, when he applied the analogy of Catholic and Protestant in Ireland to the situation of Hindu and Mohammedan in India. The device which he suggested and which was rejected because of suspicion in India was of the same type as that described here (see Keith, *Speeches and Documents on Indian Policy*, vol. ii, p.91).

18. Cmd. 6677 of 1945, chapter xiii.

19. This was aided by the use of the cumulative vote in multi-member constituencies (for 11 elected members only out of 95), and by 'weighting' in favour of rural areas, devices free from any taint of association with communalism: see S.D. Bailey, *Problems of Parliamentary Government in Colonies*, p.70; S. Namasivayam, *The Legislatures of Ceylon* (1951), pp.133—9; Sir Ivor Jennings and H.W. Tambiah, *The Dominion of Ceylon* (1952), pp.73, 79—80; Sir Ivor Jennings, *The Commonwealth in Asia* (1951), pp.38—39 and 75—79, and *The Constitution of Ceylon* (1949), chap. iv. None of these books says much about electoral practice as distinct from electoral law: a little more can be gleaned from an article by S. Namasivayam, 'Some Thoughts on the Present Constitution of Ceylon', *Parliamentary Affairs*, vol. iv, p.352 (Summer 1951).

20. A good deal of material on the introduction of electoral systems within African tribal government is to be found in the *Journal of African Administration*. I have found only the following on territorial elections: A.C. Russell, P.H. Canham, and M.J.E. Patteson, 'Gold Coast General Elections 1951', *Journal of African Administration*, vol. iii, p.65 (April 1951); J.S. Lawson, 'Operation Elections' (on the Gold Coast), *Parliamentary Affairs*, vol. iv, p.332 (Summer 1951); P.C. Lloyd, 'Some Comments on the Elections in Nigeria', *Journal of African Administration*, vol. iv, p.82 (July 1952). There is also a short *Report on the First Elections to the Western House of Assembly: General Election 1951*, published in 1952 by the Government Printer, Ibadan. There is an article on elections by Algeria and French colonies to the Chamber of Deputies under the Third Republic by R.A. Winnacker in the *American Political Science Review*, vol. xxxii, p.261 (April 1938): Mr. Campbell's article on '*Vérification des Pouvoirs* in the French National Assembly' in vol. i of *Political Studies* (p.65) suggests that *moeurs électorales* in Algeria and the Colonies have not changed much since 1938.

21. See, for instance, an illuminating article on 'small scale' politics in Japan: R.E. Ward, 'The Socio-Political Role of the Buraku (Hamlet) In Japan', *American Political Science Review*, vol. xlv, p.1025 (December 1951).

22. For reference see the index to H.G. Nicholas, *The British Election of 1950* (1951).

8 The Export of Electoral Systems[*]

The Situation

This lecture, I am afraid, is concerned primarily with some rather dry questions about the tactics of research in politics, and I hope therefore that you will excuse me if I begin by indicating, in a more personal way, the situation which may give these some present interest. Through the kindness of various sponsors I was able last summer to pay a brief visit to East and Central Africa. There are seven British territories there;[1] in all of these, and in the Sudan too, discussion about the development of elections lies close to the centre of politics. Indeed, there exists already a surprisingly large number of separate electoral systems, because of the introduction of separate electorates for separate communities. I can reckon at least fifteen of them, and this takes no account of the ingenuity of District Commissioners in devising new systems to fit local circumstances, as they are urged to do under the policy of 'democratising tribal institutions. These home-made electoral systems vary a good deal, and include some useful devices which are not in the textbooks.[2]

This outbreak of a sort of epidemic of electoral systems is at first a little startling to a politics don, more startling than the related outbreaks of Speakers and maces, Permanent Secretaries and Cabinet Secretariats, Federations and County Councils. It has been the fashion in political research, in countries where democracy is well established, to deflate the nineteenth-century notion that in a free election the voter decides rationally between persons and policies:[3] and much

*The Sidney Ball Lecture, delivered by Professor Mackenzie in the University of Oxford, 21 Feb 1957. Originally published in *Political Studies*, V no. 3 (Oct 1957).

excellent work has been done to analyse Western elections on the basis of such concepts as voting habits, the party image, the association of political attitudes with types of personality, the relation of such attitudes to more general economic and social factors. We have begun to see Western elections in terms of what Bagehot used to call 'a *cake* of custom':[4] and in doing so we have learnt much, consciously or unconsciously, from the writings of social anthropologists about the life of isolated pre-literate societies. We no longer underrate the political wisdom of non-Western peoples, and in consequence we have become increasingly sceptical about the possibility that one can in any real sense make constitutions for them; yet it is in this period that the construction of constitutions has become an industry on a grand scale. There has been much talk of the expansion of Communism, but there are few Marxist constitutions outside the USSR and China: whereas the fashion for government based on free elections has run round the world. Earlier attempts to establish Western constitutions in the Middle East and in Latin America have at least partially failed: yet to these old experiments has been added a series of new ventures in Africa, in the West Indies, the Pacific, South-East Asia, and the countries of the old Indian Empire. There have been such inconceivably gigantic operations as the introduction of universal suffrage in India:[5] at the other extreme is the spontaneous imitation of Western democracy by small groups of people like the 2,000 people of the south coast of Manus Island, where 'wait-council' time is so warmly described in Miss Margaret Mead's recent book, *New Lives for Old*.

An ingenious person might construe this as the march of a new type of imperialism, a device for captivation. On the contrary, the 'imperialists', British, French, Dutch, Belgian, Australian, to a slightly less extent American, are no longer Wilsonian: they insist nowadays that it is absurd to suppose that Western institutions can possibly be made to work in oriental or African countries without long apprenticeship. We have not imposed Western institutions; they have been demanded, one might say extorted, from us, and we are thus committed against our will to an extraordinary adventure. We share the commitment because we furnished the model and will be involved in the consequences of success or failure. But now the experiment is launched we are not invited to participate, indeed we have neither the wisdom nor the power to do so. Nevertheless, there is a challenge to gain at least an intellectual grasp of the situation: it is after all an article of faith within the cycle of beliefs to which free elections belong that it is good for a rational being to give an account of himself. If from academic observation comes knowledge useful to countries where the transition has scarcely begun, so much the better: but so far as practical justification is needed it must lie primarily in the fact that independent observation and analysis is in itself a part of free government as we understand it.

The Possibility of Research

But if political researchers are to enter this field their first problem is that of Buridan's ass, where to begin. There is a great deal of material, and it is not inaccessible to research. Electoral studies in general have this advantage over other branches of our subject, that their base is relatively secure. There is a limited range of theory about the proper character of choice by large electorates, and a limited range of devices from which to choose a prescription suited to a defined set of normative premises and of economic and social factors. The range of permutations is inexhaustible, but the materials, the pieces in the building set, are easier to grasp and to define than material about party organisation, about the interplay of pressure groups and personal cliques, or about the highest levels of executive government. Indeed, there is a certain element of ritual about elections: the doing of certain familiar things in a familiar order is part of the magic by which they command allegiance. Psephology and liturgiology are akin.[6]

This is therefore a relatively 'tidy' subject: it also offers special advantages as a a point of entry to the study of politics anywhere. In any country where elections are taken seriously they constitute a sort of bottleneck in the political process, a narrow strait or channel in which political life is for a short period concentrated under the eye of the observer. Orators, party bosses, chiefs, villagers, market women, civil servants, priests, newspapermen, all kinds of sections and pressure groups, in so far as they think about politics at all, think for a short time about one kind of politics only, electoral politics. This jostling multitude of political interests would be unmanageable, but that the formal structure of an election imposes external order on them; a student who sets out shrewdly the main influences that bear on an election thereby gives quite an orderly conspectus of the country's politics. It should be emphasised that he gives a conspectus, not an analysis, and that an electoral survey raises far more questions than it answers: but at least it is as good a way as any in which to start unravelling the skein.[7]

There are also other advantages. Many of the countries now introducing elections are small and relatively self-contained: the limits of literacy and of other channels of mass communication are such that it is not impossible for a single observer to judge what is reaching the voter from sources at the centre of politics; and both politicians and administrators have felt so much pride and enthusiasm in making new things that they have welcomed friendly observers and have accepted any comment that is not patronising. There are difficulties of language, and there are difficulties in the extreme intricacy of the local situations on which the new pattern of elections is imposed. But if these difficulties are to be accepted as final, the whole idea of the comparative study of governments separate in time or sphere must be dismissed as a delusion. Complex as are the affairs of the Gold Coast or Nyasaland, they are not — they cannot be — more complex than those of the USA or Russia, of Georgian England or France of the revolution, subjects which we attempt to teach to second- and third-year students.

Techniques

Assuming then that there is something here which is at least worth attempting, how should it be done?— in terms of method, I mean, not in terms of financial resources and men available. (This separation between methods and men is an abstraction, and is apt to do harm in discussions about the next steps in social research, but I hope that it can be excused for the moment.)

To begin with, I should like to make a working distinction between techniques and tactics, a distinction which is intended to evade certain problems, not to resolve them. Discussion about the methodology of the social sciences is apt to become a disguised sort of ethics and metaphysics and I am anxious not to become involved in this.

It seems to me that the range of techniques available is wide, the choice of tactics limited. Techniques I should classify arbitrarily as arts techniques, science techniques, and techniques of access.

The unity of arts techniques is perhaps mainly an historical one, in that they are those which most of us in this University learn first, remnants of a rather old tradition in education: the capacity to use our own language with awareness of its limits and its ambiguities; to use two or three other languages more crudely, and to grasp in general the sort of problems which arise in translation from one language to another: to handle printed or written sources in a comprehensive and orderly way: to assess the value of these and other scraps of evidence about doubtful matters: above all, to present conclusions in such a way that the reader trusts the author's judgement but is not bound by it.

To my mind, the scientific techniques have a similar unity of tradition, and seek a similar objectivity by a different route, that which combines measurement and mathematics. Probably we have now passed the time when extreme views were held one way or the other about the place of measurement in the social sciences. The problems of obtaining data worth using are now quite generally understood, and so are the limits of mathematical analysis in extracting truth from crude and inaccurate figures. Perhaps the greatest value of big experiments in social measurement (at least in the field of politics) has been not to make discoveries but to elucidate problems about standards of proof and about the status of our conclusions. Even a general notion of what is meant by 'operational definition' is a useful razor in cutting away rambling generalities: and there are many incidental ways in which a correct use of questionnaires and samples can help to buttress an argument. But full-scale experiments have generally proved too slow, cumbersome, and expensive for the ordinary man. In this country, it seems to me, the skill chiefly required is that of extemporising utility variants of elaborate schemes worked out in America, so as to get cheaply and quickly just what is wanted and no more, a business which needs judgement and administrative skill as well as competence in statistics.

My third heading, techniques of access, is, I am afraid, a piece of jargon coined merely to emphasise the importance of common sense and good manners in political research. We all know people otherwise highly qualified whom we should not care to turn loose as observers of a hotly contested election. One of Oxford's most conspicuous contributions to political studies in this country has been to establish that academic observers can be politically neutral and personally charming, and in so doing Oxford has perhaps created in the minds of British politicians a presumption very useful to the rest of us, that people from the Universities are quite trustworthy, sometimes interesting, never in the way. Obviously such success is in part due to the social tradition of this University, and it may seem inappropiate to refer to that 'easy consciousness of effortless superiority' as a technique. But it is something that can be learnt, by apprenticeship if not otherwise, and it is a necessary tool of the trade.

Doubtless the ideal research worker has all these techniques at his command: doubtless no one starts at all without some limited capacity in each branch. But being armed how then to join battle?

Tactics

1 *Electoral Law*
May I put on one side first the approach through electoral law? Every electoral system needs a code or textbook of electoral law and practice, something comparable to the massive volumes of Schofield on Parliamentary Elections and Schofield on Local Government Elections. Elections cannot work smoothly and effectively unless there is something in the nature of a prayer book or book of drill, to establish

certainty about complex procedure involving a great many people. It is an extremely difficult piece of scholarship to prepare such a textbook satisfactorily: but it is not part of its purpose to add to existing knowledge about open questions. Electoral law is not lawyer's law; it throws up few issues of importance to jurisprudence, and it is of political interest only when we come to look at the relation between form and content, between electoral law and political practice, a matter which perhaps goes beyond the sphere of law as a discipline.

If research on electoral systems has a general purpose it is to elicit new and interesting points about this relationship; an electoral system has a precise formal structure, it is set within a complex and moving political situation. How does one affect the other? How are changes in parts of one related to changes in parts of the other? Our conclusions are not likely to be very interesting or very practical unless we can achieve some analysis of this sort. It is beautiful, even comforting, to regard a political situation simply as an interacting whole, something that is 'aye growing' while men 'are sleeping'.[8] But, as Mill pointed out, this is an unrealistic sort of 'political fatalism':[9] in politics as in other branches of knowledge one must fragment in order to gain a point of leverage for action or explanation.

Are there perhaps in theory two methods of approaching this task, methods which are in practice always combined, even by those who think they have separated them? Each separately, I should maintain, is arid; the art of tactics lies in combination.

2 'Hypothetics'[10]

One method, of course, is that of conceptual framework, hypothesis, and verification; the other is that of history, or (as it is more usually called in this context) 'case-study'. The former requires that there should be a central system of interrelated propositions about the nature of man in society, from these are to be deduced more limited hypotheses about the behaviour of men in particular situations, these hypotheses are to be confirmed or refuted by carefully designed observations. If they are confirmed, the structure of the science is thus enlarged, and strengthened: if they are not confirmed, or are confirmed subject to certain reservations, there must follow a process of checking fundamental theory so as to increase its refinement and exactness. It is to this procedure, we are told, that natural science owes its power: this is what is needed to make the study of politics 'a genuine scientific discipline'.[11] I quote from a recent conference report in the *American Political Science Review*: the same sort of theme was made familiar, in a less dogmatic way, by the work of Graham Wallas and the Webbs fifty years ago. Indeed, it is no more than the latest version of the old attempt to 'introduce the experimental method of reasoning into moral subjects'.[12] In its present form its main tactical maxims are that before we start research we should settle carefully the object of each piece of research, by reference to an existing framework of interlocking definitions; that we should handle one question at a time, or at the most a small range of questions, using something analogous to the old method of concomitant variations: and that we should prove each step in the chain properly, according to some defined standard of proof, before we put our weight on it and take a step forward.

I cannot help feeling that this is too weak a hook with which to catch Leviathan. There is not 'world enough and time': political problems are too big for us and move too fast for such a method, taken alone, to be of much value. It may be that there has been some misunderstanding of the methods of the natural sciences; what is described seems to be a method of proof or criticism and of exposition, rather than a tactic of discovery. But my own judgement is affected mainly by the analogy of the rather archaic science or discipline in which I was brought up, that of classical philology. Whatever its logical status, the study of language is certainly the most highly developed and the most rigorous of the social sciences; the analogy between politics and language is (I know) vulnerable at some points, but it is at least as persuasive as those between politics and physics or between politics and biology.[13]

There are then three points which this analogy suggests to my mind. The first is that the construction of an effective grammar for a single language is not dependent on the existence of a comprehensive theory of linguistics. To know the grammar of one language may help one to grasp that of a cognate language, may perhaps hamper one in grasping a language radically different: knowledge of several grammars encourages a search for generalisation at a higher level, and perhaps this may in time require further thought about how each grammar is organised. But a grammar is valid and useful for its own language without such generalisation and revision. One can hope (on this analogy) to frame and to use a reasonably exact grammar of British, or American, or Russian politics without waiting for some new sort of Grammar of Politics' in general.[14] Secondly, making and learning grammars is a subordinate part of the business, at least for most scholars. The primary task is to understand and to translate. It is indeed possible to set out in terms of general rules, hypotheses, and verifications the business of translating a hard passage or of reconstructing and translating a fragmentary papyrus or inscription. But one is not here working from a specific experiment to a general rule, but from the rule to the meaning of this specific and unique passage; and it is most unusual to set out the structure of proof explicitly — our internal computing machine works much too fast for that, so fast that for the most part we feel we have gone straight to the meaning, and we begin to worry consciously only when we come to the business of translation.[15] Explicit appeal to deduction and verification is used as a last resort if we are stuck and need some mechanical aid in checking over what the meaning may be: or if we are involved in controversy and must defend ourselves. For the most part we proceed, as Housman said in one of his Prefaces, 'by the capricious and arbitrary method of putting forward first one foot and then, with strange inconsistency, the other'.[16] My third point is that it is extremely rare in dealing with an established literary language to attempt to amend the grammar itself by a process of hypothesis and verification. This is outside my experience, but it is doubtless a different matter if one seeks to elucidate for the first time the grammar of an unwritten language or to follow changes in the grammar of spoken English. I appreciate that some theory of general linguistics may be of value here to emancipate the searcher from the bonds of familiar grammars to set him going on the most promising line of work. But general linguistics will not help him much unless he also has direct acquaintance with several languages of different types; and even here the object of the research is not primarily to find general laws but to grasp and explain, to make intelligible the particular case.

This is as far as this analogy carries me. As the present Professor of Poetry said in his inaugural lecture, 'Man is an analogy-drawing animal; that is his great good fortune. His danger is of treating analogies as identities, of saying, for instance, "Poetry should be as much like music as possible". I suspect that the people who are most likely to say this are the tone-deaf. The more one loves another art, the less likely it is that one will wish to trespass upon its domain.'[17] I am therefore anxious not to go farther, in particular not to suggest that I think the ideas of theoretical discipline and of rigorous proof have no place in political studies. What troubles me about the analogy drawn from natural science is the conclusion deduced from it, that scholarship is idle, in language or in politics, except when it is proving new rules; and I think the assumption is a bad guide to the tactics of research in politics. For the sake of an analogy, which is no more than an analogy, it involves the researcher in grave practical difficulties. One of these is that things move very fast in contemporary politics: not faster than the human mind, but too fast for the step-by-step process of hypothesis and consolidation. Another difficulty is that we are too rich in hypotheses: hypotheses not about external verities, but about extremely interesting and pressing questions of action. To take merely the export of electoral systems, there is a bubbling fountain of hypotheses to be found in an American article on Western institutions in non-Western societies published in 1955:[18] as many more can be derived from the work of Professor Duverger and other French scholars[19] and from the handbook on electoral problems compiled by a German group as a basis for electoral reform in Germany.[20] There are enough hypotheses in circulation already to found a new science or translate all the odes of Pindar; unfortunately the only ones which can be proved easily tend (as Professor Evans-Pritchard has it) 'to become mere tautologies and platitudes on the level of common sense deduction'.[21] Rigorous proof or disproof of serious hypotheses, even quite small ones, can generally be obtained only with great expense and after considerable delay. There are some famous examples of such thoroughness, but, as I said earlier, they have perhaps been successful primarily as research into methods of research, establishing new standards and devices of proof and elucidating the difficulties of applying them. This is valuable work; but need we all do nothing else?

3 *Case-Studies*

I should prefer to call the extreme into which one reacts the method of case-studies rather than the method of history; there is some risk of confusion, but 'case-studies' is the fashionable phrase and at least it sets aside some of the problems which trouble introspective historians.[22] In particular I would like to emphasise at the outset that the tactics of description may – indeed must – use all techniques that come to hand, whether called 'humane' or 'scientific'. It would be absurd, for instance, to think of describing a large election without using electoral statistics.

As it is understood by simple souls, the case-study method is to establish the facts and let them speak for themselves; put the reader in the position of informed spectator and let him use the material as he pleases. He may wish to judge or generalise; he may merely learn by experience the feeling of a variety of situations.

It need hardly be said that this too, like the notion of an experimental method, is merely a limiting abstraction, not a practical way of proceeding. It is a commonplace that any narrative of events is in some respects both deductive and selective. A narrative is deductive in that the evidence for it is used on the basis of general experience outside the immediate field of study: it is selective in that much of the evidence is not available, and also because some choice has to be made among the evidence which might be used. Case-studies of contemporary events are usually selective in both these ways. Some important evidence is missing: sometimes one knows that it is missing, sometimes one does not know, sometimes one is left in a sort of limbo of discretion, possessing evidence, but unable to argue from it lest its source be betrayed. Other evidence must be neglected because it is too voluminous to be manageable.

Such problems are extremely hard to deal with satisfactorily, yet a case-study is pointless if what it says is determined by chance. The author, in so far as he is skilled, knows how to control his material in accordance with certain criteria of relevance. These criteria may be extremely complex; so complex that he could never explain them fully, not even if the narrative were held up indefinitely during the explanation. To understand what is being said the reader must either share the author's criteria or relevance or learn them by practice as he reads. In this sense the case-study is a means by which the student can grasp in a concrete way the judgement of a more experienced person about what is most important and interesting in a particular situation. Like good history a good case-study is comprehensive: but it is also orderly, and it is sharply, even ruthlessly, selective; and it does not waste time on explanations of its procedure.

It must be ordered also in another way, or in two closely related ways, which are more straightforward and more directly relevant to electoral studies. First, every narrative needs platforms or pausing places, where the narrator halts for a little to sketch the background of the story; however lightly this is done, the account must have form, and its form commits the writer to certain implicit generalisations about what is relevant. Secondly, a narrative must move through time, and if it relates, as electoral studies must relate, to events taking place within a set form of procedure, it falls almost as a matter of course into certain chapters, and these divisions turn up in much the same way in studies made independently. There have been differences in style and personality between the four Nuffield College studies of British general elections, but each has included chapters on the candidates, the campaign, the main organs of mass communication, and the results, and they have all dealt also with the issues of the election as defined by its immediate antecedents, with electoral machinery, and with party organisation. In addition, they have usually included a number of case-studies of separate constituencies, each study following the same sort of pattern as the main study but on a smaller scale. The four books rarely use the form of hypothesis and verification, and yet clearly they have reached some sort of generalisation about the things that are important in British elections. This generalisation could notionally (I suppose) be broken down into a set of separate propositions; many of these propositions, taken separately, would be hard to prove, taken together they give a convincing account of what happens, and this account is the expression of a coherent view set out in an orderly way. The authors believe, and their readers agree, that certain things are relevant to the narrative of a British election, and that other things are not relevant. It is usually relevant, for instance, to discuss the age and education of the candidates, but not their weights or their waist-measurements or the colour of the wives' eyes. It may well be relevant to discuss the weather: it is not deemed relevant to discuss the progress of First Division football clubs, or the state of the London theatre, or the current fashion in women's dress. These may seem outrageous examples, but such matters have sometimes been relevant to politics in the past, and they may turn up again. A future author may feel bound to bring new factors into the narrative, so that it takes a new shape. If a man can do this and convince his readers that he is talking sense, he is not only amusing them, he is also in some way establishing new knowledge, a new but acceptable variant of an existing canon of relevance.

The situation to be described varies a little from one British election to another: it varies still more between a British election and a French election, between an election in Europe and an election in Africa. The author of an electoral survey must contrive to look at each case afresh, lest he miss what is most important in it; nevertheless, he proceeds from experience of what has been found relevant elsewhere, and he contributes to and modifies this common stock. We assume when we launch ourselves on a field of study, like the study of elections, that it has order and some unity: in so far as these exist, they will emerge if shrewd observers experienced in elections expound to intelligent readers what they find, because certain themes will repeat themselves with variations more or less insistent. As Miss Margaret Mead says: 'Our capacity to see, to recognise, to isolate significant variables, is a function of which other people, how many other cultural groups, we have seen and studied, for how long and with what conceptual and practical tools.'[23]

To talk in this way is to describe one of the main currents in British political research since the war. It is a form of tactics which we know very well: and we perhaps begin to see its limits. If elections do in fact repeat themselves so that the same pattern serves for several studies without much variation, we begin to say, as the social anthropologists might, that the latest study 'lacks theoretical interest'; a case-study may be wholly admirable as a record, and yet fail to break new ground, because there is not in this area new ground to break. One might say that studies of that particular sort of election, like Greek tragedy as described by Aristotle, stop changing when they have found their true nature;[24] and there is then room for generalisation, which can be made safely and even rigorously without recourse to a step-by-step process of hypothesis and verification. A recent example of this sort of scholarship is Professor Schapera's excellent book *The Government and Politics of Tribal Societies*:[25] he had the advantage of better field material than has generally been available to political scientists, but at least one can say that this is the sort of thing that political scientists did from the time of Aristotle to the time of Bryce, and still do when they can find courage and material. This, after all, is what the Rector of Exeter has done in his book on *Government by Committee*.[26]

Of course such generalisations are more limited and less stable than those of natural science. They rest firmly enough on the opinion of experienced observers, confirmed by that of their readers, and they can be buttressed by examples which are at least rhetorically convincing. On the other hand there are no crucial instances on which a chain of reasoning can be based, there is no means of estimating the probabilities involved, there is no clear line between what changes and what is permanent. The research worker in politics is more liable than any other to be caught by events which change the emphasis of institutions, and make nonsense of his conclusions before he has published them, or very shortly afterwards. As in ancient medicine, 'opportunity is fleeting, experience treacherous, judgement difficult': and it seems natural to continue the quotation from Hippocrates, translating more freely. 'The trouble is that the research worker has to cope with the patient, the bystanders and external circumstances, as well as with his own deficiencies.'[2][7]

Summary

May I now summarise what I have said so far — and I know, or at least suspect, how many issues it has set aside? I think that for British scholars the best tactics in approaching the problem of electoral systems in non-Western countries is to begin from the method of electoral surveys, which in general we understand pretty well. I do not think that this is an evasion of the challenge to face problems and reach general conclusions, because, given a reasonably wide spread of field work, conclusions emerge from this method more swiftly than from the step-by-step method of hypothesis and verification, and do not lack standing as contributions to knowledge. And I do not think that it evades the requirements of rigorous scholarship: or that it excludes the use of techniques of measurement.

But I recommend these tactics only subject to certain reserves. Repetition of surveys contributes to political science as distinct from historical research only so long as new points of interest continue to emerge. As surveys enter the phase of diminishing returns, the time is ripe for someone to try his hand at generalisation, and for others to widen the area of research. The 'experimental method' may then be of great value to establish particular points, and also to test methods and set standards of proof. Peculiarity of local circumstances will suggest special problems for investigation: and there will be crises which deserve study simply for the record. In the end, if elections become established outside the West, they will take a settled place within a working system of politics, and it may be wise then to turn from study of the short, critical period of elections, to that of the more normal flow of political life, a more difficult task comparable to that which political scientists face in this country and in the USA.

In effect this concludes my argument, but it is hard to avoid reference to what is perhaps really a false question. This kind of research seems necessary because it is of some general importance to the world to see how this experiment goes. Will research help the experiment to succeed? And behind that question is another – will it help us to assess whether the experiment is succeeding or failing?

Practical Recommendations
As regards the first question, I cannot put the matter more succinctly than in the words of Professor Evans-Pritchard: 'Social anthropology', he says, and this applies to electoral studies, 'may occasionally resolve problems of adminis-tration. It makes for a sympathetic understanding of other peoples. It also provides valuable material for the historian of the future.'[28] This is a minimum claim; so much is certain, one might perhaps go a little further. Politics, as we understand it in developed societies, is always to some extent concerned with formal institutions, man-made and by law established. 'In studying political organisation', wrote the late Professor Radcliffe-Brown, 'we have to deal with the main-tenance or establishment of social order, within a territorial framework, by the organised use of coercive authority through the use, or the possibility of use, of physical force.'[29] This will serve for political science as well as for social anthropology: but one must add that in the analysis of Western societies we are forced to add another level of discussion. As emerges from the volume on African political systems from which I have quoted, and also from Professor Schapera's book, in tribal societies change in institutions is not itself institutionalised. In the West, on the other hand, political institutions are conspicuously institutions for changing other institutions, including political institutions. The export of elections is part of a larger movement for the export of this notion of explicit man-made forms of government. We are accustomed, as I have said, to look rather cynically at our own claim to reason, and to regard changes in electoral systems in the West as reflecting a balance of

forces rather than an effort at improvement. The objection generally made by political scientists to the introduction of a single transferable vote in Britain is not that it is impracticable or unjust, but that it is politically naïve to imagine that a great party would ever be prepared to sponsor it. But in spite of this ingrained cynicism, or positivism, we know that constitution-making goes on all the time, in large affairs and small ones, and we never dream of suggesting that it is unreasonable to talk about the success or failure of changes in the organisation of government departments, or of the nationalised industries, or of a political party machine. There may be some things which we think it unreasonable to discuss because we believe that they cannot be affected by the sort of reorganisation contemplated: but even to say this is to make a practical contribution to a discussion about organisation.

I do not think, therefore, that we can, like our colleagues in social anthropology, evade responsibility for recommendation and assessment, particularly in a matter of this sort, in which the special interest of the problem is that it is an attempt to construct new institutions on a grand scale. But what can we do in this sense is narrowly limited, by the nature of things as well as by lack of resources. Experience about the export of elections cannot be gathered and presented systematically in time to help much in this present phase, which is perhaps the decisive phase for the future of Western forms of government in non-Western societies. We can offer perhaps to the countries concerned some indication of what are in our experience reasonable and attainable standards in electoral practice,[30] some competent comment on matters of tactics and party organisation, perhaps some sense that because of its growing unity the world has a considerable interest in what may seem small matters, even to the local people, such as the franchise in British Guiana, or Mauritius, or Fiji.

In the process we will perhaps learn as much about our own political practice as about that of others. It is, for instance, obvious in non-Western countries that many of the issues of politics turn on relations between traditional authorities and a new middle-class who are educated in the

Western style and fill roles in an economy of the Western type. In each separate instance the numbers of men and women involved are quite small, and it is possible to see with some clarity how tradition, economic change, and forms of education react upon one another and upon the structure of politics. There is a similar interaction in Britain, imperfectly studied because it is very complex and changes slowly: men accustomed to observe such changes elsewhere will be better qualified to record it here. Our study of our own politics has already gained much through the opportunity to see ourselves in another guise — 'mutato nomine de te Fabula narratur' — in the politics of the Nuer and the Manus, the Zulu and the Makah Indians; it will gain more if we can grasp more clearly the relation between change of institutions and change of circumstances.

Success or Failure

There is finally the question of success or failure. It has been said that nothing imported would survive British withdrawal from Africa except the game of football: I should hazard a guess that elections would also survive, in some form. But what sort of elections? Certainly not the sort which we are seeking to export. An institution newly introduced must change unless it rests on some general public understanding of how it worked in its original place, and of how it is supposed to work now. Such understanding is of necessity dim: even formal teaching is very inadequate as a means of conveying how institutions work and is at best an adjunct to apprenticeship. The institution complete, or moderately complete, can only be taught by participation; people must move with it, as they did to the Dominions of settlement.

Professor Oakeshott's analogy of cookery books and cooking[31] and Professor Polanyi's analogy of connoisseurship[32] are in point. It is certain that, even though they continue to be based on free elections, politics in the Gold Coast or the Federation of Rhodesia and Nyasaland or Malaya or British Guiana will never in practice greatly resemble politics in Britain. These are different places and different people, and formal identity of electoral systems will do little to make them more alike.

I have forebodings, therefore, that in the future we shall hear much about how Western elections have failed in Indonesia, or failed in the Southern Sudan, or failed in British Guiana — and so on: and one is tempted to answer in advance that this sort of statement is nonsensical, because there can be neither success nor failure in this sort of venture. The only thing that can be predicted with certainty about the export of elections is that an electoral system will not work in the same way in its new setting as in its old.

Indeed this is a general point. It is not possible to measure success or failure in constitution-making by comparison with an original model. It may be true that the Presidency of the United States is modelled on the monarchy of George III, that of France on the monarchy of Queen Victoria: but it is mere nonsense to use that sort of comparison for purposes of judgement, the crudest confusion between origin and function. Is it, however, possible to seek greater generality by comparing function with function?

The trouble here is that we are not at the moment very certain of the function of elections in our own society. We have on the whole ceased to think that their function is to ensure government by the people, in any sense intelligible to Rousseau or Jefferson or John Stuart Mill: yet we continue to believe most heartily in their necessity; and this Western loyalty to elections has been strengthened by events of the last generation and of the last year. Free elections — elections in which the voters believe that they have a real though limited choice in some matter of importance to the state and to themselves — perhaps offer two advantages of a very general kind: they offer a means of continuity in succession not available to personal or party governments, and they commit the people to a sense of responsibility for their own betterment more effectively than any form of public exhortation yet devised by Ministries of Propaganda or of Information. To say this is not to offer a theory of the function of elections in Western societies, but to indicate that there is no adequate theory. Nevertheless, it seems clear enough that they are essential to us as props of the sentiment of legitimacy and the sentiment of participation: and that these sentiments break easily and are hard to repair. There is perhaps here a measure which can be at least crudely applied: elections once exported may work in odd ways, but they may be said to succeed — in India, for instance, or in Africa or in South-East Asia — if the offer of choice to the elector continues to play a vital part in the continuity of the state. In all these countries the situation demands absolutely that government should be given a new basis. Traditional government may be able to survive in a few of the larger territories, such as Morocco, Siam, Ethiopia, and Saudi Arabia, but it generally operates in units too small to be viable. The only obvious alternatives to it are army or party rule. These may solve at least temporarily the problem of order, but they have never yet solved the problem of popular participation or the problem of peaceful succession without civil war, and recent examples tell against them. At least for the present, there is a general sentiment that there is no answer available except the adoption of a régime based on free elections: and it is in this driving sense of necessity that there lies the greatest hope of success.

Notes

1. Uganda, Kenya, Tanganyika, Zanzibar, Nyasaland, the two Rhodesias. I exclude Somaliland, which has problems of rather a different kind.

2. As an example, a brief bibliography, for Tanganyika alone, is noted at the end of this paper.

3. For a clear and moderate statement and summary see D.E. Butler, *The British General Election of 1951* (1952), p.3.

4. *Physics and Politics*, Longmans ed. of 1915, vol. viii, p.18.

5. See the Report of the Chief Election Commissioner, Mr. Sukumar Sen (Manager of Publications, Delhi, 1955).

6. A political form is effective for large numbers of people only if it is $\delta\acute{\epsilon}\sigma\mu\iota os\ \phi\rho\epsilon\nu\hat{\omega}\nu$, like the song of the Erinyes: elections have form and order, but one of the difficulties of establishing them in new settings is that they do not at once appeal to the Primary and Secondary Imagination, as Auden expounds them in his lecture on 'Making, Knowing and Judging' (1956, pp.27 ff.). It is very hard to regard them as sacred or as beautiful, except in terms of some specific myth of national history such as exists in Britain, France, and the USA.

7. This resembles,but does not venture so far as, the method used by Professor Clyde Mitchell in *The Kalela Dance* (Rhodes—Livingstone Papers, no. 27, 1956): 'By working outwards from a specific social

situation in the Copperbelt the whole social fabric of the Territory is taken in' (p.1).

8. John Stuart Mill, *Representative Government* (1861 ed.), p.4.

9. Ibid., p.3.

10. Not in Samuel Butler's sense: *Erewhon*, chap. xxi.

11. Harry Eckstein, reporting a conference on 'Political Theory and the study of Politics', *American Political Science Review*, vol. 1 (June 1956), p.476.

12. Hume, *A Treatise of Human Nature*, Graham Wallas (*Men and Ideas* (1940), p.22) quotes an exact equivalent from an unpublished work of Bentham.

13. It was used also by Professor Evans-Pritchard in his Marett Lecture, to illustrate a rather different point (*Man*, no. 198, Sept. 1950). It is characteristic of the present phase of opinion that in a recent article on methodology, which casts its net very wide indeed, nothing is said about the study of language, or about research and practice in medicine, both very old political analogies (Jean M. Driscoll and Charles S. Hyneman, 'Methodology for Political Scientists: Perspectives for Study', *American Political Science Review*, vol. xlix (1955), p.192).

14. Laski's *Grammar*, whether to be approved or disapproved, was certainly not framed by the rules of 'hypothetics'.

15. This problem of how to communicate a 'meaning' in another language is one of the 'aesthetic' problems of political science referred to by W. Harrison in his article on 'Understanding Politics', *Occidente*, vol. ii (1955), p.259.

16. Preface to edition on Juvenal; reprint of 1931, p. xv.

17. W.H. Auden, *Making, Knowing and Judging*, p.24.

18. Kahin, Pauker, and Pye, 'Comparative Politics of Non-Western Countries', *American Political Science Review*, vol. xlix (1955), p.1022.

19. M. Duverger, *Political Parties*, published in French in 1951, in English translation, 1954; and (ed.) M. Duverger, *L'Influence des systémes électoraux sur la vie politique* (1950).

20. *Grundlagen eines deutschen Wahlrechts; Bericht der vom Bundesminister der Innern eingesetzten Wahlrechtscommission* (Bonn, 1955).

21. *Social Anthropology* (1951), p.57. The books of Professor Apter on the Gold Coast and of Dr. Fallers on Busoga perhaps illustrate this point. I cannot help feeling that their conceptual framework actually impedes them in sharing their great knowledge and acute sense of politics with the reader (David E. Apter, *The Gold Coast in Transition* (Princeton, 1955), and L.A. Fallers, *Bantu Bureaucracy* (1956).

22. I am inclined to think Professor Evans-Pritchard also evades these, in his comparison between history and social anthropology (*Man*, no 198, Sept. 1950) (for instance, the problems of historical 'explanation', of the historian as poet and myth-maker, of the continuous revision of history — all history is contemporary history').

23. She continues: 'Deciding what one ought to do next is tied tightly to what one has done before — in the social sciences, long experience is the analogue of the rigorous formulations essential in the natural sciences.' *New Lives for Old*, p.14.

24. Aristotle, *Poetics*, 1449.

25. 1956.

26. K.C. Wheare, *Government by Committee* (1955).

27. Hippocrates, *Aphorisms*. I, i. The first part is the translation of W.H.S. Jones in the Loeb edition, vol. iii, p.99.

28. Op. cit., p.123.

29. *African Political Systems*, ed. Fortes and Evans-Pritchard (1940), p. xiv.

30. 'Therefore to say that headmen have regular sources of income on the side is rather like saying 'water is wet'. It would be utterly incorrect to call public tribal life corrupt. The only question that matters is whether the procedure remains within traditional limits' (Hans Cory, *Sukuma Political System*, p.59). Most Western electoral systems are in some respects 'wet'.

31. Inaugural lecture, *Political Education*, now reprinted in *Philosophy, Politics and Society*, ed. Laslett (1956); see my comment on this point in 'Political Theory and Political Education', *Universities Quarterly*, vol. ix, no.4 (1955), p.351.

32. Essay on 'Skills and Connoisseurship' (Methodological Congress, Turin, 1952). See also Professor W.H. Morris-Jones's recent inaugural lecture, *Taste and Principle in Political Theory* (1957).

IV
Organisations, Systems, Decisions

The essays and articles included in this section derive largely from the interest in public administration which came partly from my own experience, partly from the Manchester environment described in the Introduction and in the essay reproduced in Section I. But they also raise by implication various questions of method, comparable to those raised in the essay on p. 132 concerning the study of elections.

For the last ten years or so 'the behavioral movement' in political science has been receding into the past, and it is perhaps best treated now as an episode in the history of American political thought. But it has left us with a much better understanding of the problems of quantification and model-building, and it is not very easy to remember how ignorant we were round about 1950. The Americans had in fact moved far ahead of us in the years since 1939, and had in the process changed the balance not perhaps of 'the discipline' but of its bibliography. Before 1939, as I have explained in the Introduction, American work had a great interest and attraction for us, but was only one aspect of what we read and taught. But from then till the 1950s virtually no academic work in politics had been done except by Americans, and one had to begin all over again to catch up and to assess.

From my point of view there were three branches of work to be grasped; voting studies, organisation theory and (a little later) the study of developing countries. I might add 'pressure groups' as a fourth, but there was much less sense of lag in that field because of the large British and European contribution to theories of pluralism, about which Americans on the whole were not very well informed.

In Manchester we paid our respects to voting studies in the work of Peter Campbell, Tony Birch, David Donnison and others: but our enthusiasm waned, or perhaps rather switched directions, as we began to understand the facts of life about data collection and processing. To put it bluntly, we ran out of questions to which we could give significant answers from samples of a size within our grasp with existing or foreseeable organisation and resources. Before the coming of the SSRC £100 was a lot of money to spend; we had to operate with student volunteers as interviewers, and if we could get 400 to 500 interviews that was pretty good. Perhaps *if* there had been money *then* our ingenuity in finding questions would have been sharpened. But in fact we switched direction and turned our limited resources towards the study of community politics from which came Tony Birch's book on *Small Town Politics* (1959), which included quantification but only as one element in building a community model. This was work on a modest scale, but it was big enough to raise the theoretical and empirical issues of a structural study of politics in context, and we were lucky to be working alongside social anthropologists who wanted to apply their experience of model-building to literate industrial communities.

As regards organisation theory, I discovered Dwight Waldo and H.A. Simon with delight; here at last were scholars who knew how to make a decent theory and who might help to demolish the intellectual slum built by the pragmatic POSDCORB school of ham-fisted efficiency men. Hence the two papers which begin this section. They date so badly that I hesitate to reproduce them; but in their context they had for me the emotion of Keats's Sonnet 'On first looking into Chapman's Homer'

> Or like stout Cortez when with eagle eyes
> He star'd at the Pacific — and all his men
> Look'd at each other with a wild surmise —
> Silent, upon a peak in Darien.

The small piece on 'Idiom' which follows is also of interest (to me and perhaps to no one else) because it was the only direct output of a sabbatical term in 1959, in which I tried to get a grasp of the tools used by Simon in *Models of Man*, and at the same time to find out about the relations between administration and administrative law in France, Germany and Italy. It was more than I could do, but perhaps the article (which is rather badly written, I now feel) is for me more central than seems at first sight. It would have been simpler to write 'Damn methodology and do your own thing – if you are good enough,' but the contorted prose represents the stress of some rather contorted thinking.

The two papers which follow arise out of this milieu, in which the theme of 'decision-making' linked organisations and communities, and there were no strict departmental divisions within our Faculty. The British Association paper was one of a group of three; the other two were by social anthropologists, Ronny Frankenberg[1] and Martin South-wold[2] – but Ronny's paper dealt with the private war within the great war, Lindemann versus Tizard, and I had been quite close to events at the time. I agreed with what was in the paper, that the 'outsiders' were in a sense stooges or unconscious advocates in a battle between organisations. But I think that analysis has never given enough account to the sheer dead weight of organisational decisions already taken.[3] In a sense, the bomber offensive (in the form it took – and I am well aware of the fire-storms at Hamburg and Dresden) flowed – from 'decisions' taken in about 1936, by different people, in a different context and with a different understanding of what bombers could and could not do. By 1941 options had been foreclosed: the imperative was either to abdicate offensive action in support of Russia or to use bombers in any way that could cause grief and pain to Germans. We had no other such weapon, and could not build one within the limits set by events.

'Decision-making' was in fact the theme of one of our staff seminars in the early 1960s, and it is worth saying two things: first, that such open seminars have always seemed to me to be a very valuable tool for gentle collective brain-storming about conceptually difficult topics, secondly that I am reminded here of two colleagues whom we have lost, the late Bruno Leoni of Pavia and the late Peter Nettl, then of Leeds, who contributed the important papers mentioned in the footnote here;[4]

Finally, two exercises in manner. 'Models of collective decision-making' tries to be austere; 'Plowden Translated' tries to be funny. But not hostile: I was astonished to find that the appalling prose of the original masked some sharp and far-sighted analysis. I fear however that Civil Service prose is 'functional' for the Civil Service, enabling it to converse in public without being understood, as Lloyd George could converse in Welsh with his Cabinet Secretary, Tom Jones.

Notes

1. 'Taking the blame and passing the buck or, The carpet of Agamemnon: an essay on the problems of responsibility, legitimacy, and triviality', in Max Gluckman (ed.), *The Allocation of Responsibility* (Manchester UP, 1972).

2. 'A Games Model of African Tribal Politics', in Ira R. Buchler and Hugo G. Nutini (eds.), *Game Theory in the Behavioral Sciences* (Pittsburgh: University of Pittsburgh Press, 1969, pp.23–43).

3. The point has been made recently in a different context in Professor Graham Allison's study of decision-making during the Cuban crisis of October 1962, *Essence of Decision* (Boston: Little Brown, 1971).

4. 'The Meaning of "Political" in Political Decisions', *Political Studies*, V (1957) p.225.

5. 'The Concept of System in Political Science', *Political Studies*, XIV (1966) p.305.

9 The Study of Public Administration in the United States*

The appearance of this important textbook[1] offers an occasion to give some account of recent developments in the study of public administration in the United States. There has been in the last five years something of a revolution and this will eventually affect our own teaching and research; but the process is likely to be slow, partly because conditions are different here both in the Universities and in the government service, partly because of the difficulty in getting American books. This article has been written with the assistance of a University library, but even so it can make no claim to completeness, for much of the literature is out of reach.

The Public Administration Movement
From the 1880s to the New Deal

A convenient starting point is Professor Dwight Waldo's book, *The Administrative State*[2], which was published in 1948. When the late Professor Laski reviewed this in *Public Administration*, he advised Professor Waldo to 'throw his enormous card catalogue' away, and to face 'really urgent' questions. With deference, this was a misconception of Professor Waldo's purpose. Professor Waldo has read practically everything that has been published on the study of public administration in the USA, and has summarised just so much as is relevant to our present interests; with the happy result that it should not be necessary for anyone to do this job again for at least another fifty years. There are for British students two points of particular interest in his summary.

*From *Public Administration* (Summer 1951).

159

First, even fifty years ago more energy was spent on the study and teaching of administration in the USA than in England. This was only in part the result of a difference in scale of organisation. American business had then been 'big business' for some time, but government became 'big government' in America later than in Britain. A more important reason was the difference in the 'shape' of government in the two countries: in the USA the federation and the 48 States were separate laboratories of administrative experiment, legally distinct but linked by private associations of reformers and by the general movement of public opinion. From the 1880s there was in most States well-grounded anxiety about the condition of government, which expressed itself in a number of parallel 'movements': a movement for the improvement of electoral machinery so as to displace the party 'bosses': a movement for the control of big business monopolies: a movement for social work and social reform in urban and rural slums: and the 'public administrative movement' which was at once a 'pressure group' active in many of the States, and a 'clearing-house' for knowledge of the best and worst in public administration.

It was also important that there are always among the multitude of American colleges and universities some which are glad to welcome new forms of practical training, without snobbery about their academic pedigree. In American government the ambitious man generally gains promotion by moving sideways and upwards (as in British local government), so that good connections and good paper qualifications are more important than seniority, and at least as important as a good record at one's job. There is thus a large potential audience for teachers of 'public administration', who are prepared to issue certificates of proficiency: it is surprising how much life develops in a subject when able teachers and able students are associated in a University, and even though the degree may be in the first instance a 'meal-ticket'.

The second point of interest is Professor Waldo's general thesis, commonplace enough, but persistently neglected, that doctrines of public administration and doctrines of business administration are in their nature doctrines about aspects of human society, and cannot exist except on the basis of assumptions about the nature of society. These assumptions may be explicit or implicit: in the first phase of American study they were largely implicit. Theorists claimed to be founding a 'science' of administration which was discovered on close examination to rest on unverified assumptions which were part of the climate of opinion in their time. On the whole, the basis of the American 'public' administration movement' was Benthamism in a form more naïve than the Benthamism of the Fabians. Its nostrums were a clean cut between policy and administration: democratic control of policy through improved electoral machinery: incorruptible administration by a unified hierarchy of professional officials. The doctrines of 'scientific management', developed for business administration, were taken over by the public administration movement, and added an authoritarian flavour to its democratic principles. In discussing reform the emphasis was on such concepts as 'unity of command', 'span of control', 'line and staff', which imply the primary importance of hierarchy and of the 'genealogical tree' of organisation.

What followed from nineteenth century (perhaps more exactly 'eighteenth century') assumptions about human nature was a programme in which a democratic political system and an authoritarian administrative system were to be combined and were to meet at a single point, the point at which policy meets administration; in American conditions in the President or Governor, for us in the Cabinet, or in the Minister's office, or the formal meetings of a local authority and its committees. A sentence or two from one of the older American text-books will illustrate this attitude.

The prime function of the legislator is to represent and translate into action the wishes of the people; that is, to determine policies and give the necessary orders for putting these policies into effect . . . The chief executive (should) be given all the duties and powers of a general manager and be made in fact, as well as in theory, the head of the administration . . . [The legislature should] look primarily to the chief executive for the efficient carrying out of its administrative determinations. The primary

responsibility of the chief executive to the legislature as
general manager is that of seeing that the administrative
affairs of the government are being honestly, efficiently,
and economically run. Unless therefore he has [adequate]
authority, neither can he meet this responsibility nor can
the legislature consistently hold him to it.'[3]

This is in many ways analogous to the language of the
Haldane Committee report; but the British attitude was
more realistic because it had for long been part of our
tradition that a body of some 600 individuals is incapable
of formulating policy except under discipline and leadership,
and that it is for the Cabinet to initiate policy, for the House
of Commons and the electorate to criticise and perhaps
punish. The British tradition was also, for different reasons,
more ready to admit that civil servants have a share in making
policy; hence the famous definition of the work of the
'administrative class' framed by the Reconstruction Committee in 1920, which has produced in British minds some
association between 'administrative' work and 'policy-
making'. The more rigid American attitude is readily compre-
hensible in terms of American problems. There is little
doubt that the 'public administration movement' indicated
the right course of reform in its own day, and its 'principles'
were persuasive arguments because they appealed to two
things dear to American sentiment; first, the eighteenth
century separation of powers, with its simple picture of the
people delegating authority to their elected servants, who
should act at the people's bidding; second the formula of
'American business' — (to which Willoughby, for instance,
regularly appeals) — in shareholders, board of directors,
general manager (in America often called the President), and
employees. These were good political principles in so far as
they helped to get things done: but no attempt has ever been
made to prove them. Indeed anyone with experience of
politics or administration in business knows that they are
grossly unrealistic as a description of what actually happens
in the making and execution of policy; they are ideals or
ethical principles, not scientific discoveries, and they make a
bad basis for a 'science' of administration. The lectures and
text-books of this period were in their own way valuable,

because they brought some order into the teaching of the
history and law of public administration, which had hitherto
been neglected or learnt haphazard on the job; and they also
helped to give administrators a consciousness of professional
unity by giving them a common background of knowledge.
But the professors certainly did not teach their students how
to administer, or even what sort of things they would find in
an administrative office; nor did they do much to bring the
other social sciences to the aid of administration.

Reorientation in the 1930s
The breakdown of this intellectual structure can be dated
conveniently by the publication in 1938 of Mr. Chester
Barnard's book on *The Functions of the Executive*.[4] There
were already cracks in the fabric,[5] and there would in any
case have been a breakdown a few years later, when the
second World War tested administrative machinery to the
limit, forced university teachers into office jobs, and mixed
all the 'social sciences' together at practical tasks in various
war agencies. But Mr. Barnard is well qualified to accelerate
history. He is a man of powerful and enquiring mind: perhaps
it is in this context more important that he has enormous
prestige as an administrator in business, in government and in
voluntary social service, and that he has read widely in the
social sciences without any of those academic commitments
to one field or another which cramp thought in the
universities. His book (one is bound to admit) is in parts
heavy going, because his doctrine is far from being final or
even clear; and it is perhaps easier to approach his work
through a recent collection of short articles and lectures[6]
which illustrate his main theme from various angles. That
theme is a simple but fertile idea, the distinction between
'formal' and 'informal' organisation.

The former is the picture which we are shown first when
we enquire about the organisation of an office; the organisation chart and the distribution of duties list. But anyone with
a little experience knows that for practical purposes even the
best of organisation charts is misleading, or at least that it
uses words in a very peculiar sense. The head of the
organisation (we are told) 'commands' or 'directs' it. Does

he? Does he not, 90 per cent of the time or more, do what he is told to do, by his private secretary, by his 'planning' staff, by his heads of divisions, by his technical experts? There is perhaps a peculiar and specialised activity called 'command' which takes up a small percentage of the 'commander's' time: but when one looks at it closely, the nearest parallel to his work is the work of the arbitrator, not that of the drill sergeant. One might almost say that he is paid to spin a coin for the organisation, when it has exhausted other means of decision. From another point of view, that of the outer world, it is true that the 'commander' in some sense 'is' the organisation; but if he is to be successful he must represent it mainly as an MP 'represents' his constituents, acting for the most part as spokesman. It is only occasionally, and only if his 'subordinates' fully trust him, that he can give a lead on the issues which he himself in virtue of his position understands best; the issues which relate to the place of the organisation in a social structure bigger than itself. This has been well summed up by a recent Swedish writer, after completing a piece of research on how general managers spend their time.

> Before we made this study, I always thought of a chief executive as the conductor of an orchestra, standing aloof on his platform. Now I am in some respects inclined to see him as a puppet in a puppet-show with hundreds of people pulling the strings and forcing him to act in one way or another.[7]

A formally authoritarian structure is usual in modern administration, and in some situations some administrators find it helpful to strike authoritarian attitudes, but it is not true, either in public or in private business, that good work is done mainly because the right orders are given from above. In practice, co-operation is many times more important than authority, and co-operation cannot be effective if it is limited to the comparatively small number of channels which can be defined by authority.[8] To give a 'true' or 'scientific' account of organisation we must bring into our field of view the factors which are not in the charts, but which all practical administrators know to be important. On the one hand, there are individual factors differentiating those who seem the same on the chart; A, B and C from different divisions habitually lunch together; D and E share the same 'old school tie'; F is not on speaking terms with his boss G; H is run entirely by his private secretary. On the other hand, there are objects of ambition common to most of them, which you have to guess from actions rather than from words; status can be symbolised by things of extreme simplicity and absurdity — the type of lamp on the desk, the form of signature to be used, the right of access to one lavatory rather than another.

This extension of the field of view is what Mr. Barnard means by 'informal' organisation. He does not mean that 'informal' factors cannot be understood and manipulated. Indeed his approach assumes that good administrators are good because they use them (consciously or unconsciously) with unusual skill; that this skill can in some degree be analysed and taught; and that such teaching will have more practical relevance than the old doctrines about the various bases of specialisation, about line and staff, about budgetary control, and so forth. His approach does not imply the abandonment of the search for a science of administration: it does imply that the science of administration must accept the implications of its place among the social sciences, and that its scope must be re-defined. The change of attitude can be seen most clearly in the change of definitions. W.F. Willoughby in 1927 defined public administration as the 'operations of the administrative branch' of government; the administrative branch consists of the agencies which are set up by Congress to carry out its policy.[9] More neatly (though more ambiguously) Professor Harvey Walker in 1937 wrote that 'the work which the government does to give effect to a law is called administration'.[10] The opening paragraph of the work under review reads as follows[11]:

> When two men co-operate to roll a stone that neither could have moved alone, the rudiments of administration have appeared. This simple act has the two basic characteristics of what has come to be called administration. There is a purpose — moving the stone — and there is co-operative action — several persons using combined

strength to accomplish something that could not have been done without such a combination. In its broadest sense, administration can be defined as the activities of groups co-operating to accomplish common goals.

One might sum up this contrast as follows. The older writers define 'public administration' in relation to the state; it is a subject within a larger and more abstract subject, what the Germans called *allgemeine Staatslehre*, the general doctrine of the state; and its most general propositions are abstract propositions derived from political theory and jurisprudence. The new definition regards an administration concretely as a number of individual men and women; these human beings are so related that they form a group, and it is possible to regard their activities as a pattern of interweaving lines with certain regularities which may be called 'group behaviour': one section or aspect of this pattern is 'administration'. There are perhaps as many theoretical difficulties about the new definition as about the old one, but the object of the present article is to state the case, not to criticise it, and there are perhaps three points to notice. *First*, the old definition related public administration to doctrines about the state, the new one relates it to doctrines about society; the most general propositions relevant to the science of administration will now be propositions about the psychology of individuals and about the sociology of groups, not propositions about the state. *Second*, it now seems better to start at the bottom, not at the top; with the simplest forms of administrative organisation, not with the most complex. The organisation of the National Coal Board is much more important to everybody than the organisation of the local tennis club; nevertheless, the latter may be a better model from which to demonstrate the principles of administration. Indeed, even the tennis club is rather complex, and it may be better to start, as do Dr. Simon and his co-adjutors, with two men combining to move a stone. *Third*, the distinction between public administration and private administration is now quite secondary: it is not necessarily unimportant, but one can go a long way in studying 'purposive group action' before one gets to it, and it may turn out in the end that the distinction is too complex for us to generalise about it in a precise and 'scientific' way.

The Interdisciplinary Approach

After Mr. Barnard's book came the upheaval of 1939—45: people (particularly academic people) learnt much about administration, but little was published, and the next convenient landmark is Dr. H.A. Simon's book, *Administrative Behaviour*, which came out in 1948.[1][2] Mr. Barnard is perhaps in the academic field a brilliant amateur: Dr. Simon is by profession a scholar, and his book was important primarily as a first attempt to put these new doctrines into academic shape. This does not mean that it is written in technical jargon or what the Americans call 'gobbledygook'. On the contrary, Dr. Simon's style is by academic standards plain enough, and on occasion it achieves a certain wry humour in the manner of Thorstein Veblen: is Dr. Simon perhaps now and then poking fun at the administrators? It is hard to say: but certainly he knows the tricks of the trade. What is academic about his approach is (first) a zeal for logic, a desire to achieve coherence and completeness as well as common sense — to create an argument which will 'stand up': (second) wide reading and a good understanding of what has been happening in the last few years in the whole field of the social sciences. It is quite easy to disagree with Dr. Simon: it is almost impossible for anyone who has academic instincts as well as an interest in administration to avoid following him on to this new ground. The theoretical issues which he raises are difficult to discuss here: but it is possible to suggest one striking point, that all or most of them arise from a sort of 'cross-fertilisation' between different branches of the social sciences. These other studies form the background of Dr. Simon's book, and also the background of the later work now under review; but Dr. Simon himself does not expound them at all fully, and a digression here may be helpful, though it is necessarily abstract and compressed.

There are at least five important branches of study in which (on this side of the Iron Curtain) a long period of development has led in the last fifteen years to profound changes in attitude.

(a) Perhaps, *honoris causa*, philosophy should be mentioned first. There is on the continent of Europe a considerable enclave of existentialism; elsewhere in the West logical positivism is formally dominant in the sense that it has imposed its manner of speech even on those who dislike its conclusions. The field of discussion has been shifted from something called 'thought' to something called 'language', on the reasonable ground that no man can get at the thought of another man except through language (using that word in a rather extended sense). This shift of emphasis from 'judgments' and 'inferences', to 'statements' and their 'implications' has been stimulating in all fields, and has perhaps simplified a number of problems in the logic of mathematics and the natural sciences. But one of its by-products has been an attempt to create a system of ethics based on a distinction between 'statements of fact' — which can be verified, and so proved or disproved — and 'statements of value', which are not verifiable, and are therefore beyond discussion, since they are not in any useful sense either true or false. Here Dr. Simon finds the basis for a restatement of the old distinction between policy and administration. Policy is concerned with decisions of 'value', which are for the administrative organisation beyond discussion: the administrative problem is to achieve the most rational solution possible to the problem of achieving a particular 'value'. In more realistic terms, an organisation exists to achieve a number of different 'values', which may compete, and 'policy' is the decision of the relative weight which is to be given to each of them. This invites much fuller discussion. But here it is perhaps enough to say that the difficulties lie in the 'fact' — 'value' antinomy of logical positivism; the advantage on the other hand is that this formula enables us to look on 'policy' not as given externally but as an integral part of the organisation — the delicate and complicated balance of values held by the group of people who *are* the organisation, and who are also susceptible to many influences of various kinds from outside the organisation.

(b) Second, there is psychology. There is nothing new now about the Freudian school and the other 'modern' schools of psychology, whose controversies began some fifty years ago: and the application of psychology to politics was a constant theme between the wars — both in the vulgar politics of Goebbels and Mussolini and 'Psychological Warfare', and in the political science of Graham Wallas and Walter Lippman. But psychology has so far had extraordinarily little impact on the study of administration. In England, the Webbs (more especially Sidney Webb) were to the end the rearguard of eighteenth century rationalism; and in the USA the 'scientific managers', who applied a little psychology at the work-bench, were much too diffident to take it with them into the Managing Director's office. It is not certain even now what psychology has to contribute except a general scepticism about the claims of men to be rational: but at least psychology has itself passed its own Messianic phase. The schools still dispute, but they begin to have doubts about the conclusive rightness of any school; and it is probable that there is now some common ground. What we require for administration are some working hypotheses about the ways in which men can learn new habits of speech, behaviour and co-operation: and a good deal is now known about the surprising conservatism and the surprising elasticity of human beings in different circumstances.

(c) Third, there is probably no sharp line between individual psychology and the various disciplines in the line of descent from Comte's attempt to found a general science of society; social anthropology, empirical sociology and social psychology. Here also there is a babel of academic schools, as well as a scum of smart journalism: but it seems clear enough that simple societies can be analysed and classified successfully in terms of social relationships. It is not so certain that the same technique can be applied to the immense complexity of what Graham Wallas called 'The Great Society'; but even for modern societies sociology has made some advances beyond the absurdities of Comte and Spencer, and the theological speculations of Marx. What has been influential, so far, is not so much sociological doctrine as the rather vague notion of sociological method.

(d) Fourth, there is the new turn which has been given to 'scientific management' by the impact of modern psychology and sociology. There seem to be two main themes, and a deduction from them. The first theme is that our habitual distinction between 'work' and 'leisure' is an abstract and arbitrary way of dissecting the single individual whom we call 'the worker'. The second theme is that if one observes a factory patiently one finds in it a social order which is not that of the organisation chart, yet influences the lives of all concerned from managing director to charwoman: this is of course closely parallel to Mr. Barnard's distinction between formal and informal organisation. The deduction from these themes is that the old 'stop-watch' methods can at the best increase productivity only within rather narrow limits, and that they are likely to fail entirely unless attention is paid to the elementary rules of 'informal organisation'. No responsible research worker would claim that he knows how to change 'informal organisation' at will: but there are various groups of researchers who think they have found the right first principles and hope to learn more.

(e) Finally, there is recent economic thought. Economics since Keynes does not seem to have produced much new economic doctrine of general interest: Dr. Simon and his partners in the present book use a good deal of economic terminology, and adapt ingeniously such notions as consumers' surplus and higher and lower indifference curves. But none of this is very new. In fact the economic theorists are now the Old Guard of the social sciences ('The Guards die but never surrender'); their algebra and their curves play much the same part in twentieth century education as did Latin and Greek verse in the nineteenth century: they demand both elegance and 'the rigour of the game'. To the outsider recent controversy seems to have been a series of demands for more and more rigour, and damn the consequences. The controversy gets nowhere, but it puts the rest of us on our mettle; it is fashionable now not to write with the vagueness and fluency which were the curse of social science before 1939, and Dr. Simon and his partners are in the fashion. Of course they leave some gaps, but the percentage of sheer nonsense which they let pass is, by the standards of the social sciences, very small.

This list of disciplines (which could be documented from Dr. Simon's footnotes) is somewhat intimidating, and indeed

Administrative Behaviour is so allusive that it would be hard reading for the average DPA candidate. It is modest enough in its claims either to certainty or to novelty: but its apparatus and its purpose are both pretty formidable. Dr. Simon describes his aim with great modesty, as if it were merely to 'construct tools', to adapt or invent a vocabulary with which to describe the facts of administration, so that future generations may at last discover its principles. But though he writes modestly no doubt he appreciates that a new vocabulary is a working hypothesis, and that an exact and final vocabulary (if we could ever reach one) would be a verified hypothesis: the vocabulary, properly used, *is* the science, not a tool which someone else will eventually use to discover the science. *Administrative Behaviour* is in effect a collection (not a complete system) of hypotheses about how people behave in some of the situations they meet in administrative organisations. Up to a point these hypotheses are confirmed by reference to Dr. Simon's own experience, to the personal experience of many of us, and to the extremely limited supply of published case-studies in administration. But they still differ totally from the old 'principles of administration'; *first*, in that they are put forward as working hypotheses, not as final truths, *second*, in that they cover only part of the field of study, that part where Dr. Simon is sure of his ground and feels (rightly) that he has something important to say.

A Text-Book on New Principles

This is as it should be: if the game is to be played by 'scientific' rules, the 'scientists' (if the scanty band of researchers can recognise themselves under that title) ought to move cautiously forward from this point, by cross-checking and criticising Dr. Simon's hypotheses and by pushing new hypotheses into unexplored territory. Unfortunately *ars longa, vita brevis*. There is a class waiting in the lecture room: we cannot teach it the old doctrine which we believe to be mainly false, or at best unimportant; nor can we fob it off with provisional hypotheses which cover only a corner of the subject advertised. At least it is impossible to do so in the USA.

Hence this book; it is a first shot at a text-book of 'Public Administration' on new principles, and in the USA this means that it is offered as a programme for courses and examinations in such colleges as decide to adopt it. Complete success was in the circumstances impossible, but the attempt is bold and ingenious, and was well worth making.

It should be said in the first place that there is nothing alarming about the book except its length, and even that is not exceptional for an American text-book. The style is clear and simple, and almost entirely free from the various forms of 'social' jargon; footnotes and bibliography are kept within bounds; and the main points are illustrated by practical examples from American experience. As a piece of writing it is extremely well done: the controversy will be about its shape and contents, and there is likely to be controversy in the USA as well as in England. This particular school of thought is not the only one in American universities, though it seems at the moment to be the most vigorous.

A brief analysis with a few comments will indicate what has happened to a once familiar subject. The headings are not those of the authors.

Chapter	Contents	Number of pages (Total 578)
1	Definition of the subject.	22
2	Brief factual account of the 'layout' of public administration in the U.S.A. (30 pages out of 578, and there is no other straight descriptive matter in the book).	30
3	Relations between individual and 'group' in *any* organisation.	37
4—5	The 'group' as a social unit within larger organisations.	38
6—7	Specialisation; by individuals within groups, by groups within larger organisations.	50
8—11	How groups are tied together for purposive action; authority, status, communication.	78
12—14	Special problems of 'tying together' in a large organisation.	52
15—17	The individual in public administration. (These chapters are relatively conventional; they set out the usual sort of principles about personnel administration in the civil service, and never reach the points at which these principles are unsatisfactory.)	69

With this we might contrast the contents of Professor
Harvey Walker's book, published in 1937; Professor Walker is
by no means a die-hard adherent of the old school.

This is a lay-out which will look much more familiar and
perhaps more sensible to readers of this journal. It follows
the chain of authority from the centre through the two
channels, 'staff' and 'line'; it is largely descriptive of practice
in the USA; and perhaps it would be fair to say that,
although it is an introduction to twelve or fifteen branches of
administrative work, each of them highly technical, it
contributes no technicality of its own. It has taken other
people's techniques, simplified them, and put them in an
orderly way within a single book; it has not even attempted
to tell the administrator anything about the special technique
of administration — if there is such a technique.

Conclusion
One's natural reaction to this contrast is that Professor
Harvey Walker was doing something obviously useful, even
though it was not very adventurous; the work of Dr. Simon
and his associates is more exciting, but of what use is it?
Would the ordinary official be right to disregard it as
something irrelevant to his business?

If it were successful, the new approach might help him in
three ways: *first*, by sending him recruits better trained, or
by training his juniors better; *second*, by making more readily
available to him the work of the various social sciences; *third*,
by research which would cast new light on problems of
administration — specifically of administration as a special
form of human collaboration, and not of cost accounting, or
budgeting, or recruitment, or grading, or the design of forms,
or business machines, or any of the other highly technical
subjects handled by administrators.

On the first of these, Messrs. Simon, Smithburg and
Thompson lay considerable emphasis in their Foreword.
They say for instance:

> We are under no illusion that an administrator can be
> trained in a college. Beyond a very definite point, the

development of his skills must take place through their actual practice. All that academic training can give him — but of course it is a very vital *all* — is a kit of fundamental tools that he will later learn to apply to practical problems. Among these tools, a realistic knowledge of how administration actually is carried on, will be at least as important as a knowledge of how it ought to be carried on. Excessive preoccupation with *ideal* or *desirable* administrative arrangements may be seriously misleading (since final truths are still a long way off in this field) and may leave the student unprepared for the realities of administration as he finds them later. In training students to advise the President, universities have not always trained them to discharge the first modest responsibilities that are placed upon them in government employment. The disillusioning shock that students of public administration have so often experienced in the past should warn us against this danger.[13]

This is perhaps not precisely applicable to British conditions, because here most students of 'Public Administration' are junior officials, and the subject is not often taught to full-time students coming straight from school to the University. But the symptoms are recognisably the same; there is an unbridged gap between the young official's experience in his own office and the lecturer's lofty talk about the structure of the Cabinet or the reorganisation of the local government system, and what he writes in his examination papers on these larger issues is often no better than mumbo-jumbo, even though the examiners pass it with distinction. It must be right to attempt to bridge this gap; the question is 'how'?

The authors' formula is to think and speak of administrators always as 'real people'; never to generalise without giving examples from actual cases; and to choose as examples small issues and organisations in preference to great ones, so as to work from the practical experience which all students already have in some measure. Surely we should all agree with this, so far? But the authors perhaps do not make it sufficiently clear that if they are not going to give descriptive teaching about the higher structure of government someone else must do it; the young administrator must be given orientation and a

sense of a larger whole, as well as practical 'insights.' This
means that the new teaching must be largely an addition to
the old, not a substitute for it, and the old descriptive
teaching cannot be carried out without some appeal to
principles. We cannot *stop* criticising the organisation of the
Cabinet, even though we know very little about it; perhaps
we should mislead our students less if we called this 'political
science' and not 'public administration'. Principles are essential here too, but they are not 'scientific' ones; their nearest
relations are the principles to be found in the political
philosophers.

Perhaps it should be said also that Dr. Simon's approach
postulates a fairly thorough preliminary course of study in
logic and scientific method, in psychology, and in sociology,
as well as in our usual preliminary subjects, economics,
modern history, and political science. In fact he postulates a
much longer course of training, and in theory he is doubtless
right; but our practical problem in teaching becomes more
than ever that of the quart and the pint pot — what is best in
the time available?

Second, would the middle level of administrators find this
book interesting? Would it give them new 'insights' into what
they have been doing? In practice there is the barrier that
most of the examples and some of the idiom are American;
but it seems certain that if a similar book could be written in
English terms it would be of great interest to administrators.
No reader can doubt that the authors are writing about
practical problems, not theoretical problems; and what they
say can help the individual administrator with his problem by
showing that it is not an isolated problem — there are close
analogies to it in the problems of the other social sciences,
and even closer ones in those of other administrators. The
authors would not claim that the analogies solve problems,
but they may help, and (to put it at the lowest) they show
the individual administrator that he is not alone. There are
plenty of other people in the same fix as he is; and that
knowledge is an excellent corrective to the alternation
between megalomania and despair which is the occupational
disease of the executive, especially the top executive. To put

it in military terms, this approach is good for the administrator's morale.

Third, there is the problem of research: can this new approach found a science of administration? This, I think, is doubtful; but flaws in theory are not always fatal to scientific research. A new theory may expose flaws in an old one, and (even though it has logical flaws of its own) it may lead to fruitful experiments. It seems clear that it will in future be much more difficult than it has been hitherto to make *ex cathedra* statements about 'span of control', 'functional organisation', 'the staff and line principle' and so forth, and to base practical arguments upon them. This is a negative gain, but a real one. The positive side is less clear.

The 'Science' of administration, if it is a science, is a very young one, and its devotees should be humble and content for the present if they can make themselves useful in small ways. The 'new approach' needs discussion and criticism, but there is some reason to hope that it may be as fruitful in teaching as it is likely to be in research.

Notes

1. *Public Administration* by H.A. Simon, Donald W. Smithburg and Victor A. Thompson. Pp.582 and xv; Knopf, New York, 1950.

2. The Ronald Press Co., New York, 1948. Reviewed in *Public Administration*, Vol. XXVI p.278 (Winter 1948).

3. W.F. Willoughby: *Principles of Public Administration* (Washington 1927) pp.2, 36, 43.

4. Harvard University Press, 1938.

5. See for instance John M. Gaus, L.D. White and Marshall E. Dimock, *The Frontiers of Public Administration* (Chicago UP 1936); Harvey Walker, *Public Administration in the USA* (Farrer and Rinehart, 1937).

6. Chester I. Barnard: *Organisation and Management*, Harvard University Press, 1948.

7. Sune Carlson: *Executive Behaviour* (Stromberg, Stockholm, 1951) p.52. It might be wise to emphasise 'in some respects' in the second sentence of the quotation. Professor Carlson does not give this either as a complete picture of the executive, or as an ideal; nor does anyone else. It is intended as a correction to an opposite exaggeration.

8. This is made very clear in mathematical form by Professor M. Polanyi in *The Manchester School*. Vol. 16, No.3, p.249 (Sept. 1948).

9. W.F. Willoughby, op. cit., p.1. Cf. Prof. L.D. White, *Introduction to the Study of Public Administration* (Macmillan 1926): 'Public administration is the management of men and materials in the accomplishment of the purposes of the state'.

10. Harvey Walker; op. cit. p.5.

11. Simon, Smithburg and Thompson; p.3.

12. Macmillan, New York, 1948. Reviewed by G.E. Milward in *Public Administration Vol. XXVI, p.274 (Winter, 1948)*.

13. Introduction *p. ix.*

10 Science in the Study of Administration*

This paper is a report by a political scientist on a field of literature which has not been much visited by political scientists, the literature of scientific administration. This is very large; an amateur in it cannot in the time available to him read more than a sample, and the picture presented here is over-simplified because of this limitation, as well as because of the limits of space.

With some notable exceptions, the books on scientific administration are not good reading. Their authors have an engaging fervour and sense of mission, but most of them use private jargons to say things which could be more accurately said without them, and they seldom appreciate the virtues of brevity and precision. In fact, there is some excuse for academic snobbery at their expense; but snobbery of this sort is always a mistake, and it has excluded political scientists from a field in which they can contribute a great deal. It is also a field in which the interest of the plain man is now engaged very actively, perhaps more actively than in the traditional problems of the State, and which is therefore important in popular thought about problems of political and social theory.

The central theme can be stated simply. It is an old commonplace that social science lags behind natural science and that most of the woes of the world are due to this deficiency. About fifty years ago, there appeared a second commonplace, that this is an age of administration, an age in which the bureaucrat takes more decisions than the politician, in which the salaried manager is more important than the board of directors or the individual entrepreneur. If we

*This paper contains the substance of a lecture given at the London School of Economics on 5 November 1951 and published in the *Manchester School of Economic and Social Studies*, XX (Jan 1952).

179

put these propositions together, it seems to follow that the first task for social scientists is to formulate a science of administration.

In the years about 1900, various people hit independently upon this train of thought. In the USA there was F. W. Taylor's gospel of scientific management in industry. In France Henri Fayol called for the formulation of *la doctrine administrative*, which was to be applicable both to industry and to public business. In Britain this was the period in which writers as diverse as Kipling, the Webbs, and H. G. Wells agreed upon government by an elite, and disagreed bitterly about the sort of elite that was required. The Webbs never seriously attempted to construct a formal science of administration, and there have been few British pioneers in the field of business management: but in its own way the movement was as strong here as in France and the USA. In Germany too there was the age of 'rationalisation', usually associated with the name of Walter Rathenau; the man who introduced *Planwirtschaft* into Germany in the first World War, made the Rapallo treaty with Russia in April 1922, and was murdered by German nationalists for his great services to the German national cause.[1]

It may be well to recall here, as it is relevant to the argument later, that in this fifty years since 1900 political theory has been largely concerned with doctrines of two kinds; doctrines of the divine right of an elite to rule, and doctrines of the divine right of the group both against the state and against the individual. In different parts of the world ambitious men have found different grounds for claiming to be the predestined elite, grounds of blood or brains or natural selection. None of them, it seems, has based a claim to rule upon knowledge of the science of administration. But James Burnham has come pretty close to it in his attempt to find a political philosophy for the American business executive; and it is worth noticing that the most important of these self-styled elites, that of the Leninists (from which Burnham deviated), founds its claim to rule on the claim that the missing social science has now been discovered, and that knowledge of it confers the right to govern. The Communist Party does not concern itself with scientific administration as such, but doubtless scientific administration can be deduced by the orthodox from scientific Marxism.

Alongside these claims to govern, there have been theories of a different sort; theories in part stated explicitly by the pluralists, in part implied by psychological and sociological doctrines in vogue. In contrast with doctrines of the individual will, there have been doctrines of the absorption of the individual in a natural whole the laws of which govern his being — or ought to govern his being; there is almost always a blur in these theories over the distinction between statements of what is and statements of what ought to be. This difficulty is present in the work of enthusiastic pluralists like Miss Mary Parker Follett, a learned and able lady who is important in this context because she has been adopted as one of the patron saints of scientific administration: it seems to the layman to be present in many of the claims of psychotherapy and group therapy.

Theories of these two types have a long history in political philosophy: the patterns of argument about them are quite familiar, and so are their uses for political persuasion, often in combinations which make good propaganda but odd logic. Their relevance here is that a period in which they were much in vogue coincided with the development of scientific administration, although few writers in that field knew enough politics to realise the bearings of political theory upon their own work.[2] The theme of this paper is that the notion of scientific administration is a point at which these imcompatible doctrines meet; and that its paradoxes arise from a use of two presuppositions, which are difficult to reconcile, although both seem to be essential to it; the presupposition that human affairs are decided by individual wills, the presupposition that it will in the end be possible to predict the actions of the individual by scientific study of the group.

For the present purpose it is unnecessary to spend time in seeking a definition of 'administration', as the word will be used only as it is used by most of the authors concerned, in a general and popular sense. The notion of 'administration' is felt vaguely by most people to have a unity of some sort, to 'make sense', and this is guidance enough at the outset of an attempt to study it. It would not be sensible to start with a full-blown definition. On the other hand, it is relevant to consider what they were saying about their proposals when they called for a new 'science'; this depends on the meaning of that word about the year 1900 in England and in the USA.

This was the end of a long story.

In Latin *scientia* is the word most commonly used to translate the Greek word ἐπιστήμη which embodies a world of thought alien to the Roman mind and language. Επιστήμη is that which can be fully understood; a body of knowledge which is systematic, which is in some sense timeless, which can be passed from mind to mind and which therefore in some sense exists independently of any single human creature. It is contrasted with τέχνη, an art or skill, which can be learnt only by practice and which therefore involves the temporal, the material, the individual. This distinction between science and art was common to all Greek philosophy after Socrates; none of the rival schools disputed it, and all subsequent European thought has been dominated by it.

The model of science in this sense is mathematics; and all knowledge in so far as it is true knowledge approximates to the condition of mathematics. But any ordered and teachable body of knowledge is ἐπιστήμη in its own degree; there is no sharp line between metaphysics, logic, mathematics, physics, biology, social science, though some sciences may be less pure than others.

This is the first sophisticated sense of the word 'science' in the English language; but the word was rather late in coming into regular use, and it was preceded by the word 'philosophy'. One still finds in Oxford a Professor of Natural Philosophy who is really a Professor of Physics; when Adam Smith lectured on the Wealth of Nations he was a Professor of Moral Philosophy; there are still in Lancashire and elsewhere 'Literary and Philosophical Societies' dating from the eighteenth century, which we should now call Literary and Scientific Societies. For some time the words 'philosophy' and 'science' run parallel courses, but even in the eighteenth century there begins to be a contrast between metaphysics and theology on the one hand, science on the

other. The latter is coloured by English empiricism so as to exclude what is revealed, transcendent, incapable of proof. By the outset of the nineteenth century, this distinction is well established; nevertheless, at this stage the word is still one of extremely wide application. Mill (in the first sentence of the *Political Economy*) in effect defines science as 'systematic enquiry into the modes of action of the powers of nature'; he has no doubt that Political Economy is a branch of science, and he devotes the sixth book of his *Logic* to the methods of the 'Moral Sciences'. In the first half of the nineteenth century Political Science was the obvious name to give to the academic study of Politics; it was the period of the Association for the Promotion of Social Science, the period of the Moral Sciences Tripos at Cambridge.

This second stage, in which 'science' meant unambiguously all organised branches of analytic and empirical study, came to an end in the Darwinian controversies of the 1860s and 1870s. A particular issue of no great importance was dramatised as a battle between 'science' and 'religion'; in the context of this controversy 'science' meant principally physics, chemistry, biology, geology and astronomy, and a scientist was a man who worked in one of these disciplines, or in other lesser disciplines closely analogous to them. 'Science' as thus defined excludes 'social science';[3] sometimes it even seems to exclude pure mathematics. The word had thus been narrowed down to a fairly small section of human knowledge. The natural scientists had earned immense prestige by their discoveries and by their swift and decisive victory over the theologians. To this they added, less legitimately, the prestige of the Western intellectual tradition, then still embodied in the word 'science'.

There followed the period in which science was a magic word: the scientist was old priest writ large. This has brought reaction, and in our divided society the word 'science' is now ambivalent. In one social world there is no limit to the craving for 'science fiction', space-ships, supermen, death-rays, scientific socialism and so forth; in another 'science' has become almost a synonym for clap-trap. The more sophisticated natural scientists prefer to be known by obscure professional titles, as astro-physicists, cryptogamic botanists, endocrinologists and so forth, and they affect attitudes of absurd diffidence about the extent of their authority. One even finds, in Professor Young's Reith Lectures, a modest attempt to disguise natural science as social science, on the ground that it involves techniques of communication between men. Social science, on its side, hastens to disclaim the methods and even the name of natural science; London is the only University in this country where the Professor of Political Science is still bold enough to use that title. In fact, we are passing beyond the attitude to 'science' expressed in the search for a 'science' of administration; or if we pursue it now, we do not act in quite the same sense as the pioneers. They sought mainly to apply the methods of natural science, but it would be fair to say that their action was affected both by the general prestige of the word 'science' and by imprecise recollections of its earlier meanings. It is not till the latest stage that one finds much self-conscious discussion of scientific method.

It would be presumptuous to attempt to say what the true method is, because this has been one of the staple tasks of philosophy for some 300 years. But there seems to be an interlocking of two processes, distinguishable but not separate: *first*, a process, more or less mathematical in character, by which definitions are decided and their necessary implications are deduced; *second*, a process by which experience is shaped into the raw material for mathematics — that is to say, it is made repetitive and countable, either by some process of abstraction or by the careful construction of experiments. The two processes can also be distinguished in the ordinary man's way of gaining knowledge: both there and in scientific method the essence of the matter lies not in either process but in their interlocking and mutual adjustment. In this each science has its own methods, of which its own experts are masters and judges; no one has produced any useful generalisations about the proper relation between deduction and experiment. It would therefore be senseless to blame pioneers for wrong procedure; their role was necessarily to fumble for a practical solution adapted to the needs of their own field of investigation. Nevertheless, the distinction will serve as a peg on which to hang a description of what has happened and what has gone wrong. It is possible to associate three lines of thought with three names – F. W. Taylor, Henri Fayol, and Elton Mayo; this will not altogether do them justice, for they were all in their way great men, and there is a great deal of caution and good judgment in their writings which is not reproduced in textbooks which purport to describe what they said. All three are associated primarily with business administration, not with public administration; there has been much big talk about the application of science to public administration, but serious writing about public administration has been largely descriptive, and its principles have been the axioms of the plain man.

Taylor and Fayol began their preaching campaigns independently and almost simultaneously in the years just before 1900. It may be convenient for the argument to take Taylor first.

Taylor is known to everyone as the apostle of time and motion study, the stop-watch in industry. The common man's visual image of 'Taylorism' has been stamped by the film 'Cheaper by the Dozen'; there is a sequence there which shows Taylor's friend F. B. Gilbreth buttoning and re-buttoning his waistcoat while Myrna Loy times the operation with a stop-watch. The film is doubtless a travesty, but it serves well enough to illustrate what is common to the development of time-study by Taylor and of motion-study by Gilbreth. These techniques are concerned with actions which can be endlessly repeated without relevant alterations, and which can be analysed into elements such that those elements in turn can be separated, repeated and recombined in various patterns. You can button up your waistcoat in the same way often enough for certain variations to be weeded out as statistically non-significant in relation to any criterion chosen; you can separate and recombine various movements, left hand or right hand, up or down, and so on. To extract general rules from these operations must always require some simple mathematics, and in the higher flights of Taylorism there may be quite advanced exercises in the mathematics of probability. But apart from mathematics, this science has very few postulates, and it has not developed any important deductive structure of its own. Its postulates about human psychology and physiology do not seem to be expressed anywhere, but they are certainly unsophisticated and perhaps ambiguous. This has run Taylorism into considerable trouble; practical trouble, because attempts to apply it have often led to resistance from workers and so to a great loss of the advantages predicted; theoretical trouble, in that experiments carefully designed on Taylor's principles sometimes fail to work consistently even though there is no conscious resistance by the participants.

Nevertheless these errors are marginal; within its limits Taylorism has certainly been a correct and successful adaptation of the methods of natural science, and it has immensely modified our attitude to all repetitive operations. Such operations are as common in public administration as in business administration; time and motion study is as well suited to a Royal Ordnance Factory as to the manufacture of motor-cars, and an expert in office routine can do the same job in the Ministry of National Insurance as in the Prudential Assurance Company. This is the staple diet of the Organisation and Methods Division of the Treasury, and 'O & M' is now an essential part of the machinery of government.

But surely this is not the science *of* management but science *for* management — an ambiguity neatly concealed by the phrase 'scientific management'. Surely repetitive routine operations are not an important part of 'administration', whatever 'administration' is. The work of the administrator, even of the administrator at the top, must contain some element of repetition, for otherwise we should not feel, as we do, that there is unity in his work, that there exists somewhere something called 'administration' about which we should like to generalise. But this unity is certainly not something that can be timed with a stop-watch; the stop-watch may be an instrument of management, and it is as useful for a manager to learn 'scientific management' as to learn cost accounting or the concise and effective use of English. But it is not more useful; he manages routine operations but he is not himself a routine operator.

The second approach is one to which it is convenient to attach the name of Henri Fayol, because his work illustrates its good points and not its bad ones. The nearest analogy here is that of economic theory. This sort of science begins with postulates and definitions, which are framed as precisely and unambiguously as possible and which seem plausible to common-sense; these are something like the axioms of Euclid, and from them necessary propositions can be deduced. These derivative propositions will be relevant to experience if two conditions are fulfilled: *first*, that the chosen postulates are more or less correct, *second*, that some unit of account or of measurement can be found by which subject-matter can be related to propositions. Economic theory is said to be a set of variations on the theme that you cannot eat your cake and have it; these variations can be translated into rules for behaviour subject to these two limitations — *first*, there are a good many exceptions to the rule that you can't eat your cake and have it; *secondly*, it is not always in real life possible to get at the cake and measure it, so as to be sure whether it is being eaten or not. Within these limitations the method is useful as well as elegant. It plays a great part in the natural sciences, above all in physics, and it is worth trying tentatively in almost any field. Professor Catlin has talked about trying it in politics, and it has been tried fairly seriously in the science of administration. Those who have tried it seem to start from postulates of three kinds.

They need (*first*) a postulate or simplified model for human nature. The game could be played with the very simple eighteenth-century model known as 'economic man'; on the whole administrative theorists seem to feel that in their field this is repugnant to common-sense, and they substitute something more complicated. One recent author[4] has a 'model man' who is moved by four instincts — love of self, love of affiliation to a group, love of accomplishment, and love of service. This is more realistic than the model of 'economic man', but it sets a new problem at the outset, because these four loves are as hard to relate to one another quantitatively as are faith, hope and charity. In seeking a realistic model we may make the whole structure of deduction useless because it cannot be applied.

Secondly, there must be a definition of administration; that commonly used is to the effect that administration is 'the organisation or disposition of men to execute a purpose through specialisation of function'. This means that we must expressly or tacitly put more details into our model of man: how far can he specialise, how fast can he learn, how many relations can he simultaneously comprehend; and so on.

Thirdly, there is an assumption about the relation of organisation to purpose. It is probably not essential in this deductive method that the purpose should be taken as external to the organisation. But whether it is inevitable or not, deductive authors invariably choose this utilitarian or rationalist or mechanist approach; they postulate a supreme author who creates the organisation for *his* purpose, sets it in motion by *his* command, and measures success in terms of advance towards *his* goal. We thus avoid (and this is one of the eternal merits of utilitarianism) the hard philosophical puzzle of 'common purpose'; but in the process a good deal is lost.

Even this limited discussion of these assumptions indicates serious difficulties; but there is nothing improper about the method. Fayol is saying something true and relevant, though its application is obscure, when he divides administration into five operations or aspects which need not be consecutive: to foresee, to construct an organisation, to set it in motion by command, to co-ordinate its parts while it is in motion, to scrutinise its performance in relation to its purpose. There are also a good many interesting tricks which can be played with the principles of subdivision by function; staff and line organisation, the different types of functional division, and so on. Yet somehow nothing much has come of this. Time and motion study has advanced beyond Taylor and Gilbreth, but the principles of administration are much where Fayol left them. This is partly because much later writing is so careless as to be disreputable, but there are also inherent difficulties in this approach, quite similar to those which dishearten the economic theorists. For one thing it must have postulates, and postulates are either tautologies or the axioms of common-sense. Tautologies are often very useful (as for instance $2 + 2 = 4$), but they invite disrespect; and the plain man's axioms are usually proverbs, which notoriously contradict one another. These points are discouraging but not fatal;

mathematics and physics are no better off. The difficulty is in the transition from deduction to experiment; no member of this school has seriously considered that crucial problem. They have not even considered whether administration as they define it is something which can be so simplified or broken down into repetitive elements as to be a possible subject for experiment. The procedure should be, in theory, to take an administrative 'proverb' (for instance, that efficiency declines if the manager's span of control covers more than five persons), give precise meanings to each term of it, deduce what would happen if this were true in a case in which the cause can be adequately isolated; and then to prove or disprove. If the proverb is a good proverb, experiment will not exactly prove or disprove it; it will refine it into a more precise and subtle statement — and that new statement will be ripe for deduction and experiment in its turn. This is a procedure of great difficulty, even in natural science; in administrative science it has not even been tried, and meantime this school can offer only tautologies, proverbs and deductions from them. The trouble with proverbs is that they contradict themselves; the trouble with tautologies is that (like $2 + 2 = 4$) they give no guide to action. It is tautology to say 'Efficiency declines if the correct span of control is exceeded': if one combines this with another tautology, for instance that 'efficiency declines if the chain of command is too long', one can arrive by a fairly strict process of reasoning at other propositions, some of which will sound interesting. But if they are fairly stated, they will be like statements in the sort of economic theory which is content to be the 'pure logic of choice'; they will indicate which courses of action are mutually exclusive, not which course of action is right. This will be a service to anyone who finds himself in a situation to which the alternatives are relevant; but it is not what we expect from natural science. We expect to be told that 'in certain circumstances the way to get A is to do B'; not that there are six alternative ways, any of which might in unknown circumstances be the right one.

However, these speculations are academic until someone produces a deductive theory worthy of the name, and this has not been done. Much has been written, but the authors seem without exception to have muddled it. They have confused tautologies with proverbs, their definitions are vague, their terminology is variable, their logic is weak, and they are intolerably apt to claim the authority of science for their own idiosyncrasies. One is reminded of the conclusion of Kipling's *Brugglesmith*: 'Though his feet were not within six inches of the ground, they paddled swiftly, and I saw that in his magnificent mind he was running — furiously running.'

This unfortunately has often been the point at which political scientists first meet scientific administration, and what they see of it shocks them.

They are less likely to be repelled by the third school with which may be associated the name of Elton Mayo. His work was mainly on the sociology of industry, at the level of the factory worker; its application to the manager is new and tentative, and it is not certain how it will work out. But enough has been done to show that the attempt is a continuation of old traditions in political science. One of these is the search for an all-embracing science of society, and in this political scientists have always been involved: as for instance, in different ways, Aristotle, Machiavelli, Bagehot, Graham Wallas. The Americans have explored this frontier between sociology and politics more methodically than have the British, but political scientists all talk a sociological language about parties and pressure-groups and public opinion, and are fairly well aware of the clash between this language and the traditional language of consent, election and representation. We use both, we are bound to use both, and we fuss a good deal about their discrepancy. A similar clash arises when sociology is applied to administration; and in some ways the issues emerge more clearly there, because it is a smaller field.

There are two problems at the outset. *First*, there is that of the relation of the manager to his organisation. Literature about the science of administration is addressed primarily to administrators; there is a proper element of idle curiosity in it, but its excuse for existing is that it will help the administrator to do his job better. Unfortunately the deductive school and the sociological school do not agree about what his job is. This is concealed by their definitions of administration, which look very similar. The older books often opened with a sentence like this: 'Administration began when five or six men first combined their efforts to achieve a purpose, for instance to move a great stone'; and this has passed over intact into the new American text-book in 'Public Administration', of which Dr H. A. Simon is the principal author. But in passing over it has quite changed its meaning.

Both schools of thought regard administration as combination to effect a purpose. For the deductive school that purpose is solely the purpose of the manager, though of course he may have received it as 'policy' from a higher level of decision. The 'data' are a purpose and a number of men; the manager's job is to organise the men so as to attain the purpose. The manager makes the organisation, but he is himself outside it; he acts upon it, and he may learn from it, but he is not changed by it. In relation to it he is God. This view of purpose does not flow from the nature of the deductive method, but from the climate of thought in which it was developed and the readers for whom it was designed; it was written for those who lived still in an atmosphere of individualism not far removed from that of Herbert Spencer, and it paid a tribute of respect to the legal fiction that shareholders govern directors, directors govern managers, managers give orders to workmen.[5] There is a chain of command; something called 'command' flows through channels which can be marked by little arrows on a chart.

Sociology by its terms of reference proceeds on other assumptions; its axiom is that social relations exist and can be known. Human beings in so far as they affect one another are in relationship, and their relationships can be studied. The object of the science is to produce rules about the behaviour of human beings in combination, as the object of chemistry is to produce rules about atoms in combination. These rules may claim only a low degree of probability, but within the limits set they will enable us to predict what combinations human beings will form in particular social circumstances. There are difficulties about this; the only one relevant here is that of the position of the administrator in relation to the group. If he affects the group he is for the sociologist in relationship with it; the more he affects it the more intimately he is a part of it, and the more necessary it is to study him in relation to the group as well as the group in relation to him. These are one social fact, not two. The sociological student of adminstration sets out to teach managers how to run their businesses better; he is apt to come back with a set of rules which say how managers are likely to behave, in relation to the various groups to which they belong. The perfect set of rules would say how managers *must* behave — meaning that if they did not behave thus they would in our society cease to be managers very soon.

This dilemma is quite familiar to us in the study of politics. We set out to improve the government of men; if we follow only the sociological school we come back with generalisations which explain why party bosses must exist, why they behave as they do, and why they would fall from power if they behaved in any other way. Most political scientists have at some stage of their careers been fascinated by the view of politics as an intricate pattern of forces in balance; but few have been able to rest content with it. Politics remains meaningless unless it has some relevance to the individual and his purposes, and is in some sense, however limited, under his control.

The second issue is closely related to this point. It seems impossible in ordinary usage to talk about administration except in terms of purpose. We administer to get something done; if there is no purpose, it is not administration. Yet purpose is particularly hard for the sociologist to handle, a difficulty common to sociology and psychology. Purpose is not a thing which we can directly observe in others. We know — at least we are convinced that we know — our own purposes, and we know what symptoms in our own actions belong to purpose. Other people's purposes we deduce from their actions, and the evidence is often difficult. Our own symptoms may not be typical; the others may deliberately or by accident mislead us; and in any case man's actions are never wholly rational. The word 'rational' is natural in this context; the idea of purpose is closely related to that of reason, and the concepts of reason and unreason, conscious, sub-conscious and unconscious, are a fruitful source of puzzles for philosophy and psychology. These difficulties are still present if we look away from the purpose of the manager, and put purpose into a group. The sociological study of administration would be the study of the organisation of a group in relation to its common purpose.

As political theorists we have been here before. 'Purpose' in ordinary speech means the purpose of some person; whose purpose is the common purpose of the group? If there is such a thing as a common purpose, the group is to that extent a person; if the group is a person, what then are the persons who compose it? If the General Will really is a Will, what becomes of you and me? Perhaps, as it is fashionable to say now, it is all a matter of using the wrong language: perhaps the word 'purpose' has meaning in regard to the individual, but is merely a source of confusion and false analogy when applied to the group.

The first difficulty, that of the leader who in one sense governs the group, in another sense is governed by it, is a paradox which we meet every day and get over well enough in practice. The second is a much more serious barrier to the sociological study of administration, and the difficulty is not eased by the determined efforts which have been made to outflank it. One successful school of sociology — that associated with Durkheim and with the British tradition in social anthropology — has set up its science on the assumption that the study of society can dispense with the concept of purpose. It has tried to use the language of physiology, not that of introspection. Sociology is treated as an analogue of physiology: purpose is rejected in sociological explanation, as teleology has been rejected by the nineteenth century in biological explanation. For the idea of 'purpose' are substituted the ideas of 'structure' and 'function'.

This is an attitude which it is difficult to sustain consistently, and few writers succeed in following their own rules. But the distinction is a real one. 'Purpose' implies a relation of means to an end. It is a 'straight line' relationship; straight lines can be linked, but in such a chain each link is related only to its neighbours. 'Function' implies a balance of parts interacting within a complex whole which tends towards equilibrium — an interlocking or circular relationship. The classical exposition is that in which Durkheim discusses at length the Division of Labour: the *purpose* of specialisation is to increase the specialist's income, the *social function* of specialisation is to maintain social solidarity. Individuals, as we know, introduce specialisation for their individual purposes: but if our point of interest is not the individual but society, for us the relevant thing about specialisation is not its relation to individual purposes, but its relation to other social facts.

This need not mean that we forget individual purpose or subordinate individual purpose to social function. The chemist in his profession disregards the physics of the atom and looks for chemical relationships: the physiologist thinks of the chemistry of the body in physiological terms of form, structure and function, and does not trouble about the nature of chemical bonds. Of course chemistry as defined is never quite adequate to the phenomena observed by the chemist; physiology is never quite adequate to the phenomena observed by the physiologist; the process of abstraction is always breaking down, but it is temporarily very fruitful in allowing progress to be made along a new line. Levels of study can be kept distinct, without implying that the thing studied is merely biological or merely chemical or merely physical. One can study the individual or study society without implying that the individual and society are eternally separate and contrasted.

All this is 'scientific' in principle; and (so far as a layman can judge) it has had real success in practice. It is true that Elton Mayo's story of the Hawthorne experiment has been told so often that it has become a sort of parable, more useful in sermons than in text-books; and probably there is not a large field in which changes in group relations can be measured by reference to a simple and uniform variable such as industrial output. But these doubts are not fatal to the claim of this sociology to be a science; at most, they suggest that it is moving away from the concept of science as a natural science, and back to the wider sense, the 'Baconian' sense, in which science includes any orderly empirical study of the natural world.

The new method ought in principle to be applicable to any group in any country; to a jungle village, or a factory, or a government office: hence the latest theme in the science of administration in the application of this sociological method to administrative groups. That is why we are being made familiar with the distinction between formal and informal organisation, and are taught to regard informal organisation as logically prior and practically more important. This is part of a general trend of thought; it is some time since the corresponding school in jurisprudence began to teach that formal law signifies nothing unless it is based on the social reality of custom.

On this analogy, formal organisation is law, informal organisation is custom. Formal organisation is to be found in the organisation chart and in the distribution of duties list, it is imposed by the manager as sovereign, or agent of the sovereign, to serve the purpose of the sovereign. Informal organisation is the structure of the group, and within the group is the manager, the titular sovereign himself; the group has its status system, its laws of solidarity and expansion, its parts are functionally related, and to its law the manager conforms. If the formal organisation does not fit the law of the social situation, so much the worse for the formal organisation; it is waste of paper.

This is a very summary view of a theme which permits many interesting variations. A good many of them invite detailed discussion; in the present context it is possible only to consider a few issues which are more general and perhaps less interesting.

There are, to begin with, three difficulties which are in theory not insuperable. In the *first* place, exponents of this new approach do not always play fair. They set out to seek conclusions about social life; they finish with conclusions about the good life. The good life, they teach, is that of the group; integration is happiness, extrusion from the group is unhappiness; unhappiness is the extreme evil, and it is our duty to eliminate it. A line of connection leads from Figgis and other pluralists, through the guild socialists and Miss Follett, to Elton Mayo and to much sociology which claims to be science and not philosophy. The science of groups can probably be disengaged from the ethics of groups; but no one has done it yet, and till it has been done this school of thought will repel many whose ethical presuppositions differ from theirs.

These remarks apply primarily to general sociologists of this school; the ethics of sociology have particularly odd effects when carried over into administration. To put the case concretely, is it the duty of miners to be happy or to produce coal? Of soldiers to be happy or to win wars? Of civil servants to be happy or to govern well? It is well enough to say that some integrated groups find happiness in efficiency; unfortunately other groups are equally happy, their morale is first-rate, and their contribution to the larger community is zero. Perhaps in time we may learn how to make the miserable happy and how to make the happy both industrious and good; but at present our repertoire of tricks is limited, and we find ourselves driving on the laggards by appeals to duty — duties towards state, duties towards one's class, duties towards humanity. Such exhortations are generally ineffectual, but everyone knows what they are meant to convey, and admits that in some circumstance or other they ought to be obeyed. In fact, it is not easy to find in modern society any group which is effectively self-contained: most men and women belong to many groups, and relations cutting across group boundaries are often more important than those within them. This is true at moments of crisis even for groups engaged in industrial production, which may still be relatively isolated in normal times; it is continuously true for public administration. Civil servants, it is true, are often deeply moved by group loyalty; but our main interest in studying the administrative group is to discover how to keep these partial loyalties within bounds. Pluralism will not do as an ethic for public servants.

Secondly, it is not derogatory to the important work which has been done on the sociology of industry to say that it is not the sociology of industrial administration; it is related to industrial administration only as social anthropology is related to colonial administration. So far the social anthropologists, though they have thought a lot, have said little about the sociology of white administrators in primitive countries; industrial sociologists and social psychologists have been equally shy in investigating the business man and the entrepreneur. There has been much talk but few experiments; good sociological books on administration are generally written by men like Mr. Chester Barnard, who use the language of industrial sociology to describe their own experience. This is a fascinating game; sociological language allows us for the first time to talk academically about things like 'empire-building', coffe-housing', office furniture, and office geography, things which we knew from experience to be important, but had hitherto been forced to classify as light relief.[6] This is a real gain; it makes it possible to talk impersonally about highly personal matters, it may make it a little easier to explain to beginners what they are likely to find in an administrative office, it may even help the administrators to think more clearly about their own problems.

All this is valuable; but the science of administration cannot grow out of the practice of administration unless empirical research is possible, and there are a good many practical difficulties about that. The managing director is likely to be a more elusive and recalcitrant guinea-pig than the factory operative. After all, what is *he* to get out of it? Even the fact of investigation may damage prestige, which is one of the administrator's main assets in dealing with his staff, his public and his superiors. As the Tavistock House 'school' suggest, the social investigator is a factor in the situation which he investigates, and the investigator of higher administration will not get far unless his presence adds to the prestige of higher administration. It would be wise for the present to avoid 'bad cases', cases in which there is public criticism and internal uncertainty, and to find administrators who are in their own and other men's estimation good administrators. It is on this basis that the researcher is most likely to be welcome, and that he is most likely to learn.

The *third* practical difficulty is that of recording experienc in an impersonal way. Most situations in public administration, and even in business administration, are extremely complicated, and different observers see different things in them; it would be possible for two honest and accurate historians to write quite different stories of the action of a government department in a crisis in its history. Notionally, there are two ways of overcoming this, which can be used singly or in combination. One is to train all researchers in a single school of thought, so that their interests are alike; they look for the same things and use the same language to describe them. The other is to abandon the study of big administration, and to look for very simple instances of administrative situations; even perhaps to create them artificially. The second trick is difficult to arrange; the first is all too easy. Schools of sociology tend to harden into cliques which are mutually hostile and unintelligible. What is more, they slip back easily into reliance on deduction as against observation; they are back in the 'spectral woof of impalpable abstractions', the 'unearthly ballet of bloodless categories',[7] from which they had hoped by science to break free.

These difficulties are quite serious; it is not easy to exclude ethics, to establish the atmosphere of confidence which is necessary to research, to maintain impersonality and objectivity in recording observation. But supposing them to be overcome, will the sociology of administration be the science of administration which we set out to find? The methods of sociology have been very successful in describing the work of offices and factories in terms of status, communications, and group solidarity; they have not been at all successful in dealing with the process of planning or with the place of the public in relation to the administrative group. Perhaps this is not accidental, but a necessary consequence of the procedure adopted by the science of sociology. The idea of administration, like the idea of government, cannot be separated from that of purpose; this form of sociology has made progress only by substituting for purpose the concept of function. Our trouble, as students of administration, is that we want to hold on to both. If we lose hold of purpose we cannot understand the administrator, because his role is to organise other men for a purpose which is not theirs; he is the government, the purpose is his purpose, even if he pursues it in the interests of the governed and under their influence.

But if we lose hold of function we are back in the old view of men as atoms, which is both false and ethically repugnant.

In this, I think, the student of administration is no worse off than other students of politics. Politics is primarily concerned with the giving of direction to human affairs. As Professor Laski used to say, the politician is the man who 'injects a stream of tendency' into affairs; so is the administrator. But politics must reckon also with the facts of the situation; the politician who ignores the laws of social equilibrium will come unstuck — so will the administrator. Is it then right to say that the study of administration is an inseparable part of political science?

This is too large an issue to pursue here. But it is safe to say that political scientists have perplexed themselves for centuries by attempting to hold together in one view two conceptions of the nature of politics, and that administrative scientists now find themselves in the same dilemma. If the analogy holds good, we cannot expect to find a science of administration based on the analogy of natural science, nor even one based on the wider eighteenth-century conception of scientific method. We can find science *for* administrators, and it is to be hoped that we shall; but the only science *of* administration will be science in the oldest sense of the word. It will be an organised body of knowledge which can be taught, but it will not claim that it conforms closely to the model of natural science, that it is in all its parts verifiable, or that is infinitely progressive. Administrative science, in fact, will be political science, and the political scientist, is in his profession condemned to live for ever upon the frontier between two worlds, the world of philosophy and the world of natural knowledge. This is a position of discomfort and responsibility: but that (after all) is politics.

Notes

1. There is a useful article on him by Dr. W. O. Henderson in *The Economic History Review*, 2nd ser., vol. IV (1951) p. 98.
2. Miss Mary Parker Follett is a conspicuous exception.

3. There is a good landmark in the year 1877, when Sir Francis Galton sought to exclude from the British Association for the Advancement of Science the section dealing with the Social Sciences, *Journal of the Royal Statistical Society* (Sept 1877), p. 468; quoted by Mr. S. G. Checkland in 'The Manchester School,' vol XIX 1951), p. 147.

4. F. C. Hooper, *Management Survey* (Pitman, 1948), p. 99.

5. Professor Dwight Waldo's book, *The Administrative State*, describes the similar effects of intellectual climate on early studies of public administration in the U.S.A.

6. Or to treat them satirically as Cornford treated them in *Microcosmographia Academica*, and Balchin in *The Small Back Room*.

7. F. H. Bradley, *Principles of Logic* (2nd ed), vol. II, p. 591.

A Note on Books

This article was written as a lecture, and few references are given in the footnotes. It may be useful to the political scientist to have a rather fuller reading list; this is not in any sense a bibliography.

General

Mary Parker Follett, *The New State*, 3rd impression, with an introduction by Lord Haldane (Longman's, 1920).

———— *Dynamic Administration*, collected papers on business administration, ed. H C. Metcalf and L. Urwick (Management Publications Trust: London, 1945—9).

L. Urwick and E. F. L. Brech, *The Making of Scientific Management*, 3 vol. (Management Publications Trust: London, 1945—9).

Dwight Waldo, *The Administrative State* (The Ronald Press Co.: N.Y., 1948).

F. C. Hooper, *Management Survey* (Pitman, 1948).

E. T. Elbourne, *Fundamentals of Industrial Administration*, 4th ed. (Macdonald and Evans, 1948).

'Taylorism'

F. W. Taylor's first influential papers ('Shop Management', 1903; 'The Art of Cutting Metals', 1906) are not very readily available. A good general survey is a symposium, *Scientific Management in American Industry*, ed. for the Taylor Society (Harper: N.Y., 1929).

Frank B. Gilbreth, *Motion Study* (D. Van Nostrand Co.) N.Y., 1911).

———— *Applied Motion Study* (Routledge, 1919).

(There are many text-books on modern practice.)

Deductive Theory
H. Fayol, *Industrial & General Administration*, trans. Coubrough (International Management Institute, 1930).
Oliver Sheldon, *The Philosophy of Management* (Pitman, 1924) ch. 2.
J. C. Mooney and A. P. Reilley, *Onward Industry; The Principles of Organisation* (1931).
L. Gulick and L. Urwick, *Papers on the Science of Administration* (Institute of Public Administration: N.Y., 1937).
L. Urwick, *The Elements of Administration* (Harper: N.Y., 1944).
E. F. L. Brech, *Management: its Nature & Significance*, 2nd ed., (Pitman, 1947).

The Sociology of Administration
Elton Mayo, *The Human Problems of an Industrial Civilisation* (Macmillan, 1933).
— ——— *The Social Problems of an Industrial Civilisation* (Routledge and Kegan Paul, 1949).
Chester Barnard, *The Functions of the Executive* (Harvard University Press, 1938).
——— *Organization and Management* (Harvard University Press, 1948).
F. J. Roethlisberger, W. J. Dickson and H. A. Wright, *Management & the Worker*, the detailed record of the 'Hawthorne Experiment' (Harvard University Press, 1941).
F. J. Roethlisberger, *Management & Morale* (Harvard University Press, 1941).
H. A. Simon, *Administrative Behavior* (Macmillan: N.Y., 1945).
H. A. Simon, D. W. Smithburg, and V. A. Thompson, *Public Administration* (Knopf: N.Y., 1950).
M. T. Copeland and A. R. Towl, *The Board of Directors & Business Management* (Harvard School of Business Administration, 1947).
W. B. D. Brown and W. Raphael, *Managers, Men and Morale* (Macdonald and Evans, 1948).
J. D. Glover and R. M. Hower, *The Administrator* (Irwin: Chicago, 1949). A book of case-studies in business administration produced by the Harvard Business School.
M. L. Mace, *The Growth & Development of Executives* (Harvard University Press, 1950).
Sune Carlson, *Executive Behaviour* (Stromberg, Stockholm, 1951).
Elliot Jaques, *The Changing Culture of a Factory* (Tavistock Publications, 1951).

11 Idiom in Political Studies*

The Carnegie Institute of Technology has been in labour for nearly ten years now: Professor Simon's last major work was the textbook on public administration published (jointly with Smithburg and Thompson) in 1950. The two books mentioned below give a first opportunity to assess the enterprise now in progress; but assessment is not easy.

Professor Simon's object has been to put the study of formal organizations on a proper basis. Three propositions: (*a*) 'In our society, preschool children and nonworking housewives are the only large groups of persons whose behavior is not substantially "organizational"'(*Organizations*, p. 2). (*b*) 'The effort devoted by social scientists to understanding organizations has not been large' (p. 5). (*c*) 'The literature leaves one with the impression that after all not a great deal has been said about organizations, but it has been said over and over in a variety of languages' (p. 5). From which follows the purpose of the book on *Organizations*: 'we wished to impose order without imposing a parochial point of view stemming from a particular or special conception of organization theory. We have tried to steer a middle course between eclecticism and provincialism' (p. 6).

So far, so good; it perhaps hardly needs saying now that Professor Simon is a man of high intelligence who aims high; he has grouped other able men round him; he has had access, cash, and technical resources beyond the reach of anyone outside the USA. If one scratches hard one may find minor points to argue about, as in any work of scholarship: but Professor Simon and his associates have passed beyond the confusion, *naiveté*, and unbalance of what he politely calls the 'classical' literature of administration theory. This is

*From *Political Studies*, VIII, no. 1 (Feb 1960).

serious work, on a subject of the highest importance; and it is
so well done that the issues it raises for debate are very large
issues. Hence the difficulty in making a quick assessment of
its permanent value.

The first point to note is that neither of these books is
easy to follow unless one knows the literature. *Organizations*
is not so much a textbook about organizations as a textbook
(highly compressed) about books about organizations. Probably the book had to be written in this way, since one of its
main objects was to order existing work by translating it into
a new 'common language', and the author's progress in this
would have been very hard to measure if it had not included
continuous references to the literature. Hence the book is a
textbook for teachers rather than a textbook for students; we
are being asked to consider whether we should cast our
teaching (perhaps also our research) about 'big organizations'
into this form. *Models of Man* is also difficult reading, for a
rather different reason: 'the essays collected here have
appeared in thirteen journals, representing statistics and all
the social sciences save anthropology' (p. vii). 'Social sciences' here excludes law, history, and philology, but includes
philosophy: the range is formidable, but one has to cope with
it if one is to grasp the game that is being played. (There is a
certain academic 'gamesmanship' about these activities, as
well as high seriousness.)

The second question then is whether it is we who are
being provincial, or Professor Simon. He is dealing with a
subject which we must agree to be central in modern political
science; he is trying to establish a common idiom; but *our*
idiom plays a very small part in *his* idiom. British political
science (including the study of big organizations) is based
largely on the study of law, history, and languages, and it is
expressed in their idioms: not in the idioms of economics,
sociology, psychology, nor in the related mathematical
formulations of games theory, input-output theory, communications theory, and statistical decision-making. The
point is not that Professor Simon writes jargon — he does
not, he writes plain English, illuminated now and then by an
agreeable deadpan humour; but that he writes in terms of
disciplines which we have not learnt, and ought perhaps to

learn from the beginning, as we learnt languages and history.

One could speculate about this gap, on the lines of Sir Charles Snow's lectures on 'The Two Cultures and the Scientific Revolution'. Have the scientific revolutionaries now become the 'establishment' in the USA? How will they stand in Britain a generation hence? This is speculation: but it seems plain that one cannot just write Professor Simon off as another simpleton dabbling in 'The *American* Science of Politics'. 'Scientism' (for good or ill) has as much claim to be international as legalism, historicism, or (to coin a word) philologism.

We therefore come (in the third place) to old and perhaps rather tedious questions about the nature and limits of scientific method, most recently expounded by Professor Brecht in his massive book on *Political Theory*. But there is at least some amusement to be got by looking at these questions again in relation to the results of very shrewd and learned work in a field where we think we can recognize the value (or otherwise) of the end-product. Professor Simon sets out to look for what is 'rigorous' and 'testable'; we applaud the contrast with what is sloppy and beyond the reach of evidence, with our nauseating daily diet of political and administrative babble. But in looking for 'rigour' and 'testability' his criteria are operational definition, mathematical deduction, statistically useful data; 'proverbial' and 'anecdotal' are bad words. Is not Professor Simon in this underrating the power of his own discipline, in which the standards should be set by its own leaders, not by logicians analysing other disciplines? To take two examples of 'innovation' and 'planning' at random, R. W. Southern on *The Making of the Middle Ages*, Professor Devons on *Planning in Practice*, cannot be rated very highly according to the logic of scientific method; but they have that solidity of scholarship which is regarded as 'rigour' and 'testability' in fields familiar to us. Indeed, they even seem to us to state 'intersubjectively transmissible knowledge', which according to Professor Brecht is the prerogative of scientific method strictly defined.

This is not to say that Professor Simon's 'scientism' is allowed to damage his 'scholarship'. Up to a point to be discussed below, what he says is compact, lucid, and well argued – what is more, it is correct, tested by the non-scientific criteria which we use every day, as small creatures living in big organizations. Professor Simon's idiom serves (up to a point) very well indeed; the suspicion suggested here is merely that one could restate his material (if one were a good enough scholar) in a 'humane' rather than a 'scientific' idiom without practical loss, and that one would have to do so in order to communicate adequately with an audience trained in the 'humaner letters'. But it must be admitted that the exercise of playing with a mathematical idiom is great fun, even for an elderly Arts don; and one almost always gains something by exercise in translation. The point is merely that one would also gain something (more, perhaps?) by setting to work to translate some pages of *Organizations* into Greek prose.

The fourth and last issue is not really one of scientism in particular, but of empirical study in general. Professor Simon is well aware that he is operating on the frontiers of political philosophy. This shows up most clearly in three ways. The first point is that a political theory must include a view of human nature. 'Propositions about organizations are statements about human behaviour, and imbedded in every such proposition, explicitly or implicitly, is a set of assumptions as to what properties of human beings have to be taken into account to explain their behavior in organizations' (*Organizations*, p. 6). For the purposes of order and idiom, Professor Simon and his associates follow good canons of method in choosing a 'naive' model of man, set out briefly in two pages (pp. 9–11) of *Organizations*. The method here is to take a simple model and see how far it carries you: this one carries a long way, but not the whole way. *Models of Man* is more ambitious. 'When these essays are viewed in juxtaposition, it can be seen that all of them are concerned with laying foundations for a science of man that will accommodate his dual nature as a social and as a rational animal' (p. vii). Professor Simon's formula for his answer is 'bounded rationality', and his 'message' is 'do not despair of rationality because you cannot be wholly rational'. This probably seems sound sense to most of us; but is it not

metaphysics, rather than science? In a scientific culture
perhaps something is gained by restating basic assumptions in
the language of science; but it does seem sometimes that
Professor Simon thinks he is demonstrating new 'truths'
when he is in fact restating old 'truths' in a new context.

The other two points also touch classic issues of political
philosophy. In this reviewer's judgment it is right that in
Models of Man Professor Simon bases his 'political' system on
'two principal mechanisms — the mechanism of influence and
the mechanism of choice' (p. viii); and that Organizations
reaches its peroration in a chapter on 'Planning and Innovation'. But it is not in the end easy to see what new points
Professor Simon has added to the old literature of power,
authority, and collective choice, except some clarification
and reformulation; and the last chapter of *Organizations*
(though it is good reading) is clinched and hammered
together much less convincingly than the rest of the book.
Professor Simon and his collaborators blame the state of the
literature for this relative weakness, which they perceive
clearly: is it not perhaps that at this stage of the argument
(the decisive one in a political theory of big organizations)
they have exhausted the possibilities of the 'naive' model of
man which they postulated at the outset?

It is worth repeating that these difficulties do not arise
because of Professor Simon's 'scientism', though
this gives them their specific form; it is at these points that
we 'empiricists' always stick and look helplessly towards the
political philosophers, who remain dumb, or talk about
something else. There is a suspicion abroad that political
philosophers do not answer because they are too lazy to find
out about modern politics for themselves, and too proud to
read the literature about it. Admittedly, a good deal of the
literature looks rather scruffy when seen in good society: but
(not in Professor Simon's group only, but in the work of
political sociologists and political economists) it has taken a
turn for the better since Professor Easton published *The
Political System* in 1953, and even since Mr. Crick submitted
his thesis in 1956. Empirical politics is no longer an
intellectual slum: perhaps some philosophers would care to
visit us?

12 Decision Making in Communities

In recent years the word "decision-making" has served as a focus for collaboration among social scientists. The word itself, in its every-day sense, indicates something of common interest to economists, sociologists, lawyers and psychologists, as well as to political scientists like myself. In the same period, electrical engineering has developed to the point that it suggests analogues for human brains and human communities. Hence mathematical formulations which can be applied directly in electronic systems have come to be regarded also as fruitful tools in analysing human systems. I refer particularly to information theory and cybernetics, games theory, and statistical decision theory: branches of mathematics in the strictest sense, but labelled by names which in themselves suggest the human analogy.

Still taking the word "decision" in its colloquial sense, it is easy to see why this field of study should seem important. We are all affected by the "decisions" of individuals and communities; as man's control of nature increases, so human "decisions" play a larger and larger part in determining his fate. We are therefore impelled to seek to understand other people's decisions, so that we can foresee and profit by our foresight; and also to improve our own decisions, so that we choose the path of action most likely to lead us to the goals we seek.

Traditional questions
This anxiety to explain and to improve decisions has an ethical and even metaphysical aspect. A political scientist, familiar with the traditions of his subject, recognises the line of descent from very old questions about the individual

*Paper read at the British Association, Aberdeen, 4 September 1963.

will and the general will. There is the problem of the individual choice.

> Of Providence, Foreknowledge, Will and Fate,
> Fixt Fate, free will, foreknowledge absolute.

There is the problem of whether many individuals can come together to choose freely in a way common to all of them: Can there be a general or political will? Or is the appearance of a common will no more than the resultant of individual will? Finally, and most important, what is a "good" will, what is a "bad will"? Can one choose ends as well as means? If not, how can there be "freedom of the will"? If so, by what criterion can one choose between ends? What could such a criterion be, but another end, chosen by no criterion?

Probably most political scientists today feel that Milton was right to set the damned angels to debate these questions in hell. This is one reason why political philosophy seems dead; we have all played all the moves so many times that we are like rats running the same maze for ever. Hence modern political scientists seek to explore decisions by logical and empirical methods, like mathematicians and naturalists, not like philosophers. Political scientists are soaked in a tradition (that of Plato, Aristotle, Machiavelli, Hobbes, Rousseau, Marx) in which philosophy and science meet, and we are not likely to forget that all social science involves value judgments. But let us see if we can make some progress as scientists with the aid of concepts and techniques new in this generation.

Decisions, power and society

To make progress at all, one must accept the fact that "decision" is not itself an operational concept. No one has ever seen a decision; is it extended in time or space, has it mass and movement, does it transmit energy? And so on. Clearly these are somehow nonsense questions: yet before we can study decisions we must have a working notion about how to recognise one when we come across it.

Different social sciences tackle this problem of defining a decision in different ways, indeed one social science (for instance, psychology) may use several different approaches. To some extent, it is a mere act of faith to think we are all talking about the same thing, and that our investigations will in the end meet. But I doubt if our state is really worse than that of the physicists who centuries ago set out to investigate something called "matter".

To take one or two examples. For mathematical decision theorists, as I understand it, decision is no more than a solution to an intellectual problem. Solution may become easier if the problem is re-stated in logically equivalent terms: and it is important to invent new procedures for solution.

In legal terms, a judge is certainly entitled to re-state his problem of decision so as to obtain a more just or elegant solution. But he may re-state it only in forms of logic legally recognised, and he can decide only within a procedure legally recognised. In law, a decision not "properly" taken is no decision; the decider is socially as well as logically constrained, and a solution logically perfect may be socially non-existent, "null and void", if proper procedure has not been observed.

The political scientists are to some extent in the same boat as lawyers; we have to ask ourselves (and advise others) about what is "constitutional". In some sense a decision which is "unconstitutional" — for instance, to march a platoon of the Guards into the Palace of Westminster and exclude half the House of Commons — is not a decision within the political system at all.

But we are also concerned with just such a situation as that; we study the exercise of political power, wherever one meets it, within the constitution or outside it. People talk about "naked power" as if it were less decent than power in full morning dress. What is the sense of this? What is the same and what is different about power exercised by (say) President Kennedy, Khrushchev, Hitler, the latest Latin American military dictator?

Of course, "power" is as slippery a word as "decision": but at least it adds the notion of a will or choice *which is in fact executed*. A man is *powerful* if his *decisions* are *effective.* Robinson Crusoe could in this sense be powerful even before Man Friday joined him on his desert island; but we are interested here in power as something *between men.* Clearly this is always a bilateral relationship; government and people, leaders and led, parent and child, master and servant, employer and employed. Such relationships inhere in a society, not in individuals: power vanishes if detached from its social context.*

Community power studies

Hence attempts to study political decision-making empirically are of necessity studies of communities, including organisations. It is true that there is a tradition of psychological study of the personalities of individual leaders: but the personality of the leader fits into a role relationship with the personalities of followers, and this role relationship varies in different societies and organisations.

Hence the existence of a field known as "community power studies". The basis of these is that public controversies about the nature of power are generally controversies about the nature of supreme power in a great society; democracy versus dictatorship, economic power versus political power, in societies on the scale of Britain, the U.S.A. and the U.S.S.R. These controversies cannot be settled empirically by study of the great societies in which they arise; the scale is too vast for research workers, the problem of access to information is too difficult. Hence, let us choose first the scale of study at which we can be reasonably certain of the validity and reliability of our observations; then let us see what questions we can answer by studies at that level.

These community studies range in scale from villages of 400 or 500 people to towns of 50,000 and perhaps larger. Similar techniques have been applied to the study of decision-making in cities as great as New York and Chicago, but only at the cost of abandoning any real attempt to study the community as a whole. No one maintains that scale

---

*I am here using "power", "will", "decision", "choice", as related but not identical terms in the political context. This needs fuller discussion.

makes no difference, and that what is learnt about power in small communities can be applied without change to great societies. But at least we are beginning to learn something fairly solid about decision-making at lower levels within the great society.

Authoritarian and democratic hypotheses

Such studies of necessity embrace a mass of details and are hard to summarise. The approach offered here may not be universally accepted.

To my mind, studies of the politics of small communities have been based on hypotheses drawn primarily from the questions which we ask about great societies. There are two groups of these hypotheses.

One group may be described as authoritarian or Machiavellian. It stresses the unity of power in any society. In so far as a society has unity it is (as it were) an interconnected hydraulic system: power may appear in separate sectors of society — political, economic, ecclesiastical, military, cultural and so on — and these sectors may appear isolated. But in fact power is attracted to power; it seeps through interconnecting channels, so that in any society, great or small, there is a single system of power.

Those who sponsor such views always state them as general descriptive truths about society. To put it in Hobbesian terms, one society can only have one "sovereign", or it will soon cease to be one society. To put it in Marxist terms, all power is one and is economic power. To put it in modern American terms, there is in every society a "power elite" which takes collective decisions for the society as a whole.

These descriptions are always in a sense normative; this is the way things are, and it cannot be right to disregard the nature of things. Some authors go further, and positively recommend unity of command, strong government, as necessary to build a strong society.

The opposite group is committed to the view that there can exist societies corresponding to the specification of radical democratic theorists. This is (very briefly) that it is possible for general law to prevail over personal power; and that by law arrangements can be made so that actual power (or at least the means of access to power) can be divided equally among a large population. In other words, there is a constitution enacting universal suffrage: that constitution is obeyed, and voters do in fact choose who shall hold public office under the constitution. What is more, "choose" here must mean to "choose deliberately between real alternatives in the light of reasonably good information" — not just to mark a cross unthinkingly or at random.

This group of concepts is more openly normative; one cannot recommend democratic ideals with confidence if no example can be found anywhere of a community, large or small, which approximates to them. But to do this it must at least find some communities in which free men choose deliberately.

Some conclusions

These two hypotheses or sets of hypotheses represent in a rough way the two "ideologies" which have in recent years divided international society; the totalitarian view and the democratic view. In fact, neither works out at all well when applied to the study of small communities. The general picture derived from these studies might perhaps be summarised in the following propositions.

(1) It is difficult to find any community in a modern society which does not comprise several different sectors. These sectors live on the whole co-operatively together and there may be cross-membership between them; the doctor and the works manager belong to the same golf club, the farmer and the works foreman go to the same church. But in each sector its own social life is dominant.

(2) The structure of sectors varies. Clearly the group of doctors, comprising general practitioners, their assistants, perhaps consultants and nurses also, has a different power-structure (or decision-making structure) from the group comprising the factory manager and his immediate subordinates, or the branch secretary of a Trade Union and his committee.

(3) In modern society virtually all groups or sectors look outwards from the small community as well as inwards. To

take those named so far — doctors, factory managers, golf clubs, churches, works foremen, farmers, Trade Union officials — each clearly is "tied into" a national situation by professional skills, national organisations, and government policies.

(4) One of these sectors may be called the "political" sector. But it is not easy to give as sharp a definition to the political sector as to other sectors. It will not do to define it as the sector primarily concerned with community decisions. There is no sector thus specially concerned. To some extent each sector acts autonomously and so decides for the community in its own sphere, not completely unchecked. To some extent, decisions go by default; nothing is decided, therefore particular (foreseeable) consequences follow.

But two criteria may be suggested:—

(a) In Western democracies the political sector consists of elected persons and those concerned to organise competition for success in elections.

(b) The role of these elected persons is in many ways specific but it also has a certain generality. The powers given to the mayor and Council by law may be specific and fairly narrow, yet the "local authority" stands for the community in a general representative capacity. At the lowest, this may be no more than a secular ritual (sometimes allied with ecclesiastical ritual): nevertheless, without it the community cannot recognise itself as a community.

(5) In other respects, the political sector (Professor Dahl of Yale calls it "the political sub-culture") does not differ essentially from other sub-sectors. It consists of people living their careers in an established pattern of senior or junior, more or less skilled, more or less ambitious people. Entry on the career is often by co-option: it runs in families, as do other jobs, and (even apart from such existing connections) one can often meet elder statesmen on local councils who say that one of their main tasks is to find good people to "bring on to the council", for all the world like industrialists talking about management succession.

(6) Yet in Western democracies the character of the political sector is stamped by electoral competition. The rules of competition differ a good deal in different places within

England, and differ still more between England and the U.S.A. In extreme cases the forms of election are no more than ritual, as success is settled in advance by the process of nomination. But even in the extreme case the ritual is a ritual of submission to the electorate, of asking as a favour that the voter should give you his vote. In normal cases there is an element of ritual and also an element of social reality. The politician is always in some degree dependent on the voter; to manipulate votes he must study voters. Thus where there is a wide suffrage and competitive elections those in the political sector must look at the whole community from the peculiar angle of the vote-getter. A doctor has other interests besides his patients, a politician has other interests besides voters. But without patients and voters these two sectors do not exist functionally at all.

(7) This brings us to the question of the voter. The idea of "the voter's choice" has been much mauled by social scientists: it has been shown that the voter is in general ill-informed, irrational and bound by habit, and that he does not make decisions in the sense called for by radical democratic theory. This is true so far as it goes: but I know of no study which attempts to apply in this field psychological findings about the relation of rationality and alertness in choice to intensity of concern. The voter is in general *less* concerned about a voting decision than about a choice of motor car, or washing machine, or hair style, or new hat. He or she generally takes *less* trouble about voting than about many other decisions, and this is relevant to the design of electoral persuasion.

But note two things to the voter's credit. First, that in the normal situation of democratic politics, the voter is pretty sensible to arrange his priorities in this way. This is a society of many sectors, and successful decisions in his own sector may mean more to a voter than anything that happens in the political sector. It is also a society of families, and family decisions may be even more vital than professional decisions. The voter would be a politician himself if he took political advertising as seriously as its authors take it. Secondly, there are recurrent exceptions to this normal pattern. If the political sector suddenly impinges on professional and family life, then the voter (both in England and America) is fairly well equipped to fight back. These sharp bouts of activity need time, skill and energy; on the whole, the higher the social and educational class of the voter, the better he or she is equipped to make a fuss successfully. The feeble are still feeble, even under universal suffrage, and elected persons cannot afford to spend much time on those who have little or no "nuisance value".

(8) It should be noted, finally, that the political sector, like other sectors, has reference outside the local community. The good G.P. has to keep abreast of medical literature and to know where to turn on behalf of his patients. Similarly, the local politician works within a framework of national politics, and his local success depends partly on his skill in this. He may (like the ambitious doctor) wish to use his skills and his local success to move upwards and away from the local community. But that issue does not concern us here.

"Who runs this place?"

John Gunther, the American journalist, has always been an intelligent amateur in this sort of enquiry, and he used a familiar catch-phrase in his reporting of local politics in the 1930s — "Who runs this place?" Methodical study in a fair number of cases suggests that one can never give a straight answer, at least in Western democracies.

The answer is never one man acting as boss, nor yet an oligarchy who fix everything behind the scenes. Yet the sector organisation of society indicates pretty clearly who are the key men and women in each sector of the community, and these people can be brought to co-operate temporarily and for limited purposes. In the U.S.A. it is often an elected person who takes the lead in co-operation; I believe that this is less common in Britain.

The answer is never that there is rational democracy of equal and reflective electors — nor is there anything at all like it. But in spite of this, elections are essential to the system: they shape the political sector in a special way (this too is not the same in the U.S.A. and in Britain) and they offer a weapon at hand for the redress of grievances, to those who know how to use it.

Small communities and great societies
These conclusions seem to me valid for the communities which have been studied. But they should not be drawn beyond that point and treated as general laws.

As was explained, this kind of study was developed because of anxieties over authoritarian and democratic government in the great society. It reveals in small societies a kind of political life which does not fit the text-book categories of either form of government. There is a temptation then to project these conclusions up to the level of political life in great societies such as America and Britain, even to treat them as sociological conclusions about political decision-making in general. I see no scientific justification for this.

First, there is the question of scale. Local studies are in their nature limited to communities in which the sociologist can study face to face relations. Scale limits observation and probably also changes the nature of the operations.

Secondly, there is the question of efficiency. A small community can react with reasonable speed to changes in its situation if the sort of pluralist institutions described are worked by intelligent people. But in a national community such institutions would work more slowly; and the time available for reaction to change is not longer. Perhaps in large states it is impossible for decisions to retain any rational quality unless they are taken in a more hierarchical and authoritarian way; or conversely, if decisions are taken in a pluralist way, they rank as decisions only by default, since events move too fast for pluralist decision-making to catch up with them. This might be a fair comment on British and American decision-making about internal affairs in the 1950s.

Thirdly, these studies of small communities within the state perhaps leave out what is for a political scientist the essence of the matter. These communities can be grasped empirically, but they are not in the fullest sense political communities, for two reasons. The question of force, internal and external is in abeyance; no one in the community has supreme power, legal or physical, over life and death. Nor is a claim made for supreme loyalty, no one is asked to die for Glyn Ceiriog or Glossop or Newhaven, and inexorably called upon to answer.

Dr. Frankenberg's analogy, I believe, carries us a long way in the analysis of decision-making about the bomber offensive, much further than we have been taken by Sir Charles Snow. It would perhaps also illuminate the decision to produce and use nuclear weapons, an affair continuous with that to which Sir Charles refers. These decisions, I have no doubt, were pluralist in structure: but they were unitary in the loyalties they compelled. The ultimate loyalties, the ultimate sanctions are rarely invoked; yet they give a special character to the political life of sovereign states.

Some British Studies

Birch, A. H. *Small Town Politics. A Study of Political Life in Glossop* (O.U.P., 1959).

Bulpitt, J. C. 'Party Systems in Local Government', *Political Studies*, XI, no. 1 (1963) p. 11.

Donnison, D. V. *Welfare Services in a Canadian Community: A Study of Brockville, Ontario* (University of Totonto Press, 1958).

Epstein, A. L. *Politics in an Urban African Community* (Manchester University Press, 1958).

Frankenberg, R. *Village on the Border* (Cohen and West, 1957).

Lee, J. M. *Social Leaders and Public Persons*, Clarendon Press (forthcoming).

Stacey. M. *Tradition and Change: A Study of Banbury* (O.U.P., 1960).

Watson, W. 'Children's Play in a Scottish Mining Community', *Folklore*, LXIV (1953).

Williams, W. M. 'The Sociology of an English Village: Gosforth', *International Library of Social Reconstruction* (London, Routledge and Kegan Paul, 1956).

Some American Studies

Banfield, E. C. *Political Influence* (with special reference to Chicago) (Chicago: Free Press of Glencoe, 1961).

Dahl, R. A. *Who Governs?* (Yale University Press, 1961).

Hunter, Floyd. *Community Power Structure* (Chapel Hill, 1953).

—— *Top Leadership, U.S.A.* (Chapel Hill, 1959).

Mills, C. Wright. *The Power Elite* (O.U.P., 1956).

Sayre, Wallace and Herbert Kaupman. *Governing New York City: Politics in the Metropolis* (Russel Sage Foundation Publication, 1960).

Decision Theory

For a brief and lucid introduction:—

Johnston, J. 'Decision Theory', *Progress* (Spring 1963) at p. 164.

13 Models of Collective Decision-making*

A Why study "collective decision-making"?
1. The attraction of this theme is that is appears to stand at a cross-road in social science, raising positive and normative issues of great complexity in various disciplines.

2. At least four issues can be distinguished, but these are closely interwoven.

1 *Positive*
How are individual and collective decisions in fact taken? This involves on the one hand individual psychology, on the other hand the disciplines which study the processes at work in collectivities of various kinds, such as social psychology, social anthropology, sociology, administration, political science, and indeed history. Such inquiries are concerned with "power" and "process" in collective decision, not with their legitimacy or their effectiveness.

2 *Normative*
Men all agree that human decisions are "imperfect" and that we need "better decisions". Analytically, it is possible to separate the moral quality of decisions and the rational quality of decisions.

a. *Ethical*. There are many variants: but at least one very strong trend in ethics places goodness in the decider, not in the decision. That is to say, a decision is important for moral evaluation only in so far as it is a choice made by a person, and is deliberate and willed.

b. *Rational*. A definition of rationality as ethically neutral is quoted below (par. 13). In the last resort, such rationality

*From *The Social Sciences: Problems and Orientations* (The Hague, Paris, La Haye: Mouton/UNESCO, 1968 pp. 356–70). © UNESCO 1968.

might be programmed on a computer. Statistical decision theory, which is concerned with maximizing the rationality of decisions in this sense, is a branch of mathematics relating to procedures for men or machines.

But this analytic procedure does violence to the ordinary use of language, which plays with paradoxes about "heart" and "reason" ("le coeur a ses raisons que la raison ne connaît pas") but does not accept a total divorce between them. Much of the "agony of decision" (whether individual or collective) arises out of this dilemma, and one is reluctant to define agony out of existence.

3 *Juristic*
The Anglo-American tradition in particular regards legal rules as being alive only in decisions; "law in action" involves judgment on a case in court, and at the same time, inseparable from the judgment, its *ratio decidendi*. But any theory of law is bound to be concerned with the relation between rules and decisions, since this is the link between legal logic and social action.

4 *Political*
This will be discussed more fully below. The problem of democracy may be formalized as that of amalgamating individual preferences so as to form a collective choice in such a way that equal weight is given to the preferences of each individual.

B Procedural conditions
3. Professor Kenneth Arrow,[1] following other models, distinguishes four methods of social choice: voting, the market, dictatorship, convention. In the following treatment "voting" becomes "aggregation", "dictatorship" becomes "authority" (the latter is the usage of J. de V. Graaff[2]); "convention" is disregarded, being (as specified by Arrow) something exogenous to the collective process discussed, like the weather. It has been difficult to decide whether to attempt any treatment of the "market model" here. This course has been rejected largely on practical grounds (the subject is a vast one) and on personal grounds (I am not

qualified to attempt it). The approach is therefore political in a very broad sense, including decision-making in all formally organized collectivities, for instance religious orders and business organizations as well as states and official public bodies within states. This does in a secondary sense involve reference to the "market model", for instance as regards unanimity and bargaining (par. 16) and as regards the treatment of urban politics as a "market place" of dealers, each seeking to maximise influence (par. 23a). But these are "markets" within a setting of formal organization. I am bound to say that I find it difficult to imagine what a market could be (except as formal model) outside a setting involving law and (in a minimal sense) politics.

4. A formally organized collectivity is one within which there is a recognized procedure for decision. This is true even for a voluntary society in so far as it has rules, including rules for the change of rules, and rules about the validity of collective acts done in specified ways. Such collectivities, voluntary but formal, may be to some extent isolated from the general legal system in force. But this is exceptional, and in most states formal procedures are part of a coherent hierarchy of rules about valid acts, in public and private capacities.

5. So far as formal individual decisions are concerned, I should adopt the late Professor J. L. Austin's analysis of "performative utterances".[3] The words "I hereby marry this woman" are not a statement, but an act, *provided that* they are said in circumstances which satisfy certain conditions specified in detail by Professor Austin. One aspect of these conditions is that the act must conform to specified rules of social recognition. The circumstances may vary from those of strict legal formality (as in the transfer of land) to those of merely social obligation (as when I promise aloud something with at least one other person present as a witness). The act of voting is in this sense a "performative utterance" procedurally determined. "I vote for Mr. A." (whether said, or performed otherwise) is a valid "unit of decision" if and only if it meets certain procedural conditions.

6. So far as these general conditions are concerned, I should adopt Professor H. L. A. Hart's analysis,[4] to the effect

that one condition necessary to the existence of a legal system is that it should have "rules of recognition specifying the criteria of legal validity, and rules of change and adjudication, which are effectively accepted as common public standards of official behaviour by its officials".

7. These formal conditions (or equivalents of them) are necessary before one can proceed to logical and operational analysis of collective decision-making.

C Forms of Procedure

8. It is then possible to distinguish two classes of procedure for this purpose, aggregation and authority. Consensus, which is not strictly speaking a form of procedure, also requires mention in this context.

1 *Aggregation*

9. Separate decisions (which might include a decision to abstain) are recorded for each qualified member of the collectivity deciding. These decisions (which may be preference schedules of some complexity) are then summed by a formally valid procedure. Such procedural rules may be extremely complex, because of political manoeuvring or because of attempts to secure either fairness or a particular weighting. But suppose as an example that one takes "voting" in its ordinary usage, as referring to a relatively simple form of procedure for aggregation. Suppose then that votes are cast on a single issue, Yes — No — Abstain, on the basis of one man one vote. Then the simple majority rule, that the target is Votes cast/2 + 1, has an intuitive appeal. But even in this one dimension the rule may vary over the whole range of requirements from the requirement of "1 + 1" (i.e. the minimum which is not pure "authority") to the requirement of unanimity. As explained in par. 16 the rule of unanimity (as an extreme case) creates a "vote market" of a peculiar kind.

2 *Authority*

10. In this case the "rule of recognition" specifies that one person (or more than one specified person) acting by defined procedures can take decisions legally binding on members of

a defined collectivity. In practice "the authority" will generally be a member of the collectivity, as defined for other purposes; that is to say, the authority will be bound by the authority's decisions till they are formally changed. But this is not itself a formal condition.

11. It should be noted that the two cases, aggregation and authority, cannot be completely separated. *Voters* in a state are never defined so as to include all its living "members", and therefore they exercise collective authority over those not enfranchised. *Authorities* will decide by aggregation except in the limiting case where the authority consists of one natural person.

3 *Consensus*

12. The word "consensus" has appeared a good deal in recent discussions about democracy, but it does not seem to have any single meaning.

(1) It might be used as a generic word for some particularly strict aggregation rule; unanimity or close to it. But this is not a common usage.

(2) It might be used to deny the presuppositions on which rules of aggregation are based, offering some other model instead of a particularistic model (see pars. 35–37 below). This seems to be implied in some forms of usage, but it is rarely made explicit, perhaps because of the difficulties involved in specification.

(3) The word is certainly used to describe authority in a rather mild form. The decisions of the authority are open to public discussion, before and after they are made. Consensus in this sense exists if the discussion is genuinely open and if its trend is on the whole favourable, or at least not hostile, to the decisions taken by authority.

(4) Attempts may be made to formalize this style of government, that of authority exercised subject to opinion. Prescribed stages of discussion may be specified as procedures binding on authority and enforceable by the intervention of an independent authority; for instance, veto by a Roman tribune, or judicial scrutiny by the American Supreme Court. This requires a formal "separation of powers", but this presents no greater or less difficulty than any other procedural stipulation (see par. 3 above).

(5) One finds (finally) that it is sometimes said that consensus exists within a society in so far as its members share values and norms. This is sometimes no more than a tautology since a society does not exist except in so far as its members share values and norms: but it also suggests the problems (not particularly relevant here) of degrees of integration, and of society's capacity to tolerate cleavage and conflict.

D Formal paradoxes

13. It is generally expected that formal decision-making, individual and collective, should be in a formal sense rational. This can be expressed as a matter of definition and axiom; or as a norm, that irrationality is intellectually and ethically "wrong" and that it is likely to tend towards the extinction of the group practicing it; or as a statement about men in general as they really exist, a statement regarded as being empirically true on the whole, even though exceptions are discovered. Various definitions of rationality in this formal sense have been offered; the following is clear and convenient: "A rational man is one who behaves as follows: (1) he can always make a decision when confronted with a range of alternatives; (2) he ranks all the alternatives facing him in order of his preference in such a way that each is either preferred to, indifferent to, or inferior to each other; (3) his preference ranking is transitive; (4) he always chooses from among the possible alternatives that which ranks highest in his preference ordering; and (5) he always makes the same decision each time he is confronted with the same alternatives."[5]

14. It should be noted that there is not necessarily anything irrational (formally or in practice) in deciding to leave a matter to chance. But this can be so only if one has "chosen chance", not if chance is accepted unawares nor if chance has to be accepted whether one likes it or not.

15. The paradoxes here described beset both *aggregation* and *authority*. As will be seen, they are largely (but not wholly) formal in character.

1 *The Condorcet paradox*

It is possible to construct cases in which a collectivity of voters, each voting consistently, will in successive votes prefer A to B, B to C and C to A.[6] This arises because voters have different orders of preference, and it may not be possible to amalgamate these consistently either by successive votes or by any aggregation rule. Prof. Duncan Black[7] has an attractive formal solution, but probably it would be of practical value only in small collectivities.

2 *Choice by multiple criteria*
The same paradox afflicts choice by authority if there are several separate criteria of choice which all rank equally. This is formally the same case as that of several voters each with his separate order of preference, each schedule counting equally towards a decision.

3 *Intensity of preference*
Procedures can be found to enable a voter to express not only rank order but intensity of preference: he may (for instance) be allowed multiple votes or fractional votes, so that he can set out scales of preference with unequal intervals, and these scales can then be amalgamated, subject to risks of a "Condorcet cycle". Authority has greater difficulty in dealing with this problem, unless it uses the price mechanism or takes what are in effect straw votes (opinion surveys) for its own guidance.

4 *Inter-personal comparisons of utility*
Authority is deemed to seek a situation which is Pareto-optimal;[8] that is to say, one in which someone is better off and none is worse off than in any other situation possible at the time. The person who is better off may of course be the authority itself if he (or they) are within the collectivity concerned. Even this weak criterion is difficult to apply inter-personally unless "good" ("utility" or "welfare") is defined in specific material or monetary terms; the problem becomes even more difficult if we seek to offset gains and losses of utility as between persons. Cardinal utility (which can be summed) can be calculated only in crudely material terms: ordinal utility is difficult to amalgamate and difficult to translate into cardinal utility. The only criterion which has

had some acceptance is that of Von Neumann and Morgenstern,[9] drawing on the probabilities of various outcomes to provide numbers with which to measure preference strength. But Arrow is right to treat this as not relevant to problems of social choice.

5 *Decision-making under risk or uncertainty*

Decisions about courses of action, whether by voters or by authority, involve calculations of uncertain future events. The orthodox view is that such events should be given a probability number based on the best evidence available, and that this figure should then be used in weighting factors and deciding on a course of action; in fact, that the decision is to accept a gamble at odds assessed as carefully as possible (on "form" and not through a betting ring or totalizator). To this G. L. S. Shackle replies that critical decisions are of a "one-off" character, and that big single things cannot properly be handled by the statistics of large numbers. Hence, his preference for "subjective probability": the use in calculations of the decision-maker's own state of mind about contingencies, expressed as his potential surprise if events should turn out against him. H. A. Simon[10] attacks the realism of using elaborate calculations in big life-and-death decisions on the rather different ground that this is not in fact how organizations survive; that in fact their decisions are not aimed at maximizing but at "satisficing", at achieving (with a margin of safety) what is necessary to survive in a given environment, and that this is in its context more "rational" than decision-making directed always to a maximum.

16. Unanimity in voting with independence of voters is exempt from these paradoxes of preference aggregation and of maximization in conditions of uncertainty. This is because it will (unless tacitly modified, as usuallly happens in practice) produce a market of a peculiar kind. Unless one postulates identity of interests between members of a collectivity, the requirement of unanimity will lead to a situation in which each participant has strong incentives to maximize the value of his vote by introducing options for decision, not so that they may be adopted but so as to establish bargaining

counters which can be used in a "game" of coalitions played for the distribution of a common stock of benefits. The theory of such "games" has been excellently formalized,[11] but in general from the point of view of players and their pay-offs. The question itself is verbal: but one is inclined to say that (as in a game of poker) the outcome is an "event", not a "collective decision". This is without prejudice to the question whether a "market model" of the usual kind should be regarded as a "model of collective decision-making". A "market decision" has no ethical content (par. 2 (2) (a)), but is does offer a rational solution to the problem of maximizing utility for a collectivity, and this the unanimity game does not do. But in discarding this method of using unanimity to evade paradoxes, it is perhaps judicious to leave the way open (Section F) for a different line of approach not based on the assumptions made in par. 9 and 10.

E Empirical studies
17. Taking the field of political science alone, one finds that an immense amount of "field-work" has been done on the study of collective decision-making, with ambiguous results. Fields of study overlap, but can perhaps be summarized under three headings:
1. Electoral behaviour
2. Community power studies
3. Administrative behaviour.

1 Electoral behaviour
18. Voting studies have attracted more research resources than any other field of political science, for three reasons. It is natural to look for a numerical basis for political study: and voting records offer the largest store of "political numbers" readily available. The prediction of electoral trends and the exercise of influence over voters affect large practical interests. The problems involved are of great importance to political theory, both normative and positive.
    19. It is impertinent to attempt to summarize this vast literature in a page; the following seven points are stated with great diffidence. They assume that voting takes place in a competitive situation, with relatively good information and relative absence of direct pressure on the voters.

a. There is a high correlation between voting and various social and economic factors: but this falls far short of 100 per cent.

b. There is generally a fairly high correlation between voting and economic class, as defined by occupation and income: but there are also strong and interesting discrepancies.

c. Higher degrees of correlation can be obtained by introducing other factors:

(i) Objective: for instance, age, sex, region, religious affiliation, social and local mobility.

(ii) Subjective: for instance, does the voter rate himself as belonging to the middle class or to the working class?

d. A corollary of this, "floating voters" — those whose vote it is difficult to predict except in terms of their own character and "choice" — are to a disproportionate extent those of mixed characteristics, a finding expressed by saying that they are subject to "crosspressures".

e. A very high proportion of voters vote consistently with their own previous votes even though political circumstances have changed. Taking an electorate as a whole, change though slow is real: but much of the change is to be explained by the succession of generations, not by transfer of voting allegiance.

f. These findings do not portray the reflective, rational, independent decision-maker of radical democratic theory. But they do not support any sort of determinism, except in the statistical sense that the total percentage of change for one country at one election can be calculated within limits of probability close enough to be of practical importance. Nor do they suggest that voters act foolishly, within the limits of the information they possess.

g. This conclusion could be formulated in terms of the concept of saliency. The voter as person operates in many spheres of activity, and these vary in their demands on his attention. Those to which he gives most "attention" (which can be operationally defined) are most "salient" to him. There is certainly some random variation in saliency; but it is in general related to the priority given to various "interests" by the agent, who is dependent on these "interests" for his existence in a given social context. For most voters, voting does not have a high degree of saliency, for two reasons:

(i) The effects of voting on the voter's interests are regarded by the voter (often correctly) as being relatively slight and remote.

(ii) Voting (even when the ballot is secret) is to some extent a social act: a voter will tend to "go along" with a group and with respected opinion-leaders, and there is a strong "threshold effect" holding him to this tendency.

20. The voter thus depicted is no fool, but it would be natural to call him a "sensible man" rather than a "rational man". His vote "makes sense", but within the whole context of his way of life. However, some voters frequently, all voters potentially, may act as rational decision-makers within the limits of the evidence available to them.

2 *Community power studies*
21. It has also been of great general interest to seek empirical evidence about problems of power and authority. It is regarded as obvious that in any society, however egalitarian and democratic, some people have more influence than others. Terminology has not been effectively standardized; but there is some tendency to use "influence" as the most general word, and to distinguish "power" as influence backed by rewards and sanctions, from "authority" as influence internalized or legitimated as meriting conformity on its own account. The use of "influence" here therefore corresponds to that of "authority" in par. 11.

22. Attempts have been made at the measurement of influence empirically in laboratory situations, and these experiments are interesting conceptually. But they hold out little prospect that numerical measurement can be obtained outside the laboratory, except in cases too simple to be interesting.

23. There are almost insuperable difficulties in making direct observations of a verifiable kind about power at the highest levels. This is particularly hard for contemporary observers, but historians also face great difficulties in securing relevant evidence. Hence there is an incentive to study influence (including power and authority) within communities which are not "sovereign" but are relatively self-

contained and are small enough for thorough investigation by academic observers. Hence a large number of studies of villages, small towns and cities, referred to as "community power studies" in so far as they are directed to testing models of the structure of influence.

24. Three quite different models have been tested in the USA, each to the satisfaction of its inventors. They may be very crudely tagged and summarized as follows:

a. *The power élite.* Any modern community (up to the level of the USA as a whole) consists of a number of distinguishable power hierarchies. By the nature of their positions, those at the top of each hierarchy communicate and negotiate. In the process they develop a sense of common interest as "top people" in a "régime";[1] [2] in spite of internal rivalries, they cohere sufficiently to be regarded as a social group or collectivity tending towards (though never wholly achieving) a monopoly of power and a common policy in the exercise of power.

b. *"Power is situational".* Contemporary society is made up of a plurality of groups and professions, and the ordinary man is influenced by different people in different contexts. Many of the people who influence us do so in professional capacities. We defer to the opinion of a doctor about health, of a teacher about preparing for examinations, of a plumber about drains, of an electrician about television repair, and so on. This obviously does not mean that doctor, teacher, plumber, electrician are in relation to us members of a power élite. Given the character of American society, the same situation arises in regard to public decisions. In the same town there are different "political communities" for different purposes, such as schoolbuilding, road development, hospitals, slum clearance and so on, and the "general public authority" (who may perhaps be the Mayor only, with a few personal henchmen) has little or no influence except as a sort of "continuity man" loosely linking each situation to the others and to the electoral process. In fact, the nature of a plural society is that in different contexts different people are powerful; and the USA is a plural society.

(c) *The market in influence.* The third view attributes much greater importance to the role of professional politi-

cians, at least in a very large city. The city is too complex to
be planned by authority; there do not exist sufficient
resources of power nor of information. But each of the class
of professional politicians is dependent for survival as politician upon his adaptability within this milieu. His "profits"
depend on his influence, and profits can be (indeed must
largely be) reinvested so as to maximize his total "holding"
of influence and to put him in a position relatively secure
against minor fluctuations. But his "influence" is always at
stake in the market unless he withdraws. If he fails to deal in
influence in such a way as to maximize influence, he cannot
survive in the role he has chosen.

25. An observer not committed to any single model would
conclude from this evidence that different things happen in
different American communities; and indeed these studies are
now entering a second phase, in which it may be possible to
map the range of variety in American communities much
more thoroughly, and to establish more complex generaliza-
tions tested within American political society. None of the
three models, and no combination of them, could ever serve
to describe the rational "Pareto-maximising" authority postulated by welfare economics. But the concept of such an
authority is intended to be normative, not descriptive, and it
is not easy to displace it empirically. Research into influence
(including power and authority) seems to be following a path
similar to that of research into voting behaviour, although the
latter has been carried much further and is much better based
on figures. We have learnt to use the concept of rational
public authority (like that of rational voter) with great
caution and with careful regard to context. But the concept
has not been destroyed.

3 *Administrative Behaviour*

26. Administration would once have been defined confident-
ly as the special sphere of *Zweck-Rationalität*, and this
concept of administration is still of value as a norm or
standard in situations where it is safe to treat administration
as purely instrumental. Indeed, it merits some defence against
the main trends of administrative research in the last forty
years, which has been concerned with administrative organ-

izations as the "social habitat" of people, and with organizations as social systems surviving in a social milieu.

27. There is no well-settled definition of "administrative
organization"; indeed, much progress has been made simply
by relaxing old formal definitions and treating organizations
in biological terms as "open systems" in continuous interchange with an environment. But there survives the concept
of an organization as something less than all-embracing: an
organization belongs to working hours, not to the whole
twenty-four hours; it is the tennis club rather than the tribe
or family. One may admit that an organization becomes a
complete way of life for some of its members: but one would
regard this as a limiting case, perhaps a pathological one. An
organization is thus an entity which can realistically be
treated as a "bounded" system within the complex of
modern society, and this has made the ecological or systems
approach to organizations particularly easy and fruitful.

28. Rigorously followed, this approach offers an adaptive
or cybernetic model of decision-making in organizations.
Does this exclude from them "decision-making" in the sense
required by this paper? A strict application of cybernetic
theory would require that organizations be treated as
"machines" in the rather specific sense defined by Ross
Ashby:[13] machines of a highly adaptable kind, capable of
programming themselves, but still "determinate" and capable
in principle of being completely specified. They "take decisions" in the same sense as a computer; is it relevant to
consider a very complex computer as a "model of collective
decision-making"? There are heuristic advantages in doing so,
provided it is kept clearly in mind that *prima facie* the cases
of determinate machine and of human organization are
analogous, not homologous. The analogy will suggest observations, tests and experiments.

29. It is certainly not incompatible with the cybernetic
model that human organizations are concerned with "rational" techniques of maximization through operational research,
cost/benefit analysis, critical path analysis and so on. These
are all "decision-making processes" which can be programmed into a machine: indeed, they owe a great deal to
computer technique. But it may well be true that the director

of an operational research unit is apt to step out of the role assigned to him and to assume another "for his own purposes". This sort of human situation is not easily handled by the "machine" model.

30. The ecological analogy has been brilliantly applied both to private and to public organizations, and naturally it generalizes in such a way as to emphasize what is common to them as organizations, and to minimize their differences. "The public interest" must in this form of analysis be defined operationally as some specific set of inputs "sensed" by the organization; and if one looks for such inputs, one is most likely to define them as interventions by specific characters, wielding specific sanctions: legislators, interest groups, voters, mass communications men and so on. These "public interest inputs" may well be expressed in a special "public interest language" appealing to norms of generality, welfare, objectivity, and so on — the language in fact in which welfare economics defines "the authority". Nevertheless, it is built into this model that these norms are nothing to the organization except in so far as they become inputs to it. Following this line of thought, one finds that the distinction between private ownership and public ownership is of no analytical importance, what matters being what impinges on the "senses" of the organization. It is in fact probable that the directors of a very large "private" business or of a "private" business strategically placed in the economy will find it necessary to have regard to the "public interest", as here defined, more than a remote and trivial office in the public service.

31. The analogy has been especially valuable in making sense of trains of action which seem to go right against the terms of reference of an organization. Things persistently happen in organizations in defiance of their *Zweck -rationalität*, yet the organizations survive; indeed, they may be placed in greater danger by attempts to impose rationality. This situation can now be understood, and can be explained to managers. But this success in analysis does not mean that the idea of purposive rationality has become irrelevant.

32. Indeed, empirical research suggests various elaborations of the cybernetic model, leaving more room for "human

rationality", individual and collective. Such human rationality has so far proved easier to find in private than in public
organizations. This may indicate only that better research
facilities are offered by the former; or there may be greater
difficulty in attaining what H. A. Simon has called "bounded
rationality" in public authorities whose "bounds" are often
hard to define. Two lines of thought are suggested.

a. *People in command.* It is not safe to disregard the old
notion of administration as a tool held in the boss's hand,
and used with "instrumental rationality" for his own
purposes. Cases do exist in which all the "cybernetic apparatus" that exists is inside the boss's head, and there are also
cases in which the boss as person seeks to behave as rational
authority. These tactics sometimes fail, and it is possible to
indicate roughly the sort of technological settings in which
they are likely to fail. But the notion of an autonomous and
rational person conducting his own business is not to be
dismissed as a piece of fantasy.

b. *Collective decisions.* By definition a decision in a formal
setting must be identified by a rule of recognition (above par.
6). But an observer talking to participants will often be told,
for instance: "That meeting was just a formality; the *real*
decision was taken elsewhere". The observer then sets of in
quest of the "real" decision, and he seems to get closer and
closer to it; but he can never find *exactly* who took it, when,
how, in what circumstances, with whose consent. This is in
part a definitional puzzle, resolved by Professors Austin and
Hart, but it also seems to be a real puzzle about choice of a
descriptive model. The model which fits best is that of
"circles" of people, each person more or less closely involved
in the issue at stake; the circles may or may not coincide with
the formal allocation of duties in an organization chart.
Possible solutions of the issue "float around" in the organization, in forms more or less precise. If the issue is a big one,
resolved slowly, the fortunes of solutions rise and fall,
solutions blend or disintegrate, and a shifting pattern can be
traced which looks different to different people in different
circles. But there will be some point in time when nearly
everyone (or everyone of importance) agrees that the issue is
settled, and that what is left is formality. From this point of

absolutely general agreement that there *has been* a "decision", one can follow the decision back; but earlier in time there are fewer people who are convinced that the matter is settled, and who prove in the event to have been right. Looking forward towards a decision analytically, the process is to set out a list of possibilities, and then narrow it till only one remains. Looking backward in time, one can see that the list of possibilities was never complete, and that at some point the path through the changing field of possibilities (perhaps after many fluctuations) became determinate in the direction of the ultimate solution.

F Final remarks

33. Each of these branches of enquiry runs into considerable difficulties, either because of logical paradoxes (for instance, that of "cyclical voting" – see par. 15 (1)), or because it is difficult to frame propositions capable of operational disproof, or because of both. Hence a recent tendency to enquire whether the enquiry is well-founded, linguistically and conceptually.

1 *Linguistically*

34. The questions referred to in Section A relate primarily to the use of words such as "decision", "choice", "preference", in the English language. Probably a really careful analysis of English usage, on the lines initiated by the late Prof. J. L. Austin, would refine very considerably (and perhaps dissolve) the notion that "decision" can satisfactorily be treated as a single concept with some central core of common usage or meaning. It is still more probable that the concept would dissolve if it were tested across linguistic frontiers, especially those between European and non-European languages. In fact, a study of linguistic usage might offer valuable clues in opening up a cross-cultural investigation of "collective decision-making".

2 *Conceptually*

35. It may be said that the analysis in Section A, and indeed the title of this paper, imply an assumption (unproven, perhaps "metaphysical" in character) that the basic "unit of account" in our enquiry should be something known as an

"individual decision", that this in some sense "exists" separately, and that the problem of collective decisions is that of aggregating individual decisions.

36. Clearly, this "particularistic" model is not very useful in describing some of the behaviour of social animals, for instance the wheeling of a flock of starlings in flight. It is said that there are forms of social behaviour in simpler societies which defy analysis by "particularistic" models, and indeed such cases are to be found readily even in developed societies. Par. 32 (b) sketched briefly the sort of case of a "slow-moving" decision which one tends to describe in terms of a changing "climate of opinion" in a collectivity within which the inter-actions between members are so complex that an aggregative model is useless. One moves as it were from the equations of the mechanics of solid bodies to those of fluid motion. Similarly, in regard to decisions within smaller complexes taken at very high speed, such as can be studied in watching really good football. Combined movements can partially be explained in terms of blackboard tactics, discipline, a signal. But this does not seem enough to explain the very rapid extemporization of new "goal-seeking" patterns by teams of brilliant individuals accustomed to combination.

37. Particularistic models have dominated recent Western thought, and this paper has been largely concerned with their paradoxes and difficulties. Much less has been done to build and test models of "fluid motion" in collective decision-making. Perhaps one reason for this is that there has been a feeling that such models do not represent the "values" of Western society. But it is easy to see that there would be difficulties, logical and empirical, perhaps as great as those which face particularistic models. It is tempting to glance at the analogy of physics and to speculate that two incompatible models can both be used, indeed that both are necessary, in exploring and handling social reality.

Notes

1. K. J. Arrow, *Social Choice and Individual Values* (New York, 1951), p. 1.

2. J. de V. Graaff, *Theoretical Welfare Economics* (Cambridge, 1957), pp. 7–8.

3. *Philosophical Papers* (Oxford, 1961) and *How to do Things with Words* (Oxford, 1962).

4. *The Concept of Law* (Oxford, 1961), p. 113.

5. Anthony Downs, *An Economic Theory of Democracy* (New York, 1957), p. 6; cf. K. J. Arrow, *op cit.*, pp. 13–14; and J. M. Buchanan and G. Tullock, *The Calculus of Consent* (Ann Arbor, 1962), p. 33.

6. Arrow, *op cit.*, p. 3.

7. *The Theory of Committees and Elections* (Cambridge, 1958).

8. J. de V. Graaff, *op cit.*, p. 8 and elsewhere.

9. *The Theory of Games and Economic Behaviour*, 3rd ed. (Princeton, 1953), pp. 17–20; and Arrow, *op cit.*, p. 10.

10. H. A. Simon, *Models of Man* (New York, 1957), introduction to Part IV; and J. March and H. A. Simon, *Organizations* (New York, 1958), Chap. 6.

11. See in particular Anthony Downs, *op cit.*; T. C. Schelling, *The Strategy of Conflict* (Harvard, 1960); W. H. Riker, *The Theory of Political Coalitions* (Yale University Press, 1962).

12. Prof. Baroja in *Honour and Shame*, ed. J. C. Peristiany (London, 1965), p. 92, refers to the "tacit friendship between nobles" deemed to exist in medieval Spain. This is similar.

13. *An Introduction to Cybernetics* (London, 1956), Chap. 3, 1. Methuen ed. p. 24.

Books cited or used

(This is not a bibliography, but may be of some help to those in search of documentation.)

Arrow, K. J., *Social Choice and Individual Values* (New York, 1951).

Ashby, W. R., *An Introduction to Cybernetics* (London, 1956).

Banfield, E. C., *Political Influence* (Glencoe, 1961).

Birch, A. H., *Small Town Politics* (Oxford University Press, 1956).

Black, Duncan, *The Theory of Committees and Elections* (Cambridge University Press, 1958).

Blau, Peter M., *Exchange and Power in Social Life* (New York, 1964).

Braybrooke, D., and Lindblom, C. E., *A Strategy of Decision* (Glencoe, 1963).

Buchanan, J. M., and Tullock, G., *The Calculus of Consent* (Michigan, 1962).

Burns, T., and Stalker, G. R. *The Management of Innovation* (Tavistock, 1961).

Dahl, R. A., *Who Governs?* (New Haven, Conn., Yale University Press, 1961).

Downs, Anthony, *An Economic Theory of Democracy* (New York, 1957).

Frankenberg, R. J., *Village on the Border* (London, 1957).

Graaff, J. de V., *Theoretical Welfare Economics* (Cambridge, 1957).

Hunter, Floyd, *Community Power Structure* (North Carolina University Press, 1953).

Lee, J. M., *Social Leaders and Public Persons* (Oxford University Press, 1964).

Little, I. D. M., *A Critique of Welfare Economics* (Oxford, 1950).

March, J., and Simon, H. A., *Organizations* (New York, 1958).

Meyerson, M., and Banfield, E. C., *Policy, Planning and the Public Interest* (Glencoe, 1955).

Mills, C. Wright, *The Power Elite* (New York, 1956).

Neumann, J. von and Morgenstern, O., *Theory of Games and Economic Behaviour*, 3rd. ed. (Princeton, 1953).

Riker, W. H., *The Theory of Political Coalitions* (New Haven, Conn., Yale University Press, 1962).

Schelling, T. C., *The Strategy of Conflict* (Harvard, 1960).

Simon, H. A., *Models of Man* (New York, 1957).

Woodward, Joan, *Industrial Organization, Theory and Practice* (London, 1965).

14 The Plowden Report: A Translation*

Translator's note. The report reached me when I was busy with other things, and a reading of the summaries, a quick perusal, conveyed nothing to me at all. My interest was reawakened by a note in Mr Anthony Sampson's book The Anatomy of Britain *at page 284, that this was a 'revolutionary and critical document' written in an unknown tongue. I used to be a philologist, sometimes I wish I still was; here is a shot at a translation. Much is of necessity conjectural, but this version has a certain internal coherence which gives it plausibility, like the stuff about clerical officers doing imprest accounts which the late Michael Ventris got out Minoan Linear B. So I hope some editor will take a chance with it.*

1. For various political reasons we were asked to attempt the impossible: to accept criticisms without accepting them, to have a public inquiry which is not public.

2. At first I was expected to carry the can alone. Then I got them to add three pretty safe people:

Sir Sam Brown, war-time Under Secretary at MAP, now a City solicitor of distinction (born 1903).

Sir Jeremy Raisman, a most distinguished member of the ICS, now Vice-chairman of Lloyds Bank (born 1892).

Mr J. E. Wall, a war-time temporary, who stuck in the Civil Service till 1952, and is now a director of EMI (born 1913).

3. Naturally, there was a great wrangle about what should be published, and this was ended by a nonsensical compro-

*From *Guardian*, May 1963, and *Public Administration*, Jun 1963. The full reference for the Report is *Control of Public Expenditure* (Chairman, Lord Plowden, KCB, KBE), Cmnd 1432 of 1961).

mise embodied in this document. The Civil Service members of the inquiry (who are officially nameless, but you can easily find who they were) do not agree to this paper, but they do not not agree in any respect whatever.

PLOWDEN
Chairman

Report

1. We proceeded on two principles: no dirty linen in public: outside critics are bores.

2. We did however chat to a great many civil servants, and two years of that is more than enough.

3. Unluckily, it turns out that the real problem is about the nature of government in general, and of British government in particular. This is what we are discussing, but of course we have to wrap it up in Mandarin prose.

4. Our general impression is that the Civil Service is extremely old-fashioned and riven by jealousies: but there is public spirit there, and some of them do try quite hard.

5. This report is just 'key-note' stuff: detailed proposals have been handed in separately.

Part 1
The need for a revolution

6. Public expenditure is not a separate problem. It involves all government action and all participants in government.

7. To be rational in government involves ranking objectives in order of priority, quantifying their rank order, and giving effect to it in action till such time as it is specifically changed.

There has been much debate as to whether this is possible in theory.

The Traditional System

8. As a matter of practice, it has not even been attempted in Britain hitherto, except to a limited extent in regard to public investment.

9. The only rational principle followed has been to resist all pressure equally, until it proved too strong or skilful.

10. This was well enough while public expenditure was

relatively small: but to follow that principle now is to
abandon the whole economy to pressure politics.

11. There is no going back now.

Principles of Reconstruction

12.
    A. Forward look.
    B. Settled decisions.
    C. Measurement.
    D. Reform of Cabinet and Commons.

A. *Forward Look*

13. This is being tried, but no one really knows how to do it.
Some of our members feel it would do more harm than good
to make a 'thing' of it at this stage.

14. It is at least notionally possible to run the exercise for
all direct expenditure by public authorities, and they ought
to be made to try it.

15. But the result could easily be misleading. Some central
government expenditure is not subject to control from year
to year: e.g. doles to unemployed and to farmers. In any
case, the line between 'public' and non-public expenditure
now has little economic meaning.

16. Similarly, on the revenue side of the account, this
really amounts to making guesses about the national income.

17. However, it would be feeble not to try: and (as we
explain later, paras. 26, 58, 75, 106) the result might be very
valuable in educating public opinion. Unfortunately we can't
believe that politicians would have the nerve to publish it,
nor could we, in our capacity as political secretaries, advise
them to take the risk.

B. *Settled decisions*

18. One can easily trace the psychological damage and actual
waste of resources caused by chopping and changing in the
1950s.

19. There is not much excuse for this where investment is
a matter of straight building programmes and the need is
uncontroversial. For instance, educational building and
motorways have been tidied up fairly well; but there is a lot

to do yet in other fields. By studied omission we note particularly the field of housing and urban renewal.

20. In some fields the results are fairly obvious, and new procedure would not make much difference. In others, like defence, the whole situation is crazy, and there is really nothing we can do about it. But let us at least have a general pro forma for expenditure over five years, the first year clear, the four later years shading off into impenetrable fog. This will make us all feel better about it.

21. But of course it may have no practical meaning for a Government caught between pressures at home which want scaling up, pressures abroad which want scaling down.

22. Let us, however, put it on record that the Keynesian idea of using public expenditure to keep the economy in balance has been completely abandoned. It makes no sense at all for current expenditure; (23) at most, there are a few small things that could be done in relation to capital programmes, if we were ready for it in time, as we never are.

24. As we said above, the worst result of the present situation is psychological. Departments think that the 'forward look' is phoney, and therefore they take little trouble about forward planning. Unfortunately they are right, but this is partly because of their own actions.

C. Measurement

25. Nobody knows how different bits of public expenditure affect the economy.

26. The public accounts are unintelligible.

27. Estimates. One thing we *have* done is to get through a revision of the form of the Estimates, which will be reflected in the form of the Accounts.

28. The next step is to train politicians, civil servants, the City, the press, to 'read' these cash accounts, alongside the economic accounts about national income and expenditure.

29. Accounts. This is just as bad a mess, but less urgent as no one uses the accounts anyhow. Progress is likely to be very slow.

30. Statisticians and Accountants (see also para. 53). The whole thing is very amateurish in method; but it is hard to see where we can find properly trained professionals in face of present competition.

D. *The Cabinet*

31. The thing is, of course, now regarded as a game. Treasury versus the Rest, at Cabinet level as well as in Whitehall.

32. We have some thoughts about this, but are not very well agreed among ourselves, and are afraid of getting dragged into public controversy. So much depends on political power, since this is a question of increasing the power of central control in government, decreasing the weight of departmental interests. You can do this up to a point by increasing the weight of the Treasury in the Cabinet (as the Prime Minister has now done); but (as some of us have pointed out) this is as likely to increase the hostility of Departments and their pressure groups as to make for closer integration.

Part II
The Treasury as holding company

33. There is much friction between Departments and the Treasury: this is to some extent routine fuss over trivialities, but it reflects an obsolete frame of mind.

34. It should be made perfectly clear in future that this is not to be regarded as a game between equal players.

35. The Departments are in effect operating companies, and the job of their managers is to manage; not to try to act as directors of the holding company.

36. The functions of policy-making are now concentrated in the Treasury, and it has been given ample power to keep lower management in its place. It is in the hands of the Treasury alone to measure the efficiency of management, and to apply rewards and sanctions by posting and promotion.

37. Supply. The old 'Estimates Cycle' is obsolete as a procedure for making policy.

38. Our alternative is:

(a) Treat Estimates procedure as Executive Class routine.
(b) Have occasional 'big dos' over the 'forward look'.
(c) Let the Treasury participate fully in each big departmental decision when it is being taken. This will slow things up, but how else can you get away from the present situation, in which the Treasury never really understands departmental policy at all, and Departments are ranked according to their strength and skill in 'bouncing' the Treasury?

39. This does not mean that we think the Treasury should keep out of small departmental decisions. It cannot train its young men except by giving them small game to chase; but it really must emphasise to them that these are only tests of speed and agility, not the real thing.

40. Establishments. The Treasury and the Staff Associations are in complete agreement that strict centralisation is essential, and the Departments realise that they are helpless in this pincer grip.

41. It is however a matter of common courtesy that there should be a show of consultation, and this can do no harm if it is confined to trivial matters.

42. Changes. Things do happen, but too slowly; we can only think of five changes in the last five years — forward look, hospital revenue (we have referred to these), general grants to local authorities, changes in agricultural price review procedure, and some minor changes in Civil Service pay negotiation.

43. The great thing is not to let these timid initiatives die out.

44. Management. One of our members got in Mr E. F. L. Brech, and he worked up the old idea that the Civil Service could learn a good deal from business practice.

45. We have all realised that 'management' is an OK word ever since Fleck got at the Coal Board in 1953. But some of us note that there are important Departments (the Foreign Office, for instance) where present doctrines about 'management' are quite irrelevant.

46. In this terminology a Department is the equivalent of an operating company within a group.

47. Within a Department the Principal Establishment Officer is supposed to be expert on managerial efficiency; but few PEOs are up to this. The job therefore falls back on the PUS, who has no time for it, and even on the Minister.

48. Hence the whole thing has to begin from the Treasury. There will be no improvement unless it assumes that normal responsibilities of top management in relation to 'management succession' throughout its group of companies.

49. What is more, it must control effective services for 'management assessment'. It is not staffed or organised at present to discharge either of these functions; and it will not

be able to do so without unrelenting and bitter opposition unless our analogy of 'holding company' and 'operating companies' is understood and accepted throughout the Civil Service.

50. 51. Management Services. A few big departments are fairly well briefed on these; to the others they mean nothing at all.

52. The Treasury does lay on courses, but the general practice is to send to these only Assistant Secretaries who have just about reached their ceiling.

53. Real progress has been made in O and M, costing, and the use of computers; but the bottleneck is in expert staff, and it is not realistic to think that these can be bought from outside at present rates. They must be home grown.

54. More could be done about common services.

55. For the hospitals, for instance; 56, 57. And perhaps for local authorities, but really we know nothing about these.

58. In fact it all needs more public discussion.

59. The Treasury. We have seemed to criticise the Departments, as independent satrapies, pressing their own ideas of public policy, ill-managed, ill-informed, and inbred. We have suggested a new model, based on that of progressive private enterprise. We realise that in doing so we have cast the Treasury for a part which it is at present ill-fitted to discharge. If it cannot adapt itself, the thing is hopeless.

Part III
The reform of Parliament

60. It is obvious that in our 'model' the role of the Commons is quite subsidiary: but it could be a help to the Government in minor ways if it were prepared to sacrifice some of its old mumbo-jumbo.

61. Annual finance procedure. The present legislative procedure is absolute gibberish: but we have not the nerve to recommend a frontal attack on it.

62. A two-year cycle has been suggested: but inflation goes too fast for that. Even private business finds it necessary to strike a fresh balance each year.

63. Penny Exercise Book Accounting. This is silly, but it has advantages as a system of policing fraud, and those who

have looked at it carefully have all looked away again, in horror at the work and dislocation involved in introducing a more logical system.

64, 65. There would be no real advantage in having sophisticated accounts except for trading services, and most of these have now been hived off to public corporations and so on. The others have trading accounts already.

66, 67. Trading accounts won't help at all in settling priorities where the determinants are political and social, and that is most of the story, as we explained earlier.

68. Claw-back. It is always said that this causes a rush to get rid of money somehow, before the financial year ends. In fact, the sums involved are not very big; it is more a question of attitudes than of accounts.

69. In an organisation as big as this, large autonomous units cannot be denied the power to 'fiddle' at the margin; this is a built-in tendency, but controlled by mutual under-standings. No tightening up can control it without ridiculous repercussions.

70. The Departments themselves know how to work with the present system.

71. and its worst defect is that subordinate authorities like HMCs don't understand it, in fact they think it is mad. It will be easier to make some concessions than to explain it to them.

72, 73. The Commons and Commitments. The Commons have at present no organisation for discussing departmental decisions at the time when they are taken.

74. A reorganisation would be useless unless the Govern-ment were prepared to give the House access to the informa-tion it possesses itself. This no Government would do.

75. Up to this point we are agreed; but some of us feel that the rest of our recommendations will fall to the ground unless something is done to secure better informed debate in public.

76, 77. PAC, EC, SCNI. The present effect of these committees on administration is bad. They are old-fashioned in approach, are interested primarily in trivialities, and waste the time of very busy men who have more important things to do.

78. The position is nearly, but not quite, intolerable; yet there is no hope of relief unless these committees begin to understand what they are doing.

79. Change. The theory of the old system, set up in the 1860s, is that the Commons control finance and the Treasury acts as its intermediary in dealing with Departments.

80. This gave paramountcy to the Commons and limited the Treasury to strict terms of reference. We recommend the paramountcy of the Treasury, and complete flexibility in its powers. There is likely to be a battle about this; fortunately or otherwise, the Commons do not realise what is at stake.

81, 82. Losses. For instance, the Public Accounts Committee have always been interested in specific cases of defalcation. But these are in total insignificant, and it is nonsense that the Treasury should be forced by the PAC to concern itself with each case individually. Its job is to see that the system is right.

83, 84. 'Regularity.' Similarly, the old business of 'policing' the appropriations is quite out of data: the risk of that sort of 'fiddle' is now negligible. The old procedure can be somewhat simplified (see Para. 27); the main thing however is to interest the PAC in the things about efficiency which now interest the Treasury.

85. Nationalised Industry. The ideas of the White Paper (Command 1337 of April, 1961) are relevant.

86, 87. The industries cost public money; the Commons therefore seek detailed control; this is likely to cost more money and to decrease efficiency further.

88. The Government's policy is to assimilate nationalised industry to other forms of big business; and this means that the Commons must be prepared to accept the limited role of shareholders.

89. They should be treated to a certain amount of blarney, stuffed with unusable figures, and allowed to take part in setpiece debates. But they really must not try to join in policy decisions when they are being made. We hope that if Dr Beeching and others can establish this rule for public enterprise the precedent will have good effects in other fields of Government expenditure.

Part IV
Summing up
90. Our main themes have been the Forward Look; the Management Model; effective Treasury control over the Commons.

91. Do not think we are very confident about success in any of these. The problem is vast and complex; (92) much of the departmental organisation is obselete and resistant to change.

93. Right strategy. There must be a group of top people sharing a picture of the situation and its difficulties.

94. They have two main instruments of control: (a) to study men and organisations at work in individual cases; (b) to set up adequate systems of comparative analysis.

95,96. Skill consists in using these two instruments judiciously in combination. (a) is quite well used now, (b) is still very poorly developed.

97. Wrong strategy. The thing not to do is to concentrate only on the total of public expenditure. This is nearly (though not completely) meaningless; and it is apt to have awkward political consequencies in the shape of a demand for percentage cuts all round. This is exactly the wrong way to proceed.

99. Danger points. We analyse these as follows: (1) The routine cost of administration must of course be screwed down; but that is a regular management job, already quite well done.

100. (2) There is always a risk of uncontrollable extravagance as a result of electoral politics. (3) But the really big waste of the 1950s has come in three ways:

101. (a) The maintenance of obsolete firms, industries, and areas, which have no hope of running except at a loss. Economic liabilities should be shed.

102. (b) Obsolete subsidies; those who are given Government money come to regard this as their right, unconditionally and for ever.

103. (c) Sudden reactions to temporary situations, military or technological.

104. In the nature of things the Treasury is bound to be 'bounced' from time to time. Its best safeguard against this

is to take decisions slowly, secure Cabinet backing, and fight attempts at sudden change.

105. The Public. We are agreed that this is a hopeless task unless the Treasury has the backing of an 'informed' public opinion. We disagree about the steps to be taken. Most of us think that public relations might easily make things worse. People can never be got to understand this kind of problem, and anything you say gives a handle to opposition.

106. A minority of us think that the risks entailed by excessive discretion are even greater. There is a national emergency, and we shall not get through unless we can somehow tap the stock of common sense used by citizens in their personal affairs.

107. Acknowledgements.

V
Constitutional Theory, Political Theory

The first term in this Section, that on Constitution Making, perhaps stands on its own, as a relic of my old Oxford interest in constitutional theory, a sort of love—hate relationship with Dicey and others of his generation, which did not find much to feed on in Manchester or Africa. In Glasgow, where I have been since 1966, the situation is different, as we are very close to the problem of constitutional engineering in Northern Ireland, as well as in Scotland itself. But perhaps I am so close to these situations as to be appalled at the character of human politics and at the limits of rationality in political contrivance. Politics is so long, the span of one's devices is so short.

The next three articles perhaps form a group, starting from the re-discovery of pressure-groups in the U.K., which Professor Sammy Finer and I launched independently and almost simultaneously in the middle 1950s, the years of Butskellism, and Churchill's tragic decline. From 1940 to the General Elections of 1950 and 1951 the commonplace about English institutions had been that they gave great power to those who controlled the executive through control of the House of Commons. The system had carried us through war and reconstruction much diminished but without disaster; and the proper questions to ask were about the risks involved in strong government: for instance, the plebiscitary position of the Prime Minister, oligarchy within the Parties (as in R. T. McKenzie's book, published in 1955), *The Passing of Parliament* (G. W. Keeton's book of 1952*), the difficulty of controlling administrators. And then suddenly things were

*And Christopher Hollis's *Can Parliament Survive?* (1949).

different; and political scientists began belatedly to dig about in the old literature of pluralism and pressures to find appropriate models. The whole field has now been so well explored that these articles are factually out of date; but they may stand as a reminder that in understanding complex situations one must have several models to hand, and that for the academic it is a matter of political judgement which models to use and in what combinations.

It should perhaps be stressed specifically that the fourth paper, the one about 'the cash basis', was written and published before the S.S.R.C. was set up in 1965. My paper may give an idea of the atmosphere then. There were some, I suppose, who had dreams of the power of social science to mould society, a concept severely attacked by what might be called the Oakeshottian Old Guard, at the S.S.R.C.'s first academic conference at the University of Kent in 1966: a turbulent and traumatic occasion. But I think the main body of opinion behind the creation of the S.S.R.C. reflected the anxieties of departmental *entrepreneurs* like myself who were under stress in the management of the academic situation as we found it. For the man devoted to the organisation of enquiry, the old Clan Cameron motto will do — 'Come to me, Sons of Dogs, and I will give you flesh': but it has to be understood in a double sense, since academics live by ideas as well as by money. The S.S.R.C. (of which I was a member from 1965 to 1969) has resolved some difficulties and has perhaps created new ones, as new institutions always do: but I feel no need to revise what I wrote in 1961.

Then there is the article on Elections for the new Encyclopaedia of the Social Sciences, which suffers from the restrictions of its form; for instance, it was not I who invented the 'functionalist' label of the article though I tried to play towards it. The article was important to me because I had always been worried that I could not identify a 'decision' except in terms of 'procedure' — and yet it is notorious that 'procedure' may be empty of reality. When I found the work on 'performative utterances' by my old colleague John Austin, I thought I had really got something; and about the same time I read Buchanan and Tullock's work on *The Calculus of Consent* on forms of procedure as the result of

bargaining. I cannot say that these two things solved the
paradox of constitutional regress set out in the paper on
Constitution Making. But at least I felt firmer ground under
my feet.

The last of these papers was written for a conference in
Paris sponsored by Bertrand de Jouvenel in relation to his
work of *Futuribles*, and one object was to take my share in
giving recognition to the contribution he had made to the
development of political thought, both speculative and practical. But by accident the conference fell in the week of Sir
Winston Churchill's funeral, 3 April 1965; and what began as
a slightly artificial exercise in method ended as a sort of
funeral oration for Churchill's England, written in a style
which I hoped was somewhat French. I don't think that it
quite worked: but perhaps it serves logically to end this
collection. 'To-morrow is a new day.'

15 Constitution Making*

I imagine that my part in this symposium is to discuss the type of relationships which we commonly call political. This is an ocean of debate, and it is unwise to set out on it without plotting a course. I want therefore to choose one train of thought about political organization and to stick to it fairly closely.

Probably the common idea of politics includes two types of relationship which are both present in our minds and are difficult to bring together in a coherent scheme: on the one hand, power and the struggle for power; on the other hand, a constitution, the idea of legitimate power or power self-limited through a choice of institutions. The contrast is familiarly expressed in the phrase, 'A government of laws, and not of men', which has a pretty continuous history in the West since the contrast was drawn between Greeks and Barbarians in the fifth century before Christ.[1]

For various reasons I wish to deal mainly with the second type of relationship, that concerned with forms of government; first because this fits in best with what Professor Macbeath has written about ritual; second, because I am rather tired of what passes for a tough-minded attitude in academic discussions of politics. Between the wars we were all disillusioned with the idea that we could by reason discover the best form of government: we were inclined (I speak in terms of my own experience) to think that it was more logical to begin by searching not for the springs of virtue, but for the springs of power. After all, there were so many things that could be done to make the world better — if only one had the power. This was a natural reaction from the type of constitution-making rather unfairly called

---

*From *Man In His Relationships*, ed. H. Westmann (London: Routledge and Kegan Paul, 1955).

Wilsonian; it could draw to its support all sorts of persuasive analogies from natural science; and it coincided with a short period (the only one) when Marxism had some real life in it as a political theory in this country.[2]

More recent experience has reinstated an older common-place, that the real problems of reform begin only when the reformers have gained power; and there has been an equally strong reaction against very simple scientific analogies, which led us to talk of political power as if it were a substance or form of energy which could be stored in tanks or batteries and drawn upon at need by the man who knew the switch. The common idea now is that power is social and not individual; that it is intelligible only as one type of relation-ship within a system which exists apart from individuals and dictates rôles to all individuals, including the most powerful. Social anthropology would, I suppose, admit the existence of temporary and unstable power held by an individual, but only as a transitional phase which must end quite quickly either in destruction or a return to stability. The modern commonplace is (in other language) very similar to that to which Dicey referred when he was explaining the real limits on the theoretical power of Parliament: 'The Soldan of Egypt, or the Emporer of Rome, might drive his harmless subjects, like brute beasts, against their sentiments and inclination: But he must, at least, have led his *mamalukes*, or *praetorian bands* like men, by their opinion.[3]

This puts the matter in an individualist frame of reference, not a sociological one, but the implication is much the same in the language of the eighteenth century or of the twentieth. All political institutions work in much the same way, and the practical differences between them lie outside politics, in the personality of the ruler or the tone of the culture. This is the theme of the 'Trimmer' in all ages:

> *For forms of government let fools contest:*
> *What'er is best administered is best,*

as Pope wrote,[4] echoing the language of those, such as Temple and Halifax, who helped to drive 'enthusiasm' out of fashion in the last years of the seventeenth century. This may be the right answer in the twentieth century too: I have

nothing against it except that while it denies the possibility
of political programmes, it is itself a programme. In fact, it
sets on one side the things that we first look for when we set
out to study politics. The impulse to study politics is an
impulse to improve institutions; it can make no headway
unless it contrives first to understand existing institutions,
but it cannot stop there. The presupposition of political
study is that men are not simply moulded by institutions, but
can by intelligence and effort make better institutions for
themselves. This is not (I think) a pre-supposition that can be
proved, indeed it is a fertile mother of paradoxes: but we
cannot abandon it without a good deal of embarrassment
here and now. After all, the British are professional constitution-makers for others if not for themselves, as one can see in
news about the colonies from one day to the next. This is an
important invisible item in our balance of payments, and one
in which political scientists cannot help getting involved.
That is one personal reason why I prefer to start from the
problem of constitution-making, rather than from the
problem of power.

Let me next narrow the issue still further. One meets
oppressive paradoxes at once if one makes a frontal attack on
the problem of making political institutions in existing
States, or in the colonies, or between States; but no one
doubts that administrative institutions are made every day,
and that they can be better or worse made. The Science of
Administration is rather too pompous a name for our limited
knowledge about these things, but no one doubts that an
army or a Ministry must have defined ranks, and defined
duties, and a regular procedure for doing business; Weber
makes rather too much of it, but no one doubts that
hierarchical organisation is an invention, not a spontaneous
growth, and that it has been as important as mechanical
inventions like the lever or the wheel.

In the last fifty years administrative science has gone
through the same phases as political science. It began with
easy optimism about the possibility of improvement by
reorganisation — 'rationalisation' as it was called in the
1920s, a period not otherwise noted for its rationalism. There
was then a reaction into extreme scepticism about the

importance of hierarchical organisation. The contrast between formal and informal organisation was beginning to be popular before 1939, but its vogue was spread by the experience of dons and authors in the civil service and the armed forces. It was a shock to learn by experience that there were actually people living behind the great facade of bureaucratic organisation in the Ministries and in the Army, and that business was done there, much as in the outer world, by winning friends and influencing people: perhaps in a more primitive way, because the bureaucratic economy runs without money, and if one wants service from a colleague one cannot get it by paying for it in cash. This is the theme of that fine book, *The Small Back Room*, and of some good stories about the forces: it has also got into the text-books, and there, I think, it has been overdone.[5] A good many students must go out with the idea that it really does not matter about organisation in an office or a factory, because everything depends on human relations; in Biblical terms, 'The letter killeth, but the spirit giveth life'. St. Paul exaggerates, and so did Elton Mayo, though his language was more cautious; the letter of the law may sometimes kill, but it is rarely irrelevant.

Let us then look rather briefly at the rôle of formal organisation in the place where it is strongest, the hierarchical structure of bureaucracy, and let us see what sort of thing it is. And do not think I am forgetting the importance of human relations because I say little about them here.

The bureaucratic situation is dominated by a formal code called 'The Regulations' — perhaps most people know best the initials KR and ACI, but a similar code is implicit in any rational organisation of this type. 'The Regulations' are the central paradox, to which we must return later; under shelter of this paradox reign order and reason. Perhaps we can analyse the system in four ways:

1. The structure of ranks and posts: in sociological jargon, a formalised status system, defining grades, qualifications, and privileges.

2. The distribution of duties; the forms of specialisation defined as it were perpendicularly and laterally, so as to settle the functions of each branch and post and to define the

powers of decision at each level. This produces the familiar
genealogical tree of his office organisation which is engraved
on the heart of every competent bureaucrat.

3. Procedures, or what the efficiency men call a 'flow-
chart': the rules which state the routes by which different
types of business are to 'flow' through the office, and the
sort of *imprimatur* to be set on business at each stage, so that
it may pass on to the next stage, and finally attain the
beatitude of decision. Once upon a time the suppliant
member of the public 'flowed' through the office himself,
paying the proper fee to the proper official whose business it
was to attach the proper seal at each point of sorting. Now,
documents flow unsupported and the public pay their fees in
taxation and not across the desk. But the principle is the
same: the proper persons must say the proper things in the
proper order, or the decision will be invalid — to speak
strictly, there will be no true decision at all.

4. It may be well to add (finally) a fourth category of
regulations: a very important category, but not on quite the
same footing as the first three. The first three define what the
office is: the fourth category tells it what it is to do. The first
three are constitutional laws; the fourth is a sort of general-
ised command. Here one is concerned with a hierarchy of
action, not with a hierarchy of posts: a line of action is given
from outside the organisation in very general terms, at each
official level it is narrowed down by regulation or precedent,
till it reaches finally the lowest official and the lowest point,
where the general becomes the particular, and the official is
in theory no more than a rubber-stamp in the hand of the
master of the organisation. I say 'in theory' to emphasize that
this is only one side of the story; an official may be given no
official discretion to grant your request, but no one can take
away his human discretion to be surly or courteous, or
perhaps even to give a hint that if you could change one or
two points of no substance to you it would be possible for
him to agree after all.

Bureaucratic regulations thus imply two hierarchies, a
hierarchy of men, or rather of men playing official parts, and
a hierarchy of action. It is scarcely necessary to illustrate that
these are interdependent; you cannot pursue a policy rationally unless you have a rational organisation — and the organi-

sation is form without meaning unless it is there to execute a policy.[6] From this one can go on to work out quite plausible and useful doctrines about types of organisation in relation to types of action; up to a point this can be done *a priori* as a kind of logical exercise, but to bring it down to earth one must relate theories about organisation to the conditions of any given society. The matter then becomes more confusing.

For instance, good organisations work much more by team-work than by command, and one can work out some general theories about the two things: but in practice team-work is largely developed by training under strict command, and as teamwork develops it displaces command, even though the command structure is kept in reserve for emergencies. Again, it is obvious that an organisation cannot be better than the men who make it up, and at first they are raw material given to the organiser by the general condition of society. But an organisation in using men changes them, so that they diverge in many ways from the rest of society and become a new social type within it: the organisation creates a new social world of its own.

These are puzzles which need to be handled carefully both in theory and in practice, but they do not make it impossible to argue rationally about (for instance) the best form of organisation for some particular purpose in Britain at the present day: the 'science of administration' or management has often made itself absurd by claiming too much, but it would be just as absurd to claim too little. It is really obvious that in any given situation different types of formal organisation will have different effects on people and on action; that some people know a good deal about this; and that with due precaution it is possible to analyse their experience in general terms. This is constitution-making as practised daily at every level of society, from the school, the football-team and the factory to Ministries and nationalised industries; and I am anxious to maintain that this sort of constitution-making is a rational operation — that by taking thought we can improve our administrative efficiency, or our dividends, or our chances of winning the World Cup.

I have called this 'constitution-making': the next thing is to consider whether the analogy is fair, and whether from relatively optimistic conclusions about the science of administration one can draw any conclusions at all about the science of politics, taking that to mean the idea of self-knowledge and self-improvement in politics.[7] The analogy can of course be followed for some distance without serious difficulty. Any constitution is in part a 'distribution of duties'; for instance, it establishes posts such as those of President or Minister or Member of Parliament and assigns duties to them, and 'organic laws' (as the French call this type of constitutional law) may regulate these things in detail. Indeed, the line between organic law and administrative law is so fine as to be imperceptible: certainly, one can criticize a constitution with reference to purpose as freely as one can administration — subject always to agreement about what the constitution is for.[8]

This proviso throws into relief the difference between politics and administration. The latter is protected from political reality by the myth of 'the Regulations': the world rests on an elephant, the elephant on a tortoise, the tortoise on what? The Regulations rest on the Minister, the Minister on Parliament, Parliament of the Constitution, the Constitution on what? It would be logical to break off here and to ask for a definition of Constitution; this is a dilemma of the Hare and Tortoise type, and as Professor Ryle has been pointing out recently, this sort of puzzle generally arises from ambiguities in definition. There is certainly ambiguity in our use of the word 'constitution'; some people take it to mean a document of a particular kind, other to mean a political system, and trouble arises if the two senses are combined.[9] But it is not easy to suggest a new formula or a compromise formula without doing violence to the goddess Constitution (constitutions have been deified before now), so that I should prefer to proceed by suggesting elements which go together in the ordinary confused idea of a constitution.

To one of these I have alluded, the element of bureaucratic organisation. This is important because orderly procedure is very valuable both for efficiency and for sentiment: but it is not the heart of the matter. I think three other elements have to be added.

The first is that a constitution implies a state: do not take this in too literal a sense, but it is perhaps the most recognisable way of saying that one cannot talk about a constitution for very long without raising difficult questions about political entities.. The problem of sovereignty became a bore in the hands of the Benthamites and the British Hegelians, and in the 1930s one's heart warmed to Sir Ivor Jennings when he wrote the whole thing off as a 'politico-theological dogma'.[10] But the dogma comes to life again as soon as one tries to talk analytically about some very practical problems of our own day: for instance, the clauses in the South African constitution which protect the 'coloured' vote, or the French attitude to the proposal for a European Defence Community, or the limits of action against political suspects in a liberal democracy. One cannot press very hard on the dry forms of constitutional law without touching the naked nerve of personal allegiance and individual decision.

The second point is that all constitutions contain an element of description. This is most obvious when one considers a constitution like the British constitution which is in the technical sense 'unwritten'; there is no document called 'The Constitution'. The nearest to it that one can find is a book by Bagehot called *The English Constitution*, and another by Sir Ivor Jennings called *The British Constitution* — books that claim to be about what the British do in politics, and what they feel they ought to do. In this sense the British constitution is the political sociology[11] of the British; this seems plain enough in this extreme case, but would it not be absurd to say this of a document like the American constitution, or of a newly made constitution like that of Nigeria or British Central Africa? I must beware of a play on words, but I think I can make the point quite fairly in two ways.

In a sense, the American constitution is, as Bryce said,[12] a document that 'may be read through aloud in twenty-three minutes', and the document is law, not description. But what political meaning could the document have for someone who read it for the first time with no knowledge of America and no knowledge of the political tradition within which is was written? The American constitution has meaning only as a document in its setting; a political system, expounded to us by great writers, in which this document is a central point for loyalties and struggles for power. One can put this in another way, if one looks at constitutions newly framed by the lawyers, which have had no time to acquire associations and tacit understandings, and which seem like new structures in an old landscape. Undoubtedly, the constitution-maker has a wide range of choice, but his choice is not infinite: he will not make a real constitution unless he uses a working political language and embodies in institutions the situation as it exists. A lawyer's constitution is dead until it strikes roots in the political soil; and it will not do so unless it contains an element of what I called above 'political sociology'. There are plenty of constitutions in the books which are no more than sham constitutions because their authors disregarded this, often deliberately and for objects of their own.

The third element is that a constitution has sanctity. In the Latin tag, *numen inest*; the language is vague, but its vagueness is less confusing than the apparent precision of language about norms and value-judgements, and about the difference between statements of fact and statements of value. One of the puzzles about constitutions is that a statement of fact is also a statement of value: a record of how men have behaved is a statement about how they ought to behave. Men seem to switch easily from one mood to the other, and even to use both together: a constitution has got to be on both sides of the fence at once, to be both political sociology and political ethics.

This way to put it may be confusing; but it seems less confusing than to put the point by emphasising that a constitution is law. I think this is true, and that all law ultimately faces the dilemma posed by the idea of constitutional law[13]. If a constitution is law, then it is law made by an authority which the law creates; the circle cannot be broken except by postulating a *Grundnorm* as the formal origin of the lawyer's system — a solution consistent in itself which frees the lawyer by transferring the problem to other disciplines which are no better equipped to handle it.

However, the paradox is acceptable enough to common sense. A people creates itself by its capacity to recognise common imperatives and to respect them. This is very loose language, but it seems to have a recognisable political meaning. For instance, there was a period after the French Revolution when the old regimes tried to compromise with the new by offering what was called a Charter or constitution *'octroyée'* — something given by the King's grace to his people. In France, the legitimist constitution of 1814 was not very different from the Orleanist constitution of 1830, except that it was enacted as of right by the people of France, not granted by the grace by 'me, Louis XVIII' to 'our people' — the 'Roi des Français' was substituted for the 'Roi de France'. The point may seem trivial: but if one is to fight for principles, this is as good a one as any on which to take a stand. The tradition of the constitution is that by it free men limit themselves, under God and the law, but under no man.[14]

One effect of proceeding in this way is to sophisticate somewhat the traditional Western distinction between true and false forms of government, and perhaps to endanger it. The distinction between democracy and dictatorship has become a nusiance, because it is so easy to twist to fit any case; but at best it was a feeble substitute for the older distinction between governments under law and governments that know no law — between constitutional government and oriental despotism.[15] This is a fortress worth defending; it may seem to weaken it if one proceeds by taking constitution and State to be correlatives, and insisting that a true constitution is both descriptive and imperative. This may have awkward consequences. For instance, has the USSR a constitution in this sense? To begin with, there is a written and enacted document, the Stalin Constitution of 1936, as later amended. One should not assume offhand that this is wholly a sham, for it was composed by clever men, and there were certainly some things in it intended to command wide allegiance in Russia. Nevertheless the document is largely futile both as a description of Russian government and as a set of rules respected by Russian leaders.

Is there then a real Russian constitution behind the sham? Is there a constitution which binds the Mamalukes who are led 'like men by their opinions'? I do not know: but I think that this is in principle an answerable question. It may be that at the centre is an anarchy like that of Hitler's court. Or it may be that there are a set of rules well understood by those who hold power: that the struggles of the ambitious are conducted within limits set by the beliefs of followers, on whom they are dependent. If the latter is true, I should feel inclined to say that there is a true Russian (or 'Communist,' or what you will) state; that it has a true constitution; and that it is in consequence formidable, because it is, in its own sense, government under law.

Hitler's Germany broke down largely because Hitler ranted about the unity of Germans, but had no conception of unity in government; indeed, his art of despotism was to break unity wherever he saw it, and in breaking unity he isolated himself from the advice of almost all able men. It may be that in the end the USSR will break in the same way, but we should be fools to assume lightly that this is not a stable regime and a true state, although an oligarchic one. Nor should it be assumed on the other side, because France, or the USA, has the traditions of a state and is arrayed in all the verbiage of constitionalism, that a true state and a true constitution exist. Lincoln remarked in his First Inaugural Address,[16] at the outset of the Civil War:

A majority held in restraint by constitutional checks and limitations, and always changing easily with deliberate changes of popular opinions and sentiments, is the only true sovereign of a free people. Whoever rejects it does, of necessity, fly to anarchy or to despotism.

'Anarchy' is as destructive of constitutional government as is 'despotism'.

I have referred to four aspects of a constitution: it is an administrative structure, it is a description of a political situation, it has binding force, and it is a *supreme* set of rules, the articulation of a political entity — 'the supreme law of the land'. Let me now work back to the problem of constitution-making; this goes on all the time in the British Commonwealth, and the possibility of it is one of the assumptions of our scheme of things. So one has strong inducements to be optimistic.

First, the political situation and its relation to the social structure. This seems to be outside our power; indeed, one certain recipe for failure is to assume facts out of existence. It is true that aspirations and loyalties are facts: it is true, as John Stuart Mill says, that 'one person with a belief is a social power equal to ninety-nine who have only interests'.[17] But this is not to the point unless the one man in a hundred exists and can be found.

Second, the mechanical construction of political institutions is no harder than the mechanical construction of administrative institutions, provided that we know and face the facts, and provided that we know what we are trying to do. This last is a large limitation because it throws us back upon the hardest question, that of political entity. How can a people have a purpose? And if they have one, how can they know authoritatively what it is except through institutions set up in the light of their purpose – to tell them what their purpose is? I do not think the logicians have yet got to work on the logic of the first person plural, but a layman may guess that it is not the same as that of the first person singular.

The dilemmas set by the idea of men acting freely yet in unity are well known: and no one is likely to produce an easy answer to them. However, they are no worse for men acting together in politics than for men acting together in any other capacity: common purpose and joint action are ideas that we have to live with, and it is not really in doubt that individuals can help or hinder the growth of this free unity, and can do it consciously. I do not say that any single man can *make* it – to do so would be to pile contradiction on contradiction, because the unity in question is jointly made and self-made. But it is a recognisable fact of politics, or of day-to-day life, that some individuals can help more than others, because they are wiser or because they try harder. Here I agree entirely with what M. Bertrand de Jouvenel said in a distinguished lecture last year:[18] this is a supreme art. But I do not like his conclusion that this art is the supreme object of political science, as Machiavelli perhaps also thought in his passion for the unity of Italy.

For one thing, this flatters the vanity of politicians too

much: there may be one man here and there who touches the
hidden springs of politics and gets the result that he ex-
pects — but most politicians are representatives, not leaders;
it is easier to be a good representative than a good leader, and
a great deal more useful than to be a bad leader. Besides, the
academic student cannot say much more about the supreme
art of politics than about the supreme arts of music or
poetry. One can define the limiting factors, one can trace the
history of the idiom common to all performers, great and
small, but one cannot capture the essence of the great man's
art. If this can be done at all it is a job for artists, not for
scholars: Thucydides on Pericles, Vergil on Augustus, even
Walt Whitman on Lincoln. But the charm of artists may be as
dangerous as the vanity of politicians, and I am not very
anxious to cement the alliance.

Nevertheless, I think one must stand firm at this central
point: the making of unity is not wholly a social process or
even one of joint will — individual will and wisdom are vital
to it. If we pass this point, we are on easier ground. The third
element to which I referred was that of the sanctity of the
constitution, and here I must in large part refer you to what
has been written by Professor Macbeath. A constitution
purports to be a rational structure: indeed the whole notion
of government under law belongs to the same realm of ideas
as right reason, natural law, and the equality of men in so far
as they realize their nature as men. Constitutions purport to
be as rational as bureaucracies, but like them they live by
myth-making and ritual. Rational organisation breeds repetition, repetition breeds habit, and habit breeds affection. An
action originally purposive is in the end performed for its
own sake: and in the process there grow up on the one hand
'rationalisations', in the new sense of false explanations, on
the other hand unexpected effects which may often be good
effects.

In a bureaucracy a piece of procedure may be well
designed for a particular purpose at a particular time: times
change, the procedure goes on: someone asks questions, and
angry defenders think of justifications for the *status quo*.
These are often so silly that they hasten reform: and reform
may take place without much thought about the problem of

whether the old operation, in losing a purpose, had gained a function. Survivals may have functions even in a bureaucracy: no one really doubts that they have functions in a constitution. The Coronation itself contained, from the first, elements purely religious, and is therefore not a good case to take: but the meeting of an enlarged Privy Council which greets the Sovereign on his or her accession has no religious implications, and yet seems a fair case of constitutional ritual. This can happen equally well with a more formal constitution such as that of the United States; the rubbish, if I may so term it, about the elected electors who elect the President serves no useful purpose, but we could not abolish these gentlemen without a good deal of disturbance to the American way of life.

I am not sure that a constitution can exist at all on a scale as large as that of a nation without this element of civil ritual, which seems mere gibberish except in so far as we find false rationalisations for it. It is hard to imagine a constitution without ritual: and yet ritual cannot be enacted. Or can it? It may be that one can enact, not ritual, but ways of acting likely to give rise to ritual, as we try to do when we impose the odd routines of Westminster on the Parliaments of West Africa. Certainly there is no other way to enact sanctity: legal safeguards written into the text of a constitution have no power other than the power of myth.

Notes

1. The line is first clearly drawn by Aeschylus and Herodotus — see in particular the words which Herodotus gives to the Spartan king in exile who was with the Persians at the Hellespont and before Thermophylae (Herodotus, VII, 114 and 209).

2. One might call this period 'middle Laski': but Laski himself was never wholly absorbed in it, because he brought with him so much from nineteenth century Oxford and from pluralism.

3. Dicey, *Law of the Constitution*, eighth ed., p. 75, quoting Hume *Essays*, *I*(1875 ed.), pp. 109—10.

4. *Essay on Man*, Epistle III, lines 303—4.

5. This has been largely an American trend, and the Americans are now coming to the same conclusion about it: see (for instance) Arthur W. Macmahon, *Administration in Foreign Affairs* (University of Alabama, 1953), at p. 168.

6. A similar point is made on p. 1 of Professor Macmahon's *Administration in Foreign Affairs*; and since writing this I have noticed that Kurt Lewin applies this analogy of 'hierarchy of purpose' to distinguish the adult personality from that of the child. (*Field Theory in Social Science*, Tavistock Publications, 1952, at pp. 102 and 110).

7. Sir Ivor Jennings, *The Law and the Constitution*, 3rd ed. (1943) at p. 314: The people in a democracy are free to learn what facts they please about their own system of government, and *to change it if they can think of a better*'. (my italics). This seems a perfect illustration of the theme and its paradoxes.

8. Sir Ivor Jennings, op. cit. at p. 131: 'As in the creation of law, the creation of a convention must be due to the reason of the thing, because it accords with the prevailing political philosophy'. Jennings, who is in principle a 'constitution-maker', though a cautious one, is here trying boldly to absorb conventions (generally supposed to be irrational) into a rational structure of politics.

9. Professor Wheare (*Modern Constitutions*, p. 3) chooses the former: Sir Ivor Jennings is close to the latter; but neither contrives to be quite consistent or free from paradox.

10. op. cit. at p. 148.

11. Or even 'political ecology'.

12. *The American Commonwealth* (1915 ed.) vol. I, p. 374.

13. Appendix III to Jennings, *The Law and the Constitution*, is much concerned with this point. Cf. A. F. Bentley, *The Process of Government* at p. 295.

14. The point is neatly made by the amendment which in 1925 added a new first section to the South African constitution, 'The people of the Union acknowledge the sovereignty and guidance of Almighty God.'

15. As characterised by Montesquieu: e.g., *Esprit des Lois*, bk. 3, chap. V.

16. Everyman Library edition of the *Speeches and Letters* at p. 171.

17. *Considerations on Representative Government* (1861 ed.), p. 14.

18. Published as 'The Nature of Politics', *Cambridge Journal*, May 1954.

16 Pressure Groups in British Government *

Readers of Professor Hancock's autobiography will remember that he refers to Disraeli's gambit — 'How is the old complaint?' — and says that if he ever meets a young social scientist whose name he has forgotten he opens conversation by asking, 'How is the conceptual framework?'[1] The subject of 'pressure groups' raises so many issues of social and political theory that one is tempted to treat it primarily as an excuse for the discussion of concepts. I think however that it would be unwise to push logical analysis very far until some attempt has been made to state the facts of the situation, and this is the primary object of the present paper. Criticism of it may provide a basis for further research and for better analysis.

Political scientists in Britain are challenged to enter this field both by the trend of academic interest in other countries and by the present state of British parties. Since 1949 we have entered a phase in which party programmes seem relatively unimportant. Parliament between 1944 and 1949 put on the statute book a programme of reconstruction which it will take at least twenty years of hard work to execute. No party is at present much tempted to look beyond the end of that period, so that the emphasis is on good administration, rather than on choice of policy. The issues in foreign policy are more profound, so profound that the public as a whole finds them hard to grasp except in terms of personalities, and is more ready to think about character and diplomatic skill than about principles. This phase might be cut short by events at any moment, but while it lasts we tend to think of politics as a continuous process of

* From *British Journal of Sociology*, VI, no. 2 (Jun 1955).

267

adjustment and not as a contest between alternative principles.

The British have not experienced this mood since the emergence of the Labour Party as a serious political force early in the 1920's. Before 1914 the more sophisticated and the more rebellious were agreed in regarding British parties, like American parties, as empty bottles bearing different labels, into which any political mixture might be poured. The composition of the mixture, it was assumed, was due to forces outside the parties, and political theory and empirical research both turned in that direction. The early work of the Webbs, on consumers' co-operation, Trade Unionism, and local government, was based on these assumptions, and they followed up their studies of working-class organisation by investigating professional associations, as they existed during the war of 1914–18[2]. All this was the background of their *Constitution of a Socialist Commonwealth of Great Britain*, published in 1920, which attempted to combine 'old' and 'new' constitutional principles into a single document. Events almost immediately turned in a different direction. Since 1920, both academic students and working politicians have discussed government primarily as a means of democratic choice between alternative policies, and not as a continuing social process.

In the historical circumstances of the time this emphasis was both inevitable and right: but its limits are indicated by the complete difference of development in the USA. The theme was set by A. F. Bentley in 1908 in a book called *The Process of Government*, and his thesis was restated by D. B. Truman in 1951 in *The Governmental Process*, a book which takes account of the immense mass of description and analysis which has accumulated in the intervening years[3]. The political theory which emerges from all this research is not very coherent, and can accommodate various conflicting conclusions about ideal forms of government. But it is extremely effective as a tool of analysis, as may be seen in the recent assessment of our situation by Professor S. H. Beer of Harvard[4]. A good deal of research inspired by the same ideas is in progress in this country, and some of what follows is based on discussion with those concerned in it, to whom I am particularly obliged. There is however little published work on which to draw except for some studies of Trade Unions and professions, which generally pay more attention to internal structure than to political and social influence. The position in other countries of Western Europe is much the same. There is an excellent study of the position in Sweden (which preceded us on this road) by Professor Gunnar Heckscher[5] : and Professor Duverger[6] has recently drawn attention to the need for research in France. But there is still little comparable material except for the USA, and it is obvious that parallels with America cannot be pushed very far.

One has therefore to deal with a subject which is wrapped in a haze of common knowledge. People everywhere are familiar with it and know a good deal about it, but they find it hard to see the situation in proportion and as a whole. It may therefore be a useful first step to seek for some agreement about what we already know, and that is the main object of the present paper. Its 'conceptual framework' is extremely amateurish, and can be justified only in so far as it arises naturally from the problem of compressing a mass of miscellaneous information into a manageable form.

A Terminology

First, terminology. The phrase 'pressure group' is now well established, but its origin is a little obscure. A. F. Bentley's book was called *The Process of Government: A Study of Social Pressures*, and it is almost entirely concerned with the concept of 'group pressures' as a tool of analysis in politics. But I do not find that he reversed the phrase so as to make it 'pressure groups': indeed it would be out of line with his scheme of thought to do so. The reversal must have been made a little later by casual usage in politics and journalism[7], and it has always had a flavour of political abuse[8]. As Bentley says[9] , there is an accepted view that politics should be conducted by reason alone — or perhaps by reason and sentiment: 'pressure' is associated with 'power', and (like 'power politics') it is repugnant to most people, if only because they believe that 'power' is always exercised by someone else, and never by themselves.

The phrase 'interest groups' is used by Bentley, and is more legitimate than 'pressure groups'. But it has acquired some unpleasant overtones, and has to be used with care. I have sometimes preferred to use the phrase 'organised groups', in a rather narrower sense explained below: but ordinary usage is too strong to displace, and 'pressure groups' they remain.

B Definition

Next, definition. We have no difficulty in recognising a pressure group when we meet one, but this does not make definition any easier. One source of difficulty is that many groups important in politics are hazy organisations of a very informal kind, the members of which do not always recognise themselves for what they are. If we are to understand British politics we must know about such things as the Clapham Sect, the Benthamites, Benjamin Jowett, Crabbet, Blooms-bury, the Morant connection in the civil service, Cliveden, the pro- and anti-German factions in the Foreign Office in the 1930's, and so on. Groups of this sort are not beyond the reach of academic study, as one can see from works like Professor Finer's book on Chadwick, Mr. Annan's on Leslie Stephen, Mr. Harrod's on J. M. Keynes. But these instances suggest that the job is one for historians: such groups are highly individual and their operation is the pith and sub-stance of the political history of a nation. There seems to be no hope of generalisation about it except at the exalted level of talk about human groups in the abstract, which is exhilarating, but not very helpful to students of politics.

It is therefore necessary, as a matter of tactics rather than of principle, to reduce this unlimited field to something more manageable, and for a political scientist it is natural as a first step to cut out groups which do not possess a specified formal organisation. Formal organisation is a subject which we are accustomed to handle in dealing with the state and its organs, and we know what its problems are.

I think however that to make the subject manageable it must somehow be reduced still further. The number of distinguishable organisations in this country is enormous —

perhaps of the same order as the number of adult inhabitants — and all organisations may have some reference to politics in the sense that all are recognised or at least tolerated by the law, and that all have some tendency to persist in their chosen course and to react against any interference, including interference by public authority. How is one to separate organisations which are politically significant from those which are not? The difficulty is that there is no logical halting-place between the least of the organised groups and the greatest. There are circumstances in which the most harmless local dramatic society or hiking club may find that it can only get on with its business if it uses tactics in local politics (or in the politics of a greater group) which are indistinguishable in principle from those used by great organised groups in national politics. Similarly, one finds that the problems of internal democracy and bureaucracy are much the same at all levels, in spite of great differences of scale.

It may be, therefore, that if one wishes to find a model or models for different types of organised groups, the best tactics will be to begin by detailed study of small pressure groups rather than of great ones. But what we are interested in as students of politics is the part played by such groups in *public* decisions, and it is therefore fair to exclude organisations which have only limited dealings with the organisation of the state. This is in its nature a shifting category, since a shift in circumstances may bring almost any organisation into a public situation. But at any given moment the number of organisations which are playing politics is relatively small. For instance the Catholic Church only comes into our scope in so far as it is involved in politics by a row about voluntary schools or about the persecution of Catholics in some foreign country. Trade Unions may sometimes be outside our scope, in so far as they are organisations which exist to bargain with employers and to organise mutual benefits for their members. But some Trade Unions are composed only of the servants of public bodies, so that all their bargaining is bargaining with the public; and all Unions are now much involved in the public regulation of wages and conditions of work. It is therefore impossible to exclude Trade Unions in general; the focus of Trade Union studies has traditionally been different, but it is sometimes illuminating to consider them from the point of view of political pressure, rather than from that of industrial democracy.

It may (finally) be wise to exclude various types of bodies which are in law organised groups but which are in practice so constituted that it is not easy to say who their real members are. ICI and the City of Manchester are in a legal sense organised groups, and they are certainly entities which exercise influence on government, but here the gap between formal and informal organisation is so wide that we shall never get outside the lawyer's world if we start from the Articles and Memorandum of Association or from the Charter of Incorporation with the relevant Acts. We cannot avoid the issue by limiting ourselves to pressure groups whose members have a free choice whether to belong to them or not, for the question of the 'closed shop' in the professions, in industry and in trade is one of the central problems: but it will be wise to exclude cases in which legal membership of the legal organisations is no more than a matter of form[10].

These exclusions leave a field which could be described as follows: *the field of organised groups possessing both formal structure and real common interests, in so far as they influence the decisions of public bodies.* This raises a difficulty about political parties, which is referred to below, and there are a number of terms in it which could be debated at great length; but it will perhaps serve as a starting-point. One can illustrate what is meant by a list; such a definition would include the influence on public policy of organised professions, trade associations and trade unions, of associations of local authorities and their officers, and of associations for the promotion of particular interests or of particular good objects: for instance, the BMA, the NUT, the Town Planning Institute, the Iron and Steel Federation, the Association of British Chambers of Commerce, the NUM, the NUR, the AMC, NALGO, the Association of Education Committees, the Association of Medical Officers of Health, the NFU, the Sabbath Day Observance Society, the Africa Bureau, the Howard League, the Road Haulage Association, the Fish Frier's Association, the educational organisation of the Catholic Church, a community association or tenant's association on a housing estate, a local Trades Council or Chamber of Trade, a golf club interested in protesting against the use of its land for building, a Mother's Union offended by BBC talks about psychology and religion.

The list is potentially enormous, yet it excludes many groups which are of great interest to sociologists. The next problem therefore is whether one can say anything important about the politics of these groups without becoming deeply involved in matters of social structure.

C The Situation

In a field like this one system of classification is bound to cut across another, and in the end the best tactics may be to choose one classification out of many, and relate everything else to it. But this will entail some sacrifices, and it may be best here to experiment briefly with various alternatives. These four seem to be the most obvious: by the type of body whose decision is influenced, by the type of interest at stake, by the internal structure of the organisation, and by the methods which it uses. What I have to say about these is based on enquiry and discussion over a pretty wide field, but there are only scraps of material here and there which can be documented up to the hilt, and very little of this documentation could be published. This is a problem not of accident but of substance: it affects all research into current politics, and its implications have not perhaps been fully considered by social scientists.

1 *By Authority Influenced*

The first heading, that of type of body influenced, raises only one point of interest. Public bodies are classifed conveniently enough in the textbooks as central, local and 'other': it is almost a commonplace that any public body has its penumbra of organised groups which form its particular public. Perhaps this is most familiar in the middle levels of administration: the Cabinet or the full Council of a large local authority are the centre of so many contending pressures that it is very hard for any single organisation other than a political party to impinge on them effectively. But each Permanent Secretary in Whitehall has to know a good deal about the troop of big and little associations which move with and around his Ministry: in a sub-department the attendant retinue may be quite small and it is the civil servant's job to know it intimately. Similarly, each Committee of a local authority will have its own pressures, and both Chairman and chief official will know them very well.

In this sense, the field of groups is organised (with much overlapping) into the clienteles of various decision-makers at various levels[11], and this is one way in which one could organise material for research: for instance, a thesis about group pressures on the homing pigeon sub-section of the pets section of the livestock division of the production depart-ment of the Ministry of Agriculture and Fisheries — or what you will. In our system the focus of decision is almost always somewhere in the field of 'administration'; an approach from this end would describe the British system in a fairly complete way, and there would scarcely be the necessity (which Professor Truman finds in the USA) to deal separately with pressure in the legislative process and on the judiciary.

This seems however to leave political parties out of the story altogether. As Professor Truman insists, the words 'political party' mean in the USA many different things in different circumstances. This is also true in Great Britain, but we tend in this country to draw a pretty sharp line between parties and pressure groups by defining party with some variant on Burke's formula: 'a body of men united for promoting by their joint endeavours the national interest upon some particular principle in which they are all agreed'[12]. This excludes a good many manifestations of party in the USA, and it also excludes the conception of party dominant in the old German and Austrian Empires (and by no means extinct), which virtually identified parties with organised interests. We also tend at present to lay a great deal of emphasis on the hierarchical organisation of the parties so well described by Mr. Robert McKenzie, and to bother less about the oddities of the informal structure. A party in this strict sense, 'Burkean' and hierarchical, may be a social class organised to transform society in its own interest: more prosaically, it may be an honest broker of many interests, a mediator between public opinion and public policy. On either interpretation of party, party is one important focus of pressure groups and channel for influence. Indeed, there is a strict view of the constitution which would assert that influence on decisions ought to be exercised *only* through parties prepared to submit to the judgment of the electors. I should guess that this is not what happens. Undoubtedly some pressure groups operate on one party or the other or on both parties, and all pressure groups are interested in MPs. But I do not think that the parties bulk very large in the day-to-day operations of the average honest pressure group; there are many ways of exercising influence nationally or locally which are accepted as proper and which do not pass through any party office.

2 *By Interest Involved*

The second line of classification is by the type of interest involved. This looks promising, but is very difficult to manage without introducing one's own judgment about the particular question at issue. One could spot at once the bias of a researcher who classified the pressures regarding television into those based on private profit and those based on interest in public service. In theory there is a distinction between selfish pressure groups and 'do-gooders': in almost all cases there is a mixture of motives. Private financial interests will campaign by using arguments derived from widely held views about the public interest, and they may end (or even begin) by convincing themselves. On the other hand, even the most high-minded organisation cannot last long or press very hard without recruiting and paying for permanent full-time employees: and there then arises the problem of the man whose job depends on his success in finding a case to make.

It would be a mistake therefore to build much on a classification of organised groups into 'self-regarding' and 'other-regarding'; and if any lines are to be drawn between types of interest it must be done more cautiously. There are for instance common local interests, such as those fostered and expressed by Industrial Development Associations[13]. There are common interests in manufacture, expressed by trade associations; there are common interests in setting standards of skill and maintaining a monopoly of jobs, expressed by professional bodies and by certain Trade Unions; there are common interests between the employees of one employer, expressed by the civil service Unions or by industrial Unions: and so on. This suggest some points of importance, but (at first sight) not many. There seems to be great similarity between all these bodies in so far as they have evolved working techniques of influence; there are also great differences of internal structure, and these seem to be related to the history and technical character of individual interests, rather than to any grouping by type of interest.

3 *By Internal Structure*

It may be convenient to take next this question of internal structure. There is a good deal to be said about this, but very little of it relates to the formal constitutional structure of the association. The constitutions of states are almost always interesting, the rules of associations are generally very dull, and contain much that is common form set out so as to conceal a sentence or two here and there on which the whole thing depends. It is therefore best to approach from the angle of informal organisation: what questions does one ask first when one is trying to get on terms with a body that one does not know? Who runs it? Who are the active members? Where does it get its money? The answer to the first question almost always turns out to be one man, full-time and paid for his services; the impression one gets is not that there is an iron law of oligarchy, but that there is a new type of entrepreneur or broker; the man who makes a living by finding and focussing common interests and grievances and by pressing them in the right way. This impression is to some extent due to the terms of our enquiry: one of the main reasons why an informal group acquires formal organisation is that it has reached the scale of hiring staff and spending money on a fairly large scale, and these are things that cannot conveniently be done except in proper form. Probably the two things develop together: the existence of a potential director encourages formal organisation, formal organisation makes it possible to have full-time staff. Without research one can only say that there is quite a large class of jobs which have much in common, in spite of social and educational differences: jobs like those of a Trade Union official, or secretary to the NUT, or the AA, or the BMA, or the NCSS, or the Howard League, or director of the FBI or of a Chamber of Commerce. It is hard to fit these men and women into accustomed categories such as administrator or entrepreneur or politician, and one must not call them 'lobbyists' because that suggests American analogies which are quite misleading. The category is a new one, and perhaps specifically British.

There is much greater variety as regards membership. One comes across organisations of all sizes and of all degrees of keenness, from small groups of business men or philanthropists keenly interested in a single topic to vast organisations which include many members whose interest in the association is very slight and who contribute nothing to it except subscriptions. There is perhaps a line to be drawn between 'do-good' organisations, which are not interested in increasing membership except to increase their funds, and may prefer to work with a few large contributors; and 'occupational' associations which will always tend towards the closed shop, because their influence depends on the completeness of their membership within the area which they attempt to control. This factor is expressed in familiar experience about standards of qualifications, pressure to join, internal jurisdiction, lines of demarcation, and growth of amalgamations, problems which have something in common at the level of the BMA, or that of the Chartered Institute of Secretaries, or that of the ASLEF. But one must be careful not to generalise too much, as the whole field except that of Trade Unions is unexplored, and even Trade Unions are imperfectly known.

The third problem is that of the link between management and members. One can call this internal democracy, or one can call it the problem of financial control: the two formulae mean much the same in practice. Trade Union studies have cast some light on the possible variety of constitutions and on different ways in which the same constitution may be worked[14]. There are some obvious points of importance in the formal drafting of a constitution: for instance, to give large powers to the annual general meeting of members will tend towards centralisation, as AGMs are generally ill-

attended and easy to handle. A plebiscitary or pyramidal
constitution may have the same effect. On the other hand,
the reference of decision to a large number of branches acting
separately is likely to delay action and also to weaken the
central authority. This sort of proposition about comparative
politics can be made *a priori* and confirmed by a few cases:
but there is very little ground for generalisation from recorded facts except about Trade Union structure.

4 *By Method of Pressure*

Much more could be said about classification by method; this
is a point at which group politics fits into the whole structure
of national politics, and one can see that there could be a
book on this which would add enormously to our understanding of the character of British government, as distinct
from American or French or Russian government. Here are
some headings, incomplete and badly documented:

(*a*) *Inducement to individuals,*   in cash or kind: or pressure
by threats, which is the correlative of this. The line drawn by
law between honesty and corruption varies very much
in different countries, and may have little practical significance. I do not know of any comparative study of the law
about corrupt practices, but my impression is that British
law, including law about financial support for candidates, is
stricter in form than the law of most other countries. This is
uncertain, but there is no doubt that British law is effectively
applied. The trickle of insignificant cases in central and local
government illustrates the small scale of such illegal corruption as there is, and makes it clear that the game is not
worth the candle. I know of no case in which there has been
even a suspicion of illegal corruption by an organised group:
as will be seen later, the good reputation of a pressure group
is one of its most effective means of influence, and it would
be insane for any group to endanger it for small temporary
gains.

There are however two important matters which are not
illegal and could scarcely be made illegal, but which raise
controversy from time to time.

(i) It is a familiar fact that particular MPs act regularly as
spokesmen of particular interests[15], and indeed this is one of

the most important parts of the work of the House of Commons. We badly need an analysis of types of MPs in the twentieth century on the lines boldly drawn by Sir Lewis Namier for the eighteenth century. Presumably all (or almost all) MPs now spend a good deal of time on the minimum of routine attention to constituency and to party which is necessary to keep a seat: and presumably there are still some who do this for reasons of social prestige and do not attempt to take a serious part in the business of the House. But probably the number who take some interest in public business is larger than it has ever been, and here there seems to be a workable distinction between those who speak mainly on specific matters related to some special interest or inter- ests, and those who speak as potential leaders of opinion or spokesmen of opinion on large matters of public policy. The protagonists of special interests are not disqualified from reaching office, and one can think of well-known cases, that of Sir Reginald Dorman Smith for instance[16]: but on the whole the way to office is not through identification with an interest, however powerful. Yet the interests are anxious to have their case stated on the floor of the House, in commit- tees, and in the smoking-rooms, and it is in the interests of the House that this should be done. It raises its prestige as Grand Inquest of the Nation, and also contributes to the efficiency of business. The Committee stage of Bills 'upstairs' is rarely effective except when there is a discussion between one set of experts speaking through the Minister and other experts speaking through various backbench MPs. Are the MPs who act as spokesmen bound in any way to the interests for whom they speak? By formal rule they are not bound and cannot be bound, without breach of privilege of the House: the matter was last thrashed out in the discussion in Mr. W. J. Brown's case in July, 1947[17]. In practice, a wide range of motives is involved; it may be the vain but human desire to have a good case and to do justice to it, the political desire to keep a good 'connection' or clientele, or some motive of social and financial ambition, honestly pursued.

(ii) The other matter that has caused anxiety is the question of whether individual public servants are influenced by the idea of good jobs in industry when they leave the service of the Crown. This is raised sometimes about politicians: there was a considerable pother about naval officers and armament firms in the 1930's, when Senator Nye and others gave currency to the idea that wars were due largely to 'Merchants of Death'[1][8]: and it is obvious now that retired Air Marshals are seldom left to beg their bread or become golf club secretaries. This is a point which requires vigilance, so long as the emoluments of public service are less than those of private industry: but it can effect only a very small part of the public service, and my guess is that even there its effect on policy is negligible[1][9].

(*b*) *Direct Pressure on Political Parties.* Here the most obvious question is that of party funds: this has attracted so much attention that it can be passed over quickly. The position about the Labour Party is clear enough, that about the Conservative Party is more obscure: all that need be said here is that the sort of groups which subscribe to political parties are very limited in numbers and type; they may be very important to the parties, but they are only a tiny part of the enormous world of organised groups.

It would be pleasant to be able to say more about pressure on parties through elections, but there is not enough evidence to enable one to be very positive. My general impression is that the plebiscitary character of elections is squeezing this out; campaigns (like that of the Catholic Church in 1950) to organise blocks of voters of particular issues are now reckoned to be a little disreputable, and in any case they do not seem to have much effect. The old nineteenth-century routine of putting specific questions to candidates also seems to be dying. But in some ways the process of selecting candidates is now more important in British politics than the process of election, and there are certainly organised groups (not Trade Unions only) which have an important influence at that stage; it is possible, but more difficult, for them to depose a sitting member or an established candidate.

(*c*) *Appeal to Public Opinion.* Pressure through elections may be declining but there is no doubt that organised attempts to alter the prevailing climate of opinion are still important in British politics. A new Corn Law League is unthinkable: and the Press Lords have passed their peak: but public agitation is still worth trying. The object perhaps is not so much to create public opinion, as to create an opinion about public opinion; both politicians and civil servants are trained to be conciliatory, and like to move with opinion, more from habit than from any specific compulsion. Expressions of opinion in the House of Commons carry extra weight if they are known to be based on wide contacts, and the status of the Parliamentary Question as an instrument of pressure depends on this. 'Write-in' campaigns of the American type may affect the atmosphere of the House of Commons a little, but under our system they rarely affect the actual vote; they may even defeat themselves by arousing suspicion and hostility. Public meetings are useful, but only if well attended and well reported in the press. Resolutions by a variety of ostensibly unconnected bodies are worth something: so are poster campaigns. But there is no doubt that the key position is held be the press, which decides what is 'news' and allocates space — editorial space, news space, and space in correspondence columns. The daily press is still held to be the best arbiter of public opinion, at its various levels, if only because its circulation figures are related in some way or other to public appreciation: but politicians are by trade pretty expert in taking the temperature of newspapers, and are not as easily deceived about public opinion as they were in the days when Northcliffe and others held the initiative. This in turn has moderated the use of stunting, and the general press is growing less important politically in relation to the various types of specialist journal, which relate to special public opinions, and belong to the next two sections of my paper as well as to this one. The BBC is of course a key point in British politics, but its importance is kept within bounds because it keeps as quiet as it can about public reactions to its programmes: ITA may prove to be more important as a sounding-board than the BBC if it has fewer inhibitions about giving publicity to what listeners and viewers think.

(*d*) *The Best Information.*   In spite of the implications of the word 'pressure', there is not much doubt that the most effective of all techniques is the appeal to reason, as the Webbs well knew. Some social and intellectual prestige is necessary in order to ensure that your information is what the best people believe to be the best: and there is an element of management in seeing that information is planted in places where it will reach decision-makers. But the essential thing is that the proper authority, whoever he may be, should be fed over a long period with relevant information which turns out to be correct. Those of us who were temporary civil servants during the war were fascinated at first by the discovery that every possible object of human consideration has its proper niche somewhere in 'Whitehall'. But one soon discovers, when one traces the man responsible for (shall we say) food for racing pigeons, that he is a chap who has never seen a racing pigeon, has only been in the job two months, and has an enquiry about pigeon-food (among his many other duties) to handle once a fortnight. But he is a conscientious chap and quite able — perhaps he got a First in Greats: he has the files: and it is easy to see from them which stories have in the past worked out right and which have worked out wrong. So he will be much influenced (for instance) by the *Pigeon Fanciers' Telegraph* if he knows that that journal has over the years been a reliable source of facts about pigeon-food.

Politicians are more accustomed than civil servants to talking generalities so as to conceal ignorance, and are vulnerable to various forms of appeal to sentiment rather than reason, which civil servants escape. But there is a vast area of decision in which politicians are concerned mainly to acquire a reputation for being right, and they too are very thankful to anyone who can keep them out of trouble.

(*e*) *Administrative Necessity*. The organised groups are often as indispensable in the execution of policy as in the making of policy. This can be found at all sorts of levels. At one extreme is blackmail by the experts: 'organise it our way or we won't cooperate'. These were the tactics of the medical profession in 1911 and 1947. The doctors overplayed their hand and became a public laughing-stock on both occasions: but their pressure has undoubtedly been responsible for the rather syndicalist look of one section of the health service

organisation. At the other extreme are associations formed
on the initiative of government because there is a job to be
done quickly and it is impracticable or politically undesirable
for the Ministry to expand its own staff and issue orders
through them. Perhaps the first famous case was the
formation of the British Iron and Steel Federation under the
pressure of tariffs in 1934: but the device of marketing
boards was introduced at about the same time for somewhat
similar reasons, and we are equally familiar with industrial
research associations, with semi-official bodies with names
like 'Bacon Importers National (Defence) Association, Ltd.',
and with Development Councils under the Act of 1947.

Often the same result may be achieved less formally, with
little said on either side; indeed it is a matter of form rather
than of substance whether business is done by an association
acting as sole agent for the government, or by an official
'control' under a temporary civil servant seconded to the
Ministry by the relevant trade association for the duration of
the emergency. One is tempted to say that in a technological
society, government is not possible except on this basis: the
political master is necessarily a layman with reference to the
experts, and he is taking grave risks if he attempts to rule
them except by discussion. It is hard to imagine what
happens in Russia in matters of this kind: certainly British
government rarely takes the risk of trying to break down a
united front of expert opinion. On the contrary, it is often
tactically important for the government to unify the experts
and interests concerned in a problem, so as to be able to
make a bargain which will stick, and (perhaps) so as to be
able to shift the burden of responsibility to their shoulders if
the scheme breaks down.

This is most marked at the lower levels of policy, since
there are some matters such as defence and foreign policy for
which the government must accept full responsibility or
abdicate. But similar considerations may have the same effect
in great matters as in small ones. The Society of British
Aircraft Constructors was reorganised during a defence crisis
in January 1938, to strengthen the industry in dealing with
the problem of rapid expansion: traditionally, various groups
in the City of London have influenced foreign policy because

of the excellence of their information about the financial situation in other centres; and we have recently seen, in the de-nationalisation of steel, an instance of the difficulty of distinguishing precisely where the line comes between control by government and control by an organised industry.

Certainly, the principle of action with and through organised groups is dominant in all ordinary affairs of government, and colours all British practice. Yet these relations are generally of a very informal kind and seem to be blighted by any attempt to tie organised groups into the formal machinery of government, on the lines familiar to theoretical reformers. In spite of Mr. Morrison's kindly references to them[20], it is hard to believe that much collective influence is wielded by the Economic Planning Board, or the National Joint Advisory Council of the Ministry of Labour, or the National Production Advisory Council for Industry of the Board of Trade. Their members are individually important, but collectively weak. Other bodies, less official in character, the Association of Municipal Corporations and the County Councils Association for instance, have achieved unofficially a status which makes them something like sub-parliaments, and they often play a very important part in legislation. But apparently this semi-official status has been achieved at the cost of effectiveness as organised groups: the local government associations are much more effective in small matters affecting local government than in great ones. Their terms of reference are so wide, their respectability so great, that they have become channels of pressure rather than pressure groups.

D Assessment

The preceding sections have raised some very general issues about British government, and perhaps cross the frontier between fact and judgment. It would be fair to end with some discussion of the political theory of pressure groups. Are they good things? Or rather, what standards do we use when we attempt to answer the question, 'Are they good things?' But my own assessment is implicit in my statement of the situation, and it is scarcely possible to go beyond this without tackling the subject again from a different point of view. I can therefore only sum the matter up in a personal way.

The structure of British government includes besides the hierarchical world of public servants and the parliamentary world of party politics a very complex world of organised groups: and public decisions are the result of interplay between these three worlds. Does the public get left out in this process? Perhaps, but then no public or publics exist politically except in so far as they can express themselves through this process: access to it is open to all, and the entry-fee can be paid in brains and energy as well as in cash. This may sound a complacent conclusion, but it is one implicit in this method of analysis. It is extremely illuminating sometimes to consider politics as a process or equilibrium, in which decisions are taken not be men but by the inter-relation of events. But one can get no assessment out of this analysis except that latent in its premises: 'The world is the best of all possible worlds, and *everything* in it is a necessary evil.'[2][1]

The answer may be different if one is asked bluntly whether one likes the thing. I think my own answer is that I don't like it very much. It seems to be one symptom among many of a general reversal of Maine's famous progress from status to contract. We are gradually shifting back into a situation in which a man is socially important only as a holder of standard qualifications and as a member of authorized groups, in fact into the new medievalism which was the promised land in the days from the younger Pugin to William Morris. This seems a good deal less romantic now than it did in the heroic age, when the English were wandering in the desert. The system is egalitarian in so far as qualifications lie freely open to talents: and its rigidity is mitigated by the fact that almost everyone has many different statuses within separate but overlapping organisations (a matter stressed· equally from different points of view by Professor D. B. Truman and Mr. T. S. Eliot[2][2]). Group managers are in general competent and clearheaded men who recognise the existence of the public interest and are moderate in action, by temperament or because in England moderation is a good way to get what you want. The worst danger to the system is from external shocks. Within its limits it is both sensible and humane, but it is technologically conservative and its political horizon is limited to problems familiar to the ordinary man in his daily business and to the organiser who represents him. Unfortunately there are a good many problems to be faced which are much wider in scope than that, and it is no use thinking that there is some specially organised group of experts which has capacity and power to deal with them. If great problems are to be handled at all it must be by a government prepared to use its majority: it is this that still gives primacy to the party system and to the traditional doctrines of the constitution[23].

Notes

1. Sir Keith Hancock, *Country and Calling* (1954), p. 223.

2. Published as a special supplement to the *New Statesman*, 21st and 28th April, 1917. Professor W. A. Robson's early work on the local government service (*From Patronage to Proficiency in the Public Service*, Fabian Society, 1922) also belongs to this phase.

3. A. F. Bentley's book was reissued in 1949 by the Principia Press, Bloomington, Indiana. The full title of Professor Truman's book is *The Governmental Process: Political Interests and Public Opinion* (New York, 1951). My debt to both these books will be obvious.

4. 'The Future of British Politics', *Political Quarterly*, Vol. 26, p. 61 (January, 1955).

5. *Staten och Organisationerna*, Stockholm, 1946: there are also two articles in English by Professor Heckscher, which I have not seen: G. Heckscher, 'Group Organisation in Sweden', *Public Opinion Quarterly*, Vol. 3, No. 4 (Winter, 1939); G. Heckscher and J. J. Robbins, 'The Constitutional Theory of Autonomous Groups', *Journal of Politics*, 1941.

6. He refers to the work being done on the French employers' movement by Professor H. W. Ehrmann, of the University of Colorado, who has already published an interesting article on 'The French Trade Associations and the Ratification of the Schuman Plan': *World Politics*, Vol. VI, p. 453 (July, 1954).

7. The usage was well established by 1928: see P. N. Odegard, *Pressure Politics: The Story of the Anti-Saloon League* (Columbia U.P., 1928), Preface, p. vii.

8. E.g. 'We do not have pressure-groups on this side of the House' — followed by an interruption (Mr. Anthony Hurd, MP, in the Crichel Down Debate: Hansard, 20th July, 1954, at Col. 1217).

9. P. 447. There was a neat example of this recently in a statement issued by the National Coal Board, which included the words: 'The action taken at Markham Main and the sympathetic action taken at

other collieries in Yorkshire is an attempt to use power instead of reason to solve disputes.' (*Manchester Guardian*, 6th May, 1955).

10. Since this paragraph was written, I have come on the following, which illustrates how hard it is to draw a working distinction between groups that are politically active and those that are not: 'The Calico Printers' Association, Ltd., has issued a booklet to each of its ten thousand employees explaining the issues involved' (in the adverse report on CPA's trade practices by the Monopolies Commission) 'and urging them to write to their members of Parliament without delay, no matter to which party they belong.' 'We fear,' writes the chairman of CPA, 'that desire for immediate political gain has been a deciding factor in the decision to force us to abandon our measures to ward off depression and unemployment when trade slackens.' (*Manchester Guardian*, 30th April, 1955.) There has also been discussion of the possible effects of ICI's profit-sharing scheme on electoral chances on Tees-side (*Manchester Guardian*, 18th May, 1955).

11. The Report of the Committee on Intermediaries (Cmd. 7904 of March, 1950) did much to explore this.

12. *Thoughts on the Present Discontents* (1770): World's Classics edition, Vol. II, p. 82.

13. See Professor M. P. Fogarty, *Plan Your Own Industries: A Study of Local and Regional Development Organisations*' (Oxford University Press, 1947).

14. See in particular V. L. Allen, *Power in Trade Unions* (London, 1954).

15. This has been excellently brought out in Sir Ivor Jennings' book on *Parliament*.

16. There are also cases, like those of Mr. Ernest Bevin and Sir Andrew Duncan, of spokesmen brought straight into office from outside the House of Commons: but House of Commons opinion is unlikely to accept this except in serious emergencies.

17. Report of the Committee of Privileges (HC 118 or 1947), and Hansard for 15th July, 1947. Similar issues arose in other privilege cases about that time.

18. Cf. Philip Noel-Baker, *The Private Manufacture of Armaments*, Vol. I, Part II, Chap. III (Gollancz, 1936): The Nye Report (74th Congress, Senate Report No. 944), in particular Part III or 3rd Part (April, 1936) and Chap. IV, Part II, of 4th Part (June, 1936): Royal Commission on the Private Manufacture and Trading in Arms (Cmd. 5292 of 1936), in particular at p. 57.

19. The case usually quoted is that of Sir Christopher Bullock, Permanent Under Secretary at the Air Ministry, who resigned after an enquiry in 1936 (Cmd. 5254); but there is still a good deal of doubt about the true circumstances.

20. *Government and Parliament* (Oxford, 1954), p. 305.

21. F. H. Bradley, Preface to *Appearance and Reality*, quoted by Professor Oakeshott in his inaugural lecture on *Political Education*. Richard Wollheim discusses the effect of 'equilibrium theory' on

Pareto's assessments, in a recent article in *Occidente* (Vol. X, p. 567, Nov. 1954).

22. *Notes towards the Definition of Culture* (London, 1948).

23. Since this paper was written the same point has been put with an attractive insularity by Mr. R. M. Jackson in quite a different context (an article on 'Ministerial Tribunals' in the *Manchester Guardian* of 22nd April, 1955): 'The underlying assumption is that the Government must always get its own way if it thinks the matter is sufficiently important, or cease to be the Government; that is a shocking doctrine to Americans and Frenchmen and their camp followers, but it happens to be our system and to work, like monarchy, because of the structure of convention and understanding.'

17 Pressure Groups: The 'Conceptual Framework'[*]

In a recent paper I implied that it was a relatively easy matter to settle a 'conceptual framework' for the analysis of politics in terms of pressure-groups.[1] A process of trial and error has convinced me that this was simple-minded, and that one must either use the phrase 'pressure-groups' as a handy and intelligible colloquialism, or go a very long way into the history of political theory in the last fifty years.

There are two major difficulties. The first is that since the 1920s there has been a growing tendency to make a separation between political theory and political description and recommendation. For instance, this is accepted as axiomatic by two authors referred to more fully later, Professor Herring and Professor Truman. In the preface to his book on *Group Representation before Congress*, published in 1929,[2] the former remarks that 'Groups, active coherent, organic are rising to a place of increased importance in the community. The full significance of such a movement must be left to the political theorist and the philosopher.' That is to say that evaluation of a state of fact is not a job for the man who knows the facts best. Professor Truman's[3] preface makes a similar point: 'it was to be expected that a large mass of essentially specialised and monographic case materials would be accumulated before an inclusive theoretical explanation appeared'. That is to say, science advances by a random assembly of material, collected by one set of persons and ordered by another. No one really believes either of these implications: and of course the excellent descriptive books written in the last thirty years are excellent partly because they order and criticise their material. Unfortunately it requires a great deal of reflective reading to grasp what

*From *Political Studies*, III no. 3 (Oct 1955).

theoretical structure each of them is using and how these
structures differ from one another.

The other difficulty is that as one reads it becomes obvious
that much of their language comes at second or third hand
from authors of books about sociology, social anthropology,
social psychology, psychoanalysis, economics, semantics, and
biology, who have invented new languages much more readily
than have political scientists. Political theory has always been
written largely in terms of such analogies, but the analogies
have not in the past been drawn from such various and
complex intellectual sources. It is like trying to theorize in six
European languages at once. A good many of the propositions expressed in this mixture of languages can be translated
back into political language of the traditional kind; and one
often has an uneasy sense of *déjà vu*. For instance, some
psychoanalytical theories have a flavour of Thracymachus:
individual urges are φύσει, social restraints are νόμῳ:[4] the
keyword 'group' does not seem to differ much in definition
from the Aristotelian κοινωνία. But these *rapprochements*
are not very helpful unless both the old and the new contexts
are known thoroughly, and it scarcely seems that this will
ever be possible again.

What is submitted here is merely a note based on a recent
reading of three books which are important in the history of
political groups: A. F. Bentley, *The Process of Government*,[5]
Pendleton Herring, *Group Representation before Congress*,
and D. B. Truman, *The Governmental Process*. Professor
Herring's second book, *Public Administration and the Public
Interest*,[6] provides a link with the related development of the
theory of groups in administration, through Mary Parker
Follett, Elton Mayo, Chester Barnard, and H. A. Simon.[7] The
object is to bring out a number of points about the
'conceptual framework' which it would be difficult to tackle
more directly.[8]

These are all American books, and it is almost certain that
the phrase 'pressure-group' was invented in America. It does
not seem to appear in the 'group' phase of British political
theory, exemplified by the early works of Professor G. D. H.
Cole, by the Webbs' *Constitution for the Socialist Commonwealth of Great Britain*,[9] and by Professor Herman Finer's
Representative Government and a Parliament of Industry:[10]

nor is it used by Mr. Walter Lippmann, as critic of Guild Socialism, in *Public Opinion*.[11]

It is still missing in the doctoral thesis about *Farmers and Workers in American Politics*, published by Professor Stuart Rice in 1924:[12] and then appears as normal usage, without apology or definition, in the preface to Professor Peter Odegard's doctoral thesis on the Anti-Saloon League,[13] which was submitted in 1928. One must assume, in default of better evidence, that it was invented by some Washington journalist during the period (Herring puts it between 1918 and 1928[14]) when the 'New Lobby' of respectable organizations was rapidly displacing the 'Old Lobby' of rather disreputable individuals. It was no doubt used from the outset to imply criticism, and it has retained that connotation in Britain. In spite of this, it is a fair enough shorthand expression for the type of 'conceptual framework' invented by A. F. Bentley.

Bentley knew American politics well, and had strong views about them; he had equally vigorous views about the logic of contemporary sociology — like Professor Ryle he will tolerate neither 'a grain-spook in the wheatfield nor a brain-spook in the class war'.[15] These two preoccupations are linked by an appeal to 'facts'. Individuals are facts, groups are facts: but individuals cannot affect government except through groups: therefore 'the process of government' must be studied as wholly a group process.

His scheme is easy to grasp, but difficult to set down specifically, because he slips round various difficulties by eloquent reiteration in language which never quite repeats itself. The basic proposition is that individuals are held together in groups by interests. A good deal of what Mr. Plamenatz wrote recently[16] about the word 'interests' is applicable to Bentley's usage. He is anxious to seem factual and tough-minded, but his 'interests' are not necessarily self-regarding, except in a tautologous sense, and various other words, such as 'wants' or 'needs' or 'wishes' or even 'purposes',[17] would serve him equally well. The existence of a group depends on an interest held in common. The group exists to get something: its existence is activity: therefore it 'presses' on its environment. The environment is in part non-human, and Bentley does allude rather casually to the economic or non-political activity of the group.[18] But he is interested only in groups pressing on one another: groups (to use language which he avoids) which are in competition for scarce goods.

Government is the resultant, and is wholly the resultant, of group pressures in this sense: and so is 'law in the broadest sense', which is 'one form of statement of the equilibrium of interests, the balancing of groups'.[19] Government 'in the narrowest sense' is defined as 'a differentiated, representative group, or set of groups (organ or set of organs), performing specified governing functions for the underlying groups of the population':[20] but this concession to traditional language is made only within his general conception of process. The process of government is an 'intelligent, felt process'[21] through and through: but reasoning and ethics are secondary, and merely 'mediate' interests.

All this (and much more) invites comment:

(a) The word 'group' became a 'blessed word' about 1900. Its semi-technical use probably began in German or French and not in English:[22] but in all three languages it had at first the convenience that it was a colourless word with which to designate human beings in the plural, more general than 'state' or 'class' or 'trade' or 'tribe' or 'village' or 'family' or any specific collectivity whatever. It was, however, almost at once mixed up with theories that groups were 'better' than various other institutions. Bentley is almost free from this sort of transference, but switches between various possible definitions of group. There are various careful formulations of these: perhaps the simplest and most useful is the working distinction between groups as (i) a number of people with the same characteristic (e.g. red-headed people); (ii) a number of people, like or unlike, who interact (the familiar film scenario of passengers faced by disaster in an aeroplane or bus); (iii) a stable pattern of interaction between a number of people who interact repeatedly. Bentley (like Professor Truman[23]) chooses the third, and is in one place[24] extremely clear that in his sense a group is 'the construction of the scientist's mind'. More usually, he blurs these senses, and it is not clear how much would be left if his vigorous language were analysed prosaically. Fog also surrounds the series of equivalences which can be drawn out from various passages (groups = intelligent felt activity = interests = pressure = inertia = process), and he is equally elusive about structure. Sometimes he anticipates later terminology about structure and function, role and status, in groups and in society; more frequently he assumes that there is structure within groups, denies that there is structure in society as a whole. Indeed he would not admit that it is possible to talk of 'society as a whole' at all.

(*b*) Bentley's idea of explanation is to set out a system of interdependent variables (the groups) tending to equilibrium. Equilibrium analysis has had a great vogue in various branches of social science,[25] but I do not know of anyone who has traced its spread and its metamorphoses in different contexts.[26] Presumably it came from the physical sciences through biology and economics.[27] It was perhaps implied in Durkheim, and it was firmly established in social anthropology by Malinowski's studies of the Trobriand Islands, made between 1914 and 1918. Bentley is vague about it, and is innocent of later problems about statics and dynamics; but he is rhetorically emphatic about the figure of groups tending to establish a balance. They never reach the position of equilibrium, because the environment is never stable: but the idea of equilibrium helps to make more intelligible what is happening in the 'process' of politics. There is always a danger lest (in Professor Lionel Robbins's[28] phrase) there be a 'penumbra of approbation round the theory of equilibrium'. 'Equilibrium is just equilibrium', he says: whereas for Bentley 'Order is bound to result, because order is now and order has been, where order is needed, though all the prophets be confounded.'[29] He is staging a drama, not drawing curves on a blackboard.

(*c*) His method is not therefore quite what it claims to be. Equilibrium is not for him (as it is supposed to be in the natural sciences) a source of hypotheses related to the practical possibilities of investigation. He is always insisting on the importance of 'facts', of asking 'how, not why':[30] but he has no notion at all about 'operational definitions' and the problems of social measurement. It is an open question (perhaps) whether 'equilibrium' *can* be used rigorously for

investigation in the social sciences: Bentley pretends to use it
for investigation, but in fact uses it didactically, and does so
with great effect. His 'conceptual framework' enables him to
hammer in one simple maxim — 'look for the interest' — with
sharp analogies from a variety of sciences, and with examples
from every part of American government. His maxim is a
good practical lesson, so long as 'interest' is loosely defined
but carefully exemplified. Indeed, it is not a bad moral
lesson, as an antidote to various forms of political oratory of
the 'will of the people' type (as General Choke said to Martin
Chuzzlewit: 'What are the Great United States for, sir, if not
for the regeneration of man?'). But the message is no
different from that of Lincoln Steffens, except that it is
preached to a different audience.

Professor Herring begins as if he intended to take a similar
line.[31] 'Democratic dogma postulates that the citizenry put
thought of national welfare before that of the individual. The
general presence of this attitude constitutes a well-disposed
public sentiment. The citizens are supposed to take a broad
view of national affairs. This makes up the "public opinion"
that is to rule the country.' But this is not to be taken
ironically: and the book raises quite different considerations
about how to use a 'group framework'. Herring refers to
Bentley in his bibliography,[32] and 'group equilibrium'
language turns up here and there.[33] But these references do
not pretend to be scientific, his definition of 'group'[34] is
quite artless, and his serious concern is with two other issues,
those of presentation and criticism.

The problem of presentation is that of getting the 'facts'
about an extremely complex situation into a continuous
account of about 270 pages. This is done intelligibly, and
without fuss, by using a framework so simple that it seems
unpremeditated: brief description of the contemporary situation, brief history, brief general account of group methods,
followed by more detailed examples under specific but
undefined headings — industry, farmers, labour, civil service,
professions, women, reform, foreign policy. This classification is thoroughly illogical, but it works. It is much more
difficult to analyse *why* it works than to comment on the
more elaborate 'conceptual frameworks' of Bentley and

Truman. The reason perhaps is that hard thought has been spent not on the framework but on the management of individual chapters, and on strict economy, relevance, and consistency of fact and style. Perhaps another framework would have served as well for so able a writer: but perhaps not — the crux is an old one in literary criticism. One can only say that this is *one* effective way to present the facts.

The same sort of remark is suggested by Professor Herring's criticism. The object of the inquiry is not to advance science, but to consider what (if anything) should be done about pressure-groups; this can only proceed on the basis of some standard of better or worse in politics. The standard offered (as the title of the book implies) is that of 'representation': this is not defined except by usage and context, and there is no attempt at the sort of sophistication about 'representative groups' introduced by Bentley. The question is how organised associations may distort or misrepresent public opinion or the opinions of various publics, and whether misrepresentation can be stopped: there are some large gaps in the answer (one of them illustrated by Professor Herring's later book about the effect of pressure-groups on administrative agencies), but within its limits the book leaves little more to be said. The job is done, yet there is no attempt to fit together consistently the disparate elements in the framework of criticism — groups, equilibrium, pressure on the one hand, individual consent, public opinion, and public interest on the other. The conclusions drawn from the latent theory are 'sensible': so presumably the theory must be 'sensible', and it would be 'sensible' to elicit it, as Professor Herring invites the philosophers to do.[3 5]

Professor Truman accepts the invitation: but leaves one in some doubt whether he was right to do so. The central portion of the book (about half of it) is a description of the American situation, closely parallel to what Herring had done twenty years before. It is a better account than Herring's, but largely because documentation has accumulated and there are more examples to hand, so that the texture of the account is closer. But it is not different in kind: it is essentially non-technical, and has the same virtues of clarity, precision, and good order.

In brief it is a scholarly piece of work: but Professor Truman (for reasons plain to all of us in the 1950s) wishes to be not a scholar but a scientist, and the rest of his book is devoted to an extremely brave and resolute attempt to pin down Bentley's ideas, and to make them fit other parts of the universe of knowledge. In particular he has to take account of a great deal of good research work not based on Bentley's scheme: and to allow much more generously than did Bentley for criticism of the group system in the name of individual rights, public opinion, and the public interest.

A group is defined (a little loosely[36]) as a pattern of interaction between individuals — 'these interactions, or relationships ... give the group its molding and guiding powers'.[37] An 'interest group' is 'any group that, on the basis of one or more shared attitudes, makes certain claims upon other groups in the society for the establishment, maintenance or enhancement of forms of behavior that are implied by the shared attitudes'. Truman defends Bentley against the accusation that the latter leaves out the individual and the public, and has no difficulty in quoting passages. But there is surely no doubt about the difference of emphasis.

In both writers the 'individual' is undefined sub-stratum: but in Bentley he exists politically only as the intersection of groups, in Truman he is the bearer of 'attitudes' which define the group. 'Attitudes' are (in Bentley's language) 'brain-spooks', interchangeable with such words as 'opinions', 'ideas', 'standards', except in so far as the word 'attitude' refers specifically to some operational definition — as it rarely does.

Further, the word 'claim' has been substituted for the word 'pressure', with no definition except by implication. Some groups are merely potential interest groups, and do not become interest groups till they make claims: these potential interest groups include the large groups whose claims are for the maintenance of the 'rules of the game'. Other interest groups claim under the shadow of potential interest groups; the government is (at least in principle) the leader of the potential interest groups,[38] it is capable of decision[39] — and is not merely a resultant of forces. All this means that the use of 'claim' is not very different from that of Victorian political philosophy: much the same thing could be said in the language of the state, law, morality, claims, rights, and duties.

There are traces elsewhere of dissent from Bentley. Secondary groups, which are deliberately constructed associations, appear and are held to be of importance:[40] due allowance is made for the real effect of difference of formal organisation (including constitutional law) both in associations and in the state:[41] political environment is only 'largely', not wholly, group-defined:[42] reasoning about the public interest, and 'norms widely recognised in society' are allowed much greater weight.[43] Professor Truman would maintain that all this is in Bentley, and could quote chapter and verse. But this inclusiveness is in the nature of Bentley's writing, and the analogies are perhaps not as important as the difference in tone between Bentley's slashing cynicism and Professor Truman's careful insistence that there is a public interest and that in the end it generally prevails. This contrast leaves one with the feeling that Professor Truman is building a system of epicycles: that he is by ingenious shifts of definition and emphasis stretching a simple doctrine till it means almost (but not quite) the opposite of what it seemed to mean at first.

This can be recorded only as a feeling: neither author is careful enough in language for it to be possible to build anything on a comparison of passages. Indeed, neither of them tries to play at theory as if it were economic theory or physical theory. They make little attempt to create a mathematical sort of elegance or pleasure, and do not seriously attempt to 'express various meanings on complex things with a scanty vocabulary of fastened senses'.[44] It would be out of place to criticise them as unsuccessful logicians.

It is perhaps, in Bentley's terms, a more serious criticism to ask whether Professor Truman's theoretical exercise helps him in what he is trying to do. His declared object is to help 'to achieve control':[45] his instruments are the same as those of Professor Herring — exposition and criticism. As regards exposition, he concludes one of his opening chapters with the remark that 'we do not at present have the data . . . on which to base a functionally more useful classification of interest groups. As adequate means of measurement are developed, such data may become available. Meanwhile conventional classifications can be employed if their limitations are kept in sight.'[46] So he goes on to use 'conventional classifications': he uses them extremely well, and adds one or two pieces of terminology (such as 'access', and 'a public' in the singular), which are very helpful. The exposition seems to owe much more to this than it does to the conceptual framework, and one is left wondering just how the progress of science will later make it possible to do the thing better.

His criticism seems less successful, perhaps because less bold. Bentley boldly hitches himself into his own system by his own boot-straps, as the initiator of 'a differentiated discussion group',[47] with its own 'interest' in pressing for the extension of a particular way of reasoning or talking. He is consciously trying to remodel the 'rules of the game' as he writes, and is himself 'pressure' or a channel of pressure. Professor Truman prefers to remain uncommitted: he does not admit that he modifies the system by describing it, and he thus seems to fall between two stools. He cannot enter the battle as a combatant, like Bentley, rather a specialised sort of combatant, but a very active one: he cannot, like Herring, be content with a 'man-in-the-street' sort of objectivity, which appeals to a well-known (though confused) set of 'rules of the game', and gives prudent advice about how to apply or modify them. The result is to give rather a complacent, almost a Morrisonian, impression of American government, which is far from his intention, for there is much that he would like to see changed. 'This rather cursory examination [he says] suggests that a pathogenic politics in the United States is possible':[48] and 'pathogenic' is used as interchangeable with other words of the same type, such as 'morbific' or 'non-viable'. But either these words are a misuse of equilibrium theory, treating equilibrium as a norm and not as an instrument or analysis; or they just mean 'bad' = 'contrary to Professor Truman's idea of what the rules of the game ought to be'. It is fair to choose the second interpretation; but surely Professor Truman's standards deserve and require analysis of rather a different kind?

Notes

1. 'Pressure-Groups in British Government', *British Journal of Sociology*, vol. vi, p. 133 (June 1955).
2. (Johns Hopkins Press), 1929, at p. vii.
3. *The Governmental Process: Political Interests and Public Opinion* (Knopf), 1951.
4. R. M. MacIver, *Encyclopaedia of the Social Sciences*: article on 'Social Pressures'.
5. First published in 1908: the references are to the reprint issued by the Principia Press in 1949.
6. (McGraw-Hill), 1936.
7. I have referred to these in two earlier articles: 'The Study of Administration in the USA.' (*Public Administration*, vol. 29 (1951), p. 131) and 'Science in the Study of Administration' (*The Manchester School*, vol. 20 (1952), p. 1).
8. I do not think that the 'direct approach' is very successful in the article by Earl Latham, on 'The Group Basis of Politics: Notes for a Theory' (*American Political Science Review*, vol. 46, p. 376, June 1952).
9. (Longmans), 1920.
10. (Allen & Unwin), 1923.
11. (Harcourt Brace), 1922.
12. (New York), 1924.
13. *Pressure Politics: the Story of the Anti-Saloon League* (Columbia UP), 1928, at p. vii.
14. p. 21.
15. p. 36.
16. *Political Studies*, vol. ii, p. 1 (Feb. 1954).
17. e.g. 'All action is purposive, with purpose strictly as process' (p. 63).
18. p. 261.
19. p. 274.
20. p. 261.
21. p. 396.
22. It appears in a quotation from Spencer's *Sociology* (1882), vol. ii, p. 135 (Durkheim, *Règles de la Méthode Sociologique* (Alcan ed. of 1938), at p. 101), but this seems to be quite without technical implications. The idea of the group as 'unit of account' in sociology is latent in Gierke and Gumplowicz from about the 1870s; it becomes more explicit in Simmel and Small in the 1890s.
23. pp. 23–24.
24. p. 245.
25. As it was put in a recent advertisement: 'Achieve natural stomach balance — *maintain it* — and you have found the way to *lasting* relief from acid indigestion pain.'
26. There is no article either on 'equilibrium' or on 'process' in the *Encyclopaedia of the Social Sciences* (1932–5). The most useful

discussion I have met is in Appendixes 2 and 3 to G. Myrdal, *An American Dilemma* (Harper), 1944.

27. For the relation between economic and social equilibrium in Pareto see Richard Wollheim's recent article in *Occidente*, vol x, p. 567 (Nov. 1954).

28. *The Nature and Significance of Economic Science*, 2nd ed. (Macmillan), 1935, at p. 143.

29. p. 267.

30. p. 90.

31. p. 4.

32. p. 294.

33. e.g. at pp. 59, 157, 251, 267.

34. p. 6.

35. Quoted above, p. 247.

36. 'An excessive preoccupation with definition will only prove a handicap' (p. 23).

37. p. 24.

38. p. 449.

39. p. 508.

40. p. 39. This suggests a reference to Professor H. A. Simon's 'Comments on the Theory of Organizations' (*American Political Science Review*, vol. 46, p. 1130, Dec. 1952), which faces a similar problem.

41. e.g. p. 322.

42. p. 338.

43. p. 351.

44. Bagehot on one style of economic writing.

45. p. 12.

46. p. 65.

47. p. 428.

48. p. 523.

18 The Conceptual Framework and the Cash Basis*

This paper is an attempt to say something in general terms about the problems of research in politics. The matter is a serious one to us professionally; but we are none of us sure that others take us as seriously as we take ourselves. Hence a certain embarrassment, from which I may sometimes take refuge in flippancy. The title of the paper (not chosen by me) has, I am afraid, that flavour.

My theme can be defined briefly as follows. It is now axiomatic that there must be 'research' in politics. I use inverted commas here to indicate that this is research in a particular context, one quite familiar to us as university people: it will appear later that it is not really practicable to stick consistently to this neat logician's trick. Politics has established itself as a university subject in almost every Western country. It has in a sense always been a university subject, in that the great books of politics, from Plato's time, have been books written for a sophisticated public, accustomed to intellectual debate, and also accustomed to look at particular questions in a wide context, so that each argument has a place in the learned or rational universe of its time. Plato and Aristotle, Academy and Lyceum, were perhaps universities in themselves: at least till the late nineteenth century, no one wrote on politics at this level unless he was prepared to attempt universality.

But now politics teaching exists in universities in a new sense. For good, or at least inescapable, reasons it has

*This is a revised version of a paper given to an academic group in Oxford in the autumn of 1958. From *Political Studies*, X, no. 1 (Feb 1962).

followed the example of other subjects, and has become the job of professionals, of people whose career (or *carrière*) this will be throughout their working lives. One of the costs of this change is that political scientists at university level no longer just argue and teach and write, like their ancestors: they must not only do their subject, they must do 'research' in their subject.

Looking back over a period of experience, one can see in pieces of 'research', one's own and other people's, structure of two kinds, which are at first sight sharply contrasted.

First, there is the structure of the argument, as it comes to a reader through the finished book or article: or (for that matter) in an answer to an examination question. In my mind the phrase 'conceptual framework' has got itself tagged to this. I do not think I understand what a conceptual framework is, but that obscure cachet, *alpha* quality, seems to be impossible without it and to be assessable easily enough by a sort of corporate judgement of peers. When it comes to analysing this, I can make only the three disconnected points, referred to below: that some (not too much) fixed terminology is necessary, that rhetorical or poetic unity is necessary, and that standards of proof are a matter for us to settle from our own experience and not from the experience of natural science.

Secondly, and at first sight independent of all this, there is what might be called the administrative structure; the plan, or series of accidents, by which a particular person was kept alive and more or less fit and sane while framing and documenting the argument in question, and by which his argument was printed and sold for distribution to a particular circle of readers at a particular time. This is the question of the cash basis, in a general and not in a crude sense. I am rather more confident about the administrative problem than about the logical problem, because I think that by experience one can narrow the margins of administrative error very considerably: there are always upsets of form (I don't know why Michael Oakeshott, a leading professor in this too,[1] never uses that very relevant metaphor), but nevertheless there *is* form. Within limits, it is true that in certain circumstances certain people (or horses) can do certain things in a certain time, and that in the same conditions they cannot do other things. The cash basis in this sense determines what is feasible: is there any point, in our subject, in brooding about conceptual frameworks for expounding arguments which it is not logistically feasible to construct?

Business men complain sometimes that academics never have to 'meet a pay-roll': this is quite misleading, at least in an organisation in which administrative responsibility rests with a specified professor or professors. The conditioning mechanism of the system is quite powerful: there is acute discomfort if one fails in the endless job of trying to match tasks and resources. My paper is in substance nothing more ambitious than an analysis of these discomforts, this 'negative feed-back' from personal experience. I seek only to pose an issue which has not (I think) been posed before, at least not in this context.

A few words first on conceptual structure. I write with little self-confidence about methodological questions in this sense: but something should be said, because my conclusion is that in our present (perhaps transient) social circumstances it is not possible to have our cake and eat it; to live by our wits and also to satisfy our intellectual consciences.

First, as against Michael Oakeshott, I think that analysis, abstaction, organisation, are good things, not bad things, in political theory, teaching and research. Or at least that they are (in his Bradleian phrase) among the 'necessary evils' in this best of all possible worlds.[2] Intimations may be the thing, at dawn in the desert, on St. Simeon's pillar, but political science in the universities is an exercise in communication and criticism. It cannot be conducted adequately in symbolical or mystical language alone: *some* at least of the words must have limited meanings allotted to them by stipulation or by reference. Logically ordered language is a tool or correlative of logically ordered exposition, exposition which 'abides our question', which can be called upon διδόναι κὰι δέχεσθαι λόγον,[3] 'to give and receive a reasoned answer'. Poetry has an order of its own, but it may be debated whether great poets and novelists do not use also an intellectual order, as a means of deploying sustained power in exposition. History lives by chronological sequence, but this is certainly not all: history is more than chronicle, it is also debate.

At the other extreme from Oakeshott are the lords of the conceptual framework, German and American, who seem to peddle two rather different notions of how we should proceed. One school (in the tradition of Hegel, Marx, Max Weber, Talcott Parsons) works from the top down, from an embracing system, derived no one quite knows how, through intermediate hypotheses, to propositions which may perhaps be verifiable or refutable. The system is (conflating two phrases of Sir Dennis Robertson's) a 'vast many-coloured umbrella',[4] a place of refuge and security: it may grow and change imperceptibly by the influence of particular observations, but it is not lightly to be questioned as a whole or thrown aside. This seems to me very different from the notion expressed a little obscurely by the key-words 'operational definition'; that nothing can be established except in terms of techniques of observation which give ranges of probability statistically measurable. We are offered not an umbrella over our heads, but ground under our feet, in the sense that within known limits observations can be repeated by independent observers, and within these limits observations may serve as grounds for organised action through limited means to a limited end. We don't claim to know much about the nature of man, but we *can* sell your soap.

I do not know how these notions, both indispensable to the structure of 'science', are to be fitted together: my point here is that 'science' for us is not enough. If one looks at successful books embodying research in politics do they not always contain two elements which would be excluded if one accepted either or both of these standards exclusively? These elements are poetical order and professional good sense.

My second point, then, is that (whether we like it or not) we are literary men — *artifices* at least, like Nero, if not artists. A good book about politics must have unity and persuasive effect. For this it must have something recognisable as a 'conceptual framework'. 'Tumult is vile; confusion is hateful: everything in a work of art should be mastered and ordered.'[5] But the framework has no merit in itself; its merit is relative to the job of organising and expounding a mass of material vastly greater than can be used. If the author is good, he can do this with a framework of a very simple kind, or even with one which is logically fraudulent (as for instance the framework used so brilliantly by A. F. Bentley).[6] Conversely, good material may be sunk without trace if the conceptual framework is too heavy for it (for instance, in Professor Apter's book about the Gold Coast).

My third point is largely a matter of the standard of validity to be looked for in one's conclusions. We have probably all had trouble with statisticians wanting to throw away the results of good research as 'not significant at the 5 per cent level, when you apply the Chi squared test'. This happens if you insist on using exact terms only, and expect an exact measurement of probabilities. Surely our duty as academics is to *advance* exactness, not to proceed at once into a world of *complete* exactness where no one is with us? I sought, rather indirectly, to make this point in the Sidney Ball lecture in 1957.[7] The Nuffield College electoral surveys are really very naughty by any elegant standard of methodology: so much the worse for methodology. It seems as clear as daylight that they have extended knowledge substantially, by what might be called the method of parallel history, a trick as old as Plutarch's parallel lives: and it is not clear that any alternative method would have served at all, for these authors in that situation.

This is very compressed, but even so it is an intolerable deal of bread to be followed by a rather small quantity of sack. It is intended only to mark points of agreement (or disagreement), and at this stage I ought to try to be more concrete, though it is not easy within the limits of time and discretion. It must be remembered that there are few precedents for research into the conduct of 'research', even in less earthy fields than ours.

The question arises in a practical way in two possible situations: *either* 'here is Mr. A: he wants to do some research and has a grant of so much for X years': *or* 'here is a problem: They (capital T, please) want us to do research about it and are prepared to pay £X over a period of X years'. Of course these problems are not for the entrepreneur separate: if he can promote an association between Mr. A and

Them he has to that extent stabilised and regularised his business. And the same elements have to be handled in each case, though in a rather different order, so that the same analysis will do for both.

What then are these elements? The order is unimportant, because each reacts on all the others. Briefly, then:

1. A body of material not hitherto explored.
2. Immediate access to it (partly a matter of censorship, partly one of time and of cost of travel and living).
3. A research worker, whose talents, training and experience are (within limits) known.
4. A channel of publication and an estimate of the 'censorship' situation; what *can* one publish?
5. A public: a body of readers 'involved' in one or both of two respects: that their attitudes or course of action will be influenced by what is published; and that their estimate of the authors and entrepreneur and financiers will go up or down, with practical effect on the reputation and fortunes of these people. (This is of course Chester Barnard on the customer as part of the organisation.)[8]
6. A form of composition related to these preceding factors: a short article or a long book, a PhD thesis or a Penguin.
7. A time schedule: how long will elapse between the inception of the plan and the impact on the public? The main time-lags are to find research workers and to get them started; for them to get through the material; for them or others to write it up; for the publisher to print and distribute. This is like building a house: whatever estimate you have made, add 50 per cent to it.

Eighth, last, and above all — Money.

To quote Bagehot, quoting Mill, 'On all great subjects "much remains to be said" ', and I could go on for hours about various aspects of this game, racket or profession. But I ought to try to pick certain plums convenient to the present argument. I find five of these.

1. First, the question of material. The stupider sort of historian is confirmed in his stupidity by the cult of 'original sources'. Much historical 'research' is determined by what has

just turned up and has not yet been looked at: and till recently historians have been concerned professionally only with periods for which the amount of material available is fairly limited — not with the nineteenth or twentieth centuries. But we, in a sense, have an unlimited field of choice: the quantity of printed matter available is appalling, and for a great many matters one can — indeed, one must — amplify printed sources by going out oneself, to look and talk. In so far as this freedom of choice exists, our situation is perplexed, since we must as reputable academics offer some criterion to explain why we begin in one place rather than another. But freedom of choice may be somewhat delusive. One is excluded from some matters — e.g. much of contemporary British administration, or the higher levels of Russian government — by censorship; from others — e.g. first-hand investigation in the USA — by problems of time and cost. Following the line of least resistance, one finds that the field narrows quickly to studies of Britain, and within Britain of parties, Parliament, local politics and pressure groups. These are important things: but not the only important things — in a period dominated by questions of foreign and colonial policy, of economic and scientific policy, of changing social structure, of the management of great industries, whether nationalised or not.

2. Secondly, there is the question of the research worker, the most uncertain element in the whole thing. There seems to be a dilemma.

On the one hand the situation of a research worker, however well backed, is a precarious one. He is expected to make a coherent and convincing story, within a limited time, out of material which is (by definition) unexplored: and he must present his material so that it appears to have a point. This is insecurity, in the sense of the psychology textbooks: and produces the textbook effects. Some people do better than could be believed possible: a higher proportion consciously or unconsciously contrive some way of escaping from an exposed position.

The other horn of the dilemma is that the most obvious way of gaining greater security is by putting faith in a conceptual framework — the Americans sometimes call it a philosophy, it would be fairer to call it a routine. To be certain (or relatively certain) of the personal factor one must have an established pattern of procedure. Indeed, it is scarcely possible to develop research on a large scale except of the basis of established procedure, and of workers selected because of proved capacity in known routine. This is the strongest practical argument for a conceptual framework: that it is in effect the standing orders of an organisation. This certainly produces results in natural science. Observing how many computer girls depend for employment on this, I hope it may produce results in econometrics. I don't think it has produced any results in politics except in the field of opinion polls, because the results are too slow and too dull. If really large sums of money are to be spent on political research this is the safest way to spend them: but I don't much want to be mixed up in it — too much routine, too little fun.

3. Thirdly, publication and the public. This is not the only point at which political research becomes part of politics, but it is the most obvious one. In every country there are some things about politics which one can find out but cannot publish: and there is not much point in engaging in political research unless it is of political interest, in the sense that it is related to controversies about action. Research is distinct from persuasion, or so at least we hope, paying tribute to the idea of academic objectivity. But research is self-defeating if (*a*) it is unpublishable: (*b*) when published it contains matter held to be offensive, so that further research is stopped: (*c*) when published it is without reference outside the closed circle of research-workers. Thus research which is entirely scrupulous may be self-destructive, just 'research'; in fact, I think, we all (or almost all) seek to publish, and we are all unscrupulous in that we do not seek to publish all that we know. We compromise by ambiguity and reserve, or by taking refuge in statistical techniques. But there is a point at which such discretion is futile, because no one any longer knows or cares what we are talking about, and self-destruction thus follows in any case. At this point it is clearly better to write fiction explicitly than to write inadequate truth. In a sense political and administrative novelists have an easier time than we do, even in the West; how much more so in Russia.[9]

Should we be bolder than we are in recognising that the 'fictionalised case-study' (excuse the jargon) is a legitimate academic form?

4. Fourthly, there is the question of time. The mechanical side of this is what one thinks of as a two-year project (a reasonable chunk of research) in fact takes about four years between inception and effective publication, and in four years much can happen. To put it metaphysically, one realises when one tries it that research is (in a Whitehead sort of way) part of process and itself process. It is not merely that politics change, as they do (Bagehot again, in the Introduction to Edition 2); it is that the researcher changes, and that what seemed a terribly good idea four years ago may seem just a bore when one sees it in print, not because it wasn't right at the time, but because one is now a different person. If one could start again four years ago one would start differently: but that is absurd. Is publication therefore absurd? No, but it involves an element of self-deception or confidence trick to achieve it with an air of boldness.

Finally, money, 'the cord which binds, the buckle which fastens' political research to the political process. Strictly speaking, one can write only what one is paid to write, and in a sense this is true even for the incredibly small number who have private means, since it is a political, not an economic, fact that they continue to enjoy their revenues. Yet for practical purposes there is one situation when research is done out of grants for projects, another when it is done by salaried teachers in a university. The teacher is of course not wholly free: for one thing he must teach, for another he needs facilities of various kinds, and his research is twisted by his chances of getting them. But the real splendour or misery of the entrepreneur is that of the Director of Research accepting from a Foundation or a Government Department (there are no other sources) a handsome grant in aid of a five-year programme or a specific project. This is a Kafka world. A man living in it wrestles for his life with continually changing shapes — material, workers, censorship, time-table, budget. Perhaps he can reckon himself modestly successful if he has kept himself and his boys alive for the time allotted, and has done no positive harm to anyone else. The permanent salaried man has at least a freer hand than this, and it is lucky that our ideology gives us a good story to back him up, since we are dedicated to the nineteenth-century view that all teaching requires research. I doubt if it is true that it requires 'research', in inverted commas: but it does require continuous first-hand contact with the subject about which we are trying to teach, and 'research' is now our best excuse for getting this, without tying ourselves with palpable strings.

Nevertheless, the strings are there: it is fairly easy to trace the ways in which political research (indeed any social research) is geared into the process which it purports to investigate. Research administration in politics draws on public funds, or on private funds dedicated to public purposes: those who give these funds think not of our spiritual improvement but of public problems (of general or selfish interest) which we may in a humble way (we cost very little) help our betters to resolve. Control is (in the British or American situation) loose in detail and much mitigated by the plurality of donors: we are free enough to feel a large share of responsibility. Yet surely what we are engaged in is itself a political activity, or at least a form of public administration? This argument is familiar though not often stated: what follows from it? My main object of course has been to ask whether familiarity with this administrative structure affects our theoretical view of the nature of the other sort of structure, that of exposition and proof.

For me it certainly does, but when I try to sum up my conclusions seem trivial. Four points:

1. First, I think the situation seems more Kafkaesque than need be because of these damnable words 'objectivity' and 'involvement'. Somewhere, I hope, some therapeutic logician has sorted this out professionally. To me it seems there is a fairly simple ambiguity. Of course political research is 'geared into' the political process in all sorts of ways; it partakes of whatever political 'values' there may be. But this is a kind of judgment about value quite different from our professional judgments about whether research is well or ill done. We share the public interest in the public values of a great society: but we are ourselves a segment of a segment of that society, a 'peculiar people' trained in peculiar ways, and we

have acquired standards of propriety which are not those of (for instance) working politicians, a group very different from us in training and experience. At the present stage, the older generation (at least in Britain) write largely as the pupils of linguistic scholars, historians, lawyers and philosophers, and from them we have inherited our scruples. This situation is changing as political science is professionalised: one may laugh at the 'research' degree as an instrument of training, but at least it is a traumatic experience, a *rite de passage*, which stamps those who suffer it.

2. This leads to my second point. There are exceptions, but on the whole our standards have been acquired by discipline in the 'humanities', not in mathematics or natural science. The position is already rather different in economics and in psychology, the balance of education in VIth forms is shifting, and things tend steadily to domination by the analogy of natural science. To live with this situation we must know enough to know what the analogy means, and how far it does not apply. It is in a remote sense true that even the work of pure mathematicians is linked to the political process: everyone has his place in the budget of national income and expenditure, and one can see for instance (around us in 1961) that the battle to produce more mathematicians is a battle to be fought by techniques of pressure with which we are professionally familiar. But, compared with us, scientists live in a relatively well-built ivory tower. We are not restricted (as most of them are) only by financial priorities. We deal with rapidly changing situations of great complexity, in which permanent elements are hard to discern; we know that there is always distortion due to the position of the observer, but we cannot measure and discount it. Hence we are always in the situation that we must say nothing, or say what we know to be (by the standards of natural science) grossly imperfect. For this reason, I think that (as is indeed the rule in this country) we should be wise to regard ourselves as scholars rather than scientists, as learned men and careful writers, not as discoverers of new truths. Perhaps that is semantically old-fashioned, and the word 'scholar' in this sense is on the way out; at any rate let us stick to it that our professional

judgment about our own business is at least as good as other people's judgment about their business.

3. My third point is that large-scale research is only possible if one can use a high proportion of second and third-class research workers, and (quite apart from administrative overheads) this involves a relatively simple and stable set of standing orders, a common 'conceptual framework'. This (I suppose) is the administrative secret of the immense power of applied science. But I don't think this is of much use to us: the results are too dull and too slow. We need learning and we need coherent exposition, but we must also have originality: we must not bore ourselves and other people. How not to be a bore is in one respect the old puzzle of the relation between order and novelty in art: but it also has something to do with the administrative puzzle about facilities for research and publication.

4. Finally, then, what excuse have we for existing? — as researchers, I mean, for the use of teaching is more obvious. It would perhaps, feeble folk as we are, be better not to insist too much that political research discovers things that help to improve society. I think it does, sometimes, and that it could do more: but our resources are small in relation to very big tasks — we are not strong enough, however well endowed we might be, to keep pace with the violent effects of research in applied science. Rather than promise what is not yet, let us emphasise what is here already, if one opens one's eyes and looks; that the existence of political research is a symptom of a particular state of society, and of a good thing in that society. About this I think we can be very bold, in various idioms, sacred and profane, from various ages of the world. You can call it, if you like that sort of language, the institutionalisation of negative feedback, a technique of survival, increasing the sensitivity of society to its situation in its environment. Or (if you prefer sacred to profane), is it not also a technique of meditation and self-criticism appropriate to a free and conscious intellectual society?

Notes

1. *A Guide to the Classics* (with G. T. Griffith): 1936, 1947.
2. *Political Education*: re-printed in Laslett, *Philosophy, Politics and Society* (1956) at p. 21.

3. See (for instance) *Protagoras* 336c, and what follows.

4. *Utility and All That* (1952), pp. 37, 39, 41: Sir Dennis was writing about something called a 'Bergson social welfare-function'.

5. Virginia Woolf, 'Granite and Rainbow'.

6. There is now an enormous literature on this: see *American Political Science Review*, vol. 54 (1960), p. 944 (a symposium on *Bentley Revisited*), and (for a personal impression) W. J. M. Mackenzie: 'Pressure Groups: the Conceptual Framework' (*Political Studies*, vol. 3 (1955), p. 247).

7. W. J. M. Mackenzie: 'The Export of Electoral Systems' (*Political Studies*, vol. 5 (1957), p. 240).

8. Chester Barnard: *The Functions of the Executive*. (13th printing, 1958) at p. 69, for instance.

9. Since I wrote this Professor Peter Campbell has shown me a remarkably apt letter about 'administrative' novels written by H. G. Wells to Henry James in 1911; *Henry James and H. G. Wells*, Hart-Davis (1958) at p. 148.

19 The Functions of Elections[*]

Elections may be regarded as one procedure for aggregating preferences of a particular kind.

Liberal democratic theories attribute special authority to the amalgamation of the expressed preferences of individuals through recognised procedures. They reject the idea that social choice can be made by some sort of group mind or interpersonal entity built out of individuals but different from them in kind. They also reject the idea that social choice is a mere illusion, that is, the notion that what appears to be a choice between alternatives is really no more than the consequence of the interplay of various forces.

But it has been argued, in the attack on welfare economics (Arrow 1951; Little 1950), that the preference schedules of individuals cannot be amalgamated without paradox except on one of two conditions: either through the operation of a market or through the compliance of individual participants with decisions by a recognised authority.

Liberal theories would certainly accept the idea that in certain cases to be defined social choice is made and should be made through the market or by relying on authority. But they postulate also that there are and should be public decisions in which citizens make an explicit choice between alternative courses of public action. This can be done in practice only through forms of procedure generally accepted as binding within the political society.

Voting is one of these procedures but not the only one. It is relevant to quote an authority on the practice of the Dominican order in the Middle Ages (Galbraith 1925, p. 33) to the effect that choice might be made by vote, by explicit

[*]From *International Encyclopedia of the Social Sciences* (N.Y.: Macmillan Co. and Free Press, 1968).

agreement after negotiation, or 'as if by the inspiration of God.' Certainly one finds everywhere, even in the most developed societies, choice by bargaining between factions and choice by acclamation, and there may be other procedures as well. It appears, however, that in 'liberal' societies voting is held in reserve as a procedure possessing special authority within the group, organisation, or state. Conversely, elections are by no means the only occasion for procedure by vote. Voting on propositions is of great practical importance in many different social and political situations, and it raises similar problems of formal analysis (Black 1958).

Voting in nationwide elections has a position of special importance in Western democracies. Its authority is strengthened because similar procedures are used for social choice in many institutions, large and small, public and private, throughout the society. (It is not greatly weakened by the existence of formal paradoxes of voting, even though these anomalies are of some tactical importance to groups seeking victory for their own interests.) This predominance has led to the export of voting in elections to countries where voting procedure has not historically possessed the same social authority as in the West: countries of the Soviet bloc on the one hand and developing countries on the other. This may give rise to situations in which the procedure exists but the element of choice does not.

Definition of elections

Thus, it is not always easy to answer the question, What is a *real* election? – and it may be useful to attempt a formal definition. What follows is based on English usage of political terms and may not have general validity, but it will serve to indicate important points for discussion.

One requires, first, the concept of recognised positions or roles ('offices') which confer certain powers and duties within an organisation. Individuals may be assigned to office either by choice or by a method independent of choice, such as a rule of inheritance, or seniority, or regulated trial by competition. Next, a general concept is needed, such as 'to choose a man for a job' or perhaps 'to decide between candidates for a job.' Within this concept, one must distinguish among 'electing', 'appointing', and 'co-opting' a man. In English each word has overtones of political evaluation. 'Election' (provided it is 'free') would be deemed 'democratic' and therefore good, but for certain positions only. 'Appointment' would be regarded as 'patronage' that tends to increase the power of the patron, except insofar as it is hedged by rules specifying the field of 'qualified' candidates. 'Co-option' smacks of oligarchy, the self-perpetuation of a ruling group, unless similarly regulated.

On this basis election might be defined as *a form of procedure, recognised by the rules of an organisation, whereby all or some of the members of the organisation choose a smaller number of persons or one person to hold an office of authority in the organisation.*

This definition raises a number of points. (1) It attempts to embrace both formal procedure and social significance — both 'rules' and 'choice'. Ideally, both elements should be present in an election. To mark a ballot paper and drop it in a ballot box is not 'electing' unless the actor 'chooses' in some socially significant sense. But equally a choice is not a 'vote in an election' unless the chooser conforms to the specified legal procedure. J. L. Austin made the same point (1961; 1962) when he said that 'I vote for Mr. A' is not a statement but a verbal act or performative utterance and that the same act can be achieved without words where this is the proper procedure. Nevertheless, it may be convenient to use the word 'election' for something that falls short of such completeness; for instance, where procedure is followed but no choice is present, or where there is a significant element of choice without close conformity to a socially recognised procedure (Akzin 1960).

(2) The rather loose word 'organisation' is chosen here deliberately. The word 'election' is not used only for 'state' elections to a hierarchy of public bodies. Indeed, it could be maintained that state elections are effective only where electoral procedure is regarded as a usual procedure throughout the society and is therefore written into the rules of all sorts of non-public bodies, such as business companies, trade unions, free churches, sports clubs, and so on. Nor would it

do to replace 'an organisation' by 'a society'. This might imply that a voter can choose only within his 'society,' whereas multiple membership of overlapping organisations is characteristic of complex societies, and one man may be a voter in many different capacities and under different rule systems.

(3) Two phrases in the definition — 'the rules of an organisation' and 'the members of an organisation choose' — refer to fundamental conceptual problems in social science. All that need be said here is that ordinary language about elections deals with persons acting within systems of ethical norms and legal procedures. It is possible to reject this language, as would happen if either economic determinism or behaviourism were strictly applied in social science. Such studies might have substantial predictive value in relation to electoral behaviour, but they would leave unanswered some fundamental questions about what men think they are doing when they participate in elections.

(4) The word 'office' implies a position designated by the same system of rules that determines the electoral procedure. The general problem is that in all social systems persons must somehow be linked to offices; election is one of many different procedures used to ensure legal succession to office in different organisations and societies.

(5) It remains to distinguish election from appointment or co-option. There are ambiguities in usage here. For instance, fellows of a college would use the word 'elect' both for choosing a Master and for choosing a junior colleague; critics of the college system might accept the former usage but would describe the latter as 'co-option'. Political advantage may be drawn from these ambiguities at various levels of political debate; in England, at least, 'election' is a good word, 'patronage' is a bad word, and 'co-option' lies in between. This usage suggests the following distinctions:

(a) In an election the choosers are a relatively numerous body. Choice by one voter would, of course, be an appointment. But how many choosers are needed to make an election?

(b) There is a question of proportion as well as of absolute number. If ten choosers voted to fill one office, one might call it election; if they filled 100 offices, one would tend to call it appointment (or even patronage). But once again there is no sharp point of division.

(c) There is a question of the relationship between the choosers and the office to be filled. A person co-opted would be a colleague; a person appointed would be a subordinate, even though he might exercise great discretionary power; a person elected would hold an office of authority, which might include authority over those who elected him.

(d) It may be said that when electing, the voters act independently of one another and more or less at the same time, whereas an appointing body acts in consultation, with each member sharing in the deliberation and expressing his point of view in turn until a conclusion is reached (Akzin 1960). This is a very important problem in the study of political development, but it seems to be a distinction between voters and councillors, rather than between election and appointment. Deliberative procedure in council is very widespread in human societies at all stages; under some circumstances (which have nowhere been seriously studied) the device of voting is used to bring issues to a conclusion. But election does not inevitably entail voting; in certain societies the proper procedure for election is by council, in others by acclamation, and in yet others by voting.

Historical developments

Elections first took a central place in politics in the Greek city-states of the eastern Mediterranean in the fifth and sixth centuries BC. There has been no systematic study of elections in societies independent of this Western tradition; certainly, traces are to be found elsewhere, but it does not seem that elections have played a central part in other societies. In the following discussion it has been assumed that electoral procedures can usefully be studied historically in terms of the diffusion of a social pattern from a single source and its modification in a great variety of situations. Further, it is assumed that these procedures correspond functionally to certain general social needs, which are particularly marked in literate, technological, and mobile societies; hence they have periodically reappeared, after setbacks, in new forms in new corners of Western society. Finally, it is assumed that where these procedures meet no social needs they may be retained as forms but are filled with a new content.

The heroic age

The poems of Homer reflect a state of society in which rule was by kings whose position was conspicuously unlike that of the 'Oriental despots' of the river valley civilisations with which they came in contact. The evidence of the mythological and epic narratives is difficult to use, but it suggests a situation roughly parallel to cases found in mobile African societies where the king, although drawn from a royal lineage, emerges as leader by a process which may include competition, conciliar election, and acclamation by the people. Clearly the leader of the war coalition, Agamemnon, had attained his precarious eminence among other kings by a process of this kind. Analogies can be drawn from Tacitus's account of the Germans and from the world of Teutonic, Scandinavian, and Icelandic epics.

The Greek democracies

The epic period of tribal mobility was succeeded by one of peasant agriculture tempered by growing commercial activity and emigration to colonies overseas. From this situation emerged the strife between the well-born and the people, which affected Greek ideas and practice about political institutions almost everywhere. Where this strife was intense, Greek elections assumed new forms, either through a complete popular victory or through attempts at compromise.

We are primarily concerned not with voting on measures in popular assemblies but with the choice of persons to fill offices of authority. Two points are of general importance. First, in voting on propositions in the assembly of the citizens the rule was apparently that of individual voting by show of hands ($\chi\epsilon\iota\rho\sigma\tau\sigma\nu\epsilon\hat{\iota}\nu$). Use was also made of written votes (in the procedure of ostracism) and of ballots in the form of pebbles ($\psi\hat{\eta}\phi\sigma\iota$) — hence, psephology. There was at times a leader of the assembly who held his informal position (for example, Pericles, Cleon, Demosthenes) because of fairly stable majority support. But holders of certain legally recognised offices (in particular, archons and generals) were elected by non-local constituencies known at tribes (φυλάι), which were held to have been instituted deliberately so as to cut across local divisions of interest within Attica. The number of voters in each tribe must have differed a good deal.

Second, the principle of election was accepted somewhat grudgingly in Athenian democratic theory; it infringed the principle of equality among citizens, and it was dangerous because it opened the way to power for ambitious, attractive, and well-trained young men of the old families (for example, Alcibiades) and equally for ambitious men of the people who were prepared to perpetuate their electoral victory by force (the common pattern of Greek 'tyranny'). The orthodox principle was that citizens should hold offices of authority in rotation, the order to be determined by lot; this was the practice for the Council of 500 and its monthly committees, which maintained continuity in the control of public business, and also for the selection of juries (methods of 'balloting' for juries are described in great detail by Aristotle, *Athenaiōn Politeia*, chapters 63—6). Similar institutions were common in early English and American practice, and rotation in office is still quite usual in small voluntary societies. But there has been no modern discussion of the relation between the principles of rotation in office and that of election by vote. It is notable, however, that in general the Athenians used voting for elections to offices requiring special skills, such as military leadership, whereas in Western countries voting is now used to fill offices of a representative character, for which the Athenians used the lot; offices requiring special skills are now generally filled by appointment from a field determined by specified professional qualifications.

The Roman republic

Even under the Republic the Romans never accepted the principle of 'one man, one vote'. Decision in legislation and in the choice of the principal officials was by a plurality of 'centuries' or by a plurality of 'tribes': within each of these constituencies one man, one vote prevailed, but the units varied in size. It was tactically important that each of them had some local basis, but locality was not decisive in their composition

The medieval church

The tradition of ancient elections was preserved in the church rather than in the state. It continued unbroken in the Roman Catholic church, but many national and nonconformist churches also developed the use of elections as the basis of a legitimate claim to hold office. (It is an interesting coincidence that 'election' has in Protestant theology a different meaning: that of the granting of spiritual grace to God's elect.)

The most ancient and continuous tradition has been that of the election of superiors (popes, bishops, deans, priors, and so on) by a relatively small electorate consisting of those next in rank. Up to a point the procedure is deliberative, tending toward a conclusion by 'sense of the meeting'. But there are also ancient and complex rules about voting procedures. These rights of election were defended, strongly but not always with success, against hierarchical and secular attempts to substitute appointment.

There is an undercurrent (almost Athenian in tone) emphasising the electoral rights of the many against the few. In Presbyterian terms, the congregation will defend the position of the elders in appointing a minister insofar as that position is endangered by the lay patron, but it claims the right to confirm or to upset the verdict of the elders. Dissent sometimes accepts the authority of a charismatic leader; but it often tends toward the equal sovereignty of all true believers, which may be shown either by election or by rotation in office.

Feudalism

The position of the feudal emperor, king, or overlord was deemed to be limited by law and custom and to some extent by the consent of his vassals.

The relation between king and lord and between lord and man was in principle one of consent leading to binding mutual obligation. The vassal chose to do homage, the lord chose whether or not to accept it. It was not a long step from this to an elected emperor and (in a few instances) an elected king. The social situation greatly limited the application of the principles of consent and election in practice; but the idea of a binding legal right of succession to office emerged slowly, along with the growth of other notions of private and heritable property.

In principle, the king was independent insofar as he could 'live of his own'. But this was a limited independence in a period of quite rapid change, and in many cases its boundaries were obscure. Hence the need for consultation, first with a feudal council, then with assemblies 'representing' others besides immediate vassals. These assemblies were the basis of the parliamentary tradition in Europe. They embodied two principles not yet wholly obsolete:

(a) The separate representation of 'estates', which might be more or less numerous; for instance, great lords, great clergy, lesser lords, lesser clergy, burghers, peasants.

(b) The representation of local communities but not of individuals. The classic case is that of the English House of Commons, based on two knights from every shire and two burgesses from every burgh. Apart from the great men of the realm, the 'units of account' in government were shires and burghs, not individuals. The choice of representatives by communities was a matter for each community, within the general law of the land. Elections thus established themselves in national government but without any national enactment about electoral procedure.

The seventeenth and eighteenth centuries

In most of Europe the assemblies of estates were displaced by autocratic, modernising monarchies. For the diffusion of elections the only important survival was in England (the parliaments of Scotland and Sweden survived but had little or no influence outside their own countries) and in colonial assemblies based on the English model. During the struggle for survival certain basic principles of consent, franchise, and representation were hammered out; although these principles were never fully applied in practice, they were recognised as the ideological basis of a system of democratic elections. The classic statements are those of English popular leaders in the 1640s and 1650s: their language recalls both that of nonconformist congregations and that of Athenian democracy. The principle, in brief, is that all governments owe their just powers to the consent of the governed and that in numerous societies this consent may be expressed by representatives freely elected on a basis of universal adult suffrage.

This principle can readily be elaborated in institutional form, for example, by the extension of the suffrage, the equalisation of constituencies, proportional representation, the elimination of intimidation and corruption, and so on. These elaborations in turn lead to political situations which illustrate ambiguities in the principle; for instance, as regards the relation between elected and electors, is there a difference between a 'representative' and a 'delegate'?

Parties in elections

By far the most important of these new problems is that of parties as intermediaries between voter and assembly. Clear recognition of this situation came first in American presidential elections, but it spread rapidly with the extension of the franchise in large states in the nineteenth century. By the last quarter of that century, parties and elections had become interdependent. Electoral parties were no longer limited to national politics: trade unions and large cooperative societies are obvious examples. But national elections are henceforth intelligible *only* in terms of parties; the traditional principles demand the scrutiny of procedure within parties, since they control the first stage of national elections.

Plebiscitary democracy and 'unfree' elections

The predominance of parties has led to a change in the character of national elections, even in countries where electoral procedure is in constant use at subnational levels. The choice of a man to hold office as a member of an assembly has given place to a national vote between different 'packages' consisting of leadership, party, and programme. The election is a choice of government or even of regime, and voting procedure is called on to bear new strains. In stable democracies the strains are mitigated because there is an understood difference between governmental structure ('regime') and government in power ('government'), and the former is not questioned by electors. But where this distinction is not drawn the strain may prove too great for the electoral system to bear, and the element of choice is removed (or greatly reduced) by various devices. The oldest of these are plebiscitary democracy, which dates from the time of Napoleon I, and the exercise of influence on elections by officials of the government in power, without blatant breach of legality. The *reductio ad absurdum* of these trends appears in 'elections' such as those of East Germany, where a vote of 99.9 per cent was recorded in favour of the government in 1964. Such a result could only be due to fraud, or pressure, or both. However, the fact that the regime deems elections necessary seems to pay tribute to the immense strength of the tradition that elections confer legitimacy.

The functions of elections

This brief historical summary illustrates the persistence and adaptability of the use of electoral procedure as a means of legitimating the assignment of a person to an office of authority. It may be said that electoral procedure is functionally analogous to procedure in a marriage ceremony: 'Do you take this man (or woman) to be your lawfully wedded husband (or wife)?' 'I do' (Austin 1962). The point in time at which 'I do' is said is not psychologically a moment of choice or decision — that came earlier; it is the point at which an individual preference becomes a social commitment. The words and acts are 'performative'; if correctly said and done in the right context, they establish new social relationships of a binding character.

Such acts are generally associated with ritual which underlies the multiple relationships linking them to a complex system of behaviour and belief. To continue the analogy with marraige ceremonies, there is a possible range of ritual complexity from ostentation to extreme simplicity — but even in marriage by registration in an advanced secular society, some elements of ritual are present. There is the same wide range in electoral ritual — for example the election of a pope and that of the directors of a manufacturing company; but in both cases there is a procedure which has binding effect if properly followed.

Thus, it is possible to speak of elections in general as a 'ritual of choice'; the binding character of elections derives from the participation of an individual as chooser in a social act, and legitimate authority is thus conferred on the person chosen. But such a generalisation tells one little about the position of elections in any given society.

Men are called by different kinds of elections to different offices in different societies. The historical sketch given above notes only a limited range of cases, but it may be sufficient to indicate that it is rash to talk of *the* function of elections. This may be illustrated by the British case. A British general election serves to choose a governing party and thus government. But (on the other hand) that government, though powerful, has not a monopoly of legitimate authority in the political system. This authority is shared by many others — those professionally qualified by education and experience, the leaders of organised interests, property owners of various kinds, and so on. On the other hand, the electoral system serves many other functions besides choice of a government; the party organisation based on it serves as a market place and reconciler of interests, a ladder for the political careers of national and local officials, a forum of national discussion, and so on. It would be quite amiss to assume at once that the same functions were filled by elections in Athens, or in the medieval church, or even in other industrial societies today.

Argument about the merits of different electoral systems is generally based on assessments of their efficiency in relation to one or more of their many possible functions. The political literature of England in the nineteenth and twentieth centuries contains a rich store of such arguments; and this has been added to in the process of 'decolonisation', since 'free elections' were assumed to be a necessary step toward independence in most of Britain's dependent territories. This is, therefore, a convenient testing ground for theories about the nature of political argument, and in particular about the relation of ideology to rationality on one flank and to self-interest on the other.

A. H. Birch (1964) has shown how contemporary debate about elections in Britain draws in arguments from various historical stages, a mixture which can be logically justified only if one assumes that elections in England serve many functions that are not necessarily compatible with one another. If one had to ground the defence of elections on a single maxim it would doubtless be that of the Puritan revolution: 'There are no laws that in their strictness and vigour of justice any man is bound to that are not made by those whom he doth consent to.' Parellels for this maxim could be found in many other political cultures. The doctrine or ideology is one of great and continuing power: but it remains empty until expressed in terms of institutions and interests, and its simplicity is then obscured and complicated by arguments drawn from other streams of political doctrine.

There has been no general study of choice as an element in the legitimation of authority. Such a study would present great difficulties. It is safe to guess that where choice is an element in determining authority in simpler societies it is entangled with other factors such as seniority, lineage, and personal ascendancy. Isolating one factor would distort the situation. In complex societies elections appear in many different contexts, private and public, and electoral procedure often survives as a ritual although the element of choice is absent; so that it would be difficult, perhaps unwise, to take the forms of electoral procedure as a guide in unraveling the complexities of modern political structure.

It would be of value, nevertheless, if pilot studies could be made of the place of elections in one or two cases of simple and complex societies. Very little work has been done on the legitimation of authority in contemporary societies; it seems probable that the part played by elections is relatively small even in established democracies, if elections are considered separately as a single factor. An attempt to isolate this factor might therefore break down; but it could hardly fail to sharpen our perception of the problem, which is of central importance in political science and is now within the grasp of empirical inquiry.

Bibliography

Theories and Concepts
Akzin, B., 1960 Election and Appointment. *American Political Science Review* 54:705–713.

Arrow, Kenneth J., (1951) 1963 *Social Choice and Individual Values.* 2d ed. New York: Wiley.

Austin, John L., 1961 Performative Utterances. Pages 220—239 in John L. Austin, *Philosophical Papers.* Oxford Univ. Press.

Austin, John L., 1962 *How to Do Things With Words.* Oxford: Clarendon.

Birch, Anthony H., 1964 *Representative and Responsible Government.* London: Allen & Unwin.

Black, Duncan, 1958 *The Theory of Committees and Elections.* Cambridge Univ. Press.

Buchanan, James M.; and Tullock, Gordon 1962 *The Calculus of Consent: Logical Foundations of Constitutional Democracy.* Ann Arbor: Univ. of Michigan Press.

Dahl, Robert A., 1956 *A Preface to Democratic Theory.* Univ. of Chicago Press.

Leibholz, Gerhard, (1929) 1960 *Das Wesen der Repräsentation und der Gestaltswandel der Demokratie im 20. Jahrhundert.* 2d ed. Berlin: Gruyter.

Little, Ian M. D., (1950) 1957 *A Critique of Welfare Economics.* 2nd ed. Oxford: Clarendon.

Riker, William H., 1961 Voting and the Summation of Preferences: An Interpretive—Bibliographical Review of Selected Developments During the Last Decade. *American Political Science Review* 55:900—911.

Ross, James F.S., 1955 *Elections and Electors: Studies in Democratic Representation.* London: Eyre & Spottiswoode.

Historical Developments

Aristotle, *Aristotle's Politics* and *Athenian Constitution.* Edited and translated by John Warrington. New York: Dutton, 1959.

Barker, Ernest, 1913 *Dominican Order and Convocation: A Study of the Growth of Representation in the Church During the Thirteenth Century.* Oxford: Clarendon.

Clarke, Maude V., (1936) 1964 *Medieval Representation and Consent: A Study of Early Parliaments in England and Ireland, With Special Reference to the* Modus tenendi parliamentum. New York: Russell.

Ehrenberg, Victor, (1932) 1964 *The Greek State.* Rev. ed. New York: Barnes & Noble. → First published as *Der griechische und der hellenische Staat.*

Galbraith, Georgina R., (Cole-Baker) 1925 *The Constitution of the Dominican Order:1216—1360.* Manchester Univ. Press.

Glotz, Gustave, (1928) 1950 *The Greek City and Its Institutions.* London: Routledge. → First published as *La cité grecque.*

Greenidge, Abel H., (1896) 1920 *A Handbook of Greek Constitutional History.* London and New York: Macmillan.

Greenidge, Abel H., (1901) 1930 *Roman Public Life.* New York: Macmillan.

Hintze, Otto, (1902–1932) 1962 *Staat und Verfassung: Gesammelte Abhandlungen zur allgemeinen Verfassungsgeschichte.* 2d enl. ed. Göttingen (Germany): Vandenhoeck & Ruprecht.

Lousse, Émile, 1943 *La société d'ancien régime: Organisation et représentation corporatives.* Louvain (Belgium): Bibliothèque de l'Université.

Moulin, Léo, 1953 Les origines religieuses des techniques électorales et délibératives modernes. *Revue internationale d'histoire politique et constitutionnelle* New Series 3: 106–148.

Palmer, Robert R., 1959 *The Age of the Democratic Revolution: A Political History of Europe and America, 1760–1800.* Volume 1: The Challenge. Princeton Univ. Press.

Ryffel, Heinrich, 1903 *Die schweizerischen Landsgemeinden.* Zurich: Schulthess.

Ullmann, Walter, 1961 *Principles of Government and Politics in the Middle Ages.* New York: Barnes & Noble.

20 Political Institutions in England*

This paper was instigated by some brilliant notes of Bertrand de Jouvenel on the weakness of the Active Power and the Surmising Forum in contemporary British institutions. The notes were by way of question. It seemed impossible to find standing ground for an answer except by going a long way round.

This outflanking manoeuver owes much methodologically to hints given by *Futuribles*. I am also influenced here by the Buchanan Report on Traffic in Towns, and by some reflections on its method which I gave in a paper at the Jubilee Conference of the Town Planning Institute, where Professor Buchanan was in the chair. The Buchanan Report (it seemed to me) was best treated not as a set of proposals but as an essay on how to analyse a problem of rational decision. I am convinced the method is in general right, but I could not agree completely with Professor Buchanan's tactics. Hence I am under some obligation to expose myself to criticism in turn, by trying a methodological exercise in the field of political institutions: a hazardous business, but not really much harder than that of traffic in towns.

Received Doctrine

I argued on that occasion that choice about the future (not necessarily 'rational' choice) depends on the availability of alternative 'models' of the future. Considering a field in which I have a professional interest, I begin to doubt whether

---

*Note: I deliberately write 'England' here. The politics of Wales, Scotland, Northern Ireland are best understood as those of 'dependent politics' or client systems under English patronage. This relationship is likely to change, and, in changing, to change the political institutions of the United Kingdom: but this is another, equally complex problem.

models of the future are intelligible without a model or models of the present; and a model of the present contains in itself a model (or alternative models) of the past.

I attempt to begin therefore with a model (or models) of political institutions as they now exist in England. A great deal of information is available; the place is like an ancient sand-dune riddled with rabbit burrows of all ages,* and a good academic ferret can run and memorise the maze of interlinked passages. But if he is asked to say what sort of place the warren is in general terms, he will certainly take refuge in explaining what sort of place the rabbits think it is. That is to say, he will try to elucidate the rabbit model (or models) of the structure of the rabbit situation. These models of the present turn out on inspection to be myths about the past.

One's first question therefore is what *were* English political institutions. I suggest three models, which I might label exoteric, esoteric and dissident.

The exoteric model will be very familiar, as it is that most generally used in public debate. The English people have always been a free people. They created Parliament in the thirteenth century, on earlier foundations, and after long struggles the people's representatives won the battle for the Sovereignty of Parliament against both Crown and Oligarchy. Hence arose a form of constitution known as responsible parliamentary government, which combines decision by the will of the people in the long run with active administrative leadership in the short run. More than this; those admirable things are combined with others equally admirable, the absolute independence of the judiciary and the right of local communities to govern themselves well or badly.

The contents of this 'package deal' can be spelt out in more detail if necessary; but they can conveniently be found in the 'independence constitutions' of ex-colonies from Canada onwards. Indeed, much of this doctrine was elaborated to provide constitutional norms for new states. Its prime source is perhaps to be found in Charles Buller's contribution to the Durham report on Canadian government in 1839: and

---

*Those who know the tales of C. R. R. Tolkien might say 'hobbit-burrows'.

the classical statements are in the works of Professor Alpheus Todd (Canada, 1866) and Professor W. E. Hearn (Australia, 1867). These set out clearly what we officially expect of Ghana — and of ourselves.

The esoteric model is very different. The classical statements are in Walter Bagehot and in what survives of the political thought of A. J. Balfour (reflecting his uncle, the great Marquess of Salisbury, and reflected in turn by the writing of Sir Sidney Low).

This doctrine has been in general taken as a matter of course in good society, but it is not appropriate to political platforms. Its basic propositions are not at all shocking; but they are not very suitable for public oratory. Perhaps they can be reduced to three.

First, social power is more fundamental than political power; politics are super-structure, and forms of political institutions don't in the last resort matter very much.

Secondly, social power (provided its social relations with the armed forces are right) has no serious rival except economic power. So strong a rival should be handled with circumspection: self-made men and their sons should not be rudely rejected, however base their sphere of operations. A deal reasserting the primacy of social power is always possible; war to the death never makes sense.

Thirdly, social power is built into the structure of society, and loses its force only with the dissolution of society. Its nature can be represented as a pyramid, or perhaps better as a nest of concentric boxes. The career of the active individual in society is one of 'climbing' or of 'penetration'; and to some extent he can hand down to his children the footholds he has gained.

The doctrine is imbedded in the ambiguities of the English language. The word 'society' can mean the whole social fabric; it can also mean the circles of those who are actively concerned with social power, circles marked off fairly sharply from the life of the ordinary unambitious Englishman. Similarly, 'the best people' can mean what it says; or it can mean the people 'on the inner circle' or closest to it.

The model is one of an astute, imperturbable, flexible oligarchy, self-perpetuating but not exclusive. Co-option is its main constitutional form; not election nor yet heredity. The model (like all these models) purports to describe the truth about a political system; but in so far as it makes good its claim to be factual it also establishes a norm. This is the myth by which successful men explain to one another their own success within what they believe to be a successful form of government.

The third model, that of English *dissidence* or dissent, is in a sense the gospel of unsuccessful men. But it sanctifies their lack of worldly success by claiming that they do not play the 'success game' at all, at least not by these rules. At the centre of the myth perhaps stand the dissident sects — Independents, Levellers, Diggers, Quakers, and so on — who animated the Parliamentary cause in the civil war of the seventeenth century. There is a good deal to be said for the dissenting view that the civil war was redeemed by its pamphleteers; through their eyes, one can see tragedy and parable in what would look to other eyes like a mean provincial scuffle about jobs.

It is probably illusory to seek for examples further back; but since the civil war there has certainly been a continuous tradition of dissent. A. J. P. Taylor has traced this in foreign policy in his book *The Trouble-Makers: Dissent over Foreign Policy, 1792–1939*; perhaps his book would be better if it did more to sketch the climate of opinion, the social institutions from which came his dissenters and their following. This has at times swollen into a mighty army, at times it has dwindled away, as CND has dwindled away in the last year or two. But so far, there have never failed to be some adherents to maintain that intellectual conviction demands action; that such action is a matter of personal rectitude, not of a quest for power (in their language the phrase might perhaps be 'to put oneself right with God', which may be the same thing as 'commitment'); and that the essential virtue of the English political system is that it admits such dissidence as a fact and recognises it as a duty. 'Ye are the salt of the earth: but if the salt have lost his savour, wherewith shall it be salted?' Bunyan's Pilgrim, Blake's Jerusalem have not yet lost their power as symbols.

I hope that these three myths of the past are recognisable as models of the present. The only evidence I can offer is that of personal impression; I think that if one could keep these three incompatible models in mind at once they would be as good a key to English political practice and principles as one could hope to get otherwise in so limited a space. Could these hunches be framed as hypotheses in operational terms? I don't think it would be impossible. But it would be a laborious and perhaps artificial exercise, and enough has been said for the purpose of the present argument.

May I then proceed to the next step?

Each of the three models purports to be a statement about the past, and a ranking of political values in the present. Suppose one could identify level-headed exponents of each doctrine, on what would they agree about the state of British government in 1965?

I think there would be two sets of propositions:

(1) There have been times of dramatic crisis in English politics; for instance, the 1640s, the 1680s, the last quarter of the eighteenth century; the 1840s; the period around 1910; the early part of the 1920s; the Spanish Civil War. This is not such a period; it could almost be described in American terms as 'an era of good feeling'. Not that the party struggle lacks excitement and loud abuse; but it does not seem to be concerned with anything very fundamental.

(2) There, would, I think, be fairly general agreement that nobody's 'ideal type' of British political society is effectively achieved at present. The conventional constitutionalists grumble continually about cabinet dictatorship, the erosion of the sovereignty of parliament, the authority of bureaucrats and technocrats, the relative impotence of the courts. The 'old oligarchs' (if I may borrow a term from the literature of ancient Greek politics) boast that the peaceful withering away of empire was the last triumph of Whig tactics, that the tradition of co-option has been strong enough to cross the barrier of colour. But there is an uneasy feeling that the magic is not what it was. The natives often seem more inclined to found their own club than to join the English one, and even in England the rising men in the newest fields of power and influence are not easy to domesticate. Oxford and Cambridge, Eton and Winchester, the Foreign Office and the Brigade of Guards, the grouse and the pheasant, the fox and the deer, begin to seem absurd rather than attractive.

The dissidents are equally at a loss. There is work to be done in the world, and the young are eager to do it. But it is hard to link it to utopian principles, because all the old principles have been accepted, and we are no better off. The principles of democracy are accepted at home, even for coloured immigrants. Colonialism and empire are dead, in principle. The British bomb is in principle now a bargaining counter, not a weapon. In principle, war is no longer an instrument of policy. But the concession of these principles has not changed the real political world; is it still possible for the English dissenter to believe as he once did that he and his principles are the salt of the whole polity, indeed of the whole earth?

So much for past and present, introduced here as the basis for deliberation about the future. My submission is that new models are emerging as hypotheses about the future, and that these models also entail norms. But unlike the old models, these are models of things that no one much likes.

I name three, which I have called the 'two peoples', 'the ungovernable interests' and 'the active power'. These models are constructed by an extrapolation of existing trends, but they should be regarded as tools of analysis, not as prophesies. The trends can be documented, but to extrapolate each of them separately proves nothing about the future.

The two peoples
First, there is a model of the development of education in relation to technology and culture. The physical condition of school buildings, the shortage of teachers, the system of examinations and the vested interests entrenched in it — all these need hard daily work which must be done in order to avoid a breakdown. But suppose we get past these difficulties, where do we arrive?

The trend of technology suggests an economy based on two kinds of being; on the one hand the man (or woman) who 'knows how things work', on the other hand the machine minder. Each of these 'peoples' will have its own complex structure: but this will not blur the broad distinction. The former acquire 'qualifications'. This is a process which begins early; the earliest 'qualification' at present is

conferred by the examination which admits children to
grammar schools at the age of eleven, or excludes them. Even
if that test is abolished the 'learners' will begin to sort
themselves out from the 'players' at much the same stage of
education, and the division will be pretty deep by the age of
sixteen. On one side there will be those who then seek work
as 'machine minders', on the other side there will be those
who proceed to 'qualify' in some branch of technical knowledge. The process of technical change means that the latter
must continue to master new ideas if they are to advance
actively in their careers. But the 'machine minders' need only
the physical dexterity required in driving a car, or working on
an assembly line, or using a typewriter; machines will necessarily be constructed so that the operator needs only adaptable capacity to use tools designed for him by others.

This pattern already exists, dividing 'professional people'
from the 'working class'. Already, the distinction is not one
of income or well-being but of way of life. The professional
stays at school after fifteen and invests effort in acquiring
qualifications, which need to be continuously renewed. His
working life is a 'career', beginning low in a hierarchy, but
leading upward like a ladder, to be climbed by effort, in
competition with peers. The points reached on the ladder will
be marked by rising income, and also by outward and visible
badges of status and rank.

The professional pattern in fact implies a 'Protestant ethic'
of a new kind; the man (and his wife) learn early to make
sacrifices in order to go one step further and then to make
sacrifices again for the next step.

Machine minders are as much in short supply as are
professionals, and average earnings may be much the same on
each side of the line. But the pattern is different. The
machine minder leaves school early, and can earn well as soon
as he or she has learnt the mores of the work-place and the
dexterity required. If he is physically and mentally active his
worst enemy is boredom, and short hours of work leave
plenty of time to seek remedies for it. Hence 'teen-age
culture': but the vast majority escape into marriage while still
young, and most marriages remain stable. The worst threat to
them is bad and expensive housing: this situation will not be

eased for a long time, and meantime it creates an urgent need for money, earned by overtime, double jobs, and part-time work by the wife. But hard work of this kind does not entail a career ladder. The machine minder in his forties may be well settled and relatively contented, but earning no more, carrying no more responsibility than he did in his early twenties.

This model suggests two ways of life based on the technological structure of production, and it can be extended to sketch types of education, types of personality, and so on. I should, however, avoid calling it a 'class model', because that begs a question — how much mobility can one expect in each generation between the two 'peoples'? Evidence mounts up that educational success is as closely connected with culture as with innate intelligence, and that the tie of family culture is very strong. But the demand for professionals has been more than enough to absorb all the competent children of the old professionals; and there has been room for children who can break away from 'working class culture' and join the professional ranks. In fact, upward mobility has exceeded downward mobility; and there seems to be no reason why this should not go on.

If it does, it becomes rather hard to regard the barrier as a 'class barrier': but it will none the less be a strong 'cultural' barrier.

The ungovernable interests

It is characteristic of a technological society that its main structure is built out of large organisations. There is room for the small organisation or even the individual entrepreneur, but only on the margin. I was startled to notice recently how many current television serials are based on the construction of a fictitious but familiar organisation; hospital, police force, factory, newspaper, research laboratory, army and so on. The formula is to take an organisation and make it personal; episodes can be invented very easily out of the clash between organisational role and personal relationships.

In addition to the big organisations, there are the big 'unions', if I may use the word here to include organised interests of all kinds. In the last ten years these have been classified almost *ad nauseam*: so carefully that one is apt to think of them as *lepidoptera* under glass — whereas they are the greatest example to be seen of individual interests harnessed (like a waterfall) to generate social power. This is something social which *can* be engineered: it would not be hard to re-phrase *The Prince* as a text-book for the organisers of interests. The central maxim perhaps is that in a technological society dominated by large organisations a man can be operationally defined as a bundle of interests arising out of different relations. Each of these interests he pursues, each within its system; each in its system is the ground for organisation; from moment to moment, day to day, nothing forces a man to know that his various interests are not compatible. Each of them becomes a ground for 'pressure'; the discordant individual is mirrored by the discordant macrocosm. The state is submerged by the interests; it continues, but only as a form of contest. The so-called 'government' is like a medieval king amid the Barons' Wars. His body is a symbol and a prize; the factions strive to possess it, but as soon as one succeeds, its success creates a coalition against it, and the cycle begins again.

This then is the second model; one which rejects as meaningless the idea of rational public choice. 'Justice is the interest of the stronger'; policy is what in fact happened, it can be seen in retrospect but gives no guide to the future.

The active power
Yet clearly this second model is only a partial model. It is true that the English lack the concept of the state; but they replace it by the concept of the Crown, alive, ambulant, recognisable in the flesh of Elizabeth II and her numerous kin. To this familiar symbol is added a solid reality in the world of organisations. It is only possible to talk vaguely of the 'public sector' of the British economy. There is in principle a board of directors called the Cabinet, giving administrative leadership to an organisation called the 'public sector'. This is far bigger than any other organisation in the country, but it is so loosely constructed that it may be misleading to call it a single organisation.

Nevertheless, it is an organisation in the text-book sense

that it is interlinked by formal communications and chains of command. If it can be made coherent, it will dominate British politics and economics.

The third model then postulates that this potential government becomes actual; some suppose (wrongly) that it is already actual; most suppose that it could be made actual, that England could be governed. This contradicts bluntly the esoteric model of the traditional system, that in which social power dominates political positions: it postulates that to seize political positions is in fact to seize power.

Only a few cranks believe that it is true now; but most people would say there are circumstances in which it must be made true, particularly those of economic or military disaster. If it came about, what would its form be? Three postulates:

(1) First, there must be a pretorian guard; the sovereign, whoever he is, cannot reign alone, but only as chairman of a consortium of the powerful, the holders of key positions. How many? Perhaps two or three thousand would be enough, if well organised and led.

(2) The government must possess sanctions, and it must take seriously the advice given to Tarquin, to lop the tallest ears of corn. At present most of us, if we know what government policy is (for instance, about universities), set to work to subvert it without the slightest risk of damage to ourselves; indeed, with the probability of gain, as the government is bound to reverse its policy soon (whatever it may be), and we shall then be well placed to profit by the swing. In the classic words used in 1952 by Mr. W. J. Keswick, a Director of the Bank of England, which is a public corporation: 'My advice therefore all round is to sell ... This is anti-British and derogatory to sterling but, on balance, if one is free to do so, it makes sense to me.*

It does not need concentration camps to stop that sort of thing; loss of career and loss of contracts would generally be enough. Government patronage now extends to so many spheres that exclusion from it could be a decisive sanction.

(3) But to achieve this or indeed to achieve anything, needs

---

*Proceedings of the Bank Rate Tribunal (Dec 1957) p. 101, Q.3850.

a working communications net. At present the two or three thousand people in key positions do not recognise themselves as a unit of any kind. (Perhaps I should make it absolutely clear that I am not talking here about the existing civil service, but about the top *echelons*, in each of many organisations: departments, public corporations, local government, research, education, mass communications, the armed forces.) This managerial revolution requires (first) communication among the managers; then, perhaps some simple central organisation through which they can pool their immense knowledge about everyone else. In the esoteric model of the past and present this function is fulfilled by the old school tie and college network, which is also an immensely extended kinship system. One could still in my time see this working; Englishmen 'on the inside' could place one another in very few moves at first meeting. But one is now equally struck by the sheer ignorance of Englishmen 'on the inside'; outside their own circle they are at sea, and comfort themselves by believing what they want to believe.

There is no *technical* (I underline 'technical') difficulty in manipulating these three things. My second model depicted England as ungovernable; the third model indicates how easy it might be to govern it if something happened to trigger off the change.

As I said earlier, part of our present perplexity is that these models might almost be called anti-models, like Orwell's *1984*. We do not like the picture of a technological society dominated by a split between the examined and the unexamined, intellectuals and 'proles'. We do not like the extrapolation of the present system of pressure by organisations till it becomes that of the *liberum veto*. We do not like the picture of a crisis, internal or external, met by tough-minded and well-planned centralisation.

But what else is there to offer? The old models are not in a very healthy condition; should we nevertheless reinstate them as norms, and seek to mould the new situation to them? What chance is there of a better model, a new More, Harington, William Morris, Blatchford? Can one realistically foresee anything ahead of us that we could positively recommend to our children, in the spirit of the old dissidents?

I should prefer to write an answer after conference
discussion, rather than before it. But it may perhaps help if I
add a page or two of analysis of a more institutional kind.

The formal model of political authority in England has
remained unchanged since it was formulated by Bagehot in
the 1860's. A Cabinet based on a strong majority in a
newly-elected House of Commons is the highest authority
there can be within this traditional system. It possesses for
the time being plebiscitary sovereignty, conferred perhaps on
a group rather than a man.

The formal nexus between authority and people is the
House of Commons. Where does the House of Commons
come from? From nomination by party organisations in some
630 constituencies. Who controls these nominations? The
small clique of caucus leaders in each constituency; these
leaders in turn owe their authority to the local *militants*, the
pretorian guard of the regime. Some 600 constituencies, not
above 1000 serious militants in each constituency, taking all
parties together; 600,000 is probably an overstatement of the
number of citizens who give a noticeable share of their time
to the business of political parties, nationally and locally.

What is the character of these worthies? This is a research-
able question, and the research has not been done. Probably
the other thirty million or so adults in the U.K. would
describe them as middle-aged conventional, unintellectual,
interested in the shadow rather than the substance of power,
continually on guard lest a new generation invade their
parishes and take away their positions of show, the positions
which give meaning to their lives. The public image of the
party worker, Conservative or Labour, is not a flattering one;
the electorate bows to the authority of elections, distrusts
the authority of party workers and their candidates.

Hence two consequences. First, there is the electoral
puzzle of the Liberal Party. For ten years it has attracted
protest votes. The meaning of the Liberal Party as an
old-fashioned machine like the others began to die out in the
1950's. It became a resource by which a citizen could vote
and yet not vote for a machine; probably this vote for
participation, against *incivisme*, against the party cliques, has
attracted at least 10 per cent of voters steadily since 1950.

But it faces an awkward choice about the future. To progress further it must organise: to organise it must secure campaign funds and routine voluntary support. If it succeeds in doing this, it will become another machine, and will depress the authority of the machines further by splitting the vote three ways and denying to any of the three machines the authority of a newly-elected House of Commons. We are on the edge of this situation in the spring of 1965; we shall enter it if (and this is very uncertain) the Liberals are capable of the sort of practical manoeuvring which enabled the Labour Party to break through to a new dimension in the election of 1905.

What then? Two alternative models are possible. One is that the House of Commons should cease to be merely a statistical link between electors and cabinet; it would become an arena of real conflict, not sham conflict; we should return in a very different century to the sort of 'government by assembly' which was dominant in the great age of *laissez-faire*, from 1846 to 1868.

Another model is that the prestige of party machines and of elected persons should continue to dwindle with their effective power. Authority would flow away from elections towards the professional elites and the leaders of the so-called non-political organisations. Technical skill would give leadership, but only in so far as it did not meet the obstacle of an organised interest.

In practice these possibilities will come together in a new blend, which I cannot foresee; indeed, I should be so bold as to say that no one can foresee, because no one can foresee technical changes and changes in the political system of the world, and also because there is no means of giving weights to the push and pull of various forces in English politics. Indeed, I can foresee only that we shall grow more and more dissatisfied with our institutions; and that perhaps will be as much gain as loss. A great deal of old England lies buried in the grave of Winston Churchill.

Index